After Apocalyptic and Wisdom

After Apocalyptic and Wisdom
Rethinking Texts in Context

Richard A. Horsley
and
Patrick A. Tiller

CASCADE *Books* · Eugene, Oregon

AFTER APOCALYPTIC AND WISDOM
Rethinking Texts in Context

Copyright © 2012 Richard A. Horsley and Patrick A. Tiller. All rights reserved. Except for brief quotations in critical publications or reviews, no part of this book may be reproduced in any manner without prior written permission from the publisher. Write: Permissions, Wipf & Stock, 199 W. 8th Ave., Eugene, OR 97401.

Cascade Books
An Imprint of Wipf and Stock Publishers
199 W. 8th Ave., Suite 3
Eugene, OR 97401
www.wipfandstock.com

ISBN 13: 978-1-61097-285-7

Cataloging-in-Publication data:

Horsley, Richard A.

 After apocalyptic and wisdom : rethinking texts in context / Richard A. Horsley and Patrick A. Tiller.

 x + 332 p. ; cm. Includes bibliographical references and index.

 ISBN 13: 978-1-61097-285-7

 1. Bible. N.T. Gospels—Criticism, interpretation, etc. 2. Apocalyptic literature—History and criticism. 3. Wisdom literature—Criticism, interpretation, etc. 4. Ethiopic book of Enoch—Criticism, interpretation, etc. 5. Bible. O.T. Apocrypha. Esdras, 2nd. 6. Syriac Apocalypse of Baruch. I. Tiller, Patrick A. II. Title.

BS646 H67 2012

Manufactured in the U.S.A.

Contents

Acknowledgments • *vii*
Abbreviations • *ix*

Introduction • 1

Part One: Social-Political Context of Apocalyptic and Wisdom Texts

1 Ben Sira and the Sociology of the Second Temple • 19
2 The Politics of Cultural Production • 56
3 The Social Settings of the Components of *1 Enoch* • 81

Part Two: Reconsideration of Texts in Historical Contexts

4 Israel at the Mercy of Demonic Powers: An Enochic Interpretation of Imperialism • 103
5 Social Relations and Social Conflict in the Epistle of Enoch • 113
6 *4 Ezra*: Anti-Apocalyptic Apocalypse • 132
7 Late Twentieth Century Scribes' Study of Late Second Temple Scribes • 141

Part Three: Questioning the Categories as Applied to the Gospels and James

8 Questions about Wisdom and Apocalypticism in Q • 163

9 Sayings of the Sages or Speeches of the Prophets? Reflections on the Genre of Q • 191

10 Apocalypticism and Wisdom: Missing in Mark • 207

11 Apocalypticism in the Gospels? The Kingdom of God and the Renewal of Israel • 230

12 The Rich and Poor in James: An Apocalyptic Ethic • 280

Epilogue • 291

Bibliography • 305

Index of Ancient Authors • 315

Acknowledgments

THE CHAPTERS IN THIS volume are revised versions of essays that originally appeared in the following publications and are used with permission. The authors and publisher are grateful for the cooperation of these journals and publishers.

Chapter 1: Richard Horsley and Patrick Tiller, "Ben Sira and the Sociology of the Second Temple." *Second Temple Studies III: Studies in Politics, Class, and Material Culture*, edited by Philip R. Davies and John M. Halligan, 74–107. JSOTSup 340. Sheffield: Sheffield Academic, 2002. By kind permission of Continuum International Publishing Group.

Chapter 2: Richard Horsley, "The Politics of Cultural Production." In *Conflicted Boundaries in Wisdom and Apocalypticism*, edited by Benjamin G. Wright III and Lawrence M. Wills, 123–45. SBL Symposium Series 35. Atlanta: Society of Biblical Literature, 2005.

Chapter 3: Patrick Tiller, "The Sociological Context of the Dream Visions of Daniel and 1 Enoch." In *Enoch and Qumran Origins: New Light on a Forgotten Connection*, edited by Gabrielle Boccaccini, 23–26. Grand Rapids: Eerdmans, 2005. All rights reserved.

Chapter 4: Patrick Tiller, "Israel at the Mercy of Demonic Powers: An Enochic Interpretation of Imperialism." *Conflicted Boundaries in Wisdom and Apocalypticism*, edited by Benjamin G. Wright III and Lawrence M. Wills, 113–22. SBL Symposium Series 35. Atlanta: Society of Biblical Literature, 2005.

Chapter 5: Richard Horsley, "Social Relations and Social Conflict in the Epistle of Enoch." In *For A Later Generation: The Transformation of Tradition in Israel, Early Judaism, and Early Christianity*, edited by Randall A. Argall et al., 100–115. Harrisburg, PA: Trinity Press

International, 2000. By kind permission of Continuum International Publishing Group.

Chapter 6: Patrick Tiller, "Anti-Apocalyptic Apocalypse." In *For A Later Generation: The Transformation of Tradition in Israel, Early Judaism, and Early Christianity*. FS Nickelsburg; ed. Randall A. Argall et al., 258–65. Harrisburg, PA: Trinity Press International, 2000. By kind permission of Continuum International Publishing Group.

Chapter 7: Richard Horsley, "Of Enoch, Nickelsburg, and Other Scribes of Righteousness." *The Review of Rabbinic Judaism* 8 (2005) 249–66. Published by E. J. Brill (Koninklijke Brill N.V.).

Chapter 8: Richard Horsley, "Questions about Redactional Strata and Social Relations in Q." In *Society of Biblical Literature 1989 Seminar Papers*, edited by David J. Lull, 186–203. Atlanta: Scholars Press, 1989; and Richard Horsley, "Wisdom Justified by All Her Children: Examining Allegedly Disparate Traditions in Q." In *Society of Biblical Literature 1994 Seminar Papers*, edited by Eugene H. Lovering, 733–51. Atlanta: Scholars Press, 1994.

Chapter 9: Richard Horsley, "*Logoi Propheton*? Reflections on the Genre of Q." In *The Future of Early Christianity: Essays in Honor of Helmut Koester*, edited by Birger A. Pearson, 195–209. Minneapolis: Fortress, 1991. Used by permission of Augsburg Fortress Publishers.

Chapter 10: Richard Horsley, "Wisdom and Apocalypticism in Mark." In *In Search of Wisdom: Essays in Memory of John Gammie*, edited by Bernard Brandon Scott, William Johnston Wiseman, 223–44. Louisville: Westminster John Knox, 1993. www.wjkbooks.com.

Chapter 11: Richard Horsley, "The Kingdom of God and the Renewal of Israel: Synoptic Gospels, Jesus Movements, and Apocalypticism." In *The Encyclopedia of Apocalypticism*, edited by John J. Collins, vol. 1, 303–44. New York: Continuum, 1998. By kind permission of Continuum International Publishing Group.

Chapter 12: Patrick Tiller, "The Rich and Poor in James: An Apocalyptic Ethic." In *Conflicted Boundaries in Wisdom and Apocalypticism*, edited by Benjamin G. Wright III and Lawrence M. Wills, 169–80. SBL Symposium Series 35. Atlanta: Society of Biblical Literature, 2005.

Abbreviations

AB	Anchor Bible
ATANT	Abhandlungen zur Theologie des Alten und Neuen Testaments
CBQ	*Catholic Biblical Quarterly*
EJL	Early Judaism and Its Literature
FOTL	Forms of the Old Testament Literature
FRLANT	Forschungen zur Religion und Literatur des Alten und Neuen Testaments
HTR	*Harvard Theological Review*
JBL	*Journal of Biblical Literature*
JJS	*Journal of Jewish Studies*
JSJSup	Journal for the Study of Judaism Supplements
JSNTSup	Journal for the Study of the New Testament Supplements
JSOTSup	Journal for the Study of the Old Testament Supplements
JSPSup	Journal for the Study of the Pseudepigraph Supplements
NovT	*Novum Testamentum*
NTS	New Testament Studies
OTP	*Old Testament Pseudepigrapha*. 2 vols. Edited by James H. Charlesworth. Garden City, NY: Doubleday, 1983, 1985
SBT	Studies in Biblical Theology

Introduction

It is virtually assumed in Jewish and Christian biblical studies that wisdom and apocalypticism were the two dominant strands of culture in early Judaism. Many second-temple texts that were included in the Hebrew Bible and many that were not are classified as either wisdom or apocalyptic. Ideas are classified and interpreted as wisdom theology or apocalyptic theology. Classification as one or the other even extends to individual sayings, images, and motifs. It is not just the interpretation of early Judaism that is dominated by these concepts. For most of the twentieth century Jesus was understood as an apocalyptic preacher. The earliest Gospel texts, Mark and Q (Jesus' teachings closely paralleled in Matthew and Luke) were understood as expressions of "apocalyptic" Christianity. Then in the last two decades it was claimed that Q consisted of a formative sapiential layer and a secondary apocalyptic layer. And liberal interpreters claimed that while John the Baptist may have been apocalyptic, Jesus was a wisdom-teacher. Meanwhile wisdom-theology was taken as the key to understanding the Gospel of John and the "opponents" of Paul in 1 Corinthians, while Paul himself was understood as arguing from an apocalyptic perspective.

Yet it would be difficult to find any two prominent concepts in biblical studies that are more vague in their lack of definition, more careless in their application, and more diverse in their understanding by biblical interpreters than wisdom and apocalyptic(ism). The problem is compounded by the tendency, particularly in New Testament interpretation, to dichotomize the two concepts. It has been clear to many that wisdom and apocalypticism are scholarly constructs developed by modern biblical scholarship, yet they continue to be assumed and used, however vaguely and diversely.

We have become convinced that discerning the social location and role of those who produced apocalyptic and wisdom texts will contribute to a more grounded understanding of these texts, and that these texts can be understood more appropriately in the particular historical context they address. We have been in close conversation for the last two decades, beginning with the intense discussions involved in collaborative research and textual analysis. The result has been a number of articles that we believe complement each other and fit well together as a revisionist analysis of wisdom and apocalyptic texts.

WHERE WE HAVE COME FROM

The field of Jewish and Christian biblical studies assumes and works in terms of broad synthetic essentialist constructs developed in modern western scholarship. Some of these are anachronistic with regard to the texts and history that biblical scholars interpret. And they tend to obscure or simply block discernment of the particulars of texts and their development in historical context. The concept "biblical," as in "biblical books" or "biblical history," for example, continues to be applied to the texts in the historical context in which they were produced. Yet most scholars in the field know that the books of the Torah and Prophets, like the Gospels and Letters, were not recognized as biblical until centuries after they were composed. Indeed text critics are saying recently that standardized texts of the books did not emerge until late antiquity or the middle ages.

The broad synthetic constructs most determinative in biblical studies are surely "(early) Judaism" and "(early) Christianity." Most biblical scholars today probably recognize, at least tacitly, that there was so much diversity of texts and areas and movements that the concepts must, at the very least, be pluralized (e.g., "Judaisms").[1] Because of the modern separation between religion and politics and economics, however, concepts such as "Judaism" and "Christianity" are understood to refer to "religions" that had simply not yet emerged. Yet these determinative concepts are programmatically reified in the naming of program units of principal professional organization, the Society of Biblical Literature, and in titles of books and articles as well as perpetuated in the standardized discourse of biblical studies.

Occasionally one of these synthetic modern scholarly constructs can be at least weakened. Beginning in the 1960s, it was gradually rec-

---

1. See, for example, Neusner et al., *Judaisms and Their Messiahs*.

ognized that there was no standard Jewish expectation of "the Messiah" in late second-temple times. Scholars suddenly realized that Judean texts give relatively few references to anointed figures. They indicate rather that different scribal circles or popular movements looked for different leaders of renewal or agents of deliverance.[2] The later synthetic Christian concept of "the Messiah/Christ" was the result of the development of the application to Jesus of Nazareth of some of these varied expectations and their synthesis into "Christology" by Christian theology. Research and rethinking in certain special areas of biblical studies and related fields have challenged other anachronistic modern scholarly constructs.[3] But the field has become so splintered into specialization on particular books, issues, or "criticisms" that it is impossible for specialists in one area or one kind of "criticism" to stay abreast of developments in others. Those who have been developing social science criticism, for example, still take verses or motifs in biblical books at face value as historical "data," when their colleagues focused on literary criticism or rhetorical criticism have long since demonstrated the necessity of critical analysis of texts for their value as historical sources. Ideological or feminist critics who have been developing sophisticated readings "against the grain" of key texts still use modern scholarly constructs such as "biblical" or "(early) Judaism" or "(early) Christianity."

"Apocalyptic(ism)" is another synthetic modern scholarly construct that continues to determine discernment and interpretation of texts and history. "Wisdom" is yet another, yet even more elusive insofar the same term is used for what were clearly different kinds or modes of wisdom. Closely related is the dichotomy of the scholarly constructs "apocalypticism/apocalyptic" and "wisdom/sapiential."

In the case of "apocalyptic(ism)," the modern scholarly construction in place by the end of the nineteenth century became entrenched in biblical studies and has simply been assumed since by specialists focused on "intertestamental" ("apocryphal" and "pseudepigraphical"—other synthetic constructs) literature, second-temple Jewish history, Paul, the Gospels, and the historical Jesus, among others). After the end of the nineteenth century, in fact, little research was done on "apocalypticism"

---

2. DeJonge, "Use of the Term 'Anointed'"; Neusner et al., *Judaisms and Their Messiahs*; Charlesworth, ed., *Messiah*.

3. On "the Zealots," for example, Horsley with Hanson, *Bandits, Prophets, and Messiahs*.

and what were labeled "apocalyptic" texts, and little innovative interpretation done on "wisdom" until well after mid-twentieth century.[4] The (texts and) translations used by those who bothered to consult them, for example, were those of Charles and Kautzsch—until the new introductions and translations published in the mid-1980s, many by scholars who were not specialists on the respective texts.[5]

Only in the last generation have a number of scholars carried out probing critical analysis and translation of Judean apocalyptic texts in the languages in which they are extant, as exemplified in the sustained scholarship of Michael E. Stone, George W. E. Nickelsburg, or John J. Collins.[6] Reinforcing interest in and investigation of apocalyptic texts, moreover, was the discovery of the Dead Sea Scrolls and early translations of key documents of the Qumran community that seemed to articulate similar ideas and concerns. The extensive investigation of apocalyptic texts, however, has adapted the scholarly construct of "apocalyptic(ism)" without mounting a fundamental challenge to it (for example the continuing characterization of "apocalyptic" texts and images as "otherworldly"). Because of the balkanization into subfields within biblical studies, however, specialists in interpretation, for example, of Qumran texts or Gospel passages or the historical Jesus, have often not found time to read the recent critical investigations of apocalyptic texts. They still assume and work with the synthetic concept of apocalypticism where it stood when they were in graduate school a generation ago, which is more or less how it had been constructed over a century ago.

In retrospect it is possible to discern how the synthetic essentialist concept of apocalypticism was constructed over a century ago, partly from the way that it has been and is still used in biblical studies. "Apocalyptic" texts that range from the third century BCE to the second century CE, codified into chapter and verse, following the pattern already established in the printing of "biblical" texts, were read in text-fragments of verses, lines, and motifs. Verses and sentences were understood as theological statements, with the imagery (such as the sun being

---

4. In Germany the first treatment after the turn of the century was Ploeger, *Theocracy and Eschatology*, which is followed by Hengel, *Judaism and Hellenism*.

5. Charlesworth, ed., *Old Testament Pseudepigrapha*.

6. See, for example, their respective magisterial Hermeneia commentaries on *4 Ezra*, *1 Enoch*, and Daniel.

darkened) taken almost literally. For reasons that have not yet become clear, what caught the eye of modern scholars were heavenly beings and statements about judgment and images of "cosmic catastrophe." With such statements and images taken more or less literally, it was assumed that "apocalypticism" was a worldview, a bizarre metaphysics, with a focus on the end of the world. Located in a history of biblical theology that reached its "Old Testament" peak in the prophets and then jumped several centuries to its climax in Jesus, "apocalypticism" was at best an awkward bridge between the two Testaments of divine revelation.

In a survey of the revival of interest in *Apokalyptik* in German theological scholarship, Klaus Koch found eight (interrelated) motifs to be prominent in the synthetic scholarly construct standardly assumed since the end of the nineteenth century:[7] (1) an urgent expectation of *the end of the world*, the impending overthrow of all earthly conditions in the immediate future; (2) the end coming as a *cosmic catastrophe*, with fire, earthquake, disorder in heavenly bodies, etc.; (3) a *determinism*, of history divided into fixed, predetermined segments; (4) clashing armies of *angels and demons* determining or intervening in earthly events (often referred to as a *dualism of heaven vs. earth*); (5) a *new salvation beyond the cosmic catastrophe*, where the *Endzeit* is like the *Urzeit*, with a tendency toward universalism; (6) transition from disaster to final redemption, from the old evil world/aeon to the higher new world/aeon by an act from the throne of God (evidently what others refer to as *the (Last) Judgment*), and thus a *dualism of the old and new worlds*; (7) a *mediator with royal functions* (with various names: the Messiah, the Son of man, the Chosen One); (8) the "glory" of *a heavenly, utopian existence* in the new world/age.

While most of these motifs also appear in nonapocalyptic literature, they are thought to comprise a sequence of events in apocalypticism. Apocalypse, moreover, entails not simply the disclosure of all this, but the inclusion of those who possess the revelation in the transformation or transition to the fantastic new heavenly reality. These motifs are the principal features of what Koch calls "an attitude of mind," an intellectual movement, what others term an unprecedented new worldview. Having been developed by around 1900, this synthetic scholarly construct with these and other stereotypical features was inscribed in handbooks by

---

7. Koch, *Rediscovery of Apocalyptic*, 28–33.

Wilhelm Bousset and Paul Volz that became the standard that shaped the subsequent scholarly understanding.[8]

Even more determinative in shaping the standard understanding of apocalypticism in New Testament studies beyond Germany, particularly in interpretation of Jesus and the Gospels, was the work of Albert Schweitzer, especially in his own sketch of Jesus in the widely read *Quest of the Historical Jesus*. More attentive to the supposed dates of the principal Judean apocalyptic texts than others, he recognized that there was a significant gap between Daniel and Enoch texts of the second century CE and the later apocalypses of *2 Baruch* and *4 Ezra* written after the destruction of Jerusalem in 70 CE. Because he and many others had already come to the conclusion that John the Baptist, Paul, and the Gospels of Mark and Matthew were completely caught up in the dominant Jewish apocalypticism, however, he believed that these Gospels and Paul's letters simply filled in the gaps, indeed that they offered a more precise sense of Jewish apocalypticism at the time of Jesus himself than could be gained from the (earlier or later) Jewish texts themselves.[9] He presented a highly influential portrayal of Jesus as utterly caught up in what he believed was an apocalyptic scenario of the cataclysmic end of the world comprised of four or five interrelated events of the end-time. Assuming that Jesus viewed himself as the coming Son of Man, he identified the Son of Man's "coming" with the *Parousia* spoken of by Paul and Matthew 25. Taking Matt 10:23 literally, Schweitzer claimed that Jesus believed that "the *Parousia of the Son of Man*," which he took as identical with the dawn of *the Kingdom* and the *Last Judgment*, would take place before the disciples sent out to gather in the 'harvest' returned from their hasty mission tour. That is, the end of the world was *imminent*.[10] In the predicted course of eschatological events, the Parousia of the Son of Man was "to be preceded by a time of strife and confusion—as it were, the birth-throes of the Messiah," the great *eschatological Tribulation*.[11] The final key feature of Schweitzer's grand apocalyptic scenario was the *Resurrection*, the eschatological metamorphosis of people into a transformed condition.

---

8. Bousset, *Religion des Judentums*; Volz, *Jüdische Eschatologie*, both of which were reprinted in the 1960s as the standard works.

9. Schweitzer, *Quest of the Historical Jesus*, 366–71.

10. Ibid., 358–59.

11. Ibid., 362.

Schweitzer viewed the resurrection and the Parousia of the son of Man as simultaneous, as "one and the same act."[12]

This scholarly construct of the Jewish apocalyptic scenario that supposedly dominated Jesus' preaching as well as Judaism at the time, as articulated by Schweitzer, became standard for much critical scholarly interpretation of Jesus and the Gospels both in Germany and in the United Kingdom and the Americas. This can be seen in Bultmann's presentation of the teaching of Jesus, and through Bultmann's work it further influenced biblical interpretation in the Anglophone countries. At the opening of his *New Testament Theology,* Bultmann declared that Jesus' message of the Kingdom of God stands *in the historical context of Jewish expectations about the end of the world and God's new future.*[13] These apocalyptic expectations look not for a change in historical (social-political) circumstances, but a "cosmic catastrophe that will do away with all conditions of the present world as it is." Bultmann's summary of the apocalyptic scenario includes the same set of events as in Schweitzer's treatment of Jesus. The new aeon will dawn with "terror and tribulation." The old aeon will end with God's "judgment of the world to be held at the determined time by [God] or his representative the Son of Man, who will come on the clouds of heaven." Thereafter "the dead will arise" and receive their reward which, for the faithful/ good deeds will be "the glory of paradise."[14]

Bultmann's scholarly work and influence also crystallized another key way in which the synthetic scholarly construct of apocalyptic(ism) has been understood and applied by interpreters of Jesus and the Gospels in particular. He included a category of "prophetic and apocalyptic" sayings of Jesus in his highly influential handbook of form criticism.[15] While he referred to only a few Jesus sayings as "apocalyptic," his students and followers extended the classification to many Jesus sayings and to verses in apocalyptic texts as well. The assumption, implication, and often the explicit claim is that even a text-fragment as tiny as an isolated individual

---

12. Ibid., 366.

13. Bultmann, *New Testament Theology*, 4; cf. his *Primitive Christianity*, 82–86, where in contrast to most New Testament scholars of his time and since, he quotes whole stanzas from Jewish apocalyptic texts, although mainly from the late *4 Ezra* and *2 Baruch*.

14. Bultmann, *New Testament Theology*, 5.

15. Bultmann, *History of the Synoptic Tradition*.

saying somehow carries and expresses a worldview. Indeed, scholars go so far as to find a worldview presupposed and expressed even in an image or motif that occurs in a saying. The assumption is, apparently, that if an image or motif occurs in a verse in an apocalyptic text, then it is an apocalyptic image or motif (in an apocalyptic saying). Hence when the same image or motif occurs in a saying in a Gospel, it is an expression of apocalypticism, an indication of an apocalyptic eschatology.

While the synthetic scholarly construct of Jewish apocalypticism had become standard in twentieth century New Testament studies, and many interpreters viewed Jesus as well as the "early Christians" as sharing and developing it, other Christian interpreters insisted that Jesus and most of the earliest Gospel tradition were not apocalyptic. The character of the synoptic tradition became more hotly debated in the 1960s, all the while hovering under the specter the apocalyptic scenario of the end of the world that had been constructed by modern scholarship.

Wisdom, or wisdom literature, had a more innocuous scholarly profile that had attracted much less debate a generation or two ago. "Wisdom" was understood mainly as proverbial wisdom, as in the protototypical book of wisdom, Proverbs. Appropriately for much of that book, wisdom literature, like apocalyptic literature, was read and interpreted as individual sayings, and it was assumed that those individual sayings carried a certain worldview, even a distinctive theology. Once theological questions were raised, however, scholarly attention focused also on "wisdom speculation" or "wisdom theology," in which wisdom was reified and even personified as a divine figure, the mediatrix of a transcendent, even remote God.

While interpretation of apocalyptic and sapiential literature proceeded along parallel separate lines in Hebrew Bible/Old Testament studies, however, in New Testament studies the two became increasingly dichotomized. This seemed most obvious in wisdom speculation, which appeared to be the background of John as the (more) "theological" Gospel, particularly in its Prologue focused on the Logos, which seemed a virtual synonym for Sophia in the Wisdom of Solomon and for Sophia/Logos in the theological reflection of Philo of Alexandria. The latter had transformed Wisdom theology into the conceptualization of Hellenistic (nascent "Middle-Platonic") philosophy. A similar dichotomy developed of "sapiential" and "apocalyptic" sayings as well. As form critics focused not on the form but the contents of individual sayings, they classified those with images of judgment or punishment or "cosmic disorder" as "apocalyptic," in contrast with the tamer proverbs or maxims or makarisms, which they classified as "sapiential." And, since scholars focused on individual sayings, often without much attention to literary or social context, the respective classes of sayings were assumed to carry and express distinctively different worldviews.

The relatively undeveloped state of the study of (proverbial) wisdom literature can be illustrated from a graduate seminar on the book of Sirach at Harvard Divinity School in the mid-1960s. Each week one of the students wrote a paper on a set of sayings in Sirach. Investigation was almost exclusively philological, saying by saying. Students received virtually no guidance from the principal professor or the other two in attendance. The role of the professors was simply blunt, acerbic criticism of the paper-writer each week for not having investigated X or thought of Y. Students learned a good deal of Greek and Hebrew philology—by painful trial and (mostly) error. In retrospect, however, it would be fair to say that neither the students nor the faculty participants in the seminar "had a clue" what wisdom literature in general or the sayings of Ben Sira in particular were about. Questions that we have subsequently learned to ask were not yet in play. Koch had suggested that German theologians in the 1960s were *Ratlos vor der Apokalyptik*. Biblical scholars in the 1960s were even more *ratlos vor der Weisheit*.

When questions of the social world behind a text were raised (which was rarely), the ideas in the texts were assumed to correspond to different groups. "Wisdom" texts were presumed to have been written by "the wise," and "apocalyptic" texts to have originated in apocalyptic conventicles interested in speculation about the cosmos and the future. Different groups were delineated by their different theological statements even within the broader construct of apocalypticism. The group that supposedly produced Daniel was read as pacifist, while the group that supposedly produced Enoch texts was taken as militant. But certainly those who produced "apocalyptic" texts and theology were deemed different from those who produced "wisdom."

QUESTIONS ABOUT THE RECEIVED WISDOM

Graduate programs in biblical studies presumably encourage critical inquiry, including the questioning of standard views, as well as the transmission of knowledge and acquisition of the tools of scholarship. While in graduate training, one of us in the late 1960s and the other in the late 1980s, both of us found ourselves questioning the received assumptions, orientation, and concepts of scholarship on apocalyptic(ism), and simply puzzled about the corresponding scholarship on wisdom literature. Questions that arose decades ago have driven much of our inquiry in our respective and collaborative research and writing behind this collection of essays. We cannot remember the sequence in which the questions arose. But they overlapped and reinforced one another, leading to alternative assumptions, approaches, and conclusions about apocalyptic and, eventually, wisdom texts and their contexts.

Basic was the literalism with which scholars tended to read statements and imagery from apocalyptic texts. In critical biblical studies, in which passages from the Gospels were supposedly not (no longer) being read literally, here was a scholarly concept constructed from phrases and statements taken fairly literally, at face value. The sun would be darkened, the moon would fail to give its light. Might the images, statements, and general rhetoric not be hyperbole, or at least metaphorical? And why should the construction of a scholarly concept key off of the most fantastic images? Why would the dawning of a new age or new "world" be construed as the End of the world in a "cosmic catastrophe"?

Students learning exegesis of Scripture were taught to delineate a "pericope" consisting usually of a paragraph or episode in a Gospel or Epistle, often corresponding to what appeared as paragraphs in the Revised Standard Version or the Jerusalem Bible. So why classify text-fragments as tiny as images and motifs as "apocalyptic," a concept constructed from texts read mainly in individual verses, as practiced in earlier generations that were using the King James Version? Even the translation of texts in R. H. Charles's edition was arranged into stanzas (as well as codified into chapter and verse). Why not read and interpret whole "paragraphs" or "stanzas" or, for that matter, a whole vision and its interpretation such as Daniel 7 or a whole hymn to Wisdom such as Sirach 24?

In the 1960s, of course, much research in biblical texts was narrowly focused as "word studies" or "motif studies." So study of apocalyptic texts or wisdom texts was not much different. But some of us were beginning to notice that, for example, Paul's letters involve sustained arguments (which rhetorical criticism has since probed and explored) and the Gospels include narrative sequences or, in Matthew, alternating steps of narrative and topical speech (which literary criticism has now analyzed). At the time, however, one had to fight to propose and get approval for a dissertation dealing with a whole gospel or epistle instead of a more manageable "word study" or thematic study. Although graduate study was primarily focused on reading secondary literature, a few of us read at least a few whole texts. It was evident, for example, that in somewhat the same way that the book of Isaiah was a composite of several collections of oracles addressing different historical contexts ("First," "Second," and "Third" Isaiah), so the book of *1 Enoch* was a composite of texts that had somewhat different forms and addressed different circumstances. Some of this was in the handbooks, of course. Yet the concept of "apocalypticism" was constructed from text-fragments selected by motif or theme from many different texts that addressed many different contexts.

Critical biblical studies had long since moved to interpretation of texts (even if still focused on text-fragments) in their particular historical context. Different sections of the book of Isaiah were seen to address different historical situations, as just noted. The Gospels were recognized to address different communities in different locations and circumstances. The deutero-Pauline letters were understood to address situations a generation or two later than those to which Paul himself addressed his letters and were not to be used as direct sources for "Pauline theology." We were warned not to naively use rabbinic texts that were centuries later as sources for what the Pharisees may have thought or to interpret Jesus' controversies with them over the law. So why was it assumed that apocalypticism was a relatively unchanging worldview from the early second century BCE to the second century CE, or specifically that several "apocalyptic motifs" (including poetic lines regarding the failing light of sun and moon taken literally) made Mark 13 or its *Vorlage* into a "Little Apocalypse" about the end of the world? Should not each apocalyptic text also be interpreted in its historical context (insofar as that is accessible)?

One of the standard generalizations was that, whereas the prophets still viewed history as the theater of God's action, apocalypticism was alienated from history, otherworldly in it orientation. A reading of the climax of the ever more precise survey of historical events in Daniel 10–11, however, indicates that the *maskilim*, who were presumably the composers of the survey, were not alienated from history in general, but struggling to maintain the traditional way of life in a particularly difficult historical situation, where they were being persecuted and martyred for their resistance to Antiochus Epiphanes. Might not a close reading of this and other apocalyptic texts find that they were affirming hope for themselves and their people despite and beyond what the emperor was doing to them?

A significant stimulus to persistent questioning of received categories and generalizations came from the discovery of the Dead Sea Scrolls in 1947. Some of the key documents appeared to expound an "apocalyptic" worldview, leading to the conclusion that the community-in-exile that produced them was an "apocalyptic" community—giving further credence to the view that "early Christianity" was an "apocalyptic" movement. Yet the scrolls also contained "wisdom" texts. That the previously unknown documents from Qumran came evidently from a community widely identified with the "sect" of the Essenes mentioned by Josephus, suggested that other/earlier apocalyptic texts also came from sect-like groups or conventicles. The vagueness of such "sociology," however, puzzled some of us, who were eager to understand how texts of systematic reflection and rigorous covenantal regulations such as the *Community Rule* from Qumran and the community that produced it were related to the Pharisees and the earlier *maskilim* of Daniel 10–12, on the one hand, and the ordinary people whom Jesus evidently addressed, on the other.

In the 1960s and certainly by the 1980s there were some sources of excitement from outside the sacred walls of biblical studies that seemed like they might lead to a "breakthrough" to new understanding of apocalyptic texts. In the 1950s and 1960s some of the sociologists and anthropologists who carried out studies of "cargo cults" in Melanesia and similar "nativistic" movements among Native Americans or "millenarian" movements in the Middle Ages borrowed phrases from "apocalyptic" texts for the titles of their books and articles (*The Trumpet Shall Sound*, *New Heaven and New Earth*, and *Millennial Dreams in Action*.[16] They did not draw significant parallels themselves, but their studies were suggestive for apocalyptic texts and what were presumed to be apocalyptic movements—and the Jesus movement(s).[17] After the

---

16. Worsley, *Trumpet Shall Sound*; Burridge, *New Heaven and New Earth*; and Thrupp, ed., *Millennial Dreams in Action*.

17. For example, Isenberg, "Millenarism"; and Gager, *Kingdom and Community*.

initial excitement, however, it was evident that cargo cults or the Ghost Dance of 1890 in the American Great Plains offered only limited parallels. Apocalyptic literature was rooted in a long tradition of Judean life under foreign empires and, at times, imperial intervention, whereas the cargo cults and Ghost Dance were responses to the initial direct impact of colonial conquest.[18]

Of much greater importance, just then emerging, we believe, was the awareness of the impact of and resistance to colonial rule that was just dawning on biblical and other scholars in the late 1960s. Interest in imperial rule and in counterinsurgency came to the fore again in the 1980s, when it became evident that the U.S. military was training and arming repressive dictatorial regimes in Central America to suppress insurgencies partly motivated by hearing and discussion of the Bible.[19] Such interest was again provoked by the U S invasion of Iraq in 1991 and finally became more widespread in biblical studies in response to the second invasion and occupation of Iraq starting in 2003.

THE OCCASIONS FOR THESE ESSAYS

The opportunities to produce the essays collected below came in three closely related steps in the late 1980s and early 1990s, followed by a fourth in the early 2000s.

Intensive study of the "Synoptic Sayings Source" Q was underway in the 1980s. Helmut Koester and James M. Robinson had laid out a systematic scheme of (hypothetical) texts (behind the Gospels) of different genres that went together with corresponding "christologies" and even with corresponding "groups." Two of these they understood in terms of the standard concepts of "wisdom" and "apocalyptic(ism)." "The Synoptic Apocalypse" in Mark 13, of course, was the key case of "apocalyptic." Q had also been understood as an example of "apocalyptic Christianity." Leaders of the SBL Section focused on Q, however, pressed the hypothesis that Q consisted of different layers, a foundational layer of "sapiential" sayings, and a secondary "apocalyptic" layer. They also argued that the "sapiential" layer advocated an individual lifestyle of "itinerant radicalism," basically that of the "wandering charismatics" hy-

---

18. See the critique in Horsley, *Sociology and the Jesus Movement*, 90–91.
19. See Horsley, *Liberation of Christmas*, chap 7, and the references there.

pothesized by Gerd Theissen for the early Jesus movement in general.[20] This schematic set of hypotheses seemed problematic and unconvincing for several interrelated reasons that boil down to two basic points. What is claimed as "sapiential" and "apocalyptic" in the (hypothetical, reconstructed) sayings of Q appears to come from modern scholarly constructs and not from the text of Q itself; much of what is labeled "sapiential" is not similar to wisdom texts and what is labeled "apocalyptic" does not resemble what is found in apocalyptic texts. Moreover, the picture of the "itinerant radicalism" is not only based on sayings taken out of context and read somewhat literally, but is rooted in the conservative structural-functional sociology developed on the basis of modern western industrial societies and heavily concerned with maintenance of the overall social order.[21]

The essays in chapters 8 and 9 below were critical responses to and alternatives to that combination of hypotheses. The concepts of "apocalyptic" and "sapiential" do not appear applicable to the text of Q, which is more prophetic in form and substance and addressed to communities of ordinary people, not individual itinerants. The essays in chapter 10, on the Gospel of Mark, and in chapter 11 on all of the Synoptic Gospels, were invited articles partly in response to the research and presentation of the essays on Q.

Second, the organization of an SBL program unit focused on "Sociology of the Second Temple" offered the occasion to explore more carefully the political-economic-religious structure of second-temple Judea. Most participating colleagues were interested in a more vague "sociology of literature." But it seemed important, underlying that, to gain a more precise sense of the particular social location and function of the learned scribes who, given the limited literacy in antiquity, presumably produced both wisdom and apocalyptic literature. Colleagues in Hebrew Bible had used the (also structural-functional) historical sociology of Gerhard Lenski to illuminate the structure of the monarchy.[22] And New Testament scholars had used Lenski to explain how the Pharisees and scribes in Josephus, the Gospels, and rabbinic texts must have been "retainers" in service of the Judean temple-state in Roman

---

20. Theissen, *Sociology of the Jesus Movement*.

21. Elliott, "Social-Scientific Criticism of the New Testament"; Horsley, *Sociology and the Jesus Movement*, chaps 1–4.

22. For example, Chaney, "Systemic Study of the Israelite Monarchy."

times.[23] Many colleagues, however, were apprehensive about "imposing" a "sociological model" onto ancient texts and history. This in fact was the occasion on which we came together for collaboration on the essay in chapter 1. It seemed possible to discern the political-economic-religious structure of second-temple Judea from the information available in the instructional speeches of Ben Sira, while both learning from the comparative material in Lenski's historical sociology and criticizing the applicability of his "model" of stratification.

Key for the utility of our sociological analysis based on Ben Sira in understanding other Judean texts, however, was the recognition that we needed to go beyond both Ben Sira and Lenski's model. Ben Sira's speeches virtually ignore that the high priestly rulers of Judea whom he and other learned scribes served as "retainers" were subject to imperial rulers, sometimes competing imperial rulers. This enabled us to realize that factions could develop in the Judean priestly aristocracy, as indeed happened under the Ptolemaic and Seleucid regimes, with corresponding factions among the learned scribes. The essays in chapters 2, 3, 4, 5, and 6 are applications of this realization to one or more particular Judean "apocalyptic" or "wisdom" texts.

Those same essays, however, were written in response to the third occasion, which led to further fruitful collaboration with many other colleagues. During a break in the verbal action at the 1993 SBL Annual Meeting, in an exciting conversation we had with our mutual friend and mentor on apocalyptic texts, George Nickelsburg, emerged the idea of forming a program unit for collaborative exploration of "Wisdom and Apocalypticism in Early Judaism and Early Christianity" (those broad synthetic essentialist constructs again). One of the motivations was to become clearer in our concerns about the dichotomy that had developed in biblical studies, especially in New Testament studies, between the two constructs "apocalyptic" and "wisdom." We agreed on certain principles of investigation, such as maintaining disciplined focus on particular texts, having separate sessions on texts produced in the Hellenistic period (that is, mainly in Judea) and the Roman period (with a wider range of provenance and contexts), and paying purposeful attention to the political-economic-religious settings. The essays in chapters 2, 4, and 12 were written for sessions of this collaborative working Group, and those in chapters 5, 7, and 11 were strongly influenced by the collaboration.

23. Saldarini, *Pharisees, Scribes, and Sadducees*.

The essay in chapter 7 is in many ways a review of the multifaceted work of this collaboration among colleagues.

The fourth occasion was the series of annual Enoch Seminars organized by Gabriele Boccaccini at which some of the implications of our sociological analysis of Sirach could be tested in discussion with Enoch scholars. Some of these ideas were also worked out in conversation with Harvard graduate students, Mark Kurtz, Nicole Kelly, and Anna-Maria Lieukendjik. Chapter 3 was originally presented at the Enoch Seminar in Venice.

Because we were working in regular conversation during the years in which these essays were researched and written, we believe that the essays in Parts One and Two have considerable coherence with one another. Both chapter 2 and chapter 3 are rooted directly in the analysis we carried out in chapter 1. That is, once we gained a sense that the "social location" and political "role" of learned scribes such as Ben Sira (and the *maskilim* who produced Daniel etc.) were as advisers of the ruling aristocracy of Judea, under higher imperial rule, it was possible to explore more precisely how both the "wisdom" texts and the "apocalyptic" texts they produced were rooted in and reflected their position "in the middle." Following through on the imperial situation to which apocalyptic texts are responding, chapter 4 explores the effect of Hellenistic imperial rule on the position and role of "Enoch" scribes. Narrowing the focus to the temple-state itself, the essay on the Epistle of Enoch in chapter 5 explores rather how the "Enoch" scribes' position "in the middle" between their patrons' exploitation of the poor and their own cultivation of and commitment to torah and prophetic traditions led to their sharp condemnation of the wealthy and powerful. With a clearer sense of the contents and concerns of third and second century "apocalyptic" texts, the essay in chapter 6 notes how *4 Ezra*, composed after the disastrous Roman destruction of Judea and Jerusalem, is no longer convinced that it is possible even for learned scribes to receive revelation of certain things. The essay in chapter 7 then reviews the last generation's remarkable advance of scholarly analysis, translation, and interpretation of wisdom and apocalyptic texts with critical assessment of key issues and of how future research can build on the foundation that has been solidly established.

PART ONE

Social-Political Context of Apocalyptic and Wisdom Texts

1

Ben Sira and the Sociology of the Second Temple

ON SOCIOLOGICAL MODELS

THE MOST INFLUENTIAL RECENT literature portrays second-temple Judea as suddenly abuzz with commercial activity in the Hellenistic period. Hengel relies heavily on the Zenon correspondence, which, he claims, gives the picture of a very active, almost hectic commercial life, originated by that host of Greek officials, agents and merchants who flooded the land in the truest sense of the word and "penetrated into the last village of the country."[1] He finds this picture confirmed by other evidence of key indicators of commercial activity: the monetarization of the economy, expanded foreign trade, and tirades against such commercial activity in traditional Jewish literature such as the book of Sirach. "Finds of coins are a further indicator of the commercial boom in Palestine at this time . . . By and large, one might say that minted money was finally established in Palestine only through Ptolemy II, and largely superseded barter."[2] Hengel finds "the increase of foreign trade in the course of the third century BCE is attested by the many stamped—and partly datable—jars from Rhodes and other parts of the Aegean which are to be found throughout Palestine west of the Jordan."[3] He further claims that "it may be assumed that in Palestine, as in Egypt, agricultural and

---

1. Hengel, *Judaism and Hellenism*, 1.43.
2. Ibid., 1.43–44.
3. Ibid., 1.44.

commercial production was considerably increased, leading not only to a substantial increase in revenue from taxes but also to an increase in the population itself."[4] Finally, Hengel states, opposition to "economic and cultural contacts with the non-Jewish environment is most clearly expressed by Ben Sira in his polemic against the hectic concern with earning money and against the . . . deceptive merchant."[5]

There are some serious problems with this picture in several interrelated respects, problems which are not peculiar to Hengel's unusually thorough scholarship, but pervade the present state of inquiry into second-temple history generally. First, Hengel and others have not asked very precise questions in their evaluation and use of numismatic, archaeological, and other evidence. In order to evaluate finds of coins, we would have to ask not only about the location of the sites at which they were found, but also about their use or function at those sites. The vast majority of coins cited as evidence for the monetarization of the economy in Palestine generally, including Judea, were found at Samaria, Shechem, and Scythopolis, i.e., outside of Judea, or at Beth Zur, which means they were probably left there by a military garrison. This is hardly evidence for the monetarization of the economy, let alone that it may have penetrated the villages! Moreover, if the economy was monetarized, why were both crown and sanctuary both collecting taxes in kind in those "great vessels" marked with the pottery stamps *jhd* and *yrslm* studied by Lapp and cited by Hengel?[6] If we look more closely at the sites where the wine jars from Rhodes were found, most of the evidence comes from cities on the coastal plain, such as Ptolemais, Strato's Tower, and Ashdod, while inland the sites are again the military fortress of Beth Zur and the Acra garrison in Jerusalem.[7] Again, there is no evidence to suggest that foreign trade had penetrated very far into Judean society. Hengel admits the lack of evidence for an increase in "agricultural and commercial production," yet extrapolates from the production of balsam around the Dead Sea, an utterly unique case which says nothing about the rest of the agrarian economy. We might also doubt whether the occurrence of literary metaphors in Qoh 2:6 and Sir 24:30–31 are solid evidence that "artificial irrigation was probably also introduced

---

4. Ibid., 1.47.
5. Ibid., 1.52.
6. Lapp, "Ptolemaic Stamped Handles"; Hengel, *Judaism and Hellenism*, 1.25.
7. See the literature cited in Hengel, *Judaism and Hellenism*, 2.35 n. 342.

into Palestine at that [second century BCE.] time."[8] Finally, except for the sharp polemics against the trader and retailer in 26:29—27:3, the passages from Ben Sira that Hengel cites as proof texts for his claim about hostility to foreigners and the busy money-making they represent require considerable imagination to be read in this way.[9]

Much of the difficulty stems from the absence of any clear sense of what the actual concrete political-economic structure of Judea or other districts of Palestine would have been like in the second-temple period. In the absence of any critically developed model of this or any other ancient society, Tcherikover, Hengel, and others continue to project back the kinds of social relations and structure they are familiar with, i. e., that of modern Western capitalist society, with its "middle class" as well as commercialized market economy. Much of the standard picture of the social and economic world in Hellenistic times generally, moreover, is based on the monumental work of Michael Rostovzeff, who himself projected back into ancient times the evolving capitalism of his native Russia in the early twentieth century.[10] It seems obvious that we should be evaluating the limited evidence available, whether coins, wine jars, or sapiental sayings, with a much more precise and complex set of questions and concepts and some overall picture of how an ancient society was put together. The obvious move would appear to be to borrow a model of how a whole society works from sociology.

We find problems, however, in the ways some biblical scholars have used sociology and with the kind of sociology they have used. Some efforts appear to do little more than illustrate from biblical texts a sociological scheme or model developed on the basis of modern societies, and pay little attention to the original literary and/or historical social context of the textual attested "data."[11] The sociological method most prominently adopted to date in biblical studies has been structural-functionalism, which dominated sociology generally in the United States in the mid-twentieth century. But that method tends to slight the importance of historical change and to obscure social conflict.[12]

---

8. Ibid., 1.46.
9. Ibid., 1.127–28; 2.40 n. 404; 2.96 n. 284.
10. Rostovzeff, *Social and Economic History*.
11. Theissen, *Sociology*.
12. See the criticism in Elliott, "Social Scientific Criticism"; and Horsley, *Sociology*.

The frequently borrowed ancient model constructed by Carney[13] does not project modern patterns back into the ancient world, but it is based primarily on evidence from Rome, and may not be readily applicable to the ancient Near East, at least until well after strong Roman influence in the East.

Given both the confusing and distorting situation in the scholarly treatment of second-temple times and the problems with borrowing sociological methods and models, we must perhaps ask some rather simple and fundamental questions and take virtually nothing for granted. It is difficult to know where to start once we recognize that even the generation of data depends on the questions we ask of our sources. It seems best to proceed dialectically back and forth between textual, archaeological, and other evidence, on the one hand, and a critical appropriation of concepts and models of traditional agrarian societies developed on the basis of comparative historical sociological studies, on the other. Thus, at the risk of repetition in this essay, we will start with what we believe is the pertinent textual information from Ben Sira, then critically adapt a widely used model of agrarian societies, and finally venture a historical sociological analysis of the Judean temple-state and temple-community based on Ben Sira's "wisdom" along with related texts. Not surprisingly, texts tell us the most about the people who produced them, in this case the scribes and sages of second-temple Judea. In an attempt to make the most of the evidence available about this crucial social stratum, which mediated structurally between the rulers and the peasantry, we will attend also to the Enoch literature apparently produced just prior to Ben Sira.

Finally, we are engaged in what is primarily a historical inquiry in which sociological models should be used to elucidate textual and historical particularity, and not to dissolve or obscure it. We are drawing primarily on evidence provided by Ben Sira and adding sociological inquiry to the usual philological, archaeological, literary, and historical investigations in an attempt to further our understanding of the social conflicts and events of second-temple Judea.

---

13. Carney, *Shape of the Past*.

INDICATIONS OF SOCIAL STRUCTURE AND ROLES IN BEN SIRA

Because we want to work from the textual and other evidence and not simply impose a sociological model that may not "fit," we begin with a search for indicators of social positions, roles, and structures in Ben Sira's "wisdom." We took this first step in our investigation, based on close reading and philological examinations of the Hebrew and Greek texts and on key secondary literature, before one of us had read for the first time and before the other had read again for the first time in twelve years the principal sociological model we will criticize and adapt just below. We hope, therefore, that the results of our investigation in this first section have not been determined by the adapted model to be utilized in a subsequent section.

We believe that Burton Mack has made an important breakthrough both in understanding what Ben Sira was about and in approaching the fundamental social structure of second-temple Judea.[14] Looking for a larger frame of reference in which to read Ben Sira's "Praise of the Fathers," Mack found help in the suggestion of structural linguistics that a text emerges from and is rooted in a larger cultural system of signs (symbol system). Like other humanities fields and social sciences, so also biblical studies can develop a discourse that treats religion and culture, literature and society, as complex interrelated systems of signs. "Regarding them as 'texts,' the scholarly endeavor is to 'read' them together, 'translating' from system to system, and so come to understand their 'meaning.'"[15] Breaking with the standard individualistic reading (exegesis) focused closely on particular terms and verses, Mack dramatically broadens the focus to take in the broader patterns that structure Ben Sira's paean of patriarchal praise. This enables him to notice the general pattern of characterization of "the pious men" in Sirach 44–50.

The great ancestors of Israel are praised not for their individual achievements but for the offices they held. It is the offices and not the individual persons which are glorious. Their virtue lies in their fulfillment of their office. Their rewards are simply the bestowal of office. In the overall pattern, there are five principal offices, besides the distinctive functions of Moses, those of "father" (Noah, Abraham, Isaac, Jacob),

---

14. Mack, *Wisdom and Hebrew Epic*.
15. Ibid., 5.

"priest" (Aaron, Phinehas, Simon), "judge" (Joshua, Caleb), "prophet" (Samuel, Nathan, Elijah, Elisha, Isaiah, Jeremiah, Ezekiel), and "king" (David, Solomon, Hezekiah, Josiah).

The focus and emphasis, however, is clearly on the priesthood, indeed the high-priesthood. Several factors make this clear. Far greater attention is lavished on Aaron than on any other historical figure including Moses and David. In fact, the role of Moses appears almost instrumental to the establishment of Aaron in the priesthood and the Aaronite priesthood takes over the only continuing function of Moses, teaching Israel the commandments (45:5, 17). The everlasting covenant (promise) of the priesthood is established for Aaron and his descendants and this is done structurally in connection with and as the sequel to the everlasting covenants (promises) made with the founding fathers, Noah, Abraham, and Jacob. By comparison, the later established covenant of kings is not characterized as everlasting and is used as a mere analogy in the assertion that "the heritage of Aaron is for his descendants" (cf. 42:25; 47:11). According to Ben Sira's characterization, even the kings appear instrumental to the temple-cult. Besides their respective fame for warfare and wisdom, David and Solomon function principally to establish the cult in Jerusalem (47:8–10, 13). The epic poem as a whole clearly climaxes in the elaborate praise of Simon, who receives more attention even than Aaron. And it is clear from the characterization of Simon that the high priesthood had taken over the functions of kingship (fortifications and water supply, cf. 48:17 and 50:2–4), while remaining focused symbolically in the temple-cult.

The overall and particular pattern of characterization thus indicates that the high priesthood is the outgrowth and continuance of all the glorious offices and their incumbents. Not only is it firmly established by the eternal covenant with Aaron and his anointing by Moses, but it is further grounded in all the glorious offices of Israel's heritage, starting with the eternal covenant/promise to the fathers. Characterization of individual office-holders, the principal themes and motifs, and the overall structure of the poem all come to a focus on the high priesthood exalted in the Temple. But just as the pious men thus praised are not merely paradigms of individual salvation, so the poem as a whole is about far more than a cult or religion called "Judaism." Ben Sira's praise of the fathers is a grand poetic and ceremonial charter of the Judean temple-state that he served in early second century BCE Jerusalem.[16]

We think that, building on what Mack has discerned, it is possible to be more precise with regard to the relationship between systems of signs, in particular, between the system of signs displayed in Ben Sira's book and that of second-temple Judea. Mack works on the assumption that the "complete system" of the hymn to the fathers "is the structure of the covenant community with its arrangements of institutions and offices organized around the temple-cult and the role of the high priest."[17] But perhaps Mack's reading has not yet brought the social structure Ben Sira portrays sufficiently and precisely into focus. The "complete system" of the hymn corresponds not to the wider "arrangement of institutions and offices organized around the temple-cult and the role of the high priest," but focuses more precisely on the office of the high priest itself. Moreover, the characterization of the office of high priest suggests that the "arrangement of institutions and offices" organized around the Temple and high priest was unusually simple and virtually monolithic or "monarchic." The office of (high) priesthood had subsumed the functions of the other offices, particularly the teaching function of Moses and the political-economic functions of king. As evidenced in the hymn of praise, there was no "structural differentiation" of separable political, economic, and religious institutions such as that found in modern Western societies. We know from outside Ben Sira's hymn, of course, that the high priesthood in Jerusalem was politically-economically subject to the Seleucid imperial regime, as it had been previously to the Ptolemies and the Persians. But in Ben Sira's view, Simon is the "head of state" in a more awesome way than David and Solomon had been. On the basis of Ben Sira's characterization, one suspects that, insofar as there may have been other offices or institutions in Judean society, they were subordinated to or delegated as part of the functions ostensibly of the high priesthood. In order to obtain access to the system of signs that corresponds to the structure of the covenant community as a whole and the wider arrangement of institutions and offices organized around the

---

16. Thus, according to Mack, ibid., 144–45, 154–55, Ben Sira's answer to the "wisdom crisis" was to accept "the dislocation of wisdom from the social fabric" that was accomplished by the "personification of wisdom as a mythic figure" and then to relocate wisdom in the social order by identifying it with the temple-state in Jerusalem.

17. Mack, *Wisdom and Hebrew Epic*, 57.

Temple and high priest, we must go to the book of Ben Sira as a whole (and whatever other texts may provide access to that wider system of signs).

Ben Sira's "Audience"

It must be noted at the outset that the meaning discerned in a particular sapiental saying or instruction depends heavily on our assumption or determination about who is being addressed. Because readings of Sirach proceed without a sense of the particular social structure it presupposed, interpreters have rather vague sense of Ben Sira's audience. E.g., usually "the broad sections of the population, sometimes . . . the wealthy."[18] Any attempt to discern more precisely who Ben Sira's addressees may have been will be dependent on our hypotheses about the basic social structure he presupposed. But some preliminary observations seem warranted by certain passages in the text. The reflection on the function of the sage in relation to those in other stations in the society indicates that the speaker's position is somewhere in the middle, i.e., above the plowmen and artisans on whose labor a city depends but below and in service to those who rule (38:24—39:11). Other passages indicate that the addressees, like the speaker, stand beneath and somewhat vulnerable to the wealthy and powerful (8:1–2) and are learning "to stand in the presence of chiefs" (μεγιστᾶσιν, שׂרים) (8:8). Yet the addressees apparently may themselves function in positions of relative power, able to rescue the oppressed when they render judgments (4:9). Much of the book, moreover, focuses on the substance and transmission of wisdom itself. It thus seems likely that Ben Sira and his book addressed primarily other sages (students of wisdom) and the prospective occupants of important scribal or judicial positions in the society. The book contains enough cautionary and critical remarks about the wealthy and powerful to suggest that they or their children were not the audience.

Some of the exhortations as well as some of the "wisdom" appears to have been addressed more generally to the society at large, including the insistence on payment of tithes and offerings to the priests. As suggested in 38:24—39:11, however, the vast majority of the people, engaged in agricultural labor or making things with their hands, would not have had the "leisure" to learn wisdom. It therefore seems likely that

---

18. Tcherikover, *Hellenistic Civilization*, 149.

these exhortations have been included because they form a part of the standard content of wisdom teaching and not because the general population was expected to read or even listen to the reading of this book.

References to Rulers and/or the Priestly Aristocracy

It is at least conceivable that "the king" from which one should not seek "a seat of honor" (καθέδραν δόξης, מושב כבוד) or authority (ἡγεμονία, ממלך) or before whom one should not display one's wisdom (7:4) is the (Seleucid or Ptolemaic) emperor.[19] On the other hand, this could simply be an archaic, traditional term from the origins of wisdom teaching under the Solomonic monarchy for the immediate societal ruler. Other references to a king (10:3, 10; 38:2; 45:3; 50:2) are not entirely consistent. According to 38:2 the physician is paid by the king, probably referring to any local ruler with the means to support the services of a physician. However, 45:3 clearly refers to the royal temple (היכל מלך). It is to be doubted that Ben Sira's readers were in a position to petition the emperor for any position of honor.

Although it is clear from the long sections on Aaron and Simon in the Praise of the Fathers, chapters 44–50, that the high priesthood ruled Judea, Ben Sira does not elsewhere refer to the rulers as (high) priests (unless this is implied in the exhortation to "honor the priest" with first fruits, etc.). He uses a variety of terms, some of which appear to be interchangeable, to refer to the rulers, often in ways that indicate the relationship in which scribes/sages stand to these their apparent superiors.

In 10:24 those of highest standing in the society are the chief (μεγιστάν, שר), the ruler (δυνάστης, מושל), and the judge (κριτής, שופט). Chief (שר) is used for chiefs and rulers, often of subordinate status. In the Greek text of Sirach, it is translated by μεγιστάν, δυνάστης, and ἡγούμενος. It does not seem to refer to a specific class of rulers; Ben Sira is a bit ambivalent about the status of his hearers (and of himself) relative to the שרים. According to 7:14 and 32:9, one (especially if young) should not speak too much in the presence of these chiefs. On the other hand, by training one can hope to be able to stand in their presence,[20] and Ben Sira advises the שרים to listen to his instruction (33:19).

---

19. In 7:4a for ממלך, ms. C reads [מא]ל, (reflected in the Greek (κυρίου) so that it is from God that one should not see authority.

20. According to the Greek text of this verse, by training one can learn to serve (λειτουργῆσθαι) chiefs. According to DiLella (*Wisdom of Ben Sira*, 212), to stand in the presence of chiefs means to be a servant or courtier.

מוֹשֵׁל ("ruler", Qal participle of מָשַׁל) is translated by ἡγούμενος, κριτής, δυνάστης, and κύριος, and seems to refer simply to anyone who rules, whether politically or otherwise (or non-political examples see 15:10; 37:18; and 44:4cd). While Ben Sira exhorts his readers not to show favoritism to a ruler (4:27), he implies that they may aspire to positions of rulership (7:6, especially if they are strong enough to oppose crime), and he identifies the skilled sage as the ruler of his people (9:17). In 30(33):27(19) Ben Sira also advises the מוֹשֵׁל to listen to his instruction. In the same vein, according to 38:33, the scribe (unlike the artisan) is found among the rulers, where presumably he expounds law, justice, and wisdom.[21] Thus Ben Sira's readers (if we can assume that they were aspiring young scribes) could be at least informally identified as rulers, and they could formally become rulers at some level.

The word שׁוֹפֵט is consistently rendered in Greek as κριτής. According to 10:1–2 a "judge" is responsible for the stability (or training[22]) of his people and has ministers (λειτουργοί, מְלִיצִים) who are subordinate to him. One of the duties of a "judge" was to settle lawsuits (see 8:14), but as in the Hebrew Bible, "judges" seem to have been responsible for administering justice in other ways as well, including promoting stability (10:1) and general administration (4:15).[23]

Perhaps even higher on the social scale is the noble (δυνάστης, נָדִיב) who according to 7:6 is in a position to dominate a judge. In 13:9 it is the נדיב from whom one is to maintain a proper distance. In the Hebrew Bible נדיב is used in poetry often as a rather neutral term for one who rules or is of high social standing. More frequently it is used in the context of the contrast between commoner and noble. For example, 1 Sam 2:8 speaks of God causing the poor to "sit with princes." Likewise Ben Sira seems to use the term to imply a contrast between the social status of the ruler and those under his authority (e.g., 11:1).

Other terms for rulers are the "master of the city" (טון עיר, μεγιστάν, 4:7)[24] before whom one should bow one's head, the "chief"

---

21. Although this verse is not extant in Hebrew, the original must have read במושלים which was misread by the Greek translator as במשלים (παραβολᾶις), as Skehan has shown (*Wisdom of Ben Sira*, 448).

22. LXX reads παιδεύσει (= יוסר) for Hebrew יוסד.

23. Note also that in 10:1 the wise judge is parallel to the understanding one who possesses authority (ממשלת, ἡγεμονια).

24. Reading עיר with Syr. for עוד of ms. A.

(נשיא, ἡγούμενος, 4:17) before whom one should be ashamed of false-hood, the officer (מחוקק, γραμματεύς, 10:5) to whom God grants majesty, and the leader (ראש) of a city, whose inhabitants emulate him (10:2). The ways in which Ben Sira uses the various terms for rulers indicates that they all refer to local rulers of the Jewish temple-state. Most of the terms are used in construct (or other indications of relationship) with words like city (עיר, 4:7 [emended text]; 10:2), people (עם, 9:17; 10:1, 2; 30(33):27[19]), assembly (קהל, 30[33]:27[19]). Assuming that Judea was a temple-state with the high priest as political ruler, then these chiefs, rulers, judges, and nobles must have been members of the priestly aristocracy of Jerusalem. In both 30(33):27(19) and 39:4 (Greek only) μεγιστᾶνες λαοῦ (שרי עם) is paralleled by οἱ ἡγούμενοι ἐκκλησίας (משלי קהל), suggesting that the priestly aristocracy were the rulers. One then has the sense that there is some overlap or relationship between μεγιστᾶνες and ἡγούμενοι among whom the scribe/sages serve in 39:4 and the πλῆθος πρεσβυτέρων among whom the sages stand and speak in 6:34 and 7:14.[25] In 10:1–2 the κριτής (שופט) of a people or city is parallel to the sagacious one who possesses authority (ממשלת, ἡγεμονία) and to "he who rules a city" (ראש עיר, ἡγούμενον τῆς πόλεως) and in 10:3 מלך (βασιλεύς) is parallel to שרים (δυναστῶν) Although the words are clearly not technical terms for specific offices, this suggests that the judge of a people was not much different from the ruler of a city and that the princes of a city were not very different from the king, the local head of state.

On the other hand, there are indications of differences in status among the ruling class. The fact that one who held authority (ממשלת, ἡγεμονία) as a מושל (κριτής) might be partial to a נדיב (δυναστής) (7:4–6) implies that the former would have been somewhat lower in rank than, or subordinate to, the latter, though even a מושל might expect a little favoritism from Ben Sira's readers (4:27). That Ben Sira exhorts his hearers not to seek authority or to become a ruler (7:4–6) suggests that not all members of the high priestly families held offices and implies that such high offices were theoretically open to scribes and/or that Ben Sira's audience included members of priestly aristocracy families. The advice not to go to law against a "judge" (κριτής, שופט, 8:14), however, suggests that ordinarily Ben Sira's audience, presumably largely nascent

---

25. The Hebrew text of 39:4 is not extant and that of 6:34 is probably corrupt. Sir 7:14 is either corrupt in Hebrew or πρεσβυτέρων is a rough translation of שרים.

sages and scribes, did not rise to such positions. His audience of scribes in the making would ordinarily be in the position of bowing their heads low to the שלטון (μεγιστᾶνες) (4:7).

Finally, it may be significant that the *gerousia* (which is often thought to have played an important role in the politics of this period) is never, or almost never mentioned by Ben Sira.[26] Sir 38:32 mentions the people's council (βουλήν λαοῦ, omitted by all witnesses except for Sc L and Syr) in parallelism with assembly (ἐκκλησία). This, however, probably does not refer to any legally constituted senate, which in any case would not be referred to as a people's council. Where the Hebrew text is extant, עדה (translated by λαός, συναγωγή, or πλῆθος) seems never to refer to anything but a band or multitude of people.

קהל is consistently translated ἐκκλησία and, as the parallelism and context shows, usually means the assembled people. Thus, there is no clear evidence of an officially constituted senatorial body in Jerusalem. These were undoubtedly various assemblies where one could speak (15:5) or refrain from speaking (7:14), where the blameless could receive praise (34(31):11; 44:15), and, and before which Simon officiated at the altar (50:13, 20), but these are not legal governing bodies.

The Wealthy

As already noted on the basis of 7:4–6, apparently not all members of the priestly aristocracy would have occupied particular offices. Yet supposedly all members of the hierocratic families would have received (and controlled) the tithes and offerings, thus having somewhat the same basis of wealth as the high priestly office-holders. Although all would have shared in the proceeds from the tithes, Ben Sira's polemics against bribery (8:2; 20:29; 40:12–13) show that those who actually held a particular office could substantially augment their income.[27] The potentially suggestive two successive warnings against "contending with the ruler" and "quarreling with the rich" (8:1–2) come in a longer series and are

---

26. Cf. ἡ γερουσία καὶ οἱ ἱερεῖς καὶ οἱ γραμματεῖς τοῦ ἱεροῦ καὶ οἱ ἱεροψάλται (Josephus, *Ant.* 12.142). Hengel mentions the possibility that the עדת־שׂרים (πλήθει πρεσβυτέρων) refers to the *gerousia* (Hengel, *Judaism and Hellenism*, 2.21). The similarity between the terms, however, is close only in the Greek version of Sirach, and עדה seems to refer only to informal groups of people.

27. One of the indications of inequality of wealth among the ruling classes is that some of Ben Sira's readers were expected to have only one slave, while most had several (33[30]:31[39]).

probably not intended as synonymous parallelism.²⁸ Hence although it seems likely on the face of it that the wealthy are basically the same as rulers, the textual references do not supply unambiguous evidence.

Also unclear and requiring further analysis is the relation between the wealthy, whom one should be cautious dealing with, and the sharp criticism of wealth generally, particularly ill-gotten riches (see 5:1, 8; 13:24–25; 14:3; 31:3–9; 40:13,18).

Tithes and Offerings

That Sirach includes four pointed passages on tithes and offerings indicates how important were such revenues to the temple-state. In the most elaborate of these passages, 35:1–12, the exhortation is framed by references to offerings as part of "keeping the law/commandments" and to giving "to the Most High as he has given to you," in the traditional understanding of tithes and offerings as something one owed to God. Two other passages, however, are more direct with regard to the actual function of such dues. The firstfruits, guilt offerings, the choice shoulder cuts from animal sacrifices, etc., were tax revenues to "honor the priest" because, in the eternal covenant bestowed on Aaron, these had been allotted to Aaron and his descendants as their "heritage" (7:29–31; 45:20–21).

Scribes, their Position and Function

The principal role or function of the scribes or sages was "to serve the chiefs" (μεγιστᾶσιν, שׂרים) (8:8). Ben Sira provides a number of indications of what particular functions the scribes served for their superiors in the ruling priestly aristocracy of Jerusalem. In the course of the prolonged reflection on the scribes' position and activities in 38:24—39:11 he mentions that scribes were sought as advisers, if not members, of the collective leadership of Jerusalem and that they attained eminence among the citizenry as a whole (38:32–33). They were members of courts that heard cases, for they understood the decisions of courts and could expound judgments (38:33). They devoted themselves to the study of the

---

28. According to Di Lella, "V 2ab is in synonymous parallelism with v. 1; as is usually the case, the rich are also the great" (*Wisdom of Ben Sira*, 211). Yet the passage implies at least a technical distinction between the great and the rich. The powerful are dangerous because they possess power; the rich are dangerous because they can use their wealth to influence those who have power.

law and to the wisdom of the ancients precisely for their service among the rulers, presumably the priestly aristocracy (39:1–4). Apparently this service of the high priestly government also involved travel in foreign lands, possibly as ambassadors. Many other passages in Sirach confirm one or another of these functions of the scribe, whether it be a prominent role in "the company of elders/chiefs" (6:34; 7:14), wise counsel in the "assembly" (15:5; 21:17, or serving on courts and the rendering of verdicts of judgment (4:9; 11:7–9; 42:2). Ben Sira also mentions that the sage "instructs his own people," although it is difficult to discern whether this means the people generally, the Jerusalemites generally, or his own circle of disciples. If the former, then this special teaching function would also be part of the sage's service of the ruling aristocracy by instructing the Jerusalemites and/or peasants in the ideological basis for the priestly oligarchy.

Although these functions are explicitly understood as service of the ruling aristocracy, Ben Sira's instruction (for other sages) displays both a clear sense of the sages' sense of superiority to the peasantry and urban artisans and a special concern for the sages' role in protecting the poor and exploited. It is clear from the unflattering comparisons of the plowman, smith and potter with the scribe's σχολή for learning wisdom that the sages understood themselves as politically more important as well as culturally superior to the "working class" below them on the social scale. Yet Ben Sira sees the scribe as responsible for protecting those vulnerable to exploitation. One of the two references to "giving a verdict" is precisely for the purpose of "rescuing the oppressed from the oppressor" (4:9). It may not be by accident of editorial arrangement that immediately following his exhortations to "honor the priest" with the lawful payment of tithes and offerings—which may well have been the basis of the scribes' own remuneration for their services by the priestly aristocracy—come corresponding admonitions concerning special attention to the poor and suffering (see 7:29–31, 32–36; 35:1–15, 16–26; and 34:21–27). Moreover, one should not show partiality to a ruler (מושל, δυναστής, 4:27). Clearly Ben Sira's view of the sage's function in society included more than simply an obligation to his aristocratic employers. It also included a perceived obligation to God to act on his behalf to limit the abuses of the powerful against the poor.

Ben Sira displays a similar ambivalence toward, as well as social-political distance from, the ruling aristocracy that he and others served with their wisdom. The sage must defer and bow low to the ruler (4:7). Not surprisingly the sages would be invited to dine at the table by their superiors and patrons. At two points Ben Sira thus offers extensive instruction for the proper deferential behavior on such occasions (13:8–11; 31:12–24). Yet despite this emphasis on subservience and deference to their superiors and patrons, Ben Sira also cautions his disciples about the potential dangers involved in dealing with the powerful (13:9).

Artisan, Smith, Potter; Physicians; Merchants

As a foil or counterpoise to the importance of the sage, Ben Sira mentions the artisan who cuts seals or paints images, the smith working with iron, and the potter making numerous vessels on his wheel (38:27–30). By comparison, physicians seem to enjoy higher social rank, like the sages themselves working among and being honored by the great ones.

Ben Sira also mentions merchants and traders (and buying and selling). Besides the brief references at 37:11 and 42:5, there is the sharp criticism in 26:29—27:2. Such a negative attitude of traders and merchants was common in ancient literature and the societies they come from.

Agricultural Workers

In contrast to trade and merchants, farm work is honorable, "created by the Most High" (7:15), and the plowman is described positively, even if of lower rank than the sage himself (38:24–25). Clearly, if the priesthood depends for its income on tithes and offerings, then there must be many more "plowmen" than priests by a factor of at least the inverse of the proportion of the crops received from the plowmen.

Slaves and Hired Workers

Interestingly, Ben Sira refers far more frequently and extensively to slaves (עבד, οἰκέτης) than to plowmen/farm workers. In these passages it seems that he is addressing people who have one or more slaves (see 6:11; 33[30]:25[33]–33[40]; 42:5), although he also gives advice to those who have only one slave (33[30]:31[39]). It would appear that these were household slaves, and not large gangs of slaves used in farming or mining. What is unclear is whether the hired laborer (שוכר, οἰκέτης), parallel to the slave in 7:21, is also a household worker (cf. 31[34]:27).

The Poor

The poor, whom Ben Sira mentions at several points, and with whom the scribes clearly have contact in the courts, are clearly not the same as beggars, whom he mentions differently (40:28). The poor have their own roofs over their heads, have some agricultural base, have holdings that can be (wrongfully) appropriated, and make appeals to the courts regarding their oppression by oppressors (see 4:1–6, 7–10; 7:32; 13:17–24; 29:1–8, 22; 34:24–27; 35:16–26).

SOCIOLOGY OF AGRARIAN SOCIETIES: A CRITICAL ADAPTATION

In recent years even biblical scholars have recognized that, consciously or not, when we (re)construct history we make use of particular models of social structure and social relations. It is not a question of whether we utilize a particular model of society, but rather of whether we do so with some critical awareness. In this study we are purposely looking for help from the comparative historical sociology of Gerhard Lenski.[29] This is partly because his study of power and privilege has already been utilized extensively in analyses of the ancient Israelite monarchy and more recently in analysis of late second-temple Palestine.[30] Thus Lenski's model has already been injected into sociological discourse among students of Hebrew Bible. But Lenski's comparative historical model has certain advantages over other sociological methods-and-models as well. By contrast with the structural-functionalism through which Theissen and others have read Synoptic Gospel materials, Lenski's approach is fully aware, indeed is structured in terms of, the historical development of societies across long periods of time through different stages or types of social structures. Thus there is far less blatant projection of modern assumptions, for example, about the divisibility of certain social functions, back into historical circumstances in which they do not apply. Moreover, although he still uses certain conceptual terms appropriate only to the emergence of capitalism in early modern Western Europe, he recognizes that agrarian societies of the past involved a pre-market economy.[31]

---

29. Lenski, *Power and Privilege*.
30. For example, Saldarini, *Pharisees, Scribes, and Sadducees*.
31. For a summary of Lenski's thesis, see *Power and Privilege*, chaps. 8–9; Saldarini, *Pharisees, Scribes, and Sadducees*, 21–25, 35–45.

We cannot simply apply Lenski's model of *agrarian societies* to second-temple Judea, however, because it has certain problems or limitations as historical sociology. Lenski himself was aware of some of them. In his overall evolutionary scheme keyed on factors such as complexity and technological developments, he sets up a limited number of stages or types, with *agrarian* societies standing between *horticultural* and *industrial*. He then lumps together all societies which appear to stand somewhere in between horticultural and industrial. In a moment of self-criticism, refreshing among scholars, he mentions in a footnote that Robert Bellah, in response to his discussion of agrarian societies, had argued for division of agrarian societies into three sub-types: city-states, bureaucratic empires, and feudal regimes.[32] It then becomes evident as one reads through Lenski's discussion that the differences in precisely those three different kinds of societies keep cropping up when Lenski discusses variations within his broad agrarian type. For example, in European feudalism (or in the Classical Greek and Roman city-states for that matter), the "state" is strikingly diffuse when compared with the far more centralized "state" of ancient Near Eastern, Indian, Aztec, Inca, and African societies. Or, in feudal Europe a good deal of mercantile or artisan specialization developed independently of feudal lords, whereas trade and artisans do not appear to have been independent of the "state" in the ancient Near East and other bureaucratic empires. Or again, in feudalism, higher lords granted "fiefs" to lower lords which included both relatively independent political jurisdiction together with a hereditary claim to the produce of the peasantry and even to the land, whereas in the ancient Near East rulers granted their high officials incomes from large landed estates without hereditary rights and without independent political jurisdiction.[33]

These differences, however, constitute a decisive systemic variation in the fundamental political-economic relations between ruler, governing class, and peasantry! And it makes a considerable difference in what catches our attention if we focus less on the different social strata or

32. See Lenski, *Power and Privilege*, 191 n. 5a.

33. To cite just one "important variable" mentioned by Lenski himself (*Power and Privilege*, 229–30), the governing class "in most of early medieval Europe . . . was made up of a feudal nobility whose power and privilege rested on their membership in a hereditary legal class. In other societies, such as the Roman, Byzantine, Ottoman, and Chinese Empires . . . the governing class consisted . . . of bureaucratic officials whose power rested on their occupancy of offices which were not usually inheritable and who did not constitute a legally defined class."

"classes" than on the basic political-economic-religious relations between those social strata, e.g., on the relations between (higher) ruler and subordinate governing class and the relations between the governing class and the peasant producers. In some of the societies among Lenski's comparative materials, the ruler is the sole as well as central political authority figure who then economically supports the governing class with goods appropriated by the state from the peasants. In others among his agrarian societies members of the governing class enjoy a combination of political authority over the peasantry and hereditary rights to the land or the produce of the land. Most of Lenski's materials illustrate the former system. For study of second-temple Judea and other ancient near Eastern societies and ancient empires, which have such decisive differences from both feudal Europe and the city-states of Greco-Roman antiquity, a far more precise comparative model of agrarian societies could be constructed by focusing on the majority of Lenski's materials. The excluded feudal European materials and city-states of Greco-Roman antiquity could then be used as illustrations of different systems for comparison and contrast. Some of the remaining problems with Lenski's model are rooted in the basic systemic difference just outlined.

In his delineation of the "priestly class" as separate and different from "the ruler," the "governing class," and the "retainer class," Lenski was apparently making the Western differentiation between church and state, spiritual power and temporal power, religious and political institutions and roles normative for his model. In much if not most of his materials, however, these dimensions of life have not been differentiated, or have been unevenly differentiated at different levels. The very use of terms such as "king" and/or "priest" or "manager" may be a projection based on a different social system. Since the category of "the priestly class" is not central or determinative in the majority of Lenski's materials, it should not be included in our model of agrarian societies. We will thus be better able to discern cases in which priests and non-priests both occupy certain social positions or carry out certain social functions.

If we were then to place Lenski's various classes not as a scheme of social stratification (the predilection of much American social sociology) but in a scheme of fundamental political-economic relations, following precisely the information provided by Lenski, it is clear that the fundamental/basic or controlling relationship lies between the rulers and the agricultural producers, the peasantry who comprise the vast majority (90 percent) of the people of such an agrarian society. By virtue of their power, military and other, the rulers are able to demand rent/tithes/tribute from the peasant producers whom they rule (but who are otherwise virtually self-sufficient). Then, as Lenski himself explains variously, the rulers (official ruler and governing class) use part of what they appropriate from the peasantry (a) to support a staff of military and legal-clerical "retainers" through whom the society is governed, (b) to organize or support traders who obtain the luxury and other goods the rulers desire, and (c) to pay or support artisans who make the various products needed by the rulers and their retainers and supporters in the cities. That is, the retainers, merchants, and even the artisans are dependent upon, as well as subordinate to, the ruling class.

Lenski is sensitive to the fact that modern Western assumptions about private property tend to obscure our understanding of political-economic-religious relations in traditional agrarian societies. This is of greatest importance in understanding how the ruler or state can lay claim to such a huge share of a society's productivity. "At the head of nearly every advanced agrarian state was a single individual, the king or emperor. Monarchy was the rule . . ." If we approach such societies with the modern capitalist concept of private property in mind, it must appear that the monarch is the "owner" of the land. But then how do we explain that the peasants in such societies are by and large not slaves but free (to a degree) and that they also have certain claim to the land and its produce? The concept of private property or ownership may simply be inapplicable. More appropriate to traditional agrarian societies would be to reconceptualize property *in terms of rights not things*, with the possibility of overlapping rights to the land, or, perhaps, to the produce of the land and the labor of the peasants. Accordingly Lenski suggests "a proprietary theory of the state," as a way of understanding what "property" or "ownership" might mean in the concrete relational terms in which such societies apparently operated. How can royal ownership be consistent with local possession or ownership? The common or corporate "ownership" can be understood as vested in the head of state. "*All agrarian rulers enjoyed significant proprietary rights in virtually all of the land in their domains.*"[34] It may thus be possible to understand how agrarian rulers appear to be "owners" or rather "part-owners," not only of their

---

34. Lenski, *Power and Privilege*, 215–16; emphasis original.

own "royal estates," but of all other lands which they grant as prebends and/or from which they extract taxes or tribute.

It is curious that in this connection, Lenski does not even raise, let alone address, the mechanism by which such "proprietary rights in virtually all of the land in their domains" is legitimated for the monarchs of traditional agrarian societies. Ironically, Lenski focuses almost exclusively on the material level, while Karl Marx provides a far less reductionist approach, one that takes the religious dimension more fully into account. Lenski does mention in passing, with regard to the advanced horticultural system of Dahomey, that the rulers "were regarded as divine or semi-divine and thus the owner of all property in the land,"[35] as well as the ancient Mesopotamian conception of the land as the estate of the society's god(s), the temple(s) as the house of the god(s) and the king or high priest as the chief servant of the god(s). But it is Marx who reflects more generally that in such societies it is by virtue of being the symbol of the society as a whole, the head of the whole body, that the god or the god's regent is the controller (and beneficiary) of the tribute taken from the members of the social body. We theologians and students of religion jealous for the importance of our subject matter can legitimately point out (over against the apparent reductionism of Lenski's comparative sociology) that the working of such a system is dependent on just such an ideology or mythology of god(s) and king and/or high priest as the representative/symbol of the whole.

Lenski's model of agrarian society, perhaps because of its part in his overall evolutionary scheme, does not take into account the fact that most concrete examples of agrarian societies are parts of larger agrarian empires. As John Kautsky explains in his *The Structure of Aristocratic Empires*,[36] the aristocratic rulers of a large agrarian empire usually comprise a different society from the peoples they rule, and the subordinate peoples often include different societies. Since many large aristocratic empires ruled their subject peoples indirectly through the native aristocracies or monarchies, the overall political-economic-religious system was usually more complex than Lenski's model allows. If we consider this point together with the previous point about how the social system was held together by an ideology of a god and/or king/high priest at its center as a symbol of the whole, we can immediately see the interrelated

35. Ibid., 154–55.
36. Kautsky, *Structure of Aristocratic Empires*.

issues of (a) the "legitimacy" of the ruler(s), local and/or imperial, and (b) the potential conflict between the levels of rulers with different legitimating ideologies.

As illustrated by that last issue, Lenski's model does not deal with social conflict, whether "manifest" or "latent." His model sets up the potential for structural conflict, by highlighting how the wealth and "privilege" of the rulers and governing class are based on their political "power" (although, as noted he fails to focus on the religious limitation of their power and privilege). But the potential lines of conflict go unexamined.

With these major adaptations or revisions of Lenski's model of a traditional agrarian society, i.e., dominated by centralized rule, as distinguished primarily from the more diffuse medieval European feudal system but also from classical Greek and Roman city states, we can bring comparative historical sociology to bear on evidence of social structure and social relations from the wisdom of Jesus Ben Sira. Finally, we should reaffirm that historical sociology should be historical, attentive to developments, conflicts, shifts, etc. from time to time insofar as they may appear through the few windows provided by our limited literary and other sources.

SOCIAL STRUCTURE AND SOCIAL RELATIONS IN BEN SIRA

In the perspective provided by comparative sociological studies of traditional agrarian societies, the evidence Ben Sira provides of the relatively simple and compact Judean temple-state and supporting community has great credibility. The picture Ben Sira sketches in the paean of praise to the High Priest Simon reflects the basic social structure. State and society are headed by the high priest, who is surrounded and assisted in ruling by the inner concentric circle of "his brothers", the aristocracy among "the sons of Aaron", who are in turn surrounded and supported by the outer concentric circle of the people, "the whole congregation of Israel" (esp. 50:1, 12). Not included in the hymnic version, of course, is the wider political-economic-cultural context in which the Judean temple-state and community fits as one tiny subordinate unit in the wider Seleucid empire. From that wide perspective the high priesthood was subordinate to, and the representative of, Seleucid imperial authority, responsible for maintaining imperial order and collecting imperial taxes.

What appears to the modern reader (accustomed to "structural differentiation" between religion and politics and economics) in Ben Sira's hymn of praise as a distinctively religious ceremony therefore includes and presupposes (or is inseparable from) the political and economic dimensions as well. From the section of the hymn in praise of Aaron, and Ben Sira's exhortations to dutifully bring such produce to the priests, it is clear that the priestly aristocracy is economically supported by the tithes and offerings of "the whole congregation of Israel," i.e., largely the Judean peasant agricultural producers (45:20–21; 7:29–31). The high priest was the political-religious "head of state" ruling Judea, while also serving as the chief political-economic Seleucid imperial officer over Judea.

From the rest of Ben Sira's book, checked at points against related textual or other evidence, we can then obtain information that further articulates the fundamental structure of priestly rulers and their peasant producers-supporters. The ruling high priest and priestly aristocracy are assisted in governing the people by the ordinary priests and, in Ben Sira, particularly by the scribes/sages. Supporting services for the priestly rulers and their functions are provided by the artisans, smiths, potters, etc. who comprise the other residents of the capital city built around the Temple. Since there would have been little or no trade in a traditional agrarian society for anyone except the ruling elite, the merchants Ben Sira castigates (26:29—27:2) must also basically have serviced the lifestyle of the priestly aristocracy in Jerusalem.

The High Priesthood and Ruling Aristocracy

Just as the high priest at the altar in all his cosmic glory had "a garland of brothers around him . . . the sons of Aaron in their splendor holding out the Lord's offerings" (50:5–13), so the high priest as head of state stood in the midst of a priestly aristocracy both in governing the people and in receiving their economic support. As noted above (pp. 27–31), Ben Sira refers to rulers in his society in what appear to be two different sets of terms. On the one hand, he has the Aaronid priesthood established with "authority over" and "inheritance in" the people. On the other hand, he speaks of "judges," "chiefs," "rulers," and "nobles," as dominant in the society and as those among whom the scribes served and (apparently) as forming various courts, assemblies, or gatherings for whose deliberations the scribes might be important (39:4; 38:33). What is the relationship between these two? The "chiefs" and "rulers" would appear to be (basically) the ruling aristocracy among "the sons of Aaron." Not all priests, perhaps not even all of the Zadokites, would have been among the ruling aristocracy. Some of the aristocracy may have held a particular office (שׁוֹפֵט/κριτής may refer to such an office), but we should not imagine that all members of a dominant aristocracy held a particular "minister's portfolio" as in the cabinets of modern governments.

The proclamation of Antiochus III about the restoration of Temple and temple-government in Jerusalem, nearly contemporary with Ben Sira, has ἡ γερουσία καὶ οἱ ἱερεῖς καὶ οἱ γραμματεῖς τοῦ ἱεροῦ καὶ οἱ ἱεροψάλται (Josephus, *Ant.* 12.142) listed as the favored ones relieved of tax burdens. The letter of the Hasmonean high priest Jonathan to Sparta a half-century later lists at the head of the people "the high priest, the γερουσία of the people, and the priests" (1 Macc 12:6). Ben Sira's references to the people governing the society fits these lists if his "chiefs," "rulers," and "judges" are understood as the same as ἡ γερουσία in the Antiochene decree and Hasmonean letter.[37] That is, a much larger number of priests served in various capacities in the Temple and other offices, but a few distinguished and well-born priestly families (designated as the *gerousia*) wielded political-economic control. Not only is it unlikely that the *gerousia* was a purely lay body,[38] but it may well have been a purely high priestly "council." Ben Sira's references to the role of sages and their relations with "chiefs" and "rulers" suggest that the sages were not "members" of the "council" (or ruling class), but merely advisers (i.e., not councilors but counselors).

The central figure in the aristocracy, as well as head of the society as a whole, was the high priest. In order to understand how the whole political-economic-religious system of second-temple Judea worked, we must devote far more attention to the religious dimension focused on the high priesthood, a dimension simply neglected in Lenski's model, as we noted above. The people are to be focused on, to fear, and to

37. The difference is that from the perspective of Antiochus III, the Greek king of a Greek empire, or from the later point of view of a head of state communicating with a Greek city-state, the chief officials in the high priest's administration would constitute a senate (γερουσία). From Ben Sira's perspective as an insider, on the other hand, there were individuals who held certain high offices and collectively formed the leadership of Jerusalem.

38. Hengel, *Judaism and Hellenism*, 1.26.

serve "the Most High," who is explicitly understood as "the king of all." Correspondingly, the whole temple-state apparatus is structured ostensibly to the service of God. Within that conceptualization, then, the high priest stands as the head of the whole (the whole people and the whole temple-state apparatus). The high priest(hood) is the people's representative to God, therefore they bring their offerings to the priesthood. The high priest(hood) is God's representative to the people, established by everlasting covenant, and given "authority and statutes and judgments" over the people, therefore the people (are to) honor the priest with their tithes and offerings as the way of "fearing the Lord" (see esp. chapter 50 and 7:29–31). Ben Sira presents what Lenski appropriately calls a "proprietary theory of the state", in a combination of theocratic and hierocratic terms. God is the ostensible "head of state" and, apparently "proprietor" of the land. But the Aaronid priesthood is God's regent and actual head of (temple) state-and-economy. In that position Aaron was granted a "heritage" but no "inheritance" (45:20–22).

The modern Western concept of private property gets in the way at this point. Ben Sira has a proprietary concept of state-land-people in hierocratic form. That is, the Aaronid priesthood (ideologically) has no land of its own because as the head of the whole it receives a (special) heritage of "first fruits and sacrifices." Ideologically, the high priest(hood) has no individual or personal wealth and power separate from his wealth and power as public figure representative of the whole. The high priest and other members of the priestly aristocracy may well have used their public wealth and power as a means of generating what would appear as private wealth or property, e.g., by charging interest on loans made from the stores/wealth they controlled (as representatives of the whole), but they were wealthy and powerful because they stood at the representative head of the whole.

This particular hierocratic understanding of the Judean state and its religious political-economy is the key to understanding both the internal relations of the temple-community and the conflicts that arose (might arise) between local and imperial rulers or between the subjects of the temple-state and the rulers, both local Judean and imperial. Insofar as the (high) priesthood is the representative of and has authority over the whole, then it would both claim support from the agricultural producers and command whatever governing apparatus was developed in addition to the priesthood itself. Both the ruler-ruled relationship and the ruler-retainer relationship will be pursued in the sections just below. The potential for conflict in the local system and in the overall imperial system is also evident once we consider how essential the hierocratic ideology articulated by Ben Sira was to the working of the Judean temple-state, both in itself and as a component political-economic unit of the overall Seleucid empire. So long as the traditional Judean hierocratic ideology and institutional forms were left intact, the Judean temple-state could operate in a semi-autonomous way, with the high priesthood serving its traditional function representative of the Judean people in their particular focus on God, Temple and high priesthood, while simultaneously serving as representatives of the imperial regime and thus maintaining the imperial as well as domestic order. But to the extent that the ruling aristocracy in Judea appeared to compromise with or sell out to the ideological or institutional forms of the imperial regime, it lost "legitimacy" among the Judeans. And such a compromise of Judean traditions and compromise with an alien culture affected Judeans according to their position and role in the social structure of the temple-state or temple-community. At such times rival parties could gain considerable support and influence as the bearers of tradition and representatives of God.

The Judean Peasantry

There would have been no glory for the high priest and no high priest at all without the peasant producers who supported the whole temple-state apparatus with their tithes and offerings. But peasants, like women, have generally been "hidden from history." While Ben Sira repeats the same information in saying after saying about sages such as himself and lauds the glory of the Aaronid high priesthood in paeans of praise, he barely mentions the ordinary people who made it all possible. Yet he does provide a few glimpses of the peasant's situation which make it possible to compare with other traditional agrarian societies. Insofar as the taxation to support the temple-state apparatus took the form of tithes and offerings from agricultural products, it was only the plowman, but not the artisan, the smith, and the potter, and the scribe mentioned in 38:24–34 on whose agricultural labor the whole system rested. Comparative studies suggest that since the level of agricultural production is traditionally low, the peasants who support the rest of the society as well as themselves with food usually must comprise about 90 percent of the population. They generally live at the subsistence level, constantly threatened with poverty and hunger since their "surplus" produce has been expropriated by their rulers. To cite Lenski's summary, "In short, the great majority of the political elite sought to use the energies of the peasantry to the full, while depriving them of all but the basic necessities of life."[39]

This is precisely the picture Ben Sira offers in the few references he makes to the peasants' situation. In striking contrast to the castigation of merchants, Ben Sira expresses admiration for agricultural labor, "which was created by the Most High" (7:15). He leaves us with no illusions about the peasants' standard of living. "Better is the life of the poor under their own crude roof than the sumptuous food in the house of others" (29:22). A survey of Ben Sira's use of the term "poor" (עָנִי, דל, אביון) suggests that more often than not it refers not to an exceptional case but to a wide range of people. "Poor," "hungry," "needy," "desperate," and other synonymous terms refer apparently to a large proportion of the people (4:1–9). Like peasants in most societies, the Judean producers were economically marginal, therefore chronically in need of loans if not alms, in response to which Ben Sira exhorts his listeners, who are better off, to respond mercifully (29:1–20, especially 29:1–2, 8–12, 14–15). Because they are marginal, however, they are all the more susceptible to the predatory practices of the wealthy and powerful. "Wild asses in the wilderness are the prey of lions; likewise the poor are the feeding grounds of the rich" (13:19). The imagery used at one point, reminiscent of the prophetic indictment in Amos 2:6–8, suggests that powerful creditors were taking advantage of the peasants who have fallen heavily into debt.

> Like one who kills a son before his father's eyes is the person who offers a sacrifice from the property of the poor. The bread of the needy is the life of the poor; whoever deprives them of it is a murderer. To take away a neighbor's living is to commit murder; to deprive an employee of wages is to shed blood. (34:24–27)

The dynamics of social relations, given the basic political-economic-religious structure, led Ben Sira to exhort his hearers to "rescue the oppressed from the oppressor" (4:9).

Some of the sayings parallel to "the poor are feeding grounds of the rich," such as "What peace is there between a hyena and a dog? And what peace between the rich and the poor" (13:18–23), suggest that this

---

39. Lenski, *Power and Privilege*, 270.

fundamental, structural opposition in the society had potential for more overt class conflict. From much of the Hebrew Bible we are aware of the fact that many components of the Israelite (and Judean) cultural heritage would have provided an ideological basis for popular resistance. In Ben Sira's book, however, typical for the wisdom tradition, historical memories (including those of the people's deliverance from Egypt or the Philistines, for example) are virtually excluded. Where historical reminiscences are present, as in the hymn of praise to the great office-holders, the judges and prophets are domesticated into the grand scheme of legitimation precisely for the high priesthood at the head of the society.

Artisans and Traders

As Ben Sira states, the artisan, smith, and potter were essential to the operations of the capital city (38:27–32). Lenski says that the artisan class may well have been "originally recruited from the ranks of the dispossessed peasantry."[40] In the case of a temple-community, one wonders the extent to which the ordinary priests and/or Levites may have performed some of these supportive services. Some of Lenski's principal points about the artisan class, however, appear to be based on evidence from medieval European towns, and may not apply to most traditional agrarian societies. There is certainly little evidence from the ancient Near East generally that would indicate that "the majority of artisans were probably employees of the merchant class."[41] Nor is there evidence of artisans rebelling against those in authority over them. In the case of a temple-city such as Jerusalem (or for that matter in any capital or royal city), the artisans would have been economically dependent on the (priestly) rulers in command of the Temple, city, and society.

Artisans would not have been employees of the merchants because any native merchants would themselves have been fellow "employees" of the rulers and governing families. Other merchants were perhaps foreigners serving the needs of the ruling families in a somewhat more independent manner. Lenski's discussion of the merchant class is flawed insofar as he is drawing heavily on medieval European, even nascent capitalist evidence, and on agrarian societies which had come into contact with and been affected by mercantile or capitalist systems. Given

---

40. Ibid., 278.
41. Ibid., 279.

the variety of societies he is considering, it is facile to generalize that "from a very early date merchants managed to free themselves from the direct and immediate authority of the ruler and governing class."[42] As has been repeatedly observed, certainly in the Ptolemaic empire which dominated Palestine just before the time of Ben Sira, trade was a virtual monopoly of the (imperial) state. It is highly unlikely that things were any different in a far smaller entity such as the Judean temple-state, but with a significant exception. The Ptolemaic regime would have been powerful enough to keep out the Greek or Phoenician traders (except for when the state did business with them!). But from Persian times on, alien traders, Phoenicians or Greeks, may well have been operating in Jerusalem, although their trade would still have been primarily in luxury goods and items desired by and paid for by the ruling elite.

Tcherikover, followed by Hengel, as noted above, fostered a picture of Jerusalem under Hellenistic rule as suddenly a-bustle with mercantile capitalism.

> Ben Sira frequently mentions merchants and their pursuit of profits, and these passages again reflect the new period which began in Judaea under Greek rule, when the money economy, the opportunity to invest one's means in profitable enterprises, and lively and absorbing commercial traffic had begun to develop.[43]

This is an anachronism, quite unwarranted by the text of Sirach. Ben Sira mentions merchants and traders (and buying and selling) explicitly at only three points: the sharp criticism in 26:29—27:2, and the brief references to merchants and bartering/buying-selling in 37:11 and 42:5. As in most ancient literature and the societies they come from, he has a negative view of trading and traders, in this case "moralized" in terms of "sin." Otherwise, Tcherikover, Hengel, *et al.* appear to be projecting nascent capitalist mercantile relations onto Ben Sira's references to "goods" (χρήματα) and wealth and "gold" and the use of other people's goods (Hengel focuses on 11:10–19; 13:24–25; 21:8; and 31:3–5). In most political-economic systems prior to the early modern Europe, however, wealth and exploitation of others' goods did not involve trading, investment, or mercantile activity.

---

42. Ibid., 250.
43. Tcherikover, *Hellenistic Civilization*, 149.

Besides the artisans of various sorts who served the needs of the priestly governing class in Jerusalem, Ben Sira mentions "(household) servants/slaves" (οἰκέται, עבדים, 6:11; 7:20–21; 42:5; 33[30]:25[33]–33[40]). Given the infrequency of references to wages, these seem to be household slaves; certainly the Greek translator thought so. There is no clear indication in the text of Sirach whether they are primarily in the households of the governing families, or also in those of the sages themselves.

Scribes and Other Retainers

The scribes, Ben Sira himself and the typical scribe-sage he writes about, clearly belonged to what Lenski called the retainer class.[44] It is worth noting that Antiochus III's decree exempting the principals of the temple-state in Jerusalem from taxation closely associates "the scribes" with the *gerousia* and the priests.[45]

There must have been other types of retainers. Presumably there was little need for military retainers insofar as the Seleucid regime would have retained a monopoly on military force, although there were temple guards and doorkeepers in the temple compound. Ben Sira mentions "physicians" who are "rewarded by the king" and are admired by "the great ones" for their skills with healing and medicines (38:1–8). The priests and Levites would have functioned somewhat as did the "retainers" Lenski describes in other agrarian societies, i.e., mediating between the governing class and the common people, including "effecting the transfer of the economic surplus from the producers to the political (and religious) elite."[46]

From Ben Sira's extensive reflection on the activities of his own "profession" it is clear that the sages were retainers with scribal-legal-cultural-religious functions, some of which may have overlapped with those of the priests. According to Ben Sira's ideology of the priesthood,

44. It is interesting that Jonathan Z. Smith (*Map is Not Territory*, 70) has made similar observations concerning the Babylonian scribes, whom he characterizes as "an elite group of learned, literate men, an intellectual aristocracy which played an invaluable role in the administration of their people in both religious and political affairs."

45. There may have been two classes of "scribes," one including only those who performed the relatively menial tasks of recording deeds, tax receipts, and other records, and the other being limited to the sages whose business was involved in the practice and dispensing of wisdom.

46. Lenski, *Power and Privilege*, 246.

the function of teaching the law, originating with Moses (45:5), belonged to the Aaronid priesthood (45:17). In second-temple Judea the (high) priesthood must have, in effect, over a period of generations, delegated that authority and function to the sages, both with regard to the people generally (37:23), and with regard to the exercise of their own governmental authority (8:8; 9:17—10:5; 38:32–33; 38:34—39:4). In 9:17—10:5 it seems particularly clear that it is the scribe who stands behind the "wise judge" and "the government of the intelligent one." As noted above, it is necessary to collapse Lenski's "priestly class" into the rulers, in the case of the high priestly families, and into the retainers, in the case of ordinary priests and scribes/sages. In Ben Sira's Judea, the sages performed the functions that Lenski ascribes to "the clergy" in societies of limited literacy, officials and diplomats as well as educators.

Of course, some "scribes" may have performed more menial tasks such as writing tax receipts and records of debts as a relatively more modest level than the role of the learned scribes serving among the rulers in their councils and assemblies, as portrayed by Ben Sira.[47] Josephus claims that a century after Ben Sira, after being out of favor under John Hyrcanus and virtually at war with Alexander Jannai, the Pharisees became, in effect, the real rulers under Alexandra Salome. That would appear to illustrate Lenski's point that at times the retainers could move into the governing class. With service in the highest temple-state offices depending on belonging to the proper high priestly lineages, however, scribes from non-priestly or ordinary priestly families could not have moved into the sacerdotal governing class even if they held considerable *de facto* power. Furthermore, Ben Sira gives no indication that scribes wielded much power in his own day.

Lenski stresses the dependence of retainers on the rulers or governing class. The sages do indeed appear to be dependent economically on the priestly aristocracy in Ben Sira. Lest anyone would project back the old notion that their successors, the Pharisees and rabbis, were artisans, the sage Ben Sira clearly looks down on artisans, potters, smiths, etc. And, like those workers with their hands, peasant plowmen would also lack the leisure for acquiring wisdom (38:24). It seems clear that when Ben Sira says, several times, that the scribes "serve the rulers" this implies that such service is the source of their livelihood. Being economically dependent on the high priestly regime, they are thus also "politically"

---

47. Ibid., 244.

vulnerable. Ben Sira's exhortations to other sages to be cautious in their dealings with rulers and wealthy-powerful figures can be read as testimony to just such a dependency.

The sages, however, also have a certain authority of their own independent of their "employment" by the high priestly regime. At least in their own mind, their own authority stems from their knowledge of wisdom and their faithful teaching of and adherence to the law of the Most High (which are evidently the same thing in Ben Sira). Just as the high priesthood has its power, privilege, and authority from God through an eternal covenant, so also the sages have their authority as the custodians of divine revelation. Besides being the heirs of earlier generations of sages, they are the successors of the prophets as well, speaking by divine inspiration. Nor would this have been simply a matter of their own self-image unmatched in the concrete power relations of early second century Jerusalem. Lenski claims that such retainers can gain in power relative to their superiors when the governing class is dominated by a hedonistic ethic. Evidence external to Ben Sira indicates that some and perhaps many in the high priestly circles were seriously distracted by the "opportunities" of Hellenistic culture and politics. Apparently these distracted aristocrats must have given lip-service to the traditional Judean ways which were ostensibly still in force until the dramatic Hellenizing reform of 175 BCE. In just such circumstances a scribal class with rigorous loyalty to the tradition of which they were the custodians could have enjoyed greater actual power in the administration of affairs.

Ben Sira repeatedly mentions the scribes' dedication to the revered covenantal laws and divinely-bestowed wisdom, from which they claim their own authority independent of the high priesthood. Viewed in the broader political-cultural context of the Hellenistic imperial situation in which they were operating, this dedication and sense of independent higher authority should alert us to the potential for eventual overt as well as latent social conflict. Insofar as the sages' professional role or function was the cultivation and administration of the traditional Judean covenantal laws as the official state law, their dedication to those laws would have been far more than a matter of individual morality. The sages had a clear sense of their own, independent of their employers, of how the temple-state should operate. in accordance with (their interpretation of) the covenantal laws. Their high priestly superiors, however, had regular dealings with the Hellenistic imperial officials and were susceptible to influence from the wider Hellenistic culture. Recognition of this potential structural conflict may help us understand the open social conflicts which erupted when ruling class elements instituted their "reform" in 175 BCE.

The strong personal (and "professional") dedication to the Mosaic covenantal laws and independent authority claimed on that basis among the sages also contributed to their concern for the poor, judging from Ben Sira's "wisdom." His exhortations include not only admonitions of personal ethics to "stretch out your hand to the poor" (7:32), but also what look like instructions to other sages not to "cheat the poor" or to "reject the suppliant" and even, more positively, to "rescue the oppressed from the oppressor" presumably in their official or professional capacities (4:1–10). Sharply criticized are those who take advantage of the desperate situation of the poor to enhance their own wealth ("offering sacrifice from the property of the poor" and "taking away a neighbor's living" in 34:24–27, reminiscent of Amos 2:6–8, may refer to creditors' "foreclosing" on debts).[48]

In both their potential opposition to certain actions or policies of the high priestly rulers (on whom they were economically dependent) and their concern for the poor, the sages display similarities to the medieval clergy described by Lenski. But their social structural position was quite different. The medieval Christian clergy was "a specially protected class," economically and politically separate and independent, whereas the second-temple sages were economically dependent and politically-religiously subordinate. Yet the claim to direct divine authority independent of the rulers was clearly asserted by the scribal class as evidenced in Ben Sira and other (Enoch) literature, and helped set a precedent for what the Christian church eventually institutionalized more securely.

Presumably the rulers accepted this semi-independent role of the sages because it was part of the foundation of their claim to divine authority and this made the sages able to provide the ideological basis for the priests' rule. Indirectly it served the interests of the wealthy in that the existence of a powerful class that defended the interests of the poor provided a legitimate (but non-threatening) outlet for the anger and frustration of the poor and oppressed.

---

48. The discussion of loans and alms in Sir 29:1–13 may imply that one should give to the poor and not loan. It seems likely that Ben Sira did not approve of foreclosing on loans to the poor.

EVALUATION AND IMPLICATION OF BEN SIRA'S PICTURE OF JUDEA

If we now place Ben Sira's picture of Judean society into comparison with the pictures of intense social conflict represented in near contemporary literature, such as certain sections of 1 Enoch or Daniel, we must evaluate the serious differences and seeming discrepancies. Is Ben Sira's picture of a social structure that is stable and quiet despite its deep divisions a reliable picture of Judea, and its differences with other sources to be explained as representing the calm of the early second century just before the storm unleashed by the Hellenizing reform of 175? Or should Ben Sira be seen as an accurate observer of the basic social structure but himself a conservative supporter of the high priesthood (and one perhaps simply oblivious to the roots of the impending social conflicts)? Or should Ben Sira's picture of a relatively simple basic social structure in Judea be dismissed as inaccurate insofar as it must miss a more complex structure and division in the society?

The last option is the most unlikely and least compelling because it would assume or project from other literature a complex social structure unique among traditional agrarian societies of the ancient Near East. The first option made sense so long as we were assuming that the social structure of second-temple Judea had been stably in place since early Persian times and it was only the sudden impact of Hellenistic influence and the especially dramatic reform of 175 BCE. that caused deep social conflicts to emerge. But, as we are finally recognizing, intense conflicts attended the various attempts to stabilize a regime in Jerusalem at least through the reform missions of Nehemiah and Ezra in mid-fifth century. Thus we would have to project a period of quiet stability during the fourth and third centuries despite the military campaigns and changes in imperial rule whirling around Jerusalem on all sides. The option that takes into account Ben Sira's own point of view as a conservative supporter of the high priesthood thus appears the more likely option. We believe that Ben Sira can be read as a relatively reliable witness to the basic social structure of second-temple Judea. Despite its relative simplicity, however, that basic social structure could produce and accommodate certain conflicts, conflicts which would likely have been exacerbated by the cultural differences between the Judean traditions and the empire at large.

Just as there had been different parties or factions among the ruling class struggling for control of the Davidic monarchy earlier in the kingdom of Judah, so there were priestly and other factions competing for power for well over a century in early second-temple times, as evident from the books of Ezra and Nehemiah. Insofar as scribes and sages had no independent economic base, they would have been associated with one or another of those (priestly) factions, and insofar as sages claimed independent divinely-given authority as the guardians of the revered traditions, they likely had their own ideas about policy and practice in the temple-state. Further, insofar as different scribes performed different functions and cultivated somewhat different forms/modes of wisdom, mantic as well as traditional/educational, different sages may have developed different interests and affiliations. Thus, although relatively simple, the structure allowed for considerable conflict between scribal-sapiental retainers and priestly rulers and between rival groups of sages as well.

We illustrate our contention with just one example. Sirach and the Book of the Watchers in *1 Enoch* 1–36 should be read as complementary sources rather than contradictory or alternative sources. The one clarifies the basic structure, while the other gives us access to a particular conflict that emerged. Furthermore, the basic structure discerned through Ben Sira can help us understand better the structural roots of the particular conflict evident in the Book of Watchers of the Enoch tradition.

The Book of the Watchers, was written and redacted during the third century BCE.[49] The dating of this book is complicated by the fact that three or four layers of composition can be detected. The oldest is chapters 6–11, itself a composite of two narratives. In one, Shemihazah and two hundred other angels descend to have intercourse with women who then bear giant offspring who in turn act violently and, along with their angelic fathers, are judged. In the other, Asael alone descends to teach forbidden secrets to humans, especially the arts of making weapons and cosmetics, both of which depend upon metallurgy. In the story

---

49. The oldest ms of the *BW* is 4QEna, dated by Milik to the first half of the second century BCE. Milik concludes from the orthography and copying errors that this ms was copied from a third century ms (*Books of Enoch*, 141). He also suggests that the script may reflect scribal customs of Northern Syria or Mesopotamia. Accordingly, the *BW* must have reached its present form by early in the second century at the latest. A third century date of composition/redaction if more likely. Hence it is contemporary to, or earlier than, Ben Sira.

as it now stands, others of Shemihaza's subordinate angels teach various mantic and astrological skills.

The other layers in the Book of the Watchers are (1) chapters 12–16, the story of Enoch's involvement in the judgment of the watchers; (2) chapters 17–36, stories about Enoch's travels to learn about world geography, including the places of judgment and the location of the mountain of God; and (3) chapters 1–5, an introduction to the Book of the Watchers with vocabulary taken from the stories of Balaam, a mantic diviner (Numbers 22–24), a warning of future judgment, and lessons for obedience taken from the regularity of nature.

The debate concerning the intellectual antecedents of Judean apocalyptic continues. Most scholars believe that there are connections to both traditional wisdom as exemplified by Proverbs and classical Israelite prophecy, as well as to various foreign influences. The "foreign" influence that seems to be determinative in Enoch literature is Mesopotamian "mantic" wisdom.[50]

Earlier analyses, such as that of von Rad, "did not distinguish sharply enough between an educational kind of wisdom and the less rational sort that found expression in divination."[51] Enochian wisdom depends upon visions, interpretations of visions, and proto-scientific speculation, especially concerning astrology/astronomy and geography.[52] These are doubtless skills that were learned by Judean sages in the Babylonian diaspora and developed in and for a Judean audience around the figure Enoch. However, from a sociological perspective, the differences between Enochic, mantic wisdom and traditional, "proverbial" or "educational" wisdom do not imply differences in social position and role. One group of sages cultivated both kinds of wisdom; another only educational.

During the period of Ptolemaic rule, Enochian sages used their mantic and astronomical wisdom as a way of articulating their opposi-

50. See Vanderkam, *Enoch*, 8; Stone, "Lists of Revealed Things."
51. Vanderkam, *Enoch*, 5.
52. This is especially clear in Book 3, the *Astronomical Book*, which probably assumed something like its present form early in the third century, if not already in the fourth century BCE. Further examples of visions and interpretations of visions can be seen in both Books 4 and 5, both written in the first half of the second century. Compare this with the Babylonian scribes, who, according to J. Z. Smith (*Map is Not Territory*, 70), "speculated about hidden heavenly tablets, about creation by divine word, about the beginning and the end and thereby claimed to possess the secrets of creation."

tion to the alliance of the high-priesthood with the Hellenistic empire. The Enochic traditions that are now found in the Book of the Watchers combined Mesopotamian traditions (the cosmic travels and geographical reports and possibly the revolt of Shemihazah and his cohorts) with Greek traditions (Asael = Prometheus). It has already been proposed that the Book of the Watchers was composed as a polemic against the Greek overlords who claimed divine descent and consumed goods and brought violence upon the land.[53] It appears to be a bit of an embarrassing contradiction, that the Watchers are condemned for bringing knowledge of divination and astrology, when those are precisely the skills for which Enoch himself is famous. Presumably the Greek diviners practiced divination and astrology that was based upon illicit sources, while that of Enoch and his followers was based upon licit revelations by God and good angels.

Various Enochic compositions refer to the fact that Enoch is passing on what he has learned from his inter-stellar travel with the angels and from his dreams to his son Methuselah. This may reflect a practice among Enochic sages to pass on their wisdom in a contest similar to that of traditional Israelite wisdom.[54] The fact that the Animal Vision (*1 Enoch* 85–90) reflects knowledge both of the traditional sources behind the Book of Watchers and of the Book of Watchers itself indicates that the Enochian traditions were being passed on from master to student, as well as in written documents. The Animal Vision (*1 Enoch* 85–90) quite clearly implies that the group to which its author belongs arose in the beginning of the second century (just about when Ben Sira wrote). It is possible that one of the forces leading to the (re-)formation of this group was the change of imperial power and the ensuing political shakeups.[55] It is difficult to say much more.

It is clear that the Enochic sages took a rather dim view of most (if not all) of those who currently held political power. None of the Enochic compositions display very much interest in the Temple, priesthood, or Mosaic Law. The Animal Vision is positively against the Second Temple,

53. See Nickelsburg, "Apocalyptic and Myth"; and Bartelmus, *Heroentum in Israel*, 175–79.

54. See J. Z. Smith, *Map is not Territory*, 74: "I would argue that wisdom and apocalyptic are related in that they are both essentially scribal phenomena. It is the paradigmatic thought of the scribe—a way of thinking that is both pragmatic and speculative—which as given rise to both."

55. Although, clearly, the Enochic sages were no fans of the Ptolemies either.

and the Ten-Week Vision (*1 Enoch* 93; 91:11–17), by implication, agrees. There is a strong possibility that already in the third century, the Book of Watchers reflects the view that while the Enochian sages fulfilled a social role identical to that of Ben Sira and his students, the Enochic sages served a priestly party that (at least in the third and second centuries) unsuccessfully competed for influence and authority. The competition between their respective patrons is probably reflected in what seems to be competition between the Enochic sages and Ben Sira. Whereas the Enochic texts consistently lay claim to knowledge about the stars and cosmic geography and the ability to interpret dreams, Ben Sira explicitly warns against such presumption (1:1–5; 3:21–24; 34:1–8; 42:17).

2

The Politics of Cultural Production in Second-Temple Judea

The Historical Context of Sirach, 1 Enoch, *and Daniel*

LITERATURE ARISES FROM AND addresses historical circumstances. This common assumption in interpretation of modern literature is also valid for ancient literature. We interpreters of ancient Judean texts, however, often have virtually no sources other than the extant texts we want to interpret for reconstruction of their historical circumstances. And we have no training in how we might go about relating ancient Judean texts classified as "wisdom" and "apocalyptic" to their historical social circumstances. The venturesome few who have inquired after who may have written "apocalyptic" literature such as Daniel and *1 Enoch* have spoken in terms of "movements," "groups," and "communities." Those concepts remain vague, with little or no indication of how they may have been comprised. Even vaguer is the "Judaism" to which they belonged. This modern construct tends to collapse the social structure, to homogenize what were historically distinctive documents, and to abstract a religion from the concrete dynamics of history. Those scholars who have investigated the circumstances that evoked the writing of apocalyptic literature such as Daniel and *1 Enoch* often focus on a "crisis." This also is conceived in vague, often essentialist terms, such as the incursion of "Hellenism."[1]

---

1. This study builds on previous examinations of the "social world" of wisdom and apocalyptic literature such as Nickelsburg, "Epistle of Enoch and Qumran Literature," and Davies, "Social World of Apocalyptic Writings."

An obvious step toward understanding who produced wisdom and apocalyptic literature and in what historical circumstances would be to investigate the structure and historical dynamics of second-temple Judean society. Our analysis, however, can move beyond the abstract synthetic "structural-functionalist" model of "advanced agrarian society" derived from Gerhard Lenski that has been applied to monarchic Israel and late second-temple Judea in recent decades, in at least two related respects.[2]

First, Lenski's scheme tends to obscure the basic division in ancient Near Eastern societies in an overly generalized scheme of horizontal stratification that attempts to accommodate evidence from feudal European and ancient Greek and Roman societies as well. In any preindustrial society where it takes ten people cultivating the soil to raise sufficient food to feed every noncultivator, there are basically two classes, the peasants who raise the crops and the rulers who take a percentage as tribute, taxes, or tithes. Moreover, if artisans, traders, and scribes cater to and are dependent on the ruling aristocracy, they do not constitute a "middle class." In ancient societies such as second-temple Judea, moreover, there was no "structural differentiation" between religious and political-economic institutions. Rather than apply Lenski's complex model, therefore, we may do better to examine closely the considerable information provided by extant texts, particularly the book of Sirach. Once we recognize that literacy was limited basically to circles of scribes, the question of who produced (and used) sapiential and apocalyptic texts becomes a simple one, at least at a superficial level: the scribes. But that does not tell us much about wisdom and apocalyptic literature, since all texts were produced by scribes. Further analysis of Sirach, Daniel, and *1 Enoch* may help us understand the particular historical social circumstances, social interests, and effective social roles of those who produced these few extant examples of "sapiential" and "apocalyptic" literature in second-temple Judea.

Second, the elaborate horizontal stratification in Lenski's model of agrarian societies may obscure the vertical divisions, the competing factions among the aristocracy. Such divisions obviously have implications for the military and scribal "retainers" who work for and are economically dependent upon the rulers. Just such vertical divisions among ruling aristocracies and their retainers, moreover, can result in historical

2. Lenski, *Power and Privilege*.

conflicts and changes. The conflicts within the Jerusalem high priestly aristocracy that led up to the Maccabean Revolt and the split in the Hasmonean dynasty that continued after the initial Roman takeover of Judea offer two prime examples.

Just those examples, however, illustrate why we cannot consider second-temple Judea in isolation. Judea was subject to a succession of empires. The imperial situation could decisively influence social-political dynamics in the temple-state. We can be more systematic in inquiring after the interaction between imperial relations and the struggle among factions for power in Judea itself. Even if some think that the basic structure was consistent through the second-temple period, the Jerusalem high priesthood was contested and its power waxed and waned in close connection with the imperial power relations.

Is it possible that the key to precisely who produced Sirach, Daniel, and Enoch literature just at certain historical junctures lies precisely in the relations between the imperial regime(s) and factions among the ruling aristocracy competing for power in Judea? Both Ben Sira's wisdom book and the Enochic and Danielic apocalyptic literature were produced by and for circles of scribes/sages. Which types of wisdom from the traditional scribal repertoire they utilized,[3] however, may have depended on their respective stance toward the temple-state and its incumbents and toward the imperial regime. Although we are plagued by a paucity of documentary evidence for the second-temple period, we can nevertheless attempt to be specific in dealing with what we do have, with regard to document, place, social location, power relations, and social interests.

BEN SIRA'S JUDEA

Ben Sira's reflections on the role of the scribe/sage in relation to others (38:24—39:11) indicates that they stand somewhere above the plowmen and artisans on whose labor Jerusalem depends, yet subordinate to and in service to the rulers.[4] Because he focuses on the city in which he himself surely lives (since he serves among rulers), he does not dwell

---

3. Outlined, with illustrations from Sirach, below. John Collins offers a brief sketch of five types of wisdom in "Wisdom, Apocalypticism," 166–68. For the types of wisdom in the broader cultural repertoire cultivated by second-temple scribes, see Horsley, *Scribes, Visionaries*, chap 6, esp. 126–29.

4. More extensive analysis and references in chap. 1 above.

long on the peasants "who handle the plow" and "drive oxen." He refers elsewhere to the "poor," "hungry," "needy," "desperate," and recites proverbial observations that "the poor are the feeding grounds for the rich" (13:19). He exhorts his fellow scribes to "stretch out your hand to the poor" with alms or loans and to rescue them from the worst predatory practices of the powerful (e.g., 29:1–20; 3:30—4:10). Peasants in such agrarian societies were almost always economically marginal, since their "surplus product" was expropriated by the rulers in the form of tithes and taxes. They were thus vulnerable to falling into debt. Those who "rely on their hands," with whom Ben Sira is more directly acquainted, include artisans, smiths, and potters. The operations of the city depends on such folks, but they are of low status, basically serving the needs of the leisured who desire "signets of seals," patterned iron work, and glazed pottery (38:27–34).

Ben Sira deploys two (juxtaposed) sets of terms in reference to the ruling aristocracy of Judea. First, for rulers or officers of state he uses, interchangeably and apparently synonymously, several traditional Hebrew terms, especially שׂר, מושׁל, and שׁופט. They are usually used in construct (hence direct relationship) with "city," "people," and "assembly." Only שׁופט is consistently translated in the Greek as κριτής. The other terms are rendered with a variety of overlapping Greek words: שׂר with μεγιστάν, δυνάστης, and ἡγούμενος; and מושׁל with ἡγούμενος, δυνάστης, κριτής, and κύριος. These terms are often used in parallel constructions, such that "chiefs of the people" and "rulers of the assembly" refer to the same figures and "the company of elders" and the "assembly of elders" refer to the same council of state (e.g., 30:27 [33:19]; 39:4; 6:34; 7:14; 10:1–2, 3). These parallel and overlapping terms thus refer apparently to the ruling aristocracy, some of whom may have had particular responsibilities and many of whom probably had similar or overlapping functions.

Second, Ben Sira pictures the high priest in the Temple surrounded by "a garland of brothers, . . . the sons of Aaron in their splendor holding out the Lord's offerings" (50:5–13). Since the (high) priests are the people's representatives to God, the people bring their offerings to the priests. Since the (high) priests are God's representatives to the people, established by everlasting covenant, so that they are given "authority and statutes and judgments" over the people, the latter are to "honor the priest" with their tithes and offerings as the way of "fearing the Lord" (7:29–31; 35:1–12; 45:20–22; 50:1–21). The "religious" relationships focused in the high priesthood in the Temple do not just legitimate but constitute the political-economic structure of Judea. The people rendered up first fruits, guilt offerings, choice shoulder cuts from animal sacrifices, etc., to "honor the priest" because in the "everlasting covenant" by which the priesthood was bestowed upon Aaron, these had been allotted to him and his descendants as their heritage (7:29–31; 45:6–7, 15–16, 20–21).

These two sets of terms—rulers and officials on one hand and (high) priests on the other—refer not to separate "lay" and "priestly" aristocracies, but to one aristocracy that held political-economic-religious power. In actual practice it was not quite this simple, for not all of the wealthy and powerful families in Judea were priestly, as we shall see below. But for the most part, the "chiefs" and "rulers" and "judges" were apparently the "high priestly" aristocracy among "the sons of Aaron." Some individual high priests, but by no means all, may have held particular offices (e.g., the "temple captain" known from the first century CE). The most prominent of Ben Sira's "chiefs," "rulers," and "judges," paralleled by "the sons of Aaron" around the high priest, therefore, appear to have constituted the *gerousia* mentioned in both Antiochus III's proclamation of restoration of the Temple government in Jerusalem (Josephus, *Ant.* 12.142) and in the letter of the Hasmonean high priest Jonathan to Sparta a half-century later (1 Macc 12:6). Of course, the incumbents could change, as happened more than once in the generation immediately following Ben Sira and in the upstart Hasmonean high priesthood.

The principal role of the wise scribes, as Ben Sira mentions repeatedly, is to serve the "chiefs" and "rulers" (8:8). In his sustained discussion in 38:24—39:11, he takes pride in the scribes as advisers of ruling councils and members of courts who understand decisions and expound judgments, even as members of embassies to foreign lands (cf. 6:34; 7:14; 15:5; 21:17; 34:12). Since they did not "rely on their [own] hands" for sustenance, however, this means that they must have been economically as well as politically dependent on patronage from the chiefs and rulers among whom they served. This explains Ben Sira's admonition to bow low to the rulers and his extensive "professional" advice on deferential behavior and caution when dealing with the powerful (4:7; 13:9–11; 31:12–24; 8:1–2, 14).

Ben Sira and his scribal colleagues, however, have a clear sense of their own authority independent of the rulers among whom they serve. They view their own authority as grounded in "the wisdom of all the ancients" and their faithful "study of the Law of the Most High" (38:34—39:1). They thus derive their authority, independent of the priestly aristocracy, from God and the revered cultural tradition (wisdom, prophecies, etc.). This suggests also that they had their own sense of how the temple-state should operate, that is, according to the sacred cultural tradition of which they were the professional guardians and interpreters. Despite their dependence on and vulnerability to their patrons among the ruling aristocracy, therefore, scribes such as Ben Sira could both criticize the aristocracy and take measures to mitigate its oppression of the poor (e.g., 4:8–10; 13:3–4, 18–19; 29:8–9; 34:21–27).

Ben Sira's representation of Judean society thus reveals two major divisions that held potential for serious conflict. The dominant division lay between the peasants and the wealthy and powerful rulers.

> What peace is there between the rich and the poor?
> Wild asses in the wilderness are the prey of lions;
> Likewise the poor are feeding ground for the rich. (13:18–19)

The less ominous division lay between the rulers and the scribes/sages. As professional cultivators and guardians of Judean cultural tradition, the latter developed both a basis of their own authority independent of the rulers and criteria for the appropriate levels of exploitation of the peasantry and codes for conducting the religious-economic relations of the temple-state. Therein lay considerable potential for serious conflict between rulers and their scribal retainers.

Ben Sira's representation of Judean society and particularly of the rulers/high priesthood, however, effectively obscures the way in which such potential for conflict might develop into actual conflict. Ben Sira treats Judea and the high priesthood as if it were an independent temple-state. In the grand hymn of praise of the ancestors at the end of the book (Sirach 44–49) he grounds the authority of the high priesthood in the sacred tradition of Israel/Judea. We who have access to texts such as Ezra and Nehemiah and the books of the Maccabees know better, that is, that the temple-state was subject to a sequence of empires.

THE INTERACTION OF LOCAL AND IMPERIAL STRUGGLES FOR POWER

Judea centered on the Second Temple was a creature of empire, initially of the Persian. The temple-state instituted in Jerusalem served several purposes simultaneously: a renewal of an indigenous people's service of their own deity, a local ruling class who owed their position to the imperial regime, and a financial administration for the imperial regime's revenues, the point of establishing an empire in the first place.[5] Besides restoring temples and their administrations throughout the empire, the Persian regime "promoted the codification and implementation of local traditional law as an instrument of the *pax Persica* throughout the empire."[6]

Far from the temple-state having been stabilized under a strong monarchical high priesthood (or a "diarchy" of high priest and local prince), there appears to have been a struggle for power in Yehud.[7] Multiple conflicts emerged during the first generations of the restoration, as is evident in Haggai, Malachi, and Isaiah 56–66. By the mid-fifth century the various "big-men" in the region vying for influence included Jerusalem aristocrats aided by the Samaritan dynast Sanballat, a sheik in the Transjordan named Tobiah, who had ties of intermarriage and mutual interest with certain (priestly?) nobles in Yehud, and an Arab magnate named Geshem (Neh 2:9; 6; 13:28–30; etc.). As indicated in his memoir, the Persian court sent Nehemiah as governor, escorted by mounted Persian troops, to reimpose order in Yehud and to regularize revenues for both the imperial regime and the Temple (Neh 5:4, 14; 10:26–29, 40).[8] Ezra's mission, also sponsored by the Persian imperial regime, aimed to consolidate the position of the previously exiled elite in Yehud. The returned (*golah*) community were defined as the only true *Yehudim*, which either excluded the indigenous "people of the land" or subordinated them to the temple-state as lesser-status people.[9] Moreover, he promulgated only one form of Yehud's legal legacy, derived from the exiled and now restored Jerusalem ruling class, as "the law of your God and the law of the king," effectually subordinating or excluding rival legal traditions and their proponents (Ezra 7:25–26). It is unlikely,

---

5. Berquist, *Judaism in Persia's Shadow*, 52–57, 63; Schaper, "Jerusalem Temple as an Instrument." See now Horsley, *Scribes, Visionaries*, chap. 1.

6. Blenkinsopp, "Mission of Udjahorresnet"; Blenkinsopp, "Temple and Society," 24.

7. Goodblatt, *Monarchic Principle*, argues for a monarchic high priesthood; the struggle for power is summarized in Horsley, *Scribes, Visionaries*, chap. 1.

8. Gottwald, *Politics of Ancient Israel*, 110; Horsley, *Scribes, Visionaries*, chap. 1.

9. Blenkinsopp, "Temple and Society," 44–47; see also Horsley, "Empire, Temple, and Community."

however, that such subordination meant destruction. Rival factions, including priestly groups who were losing ground to the dominant elite, while leaving few traces of their interests and viewpoints, would likely have cultivated alternative Judean traditions.

Under the successor empires formed in the wake of Alexander's conquests, political affairs became even more complicated and contested in the Jerusalem temple-state. The principal complicating factor was the rivalry between the Ptolemaic empire in Egypt and the Seleucid empire to the east for control of Palestine. The Ptolemies prevailed in a series of wars throughout the third century before finally yielding control to the Seleucids right around 200 BCE. Thus the dominant faction in Jerusalem and their rivals for power in Jerusalem and Judea alike had to deal regularly with competing imperial maneuvers and the potential for a sudden change in imperial overlord. And of course local power-brokers could seize any advantage as a factor in the imperial struggle for power.[10]

Several sources suggest that the high priesthood had developed into a position of considerable prominence by the end of the Persian period and the beginning of Ptolemaic rule. Hecataeus of Abdera, a Greek historian at the court of Ptolemy I, views Jerusalem as a temple-state headed by a revered high priest who has "authority over the people" (*tou plethous prostasia*) and who acts as "a messenger of God's commandments" and "announces what is ordained in assemblies" (in Diodorus Siculus 40.3). Pseudo-Aristeas (96–98), written probably by an Alexandrian Jew in the second half of the second century BCE, offers a glowing description of the awesome appearance of the high priest in the midst of the other priests offering sacrifices in the Temple. Pseudo-Hecataeus, a mid-second century BCE source cited by Josephus (*C. Ap.* 1.187–89) mentions "Ezechias, a high priest of the Judeans, highly esteemed by his countrymen, intellectual, and an able speaker and unsurpassed as a man of business." This Ezechias, moreover, may be the same person as "Hezekiah the governor" inscribed on silver coins minted in Jerusalem dating to the late fourth century or early third century, which are also inscribed in paleo-Hebrew script (not Aramaic, as under the Persians). The combination of these sources suggests that Judea was indeed headed by a high priest under early Ptolemaic rule and that, if the high priest were also the "governor," he exercised considerable power

---

10. Fuller discussion in Horsley, *Scribes, Visionaries*, chap. 2.

in the temple-state of Jerusalem/Judea.[11] As evident in subsequent developments, however, other factions and power-brokers had not disappeared from the scene in Palestine and became significant factors in the struggles for power. The considerable prominence and power of the high priest in Judah apparent at the outset of this period changed under later Ptolemaic rule.

Since Tcherikover's critical reconstructions on the basis of the Zenon Papyri and other sources, it has seemed clear that the hinterland of Palestine was dominated by a number of local figures who controlled certain limited territories and their populations.[12] Contrary to the policy in Egypt itself, the Ptolemaic regime entrusted military commands to certain local "big-men," such as "Tobias," apparently the descendent of Nehemiah's opponent east of the Jordan. Similarly, the Ptolemaic administrators "farmed" tax-collection to some of these local power–holders.[13] This ad hoc administration of Syria-Palestine had far-reaching effects in the history of the Jerusalem temple-state, as it set up the struggle between and among the Tobiads and Oniads for control of Judah. Our source is the "Tobiah romance" that Josephus draws upon in his account (*Ant.* 12.157–236). Insofar as we place credence in this "romance" as a historical source, the following would be a compelling reconstruction.[14]

In the early third century the high priests in Jerusalem held the tax contract from and/or paid the tribute to the Ptolemies. At one point the high priest Onias II stopped paying the sum of twenty talents a year, "on account of which [Onias] had received authority over the people (τοῦ λαοῦ προστασίαν) and obtained the high priestly office (τῆς ἀρχιερατικῆς τιμῆς)" (*Ant.* 12.158–161). The Tobiad Joseph, who had married into the Oniad family, took the occasion to outbid Onias for the tax-contract, indeed maneuvered himself into the position of chief tax-collector for the entire province of Syria and Phoenicia (*Ant.* 12.184). It would fit the ad hoc Ptolemaic administration of tax revenues in Syria-Palestine to separate the role of tax-collector for an area from that of the ostensible local ruler, particularly if it involved a higher bid! It is possible, of course, that Joseph also took over the high priesthood, as implied in the

---

11. Kurtz, "Social Construction of Judea in the Greek Period," 58.
12. Tcherikover, "Palestine under the Ptolemies."
13. Bagnall, *Administration of the Ptolemaic Possessions*.
14. Gera, "Tobiads," 36–57. See also Horsley, *Scribes, Visionaries*, chap. 2.

Tobiad chronicle which reports that Onias was eager to give up the high priesthood (*Ant.* 12.163).

The deal that Joseph arranged with the Ptolemaic regime had serious and far-reaching implications for power-relations within Judea, particularly insofar as the latter were closely interrelated with the shifting relations between the Ptolemaic regime and (ambitious, rival) local Palestinian power-holders. First (even if we do not find it credible that he took over the high priesthood from Onias II), in obtaining the tax-contract for Palestine Joseph gained considerable power over affairs in Judea. Second, even if he retained the high priesthood, Onias' position was relatively weakened within Judea insofar as he no longer controlled the revenue for the imperial regime, and was no longer the only or even the principal power-broker mediating between the imperial administration and the Jerusalem temple-state and people of Judea. Third, insofar as tax-farmers generally manage a considerable margin for themselves, Joseph, like other magnates in Palestine under the Ptolemies, considerably enhanced his own wealth, which in turn led to a certain acculturation of local power-brokers who developed a taste for luxurious "Greek" lifestyles, and shifted to use of the Greek language for administration and correspondence.[15] Fourth, insofar as the Tobiad family had long been maneuvering for power and position in Jerusalem, including intermarriage with the high priestly family, Joseph could consolidate and build up an already existing network in the Jerusalem aristocracy.

It should thus not be surprising that as the imperial rivalry for control of Palestine came to a head toward the turn of the century, rival Oniad and Tobiad (and perhaps other) factions were struggling for power in Jerusalem and were prepared to seek advantages from the rival imperial regimes. Those rival factions, moreover, continued to struggle for power under the Seleucids. At the very beginning of Seleucid control over Judea the high priesthood itself may have been at its nadir during the Hellenistic period. Antiochus III's charter for the temple-state (Josephus, *Ant.* 12.138–144) does not mention the high priest, but only the *gerousia*, the priests, the scribes of the temple, and the temple singers. Insofar as *gerousia* is a Greek term that corresponds to the Hebrew *sarim*, Antiochus' decree seems to confirm the priestly aristocracy as the "rulers" in the temple-state. Its inclusion of the priests and scribes in positions of privilege also confirms the conclusion above that scribes such

---

15. Schwartz, "Autonomy of Judaea," 165–66.

as Ben Sira worked for (a faction within) the aristocracy. But how do we understand the failure of Antiochus' decree to mention the "high priest." Was he simply included in the *gerousia*? Had the transition in imperial power simply caught Simon II off in exile as a result of the turmoil?

We must give credence to Ben Sira's celebration of Simon II for heading the repair of the Temple and fortifications of Jerusalem (50:1–4), taking advantage of the funding provided in accordance with Antiochus III's charter. This limited, largely indirect evidence could be read either of two ways. On the one hand, that Simon II's successor Onias III could not exert sufficient power to prevent Simon the Temple captain (προστάτης τοῦ ἱεροῦ) from appealing (successfully) over his head to the imperial governor Apollonius (2 Macc 3:4) suggests that the high priesthood remained fairly weak. On the other hand, particularly if the Seleucid regime treated the Jerusalem high priest as the local head of state and guarantor of its own revenues, the high priesthood would have been accordingly strengthened in its position in Jerusalem and Judea.[16] We thus have two possibilities for the power of the high priesthood precisely as the struggle among aristocratic factions came to a head in Jerusalem in the 170s, either of which could have led to factional struggle within the aristocracy. If it was relatively weak, the incumbent would have been more easily challenged by a Menelaus or a Jason and their supporters. If, on the other hand, the high priesthood had been strengthened by Seleucid imperial practice, it would have appeared as the greater prize for an ambitious usurper and/or a faction eager to seize power. The interest in "Westernization" in aristocratic circles that was gaining strength during these decades, of course, further complicated and exacerbated the power struggle in Jerusalem.

This general situation of rival factions in the aristocracy in interaction with the imperial regime (and its rival) sets up a number of complications for the relations between the wise/scribes and the rulers among whom they served. Rival scribal circles would understandably have been attached to rival aristocratic factions and critical of the opposing aristocratic faction(s). Given the scribes' sense of authority independent of their ruler-patrons, it is conceivable that a scribal circle could have taken a course independent of one or more dominant aristocratic factions, despite their economic dependency and political vulnerability. We appear to have examples of just such relationships between scribal circles and

---

16. Tiller, "Sirach and the Politics of Seleucid Judea," 3–5.

rival factions among the priestly aristocracy in Ben Sira and the scribes who produced the Enoch and Daniel literature.

SIRACH

The book of Sirach is apparently a representative collection of materials cultivated and expounded by a Jerusalem scribe/sage and received by his audience toward the beginning of the second century BCE. The stated purpose of the grandson's translation (Prologue), that the book serve as an instructional and inspirational book for "those who love learning," is probably a good indication of the function of the materials included in Ben Sira's book. The audience for these instructions, admonitions, meditations, and hymns must have been others of the literate elite, that is, scribes-in-training. Since much of the content concerns the relationship between the addressees and the poor (peasants and urban workers) on the one side and the aristocratic rulers on the other, neither of them can be the audience. That much of Sirach is apparently instruction for scribes-in-training is a key difference from apocalyptic literature such as *1 Enoch*. The latter also contains "sapiential" sayings and exhortation, but deploys them for purposes well beyond the instructional.

A further, more detailed review of the contents of the book may yield a more precise sense of who, in terms of social role and relations, comprise the producer and the audience of the wisdom of Ben Sira. Unlike Proverbs 10–29, Sirach is not simply a collection of proverbs and other sapiential sayings. The instructional meditations on wisdom offer reflections on wisdom's origin, character, and benefits (e.g., 1:1–20, 25–27; 4:11–19; 6:18–31; 14:20–27; 15:1–10; 19:20–24). While "the fear of the Lord" is the beginning of wisdom and keeping the law is an important aspect of wisdom, only the laudatory hymn in Sirach 24 explicitly identifies Wisdom with the law. Meditations on the order of (God's) creation draw implications for human sin and mortality; and heavenly observation (astronomical wisdom) grounds the lunar calendar, versus the solar, as authoritative (16:26–30; 17:1–24; 18:1–14; 39:16–35; 42:15–25; 43:1–33). On the other hand, Ben Sira rejects the validity of dreams and omens, that is, "mantic wisdom" (34:1–8) and simply forbids investigation of things that are "hidden," "too marvelous," or "too difficult" (speculation about the creation and/or the future? 3:21–24; cf. 42:16, 19;

43:32–33).[17] Here are major factors by which Ben Sira differs from other scribes/sages such as those who produced *1 Enoch* and Daniel.

As Ben Sira declares in the well-known and widely-quoted discourse on the scribe/sage (38:24—39:11), the acquisition of wisdom depends on having the leisure necessary for study and reflection. In that connection, he lists as the sources for his wisdom, "the law of the Most High," "the wisdom of all the ancients," and "prophecies." That the wise scribe "preserves the sayings of the famous, penetrates the subtleties of parables, and seeks out the hidden meanings of proverbs . . . and the obscurities of parables," that is, mainly traditional proverbial wisdom, is evident mainly in his poetic instructional discourses and admonitions. In the poetic meditations and reflections on creation is perhaps where he "pours forth words of wisdom of his own" (39:6).

Ben Sira occasionally refers to his activity as a teacher ("for all who seek instruction," 33:18; cf. 24:32–33; 37:23), although the "house of instruction" in the epilogue may be metaphorical, and does not attest a "school" in the modern sense. Far more prominent, in passing references laced throughout the materials as well as in the discourse on the role of the scribe/sage, is the public political role he plays and reputation he builds. The scribes/sages that Ben Sira has in mind "are sought out for the council of the people, [and] attain eminence in the public assembly" (38:32–33). Indeed, besides serving on courts, the sage "serves among the great and appears before rulers" (38:33; 39:4). At the local level of the Jerusalem temple-state, Ben Sira's and his protégés' role was the same as that of their counterparts in the Egyptian, Babylonian, and Persian imperial courts, as advisers to the rulers. Perhaps we should take seriously the passing references to the scribe's travels in foreign lands, which may well have been connected with negotiations between imperial and local regimes (39:4; cf. 34:9–13). Most impressive is Ben Sira's virtual obsession with the sage's role in the public assembly and the fame he achieves, which appears almost to be the purpose of learning wisdom (e.g., 6:33–34; 15:5–6; 21:17; 33:19; 37:22–24; 38:32–33; 39:10). And his proud references to serving among rulers takes on added credibility from his periodic admonitions to his protégés about watching their words and their step in dealing with their superiors (4:7; 8:1–2, 8–9; 11:1; 13:9; 23:14; 33:16–19; cf. 4:15).

---

17. Wright, "'Fear the Lord and Honor the Priest.'"

Ben Sira's satisfaction in serving among rulers and giving wise counsel in the public assembly fits handily with his admonition in 7:29–31 to "honor the priest and give him his portion," indeed to render up the offerings and sacrifices as commanded, presumably in the law, which he elaborates in 35:1–13.[18] Besides being required to fulfil the commandment of God, this payment of tithes, offerings, and sacrifices is parallel and virtually identical to "fearing the Lord with all your soul" (7:29).[19] Of course, it should not be surprising that scribes such as Ben Sira would encourage payment of offerings and sacrifices to God/the priest. They themselves must have been economically dependent on the priestly aristocracy, directly or indirectly. As noted, Ben Sira makes much of the fact that the scribe, unlike peasants and urban artisans, did not do manual labor, hence had leisure to study and appear in the assembly.

The most remarkable evidence of Ben Sira's and his colleagues' serving among rulers, of course, is the long paean of praise of the ancestral rulers and leaders. Some recent interpreters have found here a rehearsal of Israel's "epic history" and a sapiential development of a historical perspective on life.[20] That may be somewhat of an over-interpretation. This is hardly an epic history of Israel. It is too selective for that. And it focuses only on the leaders, indeed emphasizes rulers and ruling institutions. Tradition is being used here for contemporary purposes. The praise of ancestral heroes in Sirach 44–50 has also often been taken somewhat at face value as a representation of the commonly accepted standard view of the high priesthood and its rootage in Israelite tradition. Now that a "hermeneutics of suspicion" is more commonly exercised, however, we can recognize that this hymn expresses not an already accepted standard view but rather how its composers and users want the high priesthood to be understood. The lengthy hymn of praise in Sirach 44–50 serves primarily to articulate a foundational ideology for the high priesthood in general and the incumbency of Simon II in particular, with whose praise the hymn concludes.

A closer examination of this long paean of praise, however, indicates that Ben Sira is not just a supporter of the "establishment" in general, but an advocate of a particular understanding of the high priesthood and a particular faction of priests. Not Moses or David, but Aaron

18. See further Wright, "'Fear the Lord and Honor the Priest.'"
19. See further Olyan, "Ben Sira's Relationship to the Priesthood."
20. Mack, *Wisdom and Hebrew Epic*.

and Phinehas are the principal ancestral rulers praised, the recipients of the eternal covenant of the priesthood. Moses plays an almost subordinate instrumental role, and David and his successors, while glorious in some respects, are hopelessly flawed and disqualified. Striking is not just the absence of any mention of the Levites but even more the absence of references to Zadok or of Simon II as a Zadokite, since (according to Ezekiel, at least) the Zadokites were supposedly the legitimate high priestly lineage. While honoring Simon II with the highest praise, Ben Sira is apparently pressing the claims of all Aaronid priests, not just Zadokites (and excluding the Levites), to the (high) priesthood, its authority, and its perks.[21] It is unclear whether the emphasis on the Aaronid priesthood, along with a failure to mention Zadokites, represents merely an attempt to include all Aaronid priests in the governing (high) priesthood (or also an implicit criticism of the exclusive claim of the Zadokites?). In any case, it would have been an opportune time to press for a wider base for the priesthood. The power of the high priesthood of the incumbent Oniad family had been seriously weakened, first by the rise of the Tobiads to power in Judea and Palestine and then by the maneuvering and civil struggles entailed in the shift from the Ptolemaic to the Seleucid imperial regime.

For all his orientation to and cavorting with the high-and-mighty ruling aristocracy, however, Ben Sira insists that his fellow scribes/sages retain their mediating role in Judean society. Besides making a sharp criticism of sacrificing ill-gotten goods and an appeal to God on behalf of the humble, Ben Sira repeatedly exhorted his hearers to give special attention to the poor. Not only are they to give alms to the destitute and lend to a needy neighbor, but they should even use their positions to defend and "rescue the oppressed from the oppressor" (4:1–10; 7:32; 29:1–13; 42:2). Some of these exhortations explicitly identify this with observance of the law. Although most of Ben Sira's references to the law refer to studying and meditating on it, its observance as the beginning of wisdom was apparently more than mere sapiential piety. Modern scholars often emphasize that the scribes were the primary interpreters and teachers of the law. Yet references to teaching the law and actual citations of particular laws are rare in Ben Sira. The focus is rather observing the law, particularly in connection with mitigating the worst predatory practices of the powerful.

21. See further Olyan, "Ben Sira's Relationship to the Priesthood."

In sum, Ben Sira works creatively with traditional proverbial wisdom, cultivates astronomical lore and reflection on the created order, and composes meditations on the origin and character of wisdom, while rejecting dreams and omens. He does all this primarily for the purpose of participating in the assembly and serving the incumbent high priestly rulers of the Judean temple-state-and of course to maintain the respectable lifestyle appropriate to such an honorable position. Indeed, (reified and personified) Wisdom, identical with the Law, has made its home in Jerusalem where it endorses and supports the high priesthood and its current incumbents. Cosmological wisdom, reflective wisdom, and particularly instructional wisdom, at least in the book of Sirach, the principal collection (of different types) of wisdom from mid-second-temple history, was cultivated by scribes who supported and were dependent on the currently established priestly rulers of the temple-state.

1 ENOCH

The four earlier sections of *1 Enoch* should be dealt with in their apparent respective historical contexts. The Book of Watchers, *1 Enoch* 1–36, and the Astronomical Book, *1 Enoch* 72–82, can both be dated to the third century BCE. The Epistle of Enoch, including the Ten-Week Vision, *1 Enoch* 92–105, seems to fit sometime prior to the Maccabean Revolt. The Dream Visions, including the Animal Vision, *1 Enoch* 83–90, appears to date just before or at the beginning of the Maccabean Revolt. That these various sections are "books" (i.e., writings) indicates that scribes produced them. In at least two sections of *1 Enoch*, moreover, the "authors" explicitly identify Enoch, the ostensible writer of the books, as "scribe of righteousness," "scribe of truth" (*1 Enoch* 12:4; 15:1), and "(skilled) scribe" (92:1) and otherwise portray Enoch as writing and reading petitions, heavenly tablets, and books (e.g., 13:3–7; 81:1–2; 82:1).

The content of Enoch's books or the revelations he obtains in visions can be generally characterized as wisdom. While Enoch's wisdom includes sapiential sayings like those in much of Sirach, however, most of his wisdom is of the kind that Ben Sira includes only cautiously, rejects as invalid, or forbids as dangerous. While Ben Sira includes some astronomical wisdom about the sun, moon, and stars, one point of which is to authorize a lunar calendar that controls the festivals (all important in a temple-state economy), *1 Enoch* includes a whole book of astronomy which includes detailed treatment of a 364 day solar calendar, and passages that criticize those who do not follow it.[22] Similarly, much of the content of the Book of the Watchers is knowledge of the topography and patterns in the heavens. Enoch acquires much of his wisdom from dreams and visions (e.g., 1:2; 13:8; 14:2, 8, 18–23; 19:3), which Ben Sira rejects. And two sections of *1 Enoch* include reviews of history focused on Israel/Judah, including a projection of fantastic events of judgment and restoration of the creation, which Ben Sira simply forbids as "too marvelous" and "too difficult" (although Sirach 36 contains a psalmic appeal to God for the restoration of Israel, in very restrained language). All of the kinds of knowledge cultivated in the various books of Enoch, whether cultivated or rejected by Ben Sira, were standard in the repertoire of ancient Near Eastern scribes/sages working at various royal courts, whether in Egypt, Babylon, Ugarit, or later in Alexandria (Manetho) and Seleucid Babylon (Berossus).

Whereas Ben Sira tacitly accepts the imperial situation,[23] the producers of early Enoch literature view imperial rule as violent and oppressive. The overall purpose of the Book of the Watchers was evidently to explain the military violence and economic exploitation of imperial rule as caught up in the higher-level invasion of history by rebellious divine beings who generated the race of "giants," and to reassure "the chosen righteous ones" that God was still ultimately in control and would judge and punish the Watchers. If we were to read the Book of the Watchers as parallel in perspective to Daniel 7, then the Hellenistic empires may been particularly problematic and provocative (and Antiochus Epiphanes was not yet on the scene!). The Animal Vision in *1 Enoch* 85–90 brings forward a far more comprehensive condemnation of rulers, domestic as well as imperial. All alien enemies and rulers are portrayed as vicious predatory birds or beasts of prey and both domestic rulers and "shepherds" of imperial nations are condemned for oppression and violence against the "sheep" with whose care they are charged and their judgment is anticipated (89:59—90:27).

In contrast to Ben Sira, who spouts enthusiastic praise for the temple-state and its high priestly incumbent, the two visionary reviews

---

22. Wright, "'Fear the Lord and Honor the Priest.'"

23. While Sirach 36 expresses a hope for eventual restoration, Ben Sira praises Onias for rebuilding the Temple, for which Antiochus III had recently provided imperial funding.

of history included in *1 Enoch* both criticize the "Second Temple." In both the symbol of "house (of the kingdom)" refers to the people (i.e., the kingdom of Israel/Judah and/or of God), which will be restored in the glorious fulfillment of history (93:7, 8, 13; 89:39, 50, 66; 90:29). The Ten-Week Vision, however, while mentioning the earlier tabernacle, pointedly omits any reference to the Temple or its rebuilding, referring only to "a perverse generation" whose "deeds will be perverse" following the Babylonian conquest (93:9). The Animal Vision does refer to the Temple as a "tower built upon that house, . . . [with] a full table" (89:50, 67). The rebuilt "tower," however, had "polluted" bread and the eyes of the sheep were blind, like those of their shepherds (89:73–74). In the eschatological fulfillment the Lord of the sheep is to bring a new house, but without a tower (90:29). Both of these historical visions-and-interpretation produced by "Enoch" scribes thus articulate not simply an alienation from the incumbent high priests, but a virtual rejection of the postexilic temple-state.

The Epistle is the only section of *1 Enoch* that provides enough information for us to discern more precisely what the relation may be between the scribes/sages who produced this literature and the high priestly rulers on the one hand and the Judean people on the other. Through much of this literature, the principal division lies between "the (chosen) righteous" and the "sinners." Some have thought that the former must be a designation for the community or movement responsible for producing the literature. Closer analysis of the woes against the sinners in the Epistle, however, suggests that the relationship was more complex.[24] In the "woes" they pronounce on "the wealthy" the Enoch scribes who produced the Epistle have left a few "tracks" by which we may identify them vis-à-vis other actors in the drama. In the judgment, "the wise among men" who "will see the truth" appear to play a distinctive role among the righteous, holy, and pious who are to be vindicated by the Most High (100:5; similarly, "Enoch's" role is to provide wisdom to the chosen ones, in 5:8; 82:2–3). The righteous are a larger group among whom "the wise" have special knowledge and a special responsibility. The wealthy sinners, moreover, are addressed as "fools" precisely because they "do not listen to the wise," that is their scribal opponents (98:9). In the Epistle, therefore, one scribe ("Enoch") appears to be addressing other (a circle of) scribes/wise, pronouncing woes of destruction in the divine judgment

---

24. See the fuller analysis chap. 5 below.

against the wealthy and powerful for oppressing the righteous/pious, who will finally be vindicated.

When we look for the reason that the wealthy are condemned we find the same portrayal of the wealthy and powerful oppressing the poor that Ben Sira articulated. What are occasional observations in Sirach, however, become the basis for an almost obsessive and uncompromising condemnation in the final divine judgment in the Epistle of Enoch. As in Ben Sira's discourses and almost any ancient agrarian society, the wealthy are those who hold positions of political or political-religious power—which meant the priestly aristocracy in ancient Judea. So in the "woes" pronounced by Enoch, the "mighty" gain great riches and an easy and luxurious lifestyle by exploiting the righteous (96:8; 97:2; 96:5–6 alluding to Amos 6:4–6). The lament of the lowly that "we were not masters of our labor . . . and our enemies were our masters . . . and to our enemies we bowed our necks" (103:3, 9, 11–12; cf. 98:4) suggest that, against the covenantal norms of Judean society, the poor had been subjected to forced labor or debt-slavery by the wealthy. In this connection the repeated charge that the wealthy sinners "build their houses with sin" and "build their houses not with their own labors, [but] make the whole house of the stones and bricks of sin" (94:6–7; 99:13) similarly suggests some sort of servitude to which the poor have been subjected, again probably on the pretext of their indebtedness (cf. Neh 5:1–12). That the rich sinners "lie awake to devise evil" (100:8), like the indictment in Mic 2:1–2, suggests that the wealthy are designing schemes to take over the labor or even the land of the poor, again probably on the pretext of their indebtedness. Such actions were a direct violation of covenantal commandments: they "plunder and sin and steal and get wealth" (102:9). Indeed, these series of woes frequently allude to the violation of Mosaic covenantal principles (97:6; 98:4, 7–8, 12; 99:2). The complaint that the wealthy "weigh out injustice" (95:6) resembles the prophet Amos' charge (2:6) that "they sell the righteous for silver," referring to their manipulation of the weights in measuring out grain or oil that the peasants were borrowing. And the charge that the rich and powerful "acquire gold and silver in judgment/unjustly" (94:7; 97:8, 10), like the classical prophets' similar indictments of the ruling elite, alludes to their manipulation of the courts to gain power over the powerless.

The scribes who produced the Epistle of Enoch, like Ben Sira, saw themselves as social and culturally superior to the poor Judean peasants.

Whereas Ben Sira observed the exploitation of the poor by the rich in a relatively detached manner, however, the learned scribes who produced Enoch literature called down divine judgment against the wealthy, even saw themselves involved in retribution. They stood vehemently opposed to the wealthy, that is the aristocracy of the Judean temple-state, perhaps already in the late third century when the Book of Watchers was produced, but certainly in the early second century when the Epistle was produced.

The earliest Enoch text, the Book of Watchers, gives not a hint that the Enoch scribes were in any way actively resisting the incumbent high priestly rulers in the third century. Even in the Epistle, however they may have articulated prophetic curses against the wealthy and powerful, they appear simply as a circle of scribes/sages who had for some time sharply opposed the incumbent high priestly faction and perhaps the high priesthood. Nor is there any implication in the early Enoch texts that the "Enoch circle" hoped to replace the incumbent rulers of the temple-state, as did the Qumran community later in the second century. In the Ten-Week Vision "the righteous" would appear to have a more active role in what looks to be the current historical situation of the "seventh week). And in the Animal Vision the Enoch scribes appear to have "opened their eyes" and begun some sort of form of resistance, evidently to the invasion of Antiochus Epiphanes—or, more likely, to have joined a resistance movement against Seleucid persecution (the lambs who began to open their eyes and resist before the ram, Judah the Maccabee, sprang into action, 90:6–14). In any case, this circle of scribes projected a future age of righteousness without sin, without oppression by the wealthy and powerful, and without a Temple and its high priestly rulers.

In sum, the producers of early Enoch literature were apparently a circle of scribes opposed to the temple-state as well as hostile to its incumbent rulers. The texts they produced that are classified as "apocalyptic" (or more precisely "historical apocalypses," or even more appropriately, historical visions-and-interpretations) attempted to explain how foreign and domestic oppression had become so severe in their society and to reassure themselves at least that God was still in control and would eventually execute judgment of the rulers and restoration of the people on a renewed earth.

DANIEL

As we have emerged from the previous dichotomization of "wisdom" and "apocalyptic," it has been noted that the portrayal of Daniel and his colleagues in the tales of Daniel 1–6 closely resembles Ben Sira's reflection on the scribe/sage in Sir 39:1–11.[25] Well-born, these Judean lads are "versed in every branch of wisdom, endowed with knowledge and insight," and faithful to the Law, even active in prayer (Dan 1:4, 8–16, 17, 20). They are trained in the language and literature of the Chaldeans (1:4, 17), just as Ben Sira's sage cultivates the wisdom of the (Judean) ancients. In the later visions (9:2), Daniel is "concerned with prophecies," as well, also like Ben Sira's scribe. Daniel "explains riddles and solves problems" (Dan 5:12), just as his counterpart penetrates subtleties, hidden meanings, and obscurities (Sir 39:2–3). Neither are portrayed much as teachers, certainly not as teachers and interpreters of the law. But Daniel and his "wise" colleagues serve at court, particularly in assemblies, just as Ben Sira's wise scribe serves among rulers and public assemblies. Daniel (1:5) states explicitly what Ben Sira indicates only indirectly, that such sages are economically supported by and dependent on the rulers they serve.

What differentiates Daniel and apparently the *maskilim* who recycled the tales and produced the visions-and-interpretations in Dan 7–12 is that their principal wisdom lies in visions, and their interpretation, which Ben Sira rejects (see esp. Dan 2; 7; 8; 10–12). With regard to "mantic" wisdom of dreams and their interpretation, Daniel resembles, while excelling, all the wise men of Babylon, all the "magicians, enchanters, sorcerers, and Chaldeans (1:17, 20; 2:2, 10, 12, 19, 27, 28; 4:6, 9; 5:7, 8, 11–12). A further difference from Ben Sira emerges in the visions-and-interpretations of Dan 7–12. While the *maskilim* still function as interpreters of dream-visions in/for a ruler's court, as in the tales of Daniel 1–6, it is now (as in *1 Enoch*) the divine ruler's court rather than a human ruler's court (as with Ben Sira). While still political in their functions, Daniel and the *maskilim* have moved up several notches in the scope of political jurisdiction their ruler-patron deals with-from temple-state through imperial to the transimperial and transhistorical (see esp. Daniel 2; 7; 10–12). Far from being uninterested in politics—in their obsession with purity and communion with the angels[26]—Daniel and

---

25. See, e.g., Wills, *Jew in the Court*.
26. Cf. Collins, "Daniel and His Social World," esp. 140.

the *maskilim* are focused on politics. Indeed, their wisdom (visions and interpretations) and the insights and activities entailed are completely focused on imperial politics and its implications for political-religious life in Judea.

Similar to both Sirach and *1 Enoch*, both the tales and the visions-and-interpretations in Daniel present a completely scribal ethos. Throughout the book everything significant is accomplished by writing: the young men receive literary training in chapter 1, a hand writes on the wall in chapter 5, Daniel writes down the dream and books are opened for judgment in chapter 7, prophetic books are interpreted in chapter 9, and the deliverance of people is written in the book and Daniel seals the book in chapter 12. The scribal ethos, moreover, is relatively self-centered, as communication within the scribal circle that produced the literature. Daniel's book is not for public consumption. The mysterious divine plan (*raz/mysterion*) revealed to Daniel and the *maskilim* in chapter 2 is only ostensibly communicated to the king. Although the tales in Dan 1–6 probably circulated orally prior to their inclusion in the book of Daniel, the visions in particular and the book as a whole were produced and written down for a literate audience, perhaps only for the *maskilim* themselves (ordinary Judeans could not have read the written visions-plus-interpretation).[27] Moreover, only the *maskilim* understood what was happening. It was up to them to "give understanding to many," but presumably in oral communication and especially by their martyrdom in resistance to Antiochus Epiphanes' imperial program for Judea. Part of the secret wisdom to which they have become privy is that "the people (more generally) shall be delivered" (12:1), that "the people of the holy ones of the Most High" would be restored to (God's) sovereignty (7:27). When it comes to heroics of resistance and vindication for the martyrs, however, they are focused on themselves, on their own heroic role. The heroic *maskilim* who fall will be refined, purified, and cleansed, but apparently only as their own reward, since nothing is said of benefit for or effect on the people generally (11:35). Half of the book focuses narrowly on the role of the faithful Judean sage at the foreign imperial court who refuses to compromise his loyalty to his God–and is vindicated.[28] And

---

27. Only recently are biblical scholars recognizing that while scribes made written copies of texts, their own cultivation of texts was primarily oral, with the text "written on the tablet of their heart," whence they could recite it as appropriate to the situation. See Horsley, *Scribes, Visionaries*, chaps 5–6, and the references there.

28. Wills, *Jew in the Court*, 151–52.

at the end of the book, the glorious vindication of shining like the stars was for "those who are wise . . . and lead many to righteousness" (12:3). Daniel was produced by and for the circle of the *maskilim*.

While the *maskilim* receive revelation that the people generally will be restored and "shall give understanding to many," it would be going beyond anything suggested in the text to say that they are teachers or leaders of the people.[29] While the Epistle of Enoch envisages a future revelatory role for the wise vis-à-vis the righteous, no current or future leadership role appears for the *maskilim* in Daniel. They are almost exclusively the recipients of revelation, interpretation of the dream visions about what is happening under the suddenly super-oppressive imperial regime of Antiochus Epiphanes.

The *maskilim* who produced Daniel, however, have themselves moved into staunch resistance to the oppressive imperial forces. They, and apparently others "who are loyal to their God," are taking "action," albeit nonviolent, and to that extent they could be said to have formed, at least temporarily, a resistance movement. If the "little help" is indeed a reference to Judah the Maccabee, then it seems likely that "those who are loyal . . ." may well be the more popular resistance movement already underway, parallel but not directly linked with their own more individual nonviolent resistance. Their resistance to the imperial forces, moreover, means that they also stood in opposition to the incumbent high priestly regime that Antiochus was supporting in its "reform," headed by the usurper Menelaus, who had replaced the previous usurper Jason. The *maskilim* who produced Daniel, however, appear to have opposed more than just the usurping incumbent high priesthood. They seem to be at least de-emphasizing the very institution of the Temple and high priesthood. While the reviews of Antiochus' oppression and persecution view his actions against the Temple building and the "burnt offering" as horrendous actions (e.g., 8:13; 9:27; 11:31), the images of restoration do not include a Temple or priestly leadership. The focus is on "the people (of the holy ones of the Most High;" 7:27; 12:1). Of course this might be due to how discredited the high priesthood had become in the previous decade of its purchase and (what they would have considered disgraceful) transformation in the "reform." Yet it seems evident from chapter 9 that they did not consider that the rebuilding of the Temple after the exile had ended or overcome "the desolation of Jerusalem" (contrast

---

29. Cf. Collins, "Daniel and His Social World," 132, 139.

2 Chron 36:20–21; Zech 1:12–17). In the tales of Daniel 1–6 the Temple is conspicuous by its absence–after it was rebuilt precisely during the ostensible career of Daniel in the Babylonian court. At the end of the visions, finally, the sacrifices in the Temple are apparently superfluous for the *maskilim*, since their own suffering and martyrdom have become the means of purification, at least for themselves.[30] We must conclude that the *maskilim* who produced Daniel were decisively alienated from the ruling high priestly incumbents.

CONCLUSION

In and behind the book of Sirach, early Enoch literature, and the book of Daniel, we can discern different circles of scribes/sages. Each circle concentrated on developing particular aspects of the traditional ancient Near Eastern and Judahite scribal repertoire that ranges from proverbial and theological wisdom to astronomical and mantic wisdom.

What most differentiates these early Judean examples of apocalyptic literature and their scribal authors from Sirach is their extensive cultivation of visions and/or vision-interpretation, which Ben Sira simply rejected, and their inquiry into hidden prospects for the future, which Ben Sira forbade. A more subtle but nevertheless significant difference was their perspective on and review of Israelite and international history focused on the people as a whole, in contrast to Ben Sira's praise of ancestral leaders, particularly rulers.

What seems most determinative for which aspects of the traditional repertoire a scribal circle cultivated and developed was its relation to the rival factions in the priestly aristocracy, particularly the dominant faction, in the struggle for power in the Jerusalem temple-state, which was usually closely related to current imperial power relations. Ben Sira and his protégés served among, while the Enochic and Danielic sages opposed, the incumbent priestly rulers in Jerusalem.

Ben Sira represents a nonpriestly scribal faction that supported the Oniad incumbents and propagandized for the authority of the Aaronids. He and his circle of scribes had adjusted to imperial rule and found an honorable life in service of the high priesthood sponsored by the imperial regime. Ben Sira lauded the Oniad priesthood as thoroughly grounded in a selectively chosen and characterized ancient Israelite

---

30. Davies, "Reading Daniel Sociologically," 360.

lineage of royal and high priestly rulers–simply ignoring the concrete imperial arrangement by which the temple-state and its incumbent rulers were established. Much of his wisdom accordingly consists of professional advice on serving among the high priestly rulers, while also mitigating the worst effects of their (ab)use of power.

The wise scribes of Enoch literature and the *maskilim* of Daniel, on the other hand, employed visions both to explain the debilitating circumstances of imperial rule and to imagine a judgment of the imperial rulers and restoration of the people's independence. Apparently well prior to a situation of persecution that followed upon the "Hellenizing" crisis of 175 BCE, earliest Enoch literature sought to explain, indict, and anticipate the divine judgment of the imperial kings and, by implication, the high priestly regime sponsored by them. The Ten-Week (vision-and-) interpretation of history questioned the validity of the temple-state, labeling the postexilic arrangement as "perverse." The Animal Vision not only rejects the incumbent high priesthood but also appears to condemn the very institution of the temple-state/high priesthood. The *maskilim* who produced Daniel, however, belonged to a different scribal circle from the one that produced Enoch literature. Both of these circles were apparently alienated from the Jerusalem high priestly court. Of course, they may well also have been the clients of high priestly patrons who had (temporarily) lost out in the struggle for power. But even if that were the case, their hopes for the future restoration of the people and fulfillment of history tellingly lacked (or excluded) a temple and high priesthood.

Finally, yet another scribal circle (either priestly or allied with a faction of priests) appears to have preceded and then joined or helped form the Qumran community. The Qumran scribes/sages cultivated all of the various aspects of the conventional sapiential repertoire, including mantic and astronomical wisdom, and added to its scribal repertoire an intensive cultivation of legal traditions and concrete application of prophetic books to their own situation. The proto-Qumran scribes shared Ben Sira's positive attitude toward the temple-state and high priesthood as institutions. But like the Daniel and Enoch scribes, they sharply opposed the incumbent high priesthood, the Hasmoneans. There must have been at least four different scribal circles in Jerusalem, therefore, in the early second century. But that should not be surprising given the different and shifting factions in the aristocracy maneuvering for position in the unstable imperial situation during these decades.

3

The Social Settings of the Components of *1 Enoch*

INTRODUCTION

ASKING SOCIOLOGICAL QUESTIONS ABOUT an ancient text is a little like asking biological questions about a rock. It can be done—especially if the rock happens to be a fossil. But it is impossible to apply the same methods to a rock as one applies to a living organism. In the same way sociological studies of ancient texts are only successful with texts that happen to preserve fossilized remains of the social context in which they were produced and recorded. The methods that a sociologist would apply to the study of a living society are of little use. One must be content with the use of historical, linguistic, archeological and literary methods in answering historical questions informed by sociological sensitivities.

When we ask about the sociological settings of the components of 1 Enoch, it must be clear from the outset that we are not asking about the social groups that created the texts, as if there were some kind of correspondence between literary document and social group. We may presume that the various texts that were later collected in 1 Enoch were produced by several individuals who would have benefitted from the company of other like-minded individuals, who probably shared common theological, political, social and economic views. These, however, are not the object of our sociological inquiries. We are not asking about ideology, nor do we know the amount of ideological diversity that might have been acceptable to these people and their friends. Rather than looking for a "sect" or "conventicle," we will be trying to describe the social context in which the authors of such texts may have lived.

We are asking about social setting, and this requires some pre-understanding about the social landscape of Hellenistic Judea. For this we must content ourselves with a few observations about the political and economic structure of Judea as a subject province of larger, Greek empires—first the Egyptian, Ptolemaic Empire and then the Syrian, Seleucid Empire. We will begin by analyzing some of the available evidence. We will then attempt a synthetic description of the political, economic, and social realities. Finally, we will see whether it is possible to place the producers of the various texts of 1 Enoch somewhere within that structure.

THE SOCIAL STRUCTURE OF PTOLEMAIC JUDEA

Little is known for certain about the Ptolemaic administration of Judea, but if it were anything like that in Egypt, there would have been officials in charge of agricultural production, finances, and record keeping. In addition there would have been a military structure, somewhat independent of the rest of the bureaucracy.[1] The King probably claimed some kind of right to all of the land with direct control only over the "royal lands." Taxes in kind, as well as various monetary taxes, were collected through a system of tax farming. Royal officials collected the taxes, and the tax farmers ensured that the correct amounts were collected. On the other hand, there were clear differences between Ptolemaic administration of Egypt and that over Palestine, just as there were differences in the administration of various nomes of Egypt.[2] In particular it is evident that military administration was entrusted to local powerful families such as the sons of Tobiah who are prominent in the Zenon Papyri and virtually all other extensive accounts of the post-exilic period down to the establishment of the Hasmonean dynasty.

What little evidence we have indicates that at the beginning of Ptolemaic rule over Judea the Jerusalem high priesthood had attained a position of power at the head of what amounted to a temple-state. Hecataeus of Abdera, a Greek ethnographer in the court of Ptolemy

---

1. For a fuller review of the administration of Syria and Phoenicia see Bagnall, *Administration*, 11–24.

2. Ibid., 8.

I states that Jerusalem was a temple-state ruled by a high priest who stands in authority over the people and serves as "a messenger of God's commandments" and "announces what is ordained in assemblies" (preserved in Diodorus Siculus 40.3). Pseudo-Hecataeus (probably mid-second century BCE) refers to a chief priest Ezechias, who was a proponent of emigration to Egypt after Ptolemy became ruler of Syria. He tells us that Ezechias was "highly esteemed by his countrymen, intellectual, and moreover and able speaker and unsurpassed as a man of business" (Josephus, *C. Apion* 187–89). This Ezechias may possibly have been the "Hezekiah the governor," whose name was inscribed on silver coins minted in Jerusalem dating to the late Persian or early Ptolemaic period. If Persian, the Ezechias or Hezekiah, would have been high priest and governor of the Persian Province and would have survived until Ptolemy had seized control over Palestine. The identification, however, is speculative. Although it is not certain whether the Judean high priest functioned as governor under the Ptolemies, it is clear that the high priest was highly influential and powerful.

The power of the high priest, however, was not absolute, inasmuch as it was subject to the foreign emperor and possibly also to the local governor and, because the sphere of influence of the high priest did not necessarily extend equally over all of Judea. As the Zenon Papyri show, there were numerous powerful families, who had a certain degree of local autonomy and control. The most prominent of these were the "sons of Tobaias," presumably the descendants of Nehemiah's opponent (Neh 2:19; 4:3,7; 6:1, 14, 17–19), who was also influential among the elite in Jerusalem in his day. A certain "Toubias" is mentioned in the Zenon Papyri as a commander of Ptolemaic soldiers in and around the stronghold of Birta in Ammanitis.[3] This practice of entrusting military command to local powerful men, along with the practice of tax farming, launched the family of Tobiah into prominence and into direct conflict with the Oniads, the high-priestly family of the late third century and early second century BCE.

Josephus reports on one stage of this conflict in his "Tobiah romance," drawn from what must have been part of a "court history" of the Tobiad family. While this account should not be taken at face value, it reports events that must have had some remote correspondence to

---

3. Bagnall, *Adminstration*, 17.

actual events. According to the story Onias II[4] was responsible for paying a sum of 20 talents to the Ptolemaic rulers, which sum was somehow related to his authority over the people and his possession of the office of high priest (*Ant.* 12.158–61). This is consistent with the fact that the high priestly office was always held subject to the emperor's consent. According to the story Onias stopped paying the tax/tribute due to laziness. If indeed he had withheld payment, it would have been an act of rebellion; perhaps Onias had aligned himself with the Seleucid emperor and hoped for a Seleucid victory. Joseph, the Tobiad, now an in-law of Onias, took the opportunity to pay the amount in exchange for the position of tax farmer for all of Syria and Phoenicia (*Ant.* 12.184). No doubt such an exchange would have also carried severe consequences for Onias. If the story is true, it is extremely doubtful that Onias retained the high priesthood (see *Ant.* 12.163). It is possible, in fact, that Joseph was also appointed high priest. That Josephus fails to mention these issues is to be expected, given his tendency to present the Judean elite in a favorable light.[5]

SELEUCID JUDEA: THE DECREE OF ANTIOCHUS III

One of the most important documents that survives from the early second century is the decree of Antiochus III preserved in Josephus, *Ant.* 12.138–44. The letter has sometimes been dismissed as a Judean forgery. Its general historical verisimilitude, verifiable details, style and dialect, however guarantee that it represents, at least in general, an authentic decree issued shortly after the conquest of Coele-Syria.[6] Antiochus' decree is in the form of a letter from Antiochus to Ptolemy, the provincial governor of Coele-Syria at the time of Antiochus' conquest.[7] Its

4. Josephus' chronology is confused, but most scholars place the events in the late third century.

5. Kurtz, *Social Construction*, 62.

6. The most thorough study of this issue is that of Bickerman, "La charte séleucide," 4–35. Almost all scholars now accept Bickerman's arguments. See, for example, Tcherikover, *Hellenistic Civilization*, 82; Marcus, *Josephus*, 7:744–59; or Taylor, *Seleucid Rule*, 54–55.

7. See Taylor, *Seleucid Rule*, 108–88, for a competent treatment of Ptolemy's career, including his service in 219 BCE. Ptolemy IV as co-commander of the Macedonian phalanx in the so-called fourth Syrian war against Antiochus III (Polybius 5.63–65) and his later service to Antiochus III as strategos and archiereus of Coele-Syria. Taylor dates Ptolemy's defection to the time of the fifth Syrian was and proposes that he had formerly been strategos and archiereus of the Ptolemaic province (115–27).

importance for our purposes is that it is an official, imperial document that mentions the political realities of Judea and defines imperial policy toward Jerusalem and its local aristocracy during the transition of rule from the Ptolemaic Empire to the Seleucid Empire. Antiochus' decree was to define and cement the relationship of Antiochus as benefactor to the people and Temple of Jerusalem and to establish a new order under Seleucid sponsorship and jurisdiction.

One must assume that Antiochus published his decree partially on the basis of information provided by Judean advisors (probably not unlike Ben Sira himself) since it reflects a familiarity with Judean circumstances.[8] In fact, we know the name of one of these advisors from 2 Macc 4:11 ("He [Antiochus IV] rejected the royal concessions to the Jews that had been established through John the father of Eupolemus"). The information in it must, therefore, bear at least a rough resemblance to how things were or at least how they were represented to be by a Judean representative of the party loyal to Antiochus.

This decree depicts the centrality of the Temple in Jerusalem society and identifies the aristocracy deserving of special tax relief. The Temple was recognized by Antiochus, who promised to provide the sacrificial materials and to allow the import of tax-free timber for the rebuilding of the Temple (*Ant.* 12.140–41). The fact that Jerusalem functioned as an officially recognized temple-state is confirmed by the other proclamation of Antiochus III preserved in Josephus (*Ant.* 12.145–46), which forbids foreigners and unclean Jews from entering the Temple enclosure and forbids the introduction of non-sacrificial animals or skins into Jerusalem.

Those who were responsible for the "splendid reception" afforded to Antiochus when he arrived at the city and who were relieved of their tax burden, consisted of the "the gerousia, the priests, the scribes of the temple and the temple-singers" (*Ant.* 12.142). The importance of the gerousia (aristocratic council) in Judean civic affairs is indicated by their position at the head of the list of Judean dignitaries. This primacy is confirmed for a slightly later period by references to the gerousia

---

8. Bickerman notes, "It is obvious that the formulation of this as well as other benefits granted by the Seleucid king must have been drafted with the participation of Jewish experts. We notice, for instance, that the king does not promise to furnish the fuel for public offerings. The reason for this omission was that the wood offering was a traditional obligation of rich Jewish families in Jerusalem (Neh. 10:35, 13:31)" (*Jews in the Greek Age*, 127–28).

in 1 Maccabees, 2 Maccabees, and Judith. According to 2 Macc 4:44 the gerousia sent three men to Antiochus IV to file complaints about Menelaus. The later letter of Jonathan to the Spartans is represented as being from "Jonathan, the gerousia of the ethnos, the priests and the rest of the Judean people" (1 Macc 12:6). The answer from Sparta refers to "Simon the great priest and the elders and the priests and the rest of the Judean people."[9] Thus, the gerousia of the letter corresponds exactly to the "elders" in the letter from the Spartans.[10] Judith (probably composed in the second half of the second century) also refers anachronistically to a gerousia in Jerusalem that had the authority to waive cultic regulations concerning the eating of sacrificial food (11:14), to direct military operations (4:8), and to witness the victory over the Assyrian army and congratulate Judith for her part in it (15:8). In these passages gerousia is sometimes translated as "senate," but "aristocratic council" would be better. We have, then, evidence from 1 Maccabees, 2 Maccabees, Judith, and independently in Josephus of the powerful political-religious role of the gerousia in Judea throughout the first half of the second century.

What we lack is a clear idea of the particular powers and makeup of this council. The political upheaval that must have occurred with the transfer of power from the Ptolemies to Antiochus III would surely have effected changes that may have also had an impact on the makeup of such prominent assemblies. From the decree it is clear that the assembly had welcomed Antiochus. There seem to be several possible explanations.

1. The members of the gerousia who had sided with the Ptolemaic regime (Tobiads and other priestly and non-priestly elites) failed to sway the assembly and lost their seats, while those who sided with the Seleucids (priests and others allied with Simon II) gained new control of the assembly.

2. Or the assembly had always been in opposition to Ptolemaic rule, but had been relatively powerless. Their support for Antiochus III won them new prestige and power as a body, but involved no substantial change in membership.

---

9. 1 Macc 14:20b: Σιμῶνι ιερεῖ μεάλῳ καί τοῖς πρεσβυτέροις καὶ τοῖς ἱερεῦσιν καὶ τῷ λοιπῷ δήμῳ τῶν Ἰουδαίων.

10. Even if either letter should prove to be spurious, this demonstrates clearly that for the writer of Maccabees, the two expressions were equivalent in Greek, as we would expect anyway, given the etymology of γερουσία. See also Schürer, *History*, 2:203 n. 8. (1973–87).

3. Or finally, the power and composition of the gerousia remained relatively unchanged relative to other Judean powers, but the balance of power within the gerousia changed, with certain priestly members gaining in prestige and influence.

What we do know is that the *gerousia* was above the ordinary priests in status and sometimes (but not always) below the high priest (e.g., Jonathan), its members were rewarded for their support of Antiochus III's conquest of Judea along with the priests, and they could act independently of (and against) the high priest (e.g., Menelaus).

The decree's failure to mention the high priest is significant. The lack of mention indicates a lack of prominence. This is very significant and cannot be a mere oversight. The later letter of Jonathan to the Spartans in 1 Maccabees 12 mentions "Jonathan, the gerousia of the ethnos, the priests and the rest of the Judean people." The order of mention in the list corresponds to one's relative position in society. In both cases the gerousia is above the priests; in the decree the gerousia has the first place. There was apparently no single head of state at the time of the Seleucid entry into Jerusalem. There are a couple of possibilities that I can conjecture.

1. The Tobiad head of state (possibly Joseph the tax collector) had supported the Ptolemies and so was not among those who welcomed the Seleucid conqueror.

2. The Oniad head of state/high priest had either been exiled or executed for his failure to pay tribute due to Ptolemy, the event that led to the rise of Joseph the Tobiad to the good graces of the Egyptian monarch. There was therefore no functioning high priest.

Not long afterward the Judean high priest again attained a position of unique power. This may have been assigned by the transfer of authority to collect taxes from the house of Tobiah to the house of Simon. While it is clear that the high priest did not have exclusive control over the collection of taxes,[11] his newly regained powers would have brought him considerable new authority and wealth, including the right to use imperial troops to enforce collections. The high priest also had at least

---

11. According to 2 Macc 4:28, the collection of tax revenue was the responsibility of Sostratus, the eparch of the acropolis, while Menelaus was high priest. No Hellenistic ruler ever allowed anyone to possess exclusive financial powers over the imperial purse.

some of his own troops, as is attested by 2 Macc 4:40, according to which Lysimachus, as a representative of the high priest, raised an army of 3,000 when he had been left in charge of Jerusalem while his brother, Menelaus, was in Antioch. It was this power to levy an army that caused so much trouble later when Jason drove Menelaus out of Jerusalem after Antiochus had appointed Menelaus high priest in his place (Josephus, *Ant.* 12.239–40).

Antiochus' decree also mentions the priests, the temple-scribes, and the temple-singers. The fact that the priests are mentioned after the gerousia may only mean that the (mostly priestly) gerousia had greater status than the ordinary priests. This mention confirms the centrality of the Temple and the Temple cult in Judean society and the power of the priesthood in general. Second, it confirms the existence of a political-religious office of temple-scribe, which was subordinate to the priesthood. Unquestionably, Ben Sira was one of the these "scribes of the Temple."

SELEUCID JUDEA: THE BOOK OF SIRACH

The book of Sirach was written in the first quarter of the second century BCE by Jesus son of Eleazar son of Sira, a teacher and practitioner of wisdom in Jerusalem. This text is important for understanding Judean politics under the Seleucids for several reasons.

1. It was written by someone who was involved in the daily administration of justice and diplomacy in Jerusalem, probably not unlike John, the father of Eupolemus, who had served under Antiochus III (2 Macc 4:11).

2. It was written to instruct those who hoped to engage in similar activities.

3. It contains descriptions of various occupations (from slave to king) and prescriptions for proper behavior and relations between those of different social strata. In so doing it provides Ben Sira's idealized social structure centered on the Judean high priest.

4. Ben Sira's wisdom was written to describe and promote a new, symbolic political order with the high priest at the center and the loyal sage as the foundation.

The author identifies himself as "Jesus the son of Eleazar son of Sira" (50:27b). He invites his readers to his "house of instruction" (51:23).

Apart from these details, we know little or nothing about him personally. What is far more important for our purposes is that he describes in some detail his occupation as one "who devotes himself to the study of the law of the Most High" (38:34b). He has four basic tasks.

1. The first is to study ancient wisdom, prophecies, and parables, to meditate "on his mysteries," and to "glory in the law of the Lord's covenant" (39:1-3, 7b,8b).
2. The second is to serve in political and diplomatic roles ("He serves among the great and appears before rulers; he travels in foreign lands..." [39:4]).
3. The third is "to seek the Lord who made him and to petition the Most High" (39:5).
4. The fourth is to teach ("he will pour forth words of wisdom of his own" [39:6b]).

The sage, then, is one who studies ancient wisdom, prophecy and law; engages in bureaucracy and diplomacy; performs deeds of personal piety; and teaches. It is, therefore, a political-religious office, not a political office for religious people nor a religious office with collateral political duties.

The total integration of political and religious interests can be clearly seen in Ben Sira's agenda for global politics. According to 10:4, "The government of the earth is in the hands of the Lord, and over it he will raise up the right man from time to time." For Ben Sira, the political status of Israel in the world is wrapped up in his conviction that God "places a ruler over every nation, but Israel is the Lord's own portion" (17:17). Intermixed with the assertion that God repays individuals according to their deeds is the claim that he will also repay vengeance to the nations and judge his people's case with mercy (35[32]:18-19[23-25]).

Ben Sira's prayer for God's deliverance in fulfillment of the prophecies immediately following the threat of vengeance on the nations indicated Ben Sira's political-religious agenda. He calls for the destruction of enemies of God's people (9b), the gathering of "all tribes of Jacob" (11a), and the filling of Jerusalem and the temple with celebration and glory (13-14). Many scholars have thought that the content of this prayer is out of place in Sirach. According to Middendorp, "One recognizes sudden explosions of nationalism and particularism in a book that is otherwise filled with a humane and universalistic spirit."[12] The problem here may be a misapprehension of genre expectations. One certainly finds hints at a "humane and universalistic spirit" in Sirach (his fondness for international travel [39:4] and his use of foreign wisdom and traditions),[13] but these are not characteristic of Ben Sira or of his wisdom instruction. Wischmeyer correctly characterizes Ben Sira's religion as exclusivistic and elitist.[14] Ben Sira finds holiness, she goes on to say, at various points in Jerusalem and in the rest of Israel, the city of Jerusalem, the people of Israel, the Temple in Jerusalem are all called as holy.[15]

In retrospect this prayer seems to be more like wishful thinking than part of a real political program, but the ever-present potential for political instability may have caused hope to rise. It was only a few years later that this prayer was partially realized under the Maccabees. Nor is this wish incidental to Ben Sira's thinking. It is integral to his doctrine of opposites and his idea that all things have been created for a purpose and "will prove good in their season" (39:16–35). The purpose of things like winds, fire, hail, famine, pestilence, wild beasts, and war is to execute the vengeance of God. His wrath is directed not only at ungodly individuals (39:30), but also the nations (39:23).

A comparison of Ben Sira's claims and rhetoric with what we know from other sources about Ben Sira's society reveals certain telling discrepancies. It seems that the book does not simply describe the social reality and public duty of the sage, but seeks also to construct that reality. He does so in at least 3 ways:

1. He presents the high priest as an absolute ruler with no dependence or relation to imperial rule and provides ideological foundation for high priestly rule.

2. He exaggerates the role and authority of the scribe and provides ideological foundation for that authority.

3. He minimizes the authority and function of the gerousia to the point that it is irrelevant as a legislative or judicial body.

---

12. Middendorp, *Stellung*, 125 n. 1.

13. See Sanders, *Ben Sira*, for a study of the foreign influences on Ben Sira's wisdom. Mack, *Wisdom*, has demonstrated the influence of Greek rhetoric on chapters 44–50.

14. Wischmeyer, *Kultur*, 256–57.

15. See especially Wisdom's self-praise in chapter 24.

It is well known that the final "Hymn of the Fathers" at the end of the book of Sirach focuses on the high priest as the possessor of an eternal covenant with God and the most glorious of all the heroes of Israel's history. Far greater attention is lavished on Aaron than on any other figure, including Moses and David. Even Moses is subordinated to Aaron's office. It is Aaron who is anointed by Moses as priest and has the "lasting covenant" (45:15). The purpose of Moses' reception and transmission of divine revelation ("to teach his precepts to Jacob, his covenant decrees to Israel" [45:5]) is taken over by Aaronide priesthood (45:17). The everlasting covenant of the priesthood, established for Aaron and his descendants, is structurally connected with the everlasting covenants made with the fathers, Noah, Abraham, and Jacob. The priestly covenant is explicitly and favorably compared with the covenant with David, which was only an "individual heritage" whereas the covenant with Aaron was for all his descendants (45:25). Besides their respective fame for warfare and wisdom, David and Solomon function principally to establish the cult in Jerusalem (47:8–10, 13). The poem as a whole climaxes in the elaborate praise of Simon, who receives more attention even than Aaron. Moreover, it is clear from the characterization of Simon that the high priesthood has taken over the functions of kingship (fortifications and water supply, cf. 48:17 and 50:2–4), while remaining focused on the temple-cult.

It is significant that Ben Sira never, or almost never, mentions the gerousia. Sir 38:32 mentions the "people's council" or "council over the people" in parallelism with assembly (ἐκκλησία). This, however, probably does not refer to any regularly constituted institution. There were various assemblies where one could speak (קהל, ἐκκλησία in 15:5; עדת שרים, πλῆθος πρεσβυτέρων in 7:14), where the blameless could receive praise (קהל, ἐκκλησία in 34[31]:11; קהל, ἐκκλησία and עדה, λαοί in 44:15), and before which Simon would officiate at the altar (קהל ישראל, ἐκκλησία [υἱῶν] Ισραηλ in 50:13, 20), but these were not regular, legislative bodies (with the possible exception of the assembly of rulers in 7:14). There are a few passages that may refer to juridical councils. The reference to adulterous women being brought before the assembly (ἐκκλησία; 23:24) indicates that the assembly may have had juridical responsibilities in cases where imperial law was not involved, but we do not know what assembly he was referring to. There are also references to elders (8:9 [שבים], 25:4–5 [πρεσβυτέροις, γερόντων];

32:3 [שב], 9 [זקנים]), but none of these refer to an assembly or even an official title. They are honorific terms, and the contexts in which they are used are invariably concerned with honoring the aged. Thus, while Ben Sira refers to the people who would have been members of the gerousia, he does not mention the gerousia itself, perhaps because of his intent to accentuate the authority of the high priest and the Mosaic Law as interpreted by scribes like himself. Likewise, the temple-singers, also granted privileges by Antiochus III, are mentioned, but only to highlight the splendor of Simon as he concludes his priestly service at the altar (50:18).

The principal role or function of the scribes or sages was "to serve the chiefs" (שרים, μεγιστᾶσιν) (8:8). According to 38:24—39:11, scribes were sought as advisers, if not members, of the collective leadership of Jerusalem and they attained eminence among the citizenry as a whole (38:32–33). But in the same passage, Ben Sira clearly indicates that the sage is subordinate to the ruling class and therefore economically and politically dependent on the good will of the rulers. This explains Ben Sira's admonition to bow low to the rulers and his extensive "professional" advice on deferential behavior and caution when dealing with the powerful (4:7; 13:9–11; 31:12–24; 8:1–2, 14). Ben Sira is careful to make clear the importance of the wise scribe in government. The wise and understanding ruler will have a well-ordered rule (10:1–2) and will bring about growth instead of the ruin that results from lack of discipline (10:3). Wisdom, understanding, and discipline are precisely the qualities that Ben Sira attributes to those who study wisdom, that is the scribes. Thus the successful ruler must either be a scribe or have good scribes at his disposal.

It appears, in fact, that one of Ben Sira's goals was to enhance the authority and honor of the scribal class. His book is full of claims that the greatest honor is for the wise, those who fear the Lord and obey his commands. The role of the priests as authoritative interpreters and teachers of the law is supplanted by the sage. Besides being the heirs of earlier generations of sages, they are the successors of the prophets as well (24:33), speaking by divine inspiration. This relatively lofty social status may have been at least partly due to their unique skills; "to devise proverbs requires painful thinking" (13:26b), and not anyone could do it. Ben Sira's catalogue of honor is revealing in this regard (10:19–25). Above the nobleman, judge, and ruler in honor is "the man who fears the Lord" (24). For Ben Sira, the "fear of the Lord" can be concretely measured by obedience to the commandments, since dishonor is due anyone who transgresses the commandments (19d). The sage who is wise (as measured by his obedience to the laws of Moses) is to be honored above all. Social status and the right to speak in the assembly are for the wise (15:5).

The honor conferred by wisdom enables the sage to "rescue the oppressed from the oppressor" presumably in their official or professional capacities (4:1-10). Ben Sira criticizes those who take advantage of the poor to enhance their own wealth ("offering sacrifice from the property of the poor" and "taking away a neighbor's living" in 34:24-27, reminiscent of Amos 2:6-8, may refer to creditors' "foreclosing" on debts). The motivation for such concern for the poor is, as always for Ben Sira, the prospect of divine judgment (21:5; "The poor man's prayer goes from his lips to his [God's] ears, and his judgment comes quickly"). God refuses a bribe, shows no partiality, and executes judgment on the wicked (35:12-20), and so should the wise.

Presumably the rulers accepted this semi-independent role of the sages because it was part of the foundation of their claim to divine authority and thus made it possible for the sages to provide the ideological basis for the priests' rule. Indirectly it served the interests of the wealthy in that the existence of a powerful class, which defended the interests of the poor, also legitimated the rule of those who were in a position to oppress the poor.

The basis for the authority of the scribe was not self-evident but was the matter of debate among various groups of sages. For Ben Sira, his authority and the basis of his wisdom was firmly grounded in the Torah (although in practice Torah generally recedes to the background). This is most clearly seen in the praise of wisdom (24:1-33), which found a resting place in Jerusalem and ministered before the Lord in the holy tabernacle (24:8-12). In this hymn wisdom is explicitly identified with "the book of the covenant of the Most High God" (24:23; cf. Exod 24:7; Deut 33:4). The close identification of the person of the scribe and personified wisdom is seen in the almost imperceptible transition from wisdom's self-description (1-22) to Ben Sira's description of wisdom (23-31) to Ben Sira's self-description (30-34) in language that recalls wisdom's own speech. His authority is her authority. Like the biblical writers he "will again pour out teaching like prophecy, and leave it to all future generations" (24:33). This is not due to his own native intelligence, but he calls himself "the last on watch," "one who gleans after the grape-gatherers" (33:16). Ben Sira's authority is grounded not in himself but in the source of his wisdom, namely those who preceded him (39:1–2) and the Law, which is as reliable as Urim (36[33]:3).

Ben Sira's treatment of the rulers, if read uncritically, would lead one to conclude that Judea was ruled by an undifferentiated, aristocratic, group of honorable, wise, and fair men. They apparently had little to do with imperial politics but were active in local politics and civic affairs, beloved and respected by all people. Those who exhibited too much pride were overthrown by God, and their places were taken by their more humble associates. Otherwise, there was little competition for influence, and those who possessed the greatest authority were those who ruled men most wisely, in obedience to the Law and with the fear of God. This, however, is scarcely believable. Ben Sira's idealized view of the centrality of the high priest collides with the reality implied by Antiochus' charter, which excludes the high priest and instead grants authority to the gerousia, which is scarcely mentioned by Ben Sira at all. The office of high priest was not as monolithic as tradition tells us. Office holders had to compete for authority and received the support of scribes like Ben Sira, military officials, and other legal and bureaucratic retainers to do so.

His idealized view of the sage is in some ways more realistic, in that the sages could certainly influence political realities by their authoritative teachings. Daniel maskilim, the compilers of 1 Enoch, the "righteous teacher" of the DSS, and others would have provided competing authoritative political visions, some of which would have supported political-economic-religious individuals or groups in competition with others.

SUMMARY OF THE EVIDENCE

Even after taking the available evidence into account, very little is known with certainty about the social organization of pre-Maccabean Judea. What we do know is that it was ruled by Ptolemaic Egypt and then by Seleucid Syria as a part of the providence Coele-Syria. There was a tradition of high priestly rule, and it seems that the high priest and his fellow priests usually functioned as imperial agents and as local leaders.

The high priest had rivals, one of whom, Joseph the Tobiad, was apparently able to gain the right to collect imperial taxes toward the end of the Ptolemaic rule. By the time of Antiochus IV, however, the high priesthood had (again) become a lucrative and powerful position, as evidenced by the expensive and deadly struggles to obtain the position. In addition, there was a council of elders (the gerousia), but its makeup and responsibilities are unknown.

High priestly rule was maintained both militarily and ideologically. The imperial rulers no doubt supplied military support, but the high priest seems to have had some of his own troops as well (2 Macc 4:40; Josephus, *Ant.* 12.239–40). The ideology was traditional but needed to be renewed and maintained by the performance of the temple-cult and the teachings of the sages such as Ben Sira. The book of Sirach presupposes a society in which the high priest and his fellow priests rule an orderly society with sages like Ben Sira serving as teachers of the people, advisors, judges, diplomats, etc. This picture is partially confirmed by the decree of Antiochus III preserved in Josephus, *Ant.* 12.138–44 that established Jerusalem as the center of the temple-state within the Seleucid Empire led by a council of elders and priests with the scribes and temple-singers as privileged aristocracy. Taylor summarizes his conclusions about this decree: "Seleucid rule in Jerusalem rested on a series of privileges and benefactions that are fairly simple and direct in nature and easily paralleled ancient political life."[16] These "privileges" and benefactions" were granted to the council of elders, the priests, and other Temple personnel.

Ben Sira's portrait of Judea as a harmonious society that revolved around the political, economic, and religious rule of the high priest is, however, false. Both Ptolemaic and Seleucid rule were maintained in part by establishing competing and independent authorities, all of which reported directly to the king. There is a hint of this competition in the fact that Antiochus' decree establishes the gerousia (the council of elders) as the chief in the Jerusalem hierarchy, but by the time of Antiochus IV it is the high priest. The Scythopolis Inscription, first published by Landau[17] and studied in detail by Taylor,[18] illustrates the fact that provincial officials were dependent directly on the king and not on some local chief. The inscription is a record of correspondence with

---

16. Taylor, *Seleucid Rule*, 170.
17. Landau, "Greek Inscription," 54–70.
18. Taylor, *Seleucid Rule*, 108–68.

the Syrian king concerning disputes between Ptolemy and other agents of the empire, including even local garrison commanders. Taylor has shown that Ptolemy, the strategos and high priest of Coele-Syria and the addressee of Antiochus's decree concerning Jerusalem, functioned as governor with supervisory role over all of the sanctuaries in the land, including the one in Jerusalem. Yet, despite his apparently powerful position, Ptolemy had little or no authority over other local financial and logistical administrators (dioiketai) and had to appeal to the king to resolve disputes. In addition, there was the very real conflict between the two external powers as they fought war after war over Syro-Phoenicia.

Sages were members of the privileged aristocracy that depended in part upon imperial and/or priestly benefactions for their position and stature in society. Inasmuch as their patrons had conflicting interests and loyalties, the interests and loyalties of the sages/scribes would also conflict.[19] It is in this context that we should think about the social context in which the Enochic visions and other literature were produced.

THE SOCIAL SETTING OF THE EARLY BOOKS OF ENOCH

There is little information about social locations in the books of 1Enoch, but there are a few hints. All of the Enochic books reflect a scribal origin. The simple fact that only professional scribes would have had the skill to write these books gives us a pretty clear indication that the compilers of Enochic traditions belonged to the scribal class. In several passages, Enoch (with whom the writers presumably identify) is called a scribe (12:3–4; 15:1; 92:1). Moreover he functions as a teacher of wisdom for his children (82:1–3; 91:1–4), using vocabulary that is reminiscent of instruction of "sons" in wisdom literature. The emphasis on reading and writing also points to a scribal milieu (13:3–7; 81:1–2; 82:1; 93:2; 89:61, 68, 76–77).

That the writers of 1 Enoch and Ben Sira both belonged to the same socio-economic class does not mean that they would agree on ideology. Ben Sira provides the theological and ideological underpinnings for Oniad priestly rule subject to the foreign emperor. The Enochic writers oppose both Oniad priestly rule and foreign dominance. The Book of Watchers, collected and composed during the rule of the Ptolemies re-

---

19. Horsley and Tiller, "Ben Sira," 74–107.

flects an anti-imperial stance that rejects not only the foreign rulers, but also their local, priestly representatives. Nickelsburg and Bartelmus have both proposed that the Book of Watchers was composed as a polemic against the Greek overlords who claimed divine descent, consumed goods, and brought violence upon the land.[20] It was apparently expanded to provide a more pointed critique of the priesthood over the issue of family purity and intermarriage.[21] None of the Enochic compositions displays very much interest in the Temple, priesthood, or Mosaic Law. The Animal vision is positively against the Second Temple as such, and the Ten-Week Vision (*1 Enoch* 93; 91:11–17), by implication agrees.[22] It seems, therefore that while the Enochic sages, fulfilled a sociological role identical to that of Ben Sira and his students, the Enochic sages served priestly powers that (at least in the third and second centuries) unsuccessfully competed for the influence and authority and resisted or opposed the cooperation of the high priests with the Hellenistic empires.[23]

The Epistle of Enoch, written probably in the first third of the second century BCE is also reflects a scribal ethos that formally agrees with Ben Sira, but probably does so in opposition to the leaders that Ben Sira supports. The writers pronounce judgment against the wealthy for their oppression of the righteous. In one case the righteous are identified with "lowly" (96:5), but the word "poor" is never used.[24] It seems likely that the Israelite traditions about justice for the poor and oppressed have been applied by the writers to the oppression of the powerful against themselves, the righteous.

Indications in both Sirach and *1 Enoch* (especially book 5) show that Ben Sira and the Enochic sages have operated in conscious op-

---

20. Nickelsburg, "Apocalyptic and Myth," 383–405; and Bartelmus, *Heroentum*, 175–79 (cited by VanderKam, *Enoch*, 128 n. 67). It might appear to be inconsistent that the watchers are condemned for bringing knowledge of divination and astrology, when those are very similar to the skills for which Enoch himself is famous. Presumably the Greek diviners practiced divination and astrology that was based upon elicit sources and included kinds of divination that were unacceptable to the Enochic sages, while that of Enoch and his followers was based upon licit revelations by God and good angels and include interpretations of visions but not other sorts of auguries.

21. Suter, "Fallen Angel," 115–35; and Nickelsburg, "Enoch, Levi and Peter," 575–600.

22. Tiller, *Commentary*, 39–40, 97.

23. See Bryan, *Cosmos*, 168–85, for an argument for "the strong priestly background of the seer" (183).

24. Nickelsburg, *Commentary*, 426–27.

position to each other.²⁵ Both books present their authors as sages and teachers, each with their own unique traditions. Both make use of the same Israelite traditions. One appeals to dreams and visions, while the other warns against them. Both propose innovations over against the structure prescribed by Antiochus's decree, which seems to establish the gerousia over the priests and does not mention the high priest at all. Ben Sira wants to rearrange the power structure, while the Enochic visionaries want to dismantle and replace it with something radically different.

The close literary (and/or oral) relationship between the Book of Watchers and the Animal Vision indicates a succession of Enochic teachers who maintained and passed on the Enochic traditions.²⁶ This is different from the *Jubilees* where traditions about Enoch are retold, but with less faithfulness to the traditions told in the name of Enoch. This, however, does not imply the existence of a social group. When we speak of community or sociological group, we usually have in mind an organized social structure with defined boundaries and constraints. Having a common hero and theology does not imply social structure. Horsley makes a similar argument concerning the Epistle of Enoch: "We should not think that *1 Enoch* 92–105 is the product of a movement or group any more than we would understand a text of Sirach as testimony to Ben Sira heading a social movement."²⁷ Nothing in any of the books of Enoch implies a social structure for the wise/righteous or that they have any exclusive claim to election. Like Daniel the books assume that the wise will function as teachers for many others who are not among the wise and that this teaching will be based on revealed wisdom.²⁸ It seems extremely unlikely that any real social groups ever defined boundaries in terms of adherence to the teachings of "Enoch" or "Daniel." As we are reminded by Grabbe, "There is no necessary connection between apocalypses and apocalyptic communities."²⁹ It is, in fact, difficult to imagine what sort of community or social movement could have been devoted to the cultivation of Enochic wisdom. It is far more likely that the sages who produced this literature were members of a larger social group and that their teachings were largely compatible with the ideals of the group.

25. Wright, "Fear the Lord," 189–222; and Argall, *1 Enoch and Sirach*, 249–55.
26. Tiller, *Commentary*, 88–89.
27. Horsley, "Social Relations," 115.
28. Nickelsburg, "Epistle of Enoch," 333–48
29. Grabbe, "Social Setting," 29.

Books like Daniel, Enoch, Sirach, or other books of the period should no longer be mined for theological evidence of groups that were either the same or different. Rather they are evidence that their writers and compliers belonged to a class of professional sages and teachers, trained in the tradition of aristocratic and/or apocalyptic wisdom (whether native or foreign), whose politically charged teachings had an impact on their own and subsequent generations.

PART TWO

Reconsideration of Texts in Historical Contexts

4

Israel at the Mercy of Demonic Powers

An Enochic Interpretation of Post-Exilic Imperialism

INTRODUCTION

THE SECOND DREAM VISION of book 4 of *1 Enoch* (the Animal Vision) is an allegorical review of human history from Adam until the ideal future age.[1] The period from the Babylonian exile until the predicted end of the present age (apparently meant to arrive during the Maccabean revolt) is included in what we may call the allegory of the seventy shepherds. This section is an interpretation of the history of exilic and post-exilic Judea (the author is not so interested in the rest of Israel) under various foreign dominions. In the process of interpreting history (including the author's present), the text promotes an ideology that competes with the dominant ideology of the temple-state and with that of the Seleucid Empire. The interpretation of the allegory is relatively straightforward because the writer has embedded in the text two sets of indicators of meaning. The first is the allegorical component. The second is the reuse of older textual (and oral, though these are harder to discover) traditions. We will first consider the external referent of the shepherds by investigating the internal workings of the allegory. We will then consider the antecedent traditions that seem to be incorporated within the story. Finally we will consider whether we can use these

---

1. On the characterization of the Animal Vision as an allegory and the implications of that characterization for understanding it, see Tiller, *Commentary*, 21–28.

two sets of interpretive clues to understand the implied interpretation of Judean history. According to this Dream Vision, imperial rule over Judea is nothing less than a replay of the descent of the Watchers with disastrous results for the whole earth.

THE ALLEGORY

The controlling allegory of the Animal Vision is Israel as God's sheep. Before Jacob, the Sethite progenitors up to and including Isaac are symbolized as white cattle; the non-Sethites (particularly the Cainites) are symbolized as black cattle. The descent of the Watchers is represented by stars that fall to earth and cohabit with cows. The cows, in turn, give birth to elephants, camels, and asses (the giants). Seven beings "like white men" who represent the archangels carry out temporary judgment against the stars and the unnatural offspring of the stars and cows. After the flood in which most of the cattle are drowned, the surviving cattle again give birth to strange offspring. From one white bull comes a white sheep, which represents Jacob. From other cattle come various unclean, predatory or scavenging animals and birds that threaten the sheep. These animals represent gentile contemporaries of Israel. The account contains an allegorical representation of the construction of the Jerusalem Temple under Solomon and the subsequent abandonment of the Temple, first by Israel and then by God. After the destruction of the First Temple, the sheep-master (God) delivers the sheep (Israel) into the care of a series of seventy shepherds (angels) who are to tend the sheep and kill some of them (89:59-60). One may perhaps presume that this slaughter is not for food or sacrifice, but that it is a punishment for the sheep's abandonment of their house (Jerusalem) in 89:51. The sheep-master also appoints an auditor to count and record the actual number of sheep killed, because he knows that the shepherds will prove too zealous in their killing. This situation lasts until the final battle, which immediately precedes the final judgment, when the shepherds are punished for exceeding the sheep owner's command. The final age is marked by a transformation into white cattle of all who survive the judgment, a change that represents a restoration to adamic conditions.

The most important clue to the meaning and significance of the seventy shepherds is the internal function of the sign/symbol as indicated by its relationship to other signs within the allegory. When R. H.

Charles published his masterful commentary on *1 Enoch*, the identity of the shepherds was still "the most vexed question in Enoch."[2] Until the beginning of this century, most attempts to explain the seventy shepherds assumed the identification of angels either with a series of 70 foreign or native kings or of 70 years.[3] By the time of Charles, however, there was a new consensus that the shepherds represent angels.[4] Charles' argument was based first on the fact that all other human figures in the allegory represent either angels or God. Second, these shepherds also correspond to the stars that fell to earth among the cattle earlier in the allegory, because they are judged together in the final judgment. According to 90:24–25, the stars were the first to be judged, and they were put into a deep, fiery, abyss. The shepherds were judged next and placed into the same abyss. The blinded sheep are the only other group to be judged, and they were placed in a separate abyss. Apparently there is one abyss for angels and one for humans. Since the shepherds and stars share a common judgment, they must both be angels. Third, the shepherds are associated with the angelic auditor who observed and recorded their deeds, since he is called "another" (89:61) one of them. That the auditor is an angel is clear from the fact that in 90:14, 17, and 22 he is said to be one of the seven white men of 87:2 who represent the seven archangels otherwise mentioned in *1 Enoch* 20 and 81:5. If the angelic auditor can be called "another" of them, then they must also be angels.

The implications of these identifications go far beyond the simple determination of referents external to the allegory. They extend to the signification of the allegory itself. The close association of the stars and shepherds in the final judgment is an indication they both groups play a similar role in the allegory. Not only do the seventy shepherds and the "fallen" stars share a common judgment, but they also face common foes in both the determination and the execution of that judgment. According to 88:1–3 three of seven individuals "like white men" (87:2) cast the stars into deep crevices in the earth to await judgment and send the elephants, camels and asses into battle against each other. These events correspond

---

2. Charles, *The Book of Enoch*, 200.

3. For a review of previous attempts at a solution, see Gebhardt, "Die 70 Hirten," 163–246. Gebhardt concluded that a solution was impossible without further textual evidence.

4. This was first suggested by von Hofmann, *Der Schriftbefwies*, 1.422. It was argued most carefully be Charles, *Book of Enoch*, 200; and Martin, *Le livre d'Hénoch*, 217–18. See also Tiller, *Commentary*, 51–53.

quite transparently to the story as recorded in the Book of the Watchers (*1 Enoch* 1–36). In *1 Enoch* 10:4–5, Raphael binds Asael and casts him into a rocky hole in the desert. In 10:9 God tells Gabriel to send the children of the Watchers into battle against each other. The judgment of the shepherds is closely modeled after that of the Watchers.

According to 90:22, one of the same seven white men was the auditor who was to count and record the number of sheep killed by the shepherds. Apparently God's economy is not completely different from that of the foreign empires with their official recorders and census takers. The function of this auditor was to guard against fraud. And, in fact, it was this auditor's report on the fraudulent (excessive) killing that instigated the sheep-master's violent intervention in 90:17. Again this series of events corresponds precisely to the account of the Book of the Watchers. According to *1 Enoch* 9 it was the archangels Michael, Sariel, Raphael and Gabriel who noticed the violence brought about on earth by the giants and brought the Watchers' sins to God's attention. It was the angelic auditor who notified God of the excesses of the seventy shepherds and brought them bound to judgment before the sheep-master (90:22). Thus, the angelic auditor is explicitly identified as one of the archangels, and like the archangels of the Enochic tale of the Watchers (*1 Enoch* 9–10), it was his task to report to God on the misdeeds of errant angelic beings and then to bind them for judgment.

Thus the allegory of the seventy shepherds is designed with reference to the older myth of the Watchers. The larger allegory has within it the story of the descent and judgment of the Watchers who are allegorized as stars that fell from the sky and cohabited with cows. This, however, is not the end of the story. Like so much in apocalyptic literature, older myths become the key to understanding the present. The past is not only the past; it is also the model for understanding the present.

INTERPRETATION OF ANTECEDENT TRADITIONS

The Animal Vision of *1 Enoch* clearly incorporates several earlier biblical and Enochic texts, though never by quotation and only rarely by the use of common words or phrases. As an allegory, it points to earlier texts by relating in allegorical form the events and situations described by these texts or by adapting the symbols of earlier texts. The allegorist has brought together a rich array of sacred Judean traditions to provide an allegorical retelling of Israel's history, which implicitly interprets the present condition of Judea as exile under the deficient care of delinquent angels. He combines the notions of 70 years (or periods) of exile, oppression by angelic beings, and divine punishment for sins to create a tapestry of traditions, woven together into a critique of the current Judean political establishment with its cooperation with foreign rulers.[5] Our task at this point is to define these traditions more precisely and show how the writer of the Animal Vision has interpreted these traditions and how they contribute to the development of the allegory.

Some of the traditions are too general to be traced to a particular text. The basic symbol of the Animal Vision is that of shepherd/sheep. This is an ancient and common metaphor that is by no means limited to Israelite traditions. Paul Porter has conducted a careful investigation into the semantic domain of the animal metaphors of Daniel 7–8, in the course of which he considers also the Animal Apocalypse. He has shown that the metaphor of the shepherd is used not only in the Hebrew Bible, but also throughout ancient Mesopotamia. It is used of the relationships between political and divine rulers and their subjects. As in the Animal Vision, these rulers are sometimes criticized as wicked shepherds.[6] Ezekiel 34 and Zechariah 11 provide excellent parallels and may even have influenced the shaping of the allegory. Ezekiel 34 contains a condemnation of the "shepherds of Israel" who failed to care for the sheep and a promise that God himself would gather the flock and personally shepherd his sheep, restoring those who had been harmed and establishing justice (Ezek 34:16). In Zechariah 11 the Lord declares that he will raise up a foolish shepherd who will eat the sheep instead of caring for the flock and then will be punished. In the Animal Vision, as in Ezekiel 34, the shepherds are explicitly contrasted with the sheep-master. This provides a poignant reminder of the relationship that the Judeans' ancestors had once had with God, but which has been replaced by a destructive relationship with angelic substitutes. Plainly pseudo-Enoch sees his present time as one in which Judah is in some sense estranged from God as punishment for past failures. The real rulers of Judah, however,

---

5. The use of multiple traditions is also recognized by Newsom, "Enoch 83–90," 24–27. Although she understands the seventy shepherds primarily as "a systematic exegesis of Jeremiah 25" (25), she acknowledges that "the influence of Ez. 34 and Zech. 11 must not be discounted," and she accepts the possibility of the multivalence of the number seventy (27).

6. Porter, *Metaphors*.

are not the local chieftains, priests, or elders (however one imagines the precise political organization of Judea at this time) or even the foreign representatives of the imperial court, but angelic beings whom God has commissioned to take his place in the care of his people. This turns the imperial claims to divine descent on its head. Yes, there is something otherworldly behind the empire, but it is demonic, not divine.

Another of the more general traditions presupposed in the allegory is what David Bryan calls the "kosher mentality." Using an anthropological approach, Bryan argues that the strict and consistent use of only non-kosher animals for all but the patriarchs before Jacob and Israel is a reflection of the idea of clean and unclean. The unclean animals evoke a sense of chaos, while the conflict between the unclean animals and the sheep evokes the perennial conflict between order and chaos. The whole history of Israel, then, is symbolically represented as an ongoing battle between the forces of chaos and the created order. Final restoration of all humans in the form of white cattle represents the final victory of order. The references during the period of the seventy shepherds to blind sheep in 89:74 and blind and deaf sheep in 90:7 bring the notion of anomaly even into the sheepfold. The author's present is one in which order is threatened by chaos.[7] The problem, however, is not simply that life is chaotic. The real opponents are the angelic caretakers of Israel and the gentile nations that oppress the Judean people. The symbolism marks the foreign rulers as disordered, unnatural, and unclean—unfit for mixing with the Judean faithful. With this the allegory denies the claim that imperial rule is somehow benevolent; whatever so-called benefactions it may bestow bring only disorder and chaos.

One somewhat more specific tradition that is presupposed in the allegory of the seventy shepherds is the interpretation of Jeremiah's predicted seventy years of exile, popularized by Daniel's seventy weeks of years (Dan 9:24–27).[8] Jeremiah 25 and the allegory of the shepherds share a common condemnation of Israel, a common punishment, a

---

7. Bryan, *Cosmos*.

8. Newsom ("Enoch 83–90," 24–27) and VanderKam (*Enoch*, 165–67) derive most of the imagery from Jeremiah 25 with a great deal of justification. The following discussion is heavily dependent upon their analyses. The richness of the traditions brought together here, however, seems to require a broader search. One of the traditions that scholars frequently appeal to in studies of this passage is the idea that each of the seventy nations of the world has an angel assigned to it. This seems unlikely. See Tiller, *Commentary*, 53.

common time period, a common judgment upon the instruments of Israel's punishment (including the metaphorical sword in both cases), and significantly a common use of the shepherd symbol. Jeremiah is somewhat unique in the Hebrew Bible in that it uses "shepherd" to symbolize foreign rulers. The reinterpretation of Jeremiah's prophecy in the Animal Vision is a clear sign of the rejection of the legitimacy of the contemporary temple-state. The seventy years of exile are not over. There is still a shepherd or two to go before the end.

What is by far the most important of Israel's sacred traditions for our text, however, is often overlooked in contemporary scholarship. That tradition is the specifically Enochic tradition of the Watchers. Over a century before the composition of the Animal Vision, another Enochic sage composed the Book of the Watchers by bringing together two separate myths of divine or angelic descent. George Nickelsburg has already proposed that the Book of the Watchers was written near the end of the fourth century in response to the wars of the diadochi, "a time of bitter military conflict by a foreign power, and among foreign powers—conflict so fierce, incessant, and widespread as to lead our author to claim that the existence of the human race was threatened."[9]

In the Book of the Watchers, contemporary events are compared to the ancient myth of the Watchers. The reader understands that like the ancient giants, Alexander's heirs are consuming and destroying the earth. The Animal Vision goes even further. The allegory of the shepherds declares that current status of Judea under the domination of foreign powers is the direct result of disobedience to God. The ruin experienced by the faithful of Israel is being orchestrated by disobedient angels. The only proper response to such a situation is resistance. Those who cooperate are blind, apostate sheep. The foreign emperor falsely claims legitimacy on the grounds that the conqueror has the right to rule and that he can trace his ancestry to the gods. The true basis for his rule over Israel is that God has abandoned his people into the care of false shepherds. They are illegitimate rulers, whose place has been secured by disobedient angels. Fellow Judeans are called to spiritual vision and military resistance. Those who cooperate with such rule are cooperating with angelic rebellion against God as serious as the rebellion of the ancient Watchers whose sin brought about the flood. The story carefully identifies the shepherds with the stars in order to demonstrate that the

---

9. Nickelsburg, "Apocalyptic," 391.

ancient ante-diluvian events described in the Book of the Watchers correspond to the contemporary situation, and not only by analogy.

It is certainly possible to understand each of these adaptations of tradition in purely theological terms, but that is probably not the most satisfactory frame of reference. The one common thread that unifies all of the variegated elements of this allegorical tapestry is that each implies a critique of the current political regime. This critique is certainly aimed at the high priestly regimes of Jason and Menelaus. It would be a mistake, however, to assume that the critique is aimed solely at these "Hellenizing" high priests. The Animal Vision itself is very clear about the scope of the critique. It goes back at least as far back as the founding of the Second Temple, the sacrifices of which were "polluted" and "not pure" (89:73). If we follow the allegory, we are brought all the way back to the beginning of the exile when the seventy shepherds were first commissioned by the sheep owner.

CONCLUSIONS

In an Enochic book that plainly refers to the famous Enochic story of the fall of the watchers the inter-textual clues lead one inexorably to understand the seventy shepherds in terms of a kind of *Urzeit–Endzeit* scheme. The writer and his fellow Judeans are now (at the time of composition) experiencing the horrors that were inflicted upon the earth by the Watchers and their giant offspring. The writer acknowledges that God is rightfully punishing his people for past wrongs, but the rightful limits to that punishment have been violated. Like the shepherds of Ezekiel 34:8 or Zechariah 11, the foreign nations and the domestic political leaders have made fodder of the Judeans. Instead of feeding and caring for the flock, while killing a predetermined number, the angelic guardians have slaughtered the Judeans and allowed other nations to oppress them as well. Political rule has become a tool of supernatural oppression and exploitation.

It should now be clear that the allegory is a political allegory. The story begins with cattle, which represent people differentiated only as Sethite and non-Sethite. It then moves to the birth of all kinds of animals, each of which represents a nation or ethnic group, and in the end returns to the transformation of all animals back into white cattle. This must be understood as the ultimate elimination of the separate identities of different nations. Even Israel does not survive as Israel, but in the form of the original patriarchs of the Sethite line. There is no restored Temple in the rebuilt Jerusalem. In this connection the use of Enoch as the hero begins to make sense. He represents the pious individual, not of Israel, but of generic humanity. The Animal Vision is an extremely radical document. It criticizes not only enemy regimes, but even the propriety of any political, ethnically based regime. Granted, the history of Israel under Solomon was good, but it quickly degenerated when the people neglected God and his messengers.

In the light of these conclusions, we must reconsider how we understand the alignment of the Enochic writer in the context of Judean politics of the second century BCE. It is impossible to imagine that any of the claimants to power during the post-exilic period could have won the loyalty of the allegorist. The usual view that this text supports Judas Maccabeus and other rebels against the Seleucid rule and against the Seleucid-appointed high priests is undoubtedly correct. The Maccabees are supported, however, not as national rulers, but as rebels. The text is not an anti-Hellenizing document, supporting traditional high-priestly rule against political and religious change. The basis of all post-exilic rule in Jerusalem has been cooperation with and subordination to the reigning foreign empire. Onias, no less than Tobias, could only rule with the approval of the Greek king. The Second Temple was understood to be impure and its offerings were polluted.

In the books of *Enoch*, then, we have evidence of a group of pious sages who trace their existence back at least to the beginning of Seleucid rule.[10] They were as opposed to so-called theocratic rule of Simon and Onias as to the so-called Hellenizing rule of Jason, Menelaus, and the compromise high priest, Alcimus. Religious opposition did not begin with Jason, but at the latest with the transfer of power from Ptolemaic Egypt to Seleucid Syria. If one assumes that the Book of the Watchers was motivated by a similar sentiment, then the opposition began with the conquest of Alexander the Great or shortly thereafter. The simplistic view that the political scene of early second century Judea was characterized by competition between faithful Torah observance against in-

---

10. The statement in *1 Enoch* 90:6, that "lambs were born from those white sheep, and they began to open their eyes and to see and to cry out to the sheep," seems to indicate that the writer identifies with the reform group symbolized by the lambs. See Tiller, *Commentary*, 102–16, 350–51.

novative Hellenism is false. The books of *Enoch* display a third, more radical way.[11] The goal of history is an end of all political divisions. No longer will one people rule another. Rather the God of Israel will personally rule a unified people without the need for Temple or king.

This study has further implications for how we interpret historical apocalypses. The historical review of the Animal Vision has a real, interpretive function. It is not there simply to confirm the predictive powers of the claimed author, in this case, Enoch. At least for this apocalypse, the purpose of the historical review is to interpret history and to create a meaningful vision of reality. This reality includes the day-to-day realities of everyday experience, but it encompasses also the larger realities where God and the angels act and compete for power over this world.

---

11. See Argall for speculation about one of the contexts in which Enochic opposition may have been expressed and nurtured (*1 Enoch and Sirach*, 249–55).

5

Social Relations and Social Conflict in the Epistle of Enoch

GEORGE NICKELSBURG'S TREATMENT OF the "social aspects" of Judean apocalyptic literature enabled us to appreciate the inadequacies of previous constructions of the social context of apocalyptic literature and to established some important procedural principles.[1] For example, Plöger's theory that the Hasidim, already a "hard-and-fast group" prior to the Maccabean revolt, were not only the authors of Daniel but the ancestors of the Pharisees was far too simple an explanation for the complicated details of so much second-temple history, particularly considering the serious lack of solid historical evidence.[2] Similarly, Hengel's extension of Plöger's thesis to explain the origins of the Essenes, who supposedly produced the Dead Sea Scrolls, resulted in a hypothesis too grand to be convincing about any particular document or community. While taking social factors into account, moreover, Hengel had offered a mainly cultural explanation: the apocalyptic worldview was basically a negative response to Hellenistic forms of thinking that were perceived as a threat to the existence of Judaism.[3] Nickelsburg rather pressed the case for addressing more genuinely sociological questions to the documents and stressed the importance of interrelating a range of social factors. Most important perhaps, given the now-passing

---

1. Nickelsburg, "Social Aspects." Cf. subsequent critical surveys by Davies, "Social World"; and Grabbe, "Social Setting."

2. See Nickelsburg, "Social Aspects," 641–43; similarly, Davies, "Social World," 256–57.

3. See Nickelsburg, "Social Aspects," 642–43; cf. Davies, "Social World," 258–60.

intellectual fad of constructing social-scientific "models," which tend to obscure rather than illuminate particular social relations and dynamics, Nickelsburg insisted that inquiry not only begin with but proceed by focusing on particular Judean apocalyptic writings.[4] In pursuing the kind of agenda Nickelsburg outlined, this brief study will focus on the same text he used as a "case study," the Epistle of Enoch (*1 Enoch* 92–105).[5]

In the Epistle of Enoch appears "a bitter conflict between two groups generally called 'the righteous' and 'the sinners.'" Despite other vague designations (*eusebeis* vs. *adikoi*), Nickelsburg finds "evildoing" of two kinds in the descriptions of the sinners' behavior.

> First, the sinners are the rich and powerful, who persecute and oppress the righteous and lowly. They hoard wealth which they have obtained unrighteously, they banquet sumptuously . . . (96:5–6; 97:8—98:2). They impress others into their service to construct their lavish houses (99:13; cf. 94:6–7). They are accused of robbing, torturing, and "devouring" the righteous, or treating them like beasts of burden, and of murdering them. They connive with the rulers, who support their oppressive deeds (103:9–15).[6]

Second, in a set of "religious charges" the sinners are described "as pagans or apostates [who] practice idolatry (99:7), consume blood (98:11), and blaspheme (94:9; 96:7)." Other sinners are blamed for disregarding and perverting Torah (99:2, 14). They do not listen to the wise (98:9); they write tying and deceitful words (98:15).

> Built into these latter passages is a sharp dichotomy between the members of the author's group, who are the protagonists of wisdom, and their opponents, who are false teachers and who can violate Torah while claiming that they are innocent Although the Epistle discloses nothing about the structure or organization of the author's group or community, evidence in the *Apocalypse of Weeks* (93:9–10 + 91:11–13) indicates that they understand themselves as the recipient of the revealed, eschatological gift of

---

4. Nickelsburg, "Social Aspects," 643–45; similarly, Davies, "Social World," 264. Grabbe, "Social Setting," reverts to the wide-ranging discussions of the 1960s and 1970s, borrowing from earlier social science and discussing a wide variety of materials, from medieval Europe to modern California, under the broad and vague concepts of "apocalypticism" and "millennialism."

5. In addition to his "Social Aspects," Nickelsburg provides close analysis of the *Epistle of Enoch* in "The Epistle of Enoch and the Qumran Literature"; and "Riches, The Rich, and God's Judgment in *1 Enoch* 92–105."

6. Nickelsburg, "Social Aspects," 651.

full wisdom and knowledge ... who will function as God's agents in the coming judgment.[7]

It remained unclear thirty years ago just how to understand the *Epistle*'s rhetoric, such "loaded legal categories as 'robbery, injustice, and murder.'"[8] Hesitating to press for further precision in their analysis of the historical situation underlying such rhetoric, biblical scholars found some satisfaction in categories borrowed from social science of the 1950s (which they had discovered in the 1970s). In language scarcely less vague than "the sinners" or "the righteous," those involved in ancient Palestinian Jewish apocalypticism, like those caught up in millenarianism, were seen to have acquired a "sense of alienation" during "times of social upheaval and turmoil." What mattered was their own sense of *relative deprivation*.[9] This social-psychological explanation was sufficiently satisfying to interpreters that it seemed unimportant to determine more precisely the social location of literature such as the Epistle of Enoch in historical political-economic structures and power relations. Cross-cultural studies of "millenarianism," however, are so broadly conceived and couched in such vague terms that they may obscure rather than illuminate the historical, political, economic, and religious dynamics from which Judean apocalyptic literature emerged. Indeed, insofar as much of the cross-cultural material comes from societies without sharp class divisions that are undergoing the initial impact of Western colonization, studies of millenarianism maybe misleading with regard to ancient Judean society. In contrast with the former, the latter was sharply divided between rulers and ruled and had for centuries been subject to imperial domination.

THE SOCIAL LOCATION AND ROLE OF THE SCRIBES: THE EVIDENCE FROM BEN SIRA

What study of ancient Judean apocalyptic texts has not yet done, therefore, is to consider more precisely their social location in the broader

---

7. Ibid., 652.
8. Ibid., 651.
9. Isenberg, "Millenarianism in Greco-Roman Palestine," 35; Grabbe, "Social Setting," 30–31, is still convinced, despite the broad generalizations involved, that "millenarianism" provides an "important resource for building models to help with the social setting of Jewish apocalypticism."

political-economic-religious structure of Judea in the context of the Ptolemaic and Seleucid (and later, the Roman) Empires.[10] The dominant conceptual apparatus of biblical studies has tended to block such questions. Insofar as we think of such literature as expressions of "Judaism" then the context is conceived of as an undifferentiated "-ism" without social structure and social dynamics. Strictly speaking, however, what scholars think of as "Judaism" did not yet exist in the second-temple period. Rather, under the sponsorship of the Persian and then the Ptolemaic and Seleucid imperial regimes, the temple-state in Jerusalem dominated a number of village communities in a somewhat limited surrounding area. As historians, we are dealing not with a religion separable from other dimensions of life, but with a society in which the religious dimension was inseparable from political-economic relations. The Temple stood at the center of a temple-state and its political economy, in which tithes and offerings were religiously motivated and legitimated taxes that supported the governing temple apparatus as well as the priesthood. Under the influence of Protestant scholarship based in modern European religious and political history, biblical scholars and Jewish historians have projected the concept of "sect" onto vaguely defined movements or groups, such as the "Pharisees" and "Essenes." It is often assumed that some "group" or "community" constituted the source and/or addressees of each extant piece of literature, an assumption reinforced by the linking of the Dead Sea Scrolls with the "community" at Qumran.[11] Such an assumption is utterly unwarranted, however, as a consideration of the extremely low rate of literacy in ancient society should indicate. Virtually the only people who could read and write—and therefore produce and leave texts—were the scribes, who were usually

---

10. Davies, "Social World," 269, makes some suggestive passing observations that move in the direction of the needed social-structural analysis but prescinds from pursuing it, apparently out of his concern to "rescue" the term "apocalyptic" from "amateur sociology" as well as from theological dogmatics. M. E. Stone, "Ideal Figures and Social Context," mentions the concept of "social role," but offers no more precise delineation of the "particular context" of Ben Sira or of the "group or tendency within Judaism" from which Aramaic Levi stems. J. Collins, "Genre, Ideology, and Social Movements," discusses mainly ideology and genre.

11. While objecting to the scholarly habit of assigning apocalypses and apocalypticism to "conventicles" or "small groups," Davies ("Social World," 257, 262, 267) still speaks in terms of undefined "social groups" and "sectarianism." Nickelsburg ("*Epistle of Enoch* and the Qumran Literature," 346) finds that there is little basis in the *Epistle* itself for concluding that the author represents a specific group or community or conventicle.

dependent economically on the rulers (whether directly or indirectly). Thus very few movements among the ordinary people would have left literary remains (the movements focused on Jesus of Nazareth were significant exceptions!). And scribes who produced literary remains would not necessarily have been participants in some identifiable community or socially defined group.[12] We should proceed rather in terms of the concrete historical political-economic-religious structures and dynamics identifiable in our sources.

Once we recognize that the rate of literacy was extremely limited, then it is possible to recognize also that, by definition, literature such as the Epistle of Enoch was produced by someone or some circle (as opposed to an identifiable "community" or "sect" on the model of Qumran) among the tiny educated elite that were literate. Indeed, evidence internal to the literature now combined into the collection called *1 Enoch* confirms that it was produced by "scribes" (*1 Enoch* 12:3-4; 15:1; 92:1)—to which "Daniel" the scribal sage is comparable, given his education in letters and his writing and reading activity (Dan 1:3-7). Thus, whatever differences they may display, both "apocalyptic" literature such as that collected in *1 Enoch* and "wisdom" literature such as the Book of Sirach were produced by scribes or scribal circles. The first step toward defining more precisely where such texts and their concerns fit in the wider society would appear to be to probe more carefully for information precisely in such texts. The written sources are few. And in the case of apocalyptic literature, it has been difficult to identify clear indicators of the authors' social location and particularly the power relations in which they were involved, including social conflicts. In the case of wisdom literature, however, the indications are abundant indeed, if we have eyes to see and ears to hear.[13]

Because they usually read Sirach without a sense of the particular social structure it presupposes, scholars have a rather vague impression of Ben Sira's audience, usually as "the broad sections of the population, sometimes . . . the wealthy."[14] The book contains so many comments critical of the wealthy and powerful, however, that they or their children

---

12. See now Horsley, *Scribes, Visionaries*, chaps 4 and 5.

13. The following sketch of social relations in Judea evident in Sirach draws on Horsley and Tiller, "Ben Sira and the Sociology of the Second Temple," reprinted as chapter 1 above.

14. Tcherikover, *Hellenistic Civilization and the Jews*, 149.

were almost certainly not the intended audience. Its focused reflection on the functions of the sage/scribe in relation to those in other positions in the social structure, particularly the long section in Sir 38:24—39:11, indicates that the speaker's position is somewhere above the plowmen and artisans on whose labor a city depends but below and in service to those who rule. Ben Sira gives other indications that the addressees, like himself, stand beneath and somewhat vulnerable to the wealthy and powerful (8:1–2) and are learning "to serve princes" ("to stand in the presence of chiefs," 8:8).

Ben Sira refers to the rulers of the Jerusalem temple-state in what appear to be two (juxtaposed) sets of terms. He apparently uses several traditional Hebrew terms—especially שר, מושל, and שופט—for rulers or officers of state almost interchangeably and synonymously. Of these only the last is translated consistently in the Greek as κριτής. Other positions are rendered with a variety of overlapping Greek terms, שר with μεγιστάν, δυνάστης, and ἡγούμενος; and מושל with ἡγούμενος, δυνάστης, κριτής, and κύριος. In the following discussion, I will attempt to use the terms "chief," "ruler," and "judge," respectively, for שר, שמול, and שופט. Most of these terms are used in construct (or other indications of relationship) with words such as "city," "people," and "assembly." In both Sir 30:27 (33:19) and 39:4, "chiefs of the people" is paralleled by "rulers of the assembly." One also has the sense that there is some overlap or relationship between the "chiefs" and "rulers" among whom the scribes/sages serve in 39:4 and the πλῆθος πρεσβυτέρων among whom the wise stand and speak in 6:34 and 7:14. In 10:1–2 the "judge" of a people or city is parallel to the sagacious one who possesses "authority" and to "he who rules a city," and in 10:3 "king" is parallel to "chiefs." These interchangeable words thus appear not to be technical terms for specific offices of state. They are rather parallel, overlapping, almost synonymous terms for the ruling aristocracy, some but not all of whom may have had particular responsibilities and many of whom probably had similar or overlapping functions. Since Judean society was apparently headed by a temple-state, these terms all seem to have referred to members of the priestly aristocracy, as confirmed by Ben Sira's second set of terms.

Ben Sira's references to the high priest and his "brothers" indicate clearly that they were the rulers of the temple-state based in Jerusalem. Just as the high priest at the Temple altar had "a garland of brothers around him . . . the sons of Aaron in their splendor holding out the

Lord's offerings" (50:5–13), so the high priest as head of state stood in the midst of a priestly aristocracy both in governing the people and in receiving their economic support. The Judean people are to serve "the Most High," who is understood as "the king of all." Since the (high) priests are the people's representatives to God, the latter bring their offerings to the priests. Since the (high) priests are God's representative to the people, established by everlasting covenant and given "authority and statutes and judgments" over the people, the people are to "honor the priest" with their tithes and offerings as the way of "fearing the Lord" (see esp. Sir 7:29–31; 35:1–12; 45:20–22; and chap. 50). In this second set of terms referring to the rulers of the temple-state, it is clear that economics as well as politics is inseparable from and closely articulated with religion. The first fruits, guilt offerings, choice shoulder cuts from animal sacrifices, and so on were also tax revenues to "honor the priest," because in the eternal covenant bestowed on Aaron, these had been allotted to Aaron and his descendants as their "heritage" (see esp. 7:29–31; 45:20–21).

What then is the relationship between the people referred to by these two sets of terms? The "chiefs" and "rulers" and "judges" were apparently the ruling aristocracy among "the sons of Aaron." Not all priests, not even all of the Aaronides, would have belonged to the ruling aristocracy. Some individual high priests may have held a particular office (similar, e.g., to the "temple captain" in the first century CE). But we should not presume that all members of the dominant aristocracy held a particular "minister's portfolio," as in the cabinets of modern parliamentary governments. Although Ben Sira never explicitly mentions a *gerousia*, often presumed to have been the governing aristocracy in the temple-state, his "chiefs," "rulers," and "judges," would appear to match the gerousia mentioned in both Antiochus III's proclamation of restoration of the temple government in Jerusalem (Josephus, *Ant.* 12.142) and in the letter of the Hasmonean high priest Jonathan to Sparta a half-century later (1 Macc 12:6).

A (the?) principal role of the scribes and sages such as himself, according to Ben Sira, was to serve the "chiefs" (8:8). In the sustained discussion of the scribes' position and activities in 38:24—39:11, he portrays the scribes as advisers of the ruling councils, as members or advisers of courts who understood decisions and could expound judgments, and as members of embassies to foreign lands (cf. 4:9; 6:34; 7:14; 11:7–9; 15:5;

21:17; 34:12; 42:2). Their devotion to the study of covenantal law and to the wisdom of the ancients was precisely for the purpose of their service to the ruling aristocracy. The teaching of the law, which had originated with Moses and been vested in the Aaronide priesthood (45:5, 17), had been delegated (perhaps gradually, over a period of generations) to the sages, both with regard to the people (37:23) and with regard to the aristocracy's exercise of its own governing authority (8:8; 9:17—10:5; 38:32-33; 38:34—39:4). The scribe stands behind "the wise judge" and "the government of the intelligent one" (9:17—10:5).

Insofar as they served the ruling aristocracy, scribes/sages must have been economically as well as politically dependent on patrons among the ruling families. Not surprisingly, Ben Sira advises aspiring sages to defer and to bow low to the ruler (4:7). He also offers extensive advice on the proper deferential behavior for the scribes when invited to dine with their patrons (13:9-11; 31:12-24). He also warns about the potential dangers involved in dealing with the powerful (13:9). Particularly dangerous, of course, would be "contending with the powerful" or "quarreling with the rich," lest the scribe "fall into their hands" (8:1-2, 14).

Yet the scribes/sages have a clear sense of their own authority independent of their dependence on the aristocracy. Their authority, at least in their own mind, came from their knowledge of wisdom and their faithful adherence to and teaching of the law of the Most High (which are the same thing for Ben Sira). Ben Sira refers repeatedly to the scribes' dedication to the covenantal laws and to divinely bestowed wisdom, from which they claim their own authority directly from God, independent of the high priesthood. Moreover, they also understood themselves as the successors of the prophets as well as their interpreters, speaking by divine inspiration (39:1-3, 6). They had their own sense of how the temple-state should operate—according to the law, the sacred traditions of the people, of which they themselves were the proper interpreters.

SCRIBES IN THE MIDDLE OF POLITICAL-ECONOMIC CONFLICT

Thus, despite their dependence on and vulnerability to their patrons among the aristocracy, scribes such as Ben Sira speak both of criticizing the aristocracy and of attempting to mitigate oppression of the poor by the powerful. This is worth exploring in itself but also because it may shed some light on woes against the rich sinners in the Epistle of Enoch.

The scribes/sages understood themselves as a cut above the peasant farmers and urban artisans politically and culturally. Such ordinary folk did not enjoy the leisure necessary to acquire and practice wisdom (38:24–34). Yet Ben Sira articulates an unmistakable sympathy and concern for the plight of the poor and urges his scribal protégés to assume responsibility to mitigate their exploitation by the wealthy and powerful. He explicitly mentions the "plowman" or other synonyms for the peasantry, which formed the economic base of any traditional agrarian society such as the ancient Judean temple community, more than he does artisans or household slaves. A survey of Ben Sira's use of terms often translated with "poor," however, suggests that they usually refer to a wide range of people. "Poor," "hungry," "needy," "desperate," and other synonymous terms refer apparently to a large proportion of the peasant producers. Like peasants in most agrarian societies, the Judean producers would have been economically marginal. They would therefore have been chronically in need of loans and even alms. They were thus vulnerable to the predatory practices of the wealthy and powerful.

Ben Sira articulates his concern for the poor in three ways. First, he urges his scribal proteges, in their own personal ethical behavior, to respond mercifully. "Stretch out your hand to the poor" with almsgiving, and do not "cheat the poor" or "reject the supplicant" (29:1–20, esp. vv. 1–2, 8–12, 14–15).

Second, Ben Sira offers some strikingly sharp criticism of those who take advantage of the desperate situation of the poor to enhance their own wealth,

> A rich person does wrong, and even adds insults;
> a poor person suffers wrong, and must add apologies.
> A rich person will exploit you if you can be of use to him,
> but if you are in need he will abandon you . . .
> What peace is there between a hyena and a dog?
> And what peace between the rich and the poor?
> Wild asses in the wilderness are the prey of lions;
> likewise the poor are feeding grounds for the rich.
> (13:3–4, 18–19)

Such sayings may sound like matter-of-fact observations about the "natural" state of affairs, what life is like. Yet if heard from Ben Sira's own viewpoint, rooted in Mosaic covenantal concern for the Israelite people's continuing economic viability, such sayings have an edge. Although couched in traditional form and style of sapiential observations about life, they are in effect an indictment of the perpetual economic exploitation inherent in a political-economic-religious system in which the peasants are vulnerable to the power holders.

It goes almost without saying that the wealthy and powerful criticized in these passages were members of the priestly aristocracy. As in other pre-industrial agrarian societies, the productive forces in second-temple Judea would not have been sufficiently developed to support a lay as well as a priestly aristocracy. The rise of the Tobiads to prominence in Jerusalem was based on their own economic base across the Jordan and on their maneuvering for position in the imperial mechanism of tribute collection from Palestine. To the extent that they exploited their wealth for further economic advantage within the Judean temple community, they may well have contributed to the crisis that emerged in the first quarter of the second century. Over against Tcherikover's and Hengel's influential earlier projections onto Hellenistic Judea as suddenly abuzz with commercial activity, it is simply not true that "Ben Sira frequently mentions merchants... and that these passages reflect...the money economy, the opportunity to invest one's means in profitable enterprises, and lively commercial traffic . . ."[15] Ben Sira mentions traders only at three points (26:29—27:2; 37:11; 42:5), where he articulates the negative view of merchants typical of traditional agrarian aristocratic societies. Otherwise Tcherikover and Hengel are projecting nascent capitalist mercantile relations onto Ben Sira's references to the acquisition/stockpiling/possession of "goods" (χρήματα), wealth, and "gold" and to the use of other people's goods (Hengel focuses on 11:10–19; 13:24–25; 21:8; and 31:3–8). One of those passages ("Whoever builds his house with other people's goods . . . ," 21:8), in fact, indicates precisely the way that the wealthy and/or powerful exploited the poor in an agrarian society: by taking as tribute/tax/tithes what the peasant considered wrongfully taken or by charging interest on loans (which was prohibited in Israelite covenantal law; e.g., Exod 22:25).

Ben Sira even gives some indications that it was the priestly aristocracy that was exploiting the peasants, even though he does not explicitly identify the high priests, the wealthy, and the chiefs, rulers, and judges,

15. Ibid.

as mentioned above. In an unusually long discourse for Ben Sira (35:1–26), his discussion of sacrifices and offerings suddenly turns instead to a sustained declaration that the Most High will heed the supplication and appeal of the oppressed and do justice for the righteous, "breaking the scepters of the unrighteous." We notice also that several couplets at the opening of the passage relativize temple offerings by declaring that commandment-keeping and almsgiving are their equivalent. It seems that Ben Sira almost overshadows his exhortation to make sacrifices and offerings in the Temple with an ominous warning to the "rulers" about exploiting the poor and humble. A shorter section (34:21–27) seems to be directed pointedly at the ruling priesthood.

> If one sacrifices ill-gotten goods, the offering is blemished . . .
> Like one who kills a son before his father's eyes
> is the person who offers a sacrifice from the property of the poor
> . . .
> To take away a neighbor's living is to commit murder;
> to deprive an employee of wages is to shed blood.

These are serious charges. The imagery used in this blunt warning is reminiscent of prophetic indictments in Amos. This passage approaches the severity of Amos 4:4–5 and 5:21–24, where God rejects sacrifices outright as sin, demanding justice instead. Even more important, this passage is reminiscent of Amos 2:6–8 in its suggestion that the wealthy and powerful, as creditors, were taking advantage of the peasants who had fallen heavily into debt and were "foreclosing" on their goods.

Third, however, and even more striking than Ben Sira's criticism of the wealthy and powerful priestly aristocracy, because of the potential "conflict of interest" involved, are some of Ben Sira's other exhortations to his scribal proteges/listeners. He urges them not simply to give alms and otherwise to attend to the needs of the poor themselves (4:1–4; cf. 29:8–9), but even to "rescue" the oppressed from the oppressor, and not to hesitate in giving a "verdict," presumably in their professional (or official) capacities (4:9). That would likely have entailed some form of opposition to the behavior of the ruling families on whom they themselves were politically and economically dependent. Yet he insists that his scribal listeners not "show partiality to a ruler" (4:17). Indeed, they should not aspire to a high office such as that of judge, or they would "be unable to root out injustice" and would be in situations where they would "be partial to the powerful, and so mar [their] integrity" (7:4–7).

What Ben Sira and his scribal colleagues were apparently facing was a recurrent problem in the history of Israel and Judah, as in other agrarian societies in which a small coterie of rulers held political or political-religious power over the peasant producers. They would have known such famous conflicts as Jeremiah's indictment of King Jehoiakim for rebuilding his royal palace with forced labor at a time of acute crisis for Judah (Jer 22:13–19). Closer in time and in pattern to the exploitation Ben Sira complains about was the crisis Nehemiah had dealt with, when the rulers of the temple-state had taken advantage of the desperate economic plight of the Judean peasants in the mid-fifth century to get them into debt and to seize their lands:

> Now there was a great outcry of the people and of their wives against their Judean kin . . . "We are having to pledge our fields, our vineyards, and our houses in order to get grain during the famine . . . We are having to borrow money on our fields and vineyards to pay the king's tax. [They] are forcing our sons and daughters to be slaves, and some of our daughters have been ravished; we are powerless and our fields and vineyards now belong to others." (Neh 5:1–5)

The ensuing account of Nehemiah's response also indicates precisely how the wealthy and powerful ruling aristocracy of the temple-state had been manipulating the desperate peasantry to aggrandize their own hold over the peasants' land and labor.

> I brought charges against the nobles and the officials; I said to them, "You are all taking interest from your own people—Let us stop this taking of interest. Restore to them, this very day, their fields, their vineyards, their olive orchards, and their houses, and the interest on money, grain, wine, and oil that you have been exacting from them." (Neh 5:7–11)

This illustration from the mission of Nehemiah, the Persian governor for Judea, about how the ruling elite of the temple-state exploited their subjects, moreover, points to a determining aspect of the political-economic-religious structure of second-temple Judea that is often ignored in treatments of Judean apocalyptic and wisdom literature. Contrary to the appearance from Ben Sira's ideology of Aaronide/Oniad rule grounded in the glorious Israelite tradition of officeholders, from Moses to Simon (chaps. 44–50), the Judean temple-state was not autonomous, not sovereign over its own affairs. From the outset the temple-state had been the creature of empire. Just prior to the time of Ben Sira, the high priestly regime in Jerusalem was dependent on its approval by the Ptolemies, and after about 200 BCE was subject to the Seleucids.

This potentially determinative subjection of the temple-state to and dependence on imperial rule set up two interrelated structural conflicts that had a profound effect on events in second-temple Judean history. First, it set up almost certain situations of conflict between the rulers of the temple-state and their scribal clients. The Judean priestly rulers depended on their imperial sponsors and were vulnerable to whatever influence and pressures they might receive in that connection. The scribes/sages such as Ben Sira, however, who functioned as the guardians and interpreters of sacred Israelite traditions, including Mosaic covenant principles, believed that the temple-state as well as Judean society should operate according to these sacred traditions. As can be seen in his paean of praise that climaxes in the exordium to the high priest Simon, Ben Sira had constructed a grand ideology of high priestly rule out of Israelite tradition.

Second, subjection of the temple-state set up potential conflict between rival cliques within the ruling aristocracy. Already under the Davidic monarchy, different factions within the royal family and their protégés competed for power. It is evident from the Books of Ezra and Nehemiah and other sources that priestly and other factions had been competing in early second-temple times. The struggle between the Ptolemies and Seleucids for control of Palestine set up a situation in which rival factions in Jerusalem would make alliances with the opposing imperial regimes. The rise of the Tobiad family across the Jordan River, its intermarriage with the high priestly family, and its intrigue with the Ptolemaic regime further complicated the struggle for power in Jerusalem. Insofar as scribes and sages had no independent economic base, they would have associated with one of the rival factions among the ruling aristocracy. And insofar as scribes had varying ideas about policy and practice in the temple-state, they formed rival scribal circles, and their pursuit of their own political-religious agenda further complicated the struggle among rival factions among the aristocracy. Thus, although the structure of the temple-state under imperial rule was fairly simple, once the imperial situation and the cultural factor of the scribal commitment to indigenous Judean tradition are taken into account, this set up potential conflict between scribes and rulers, between rival ruling factions, and even between rival groups of scribes.

"ENOCH'S" WOES AGAINST THE WEALTHY RULERS FOR OPPRESSING THE POOR

Read in this context, deduced largely from the near-contemporary wisdom of Jesus ben Sira, the intense sets of woes pronounced against the rich sinners in the Epistle of Enoch appear to emerge from just such a conflict, between the rulers in Jerusalem and the scribal circle that produced the Enoch literature. Judging from other sections of the composite book of *1 Enoch*, the scribal circle from which the texts emerged viewed the Second Temple generally as illegitimate. In the Animal Vision, the rebuilt "tower" (temple) has polluted bread on its table and the shepherds (rulers) of the sheep are blind (*1 Enoch* 89:72–80). In the Ten-Week Vision, a "perverse generation" whose deeds are all "perverse" arises in the seventh week (*1 Enoch* 93:9).

The simple fact that the Epistle of Enoch is literature means that it was produced by scribes. Despite the lack of obvious indications in the text, the composer(s) left a few tracks here and there by which we can identify both composer(s) and addressees as scribes/sages. In a description of judgment, the Most High is expected to "set a guard of holy angels over all the righteous and holy" so that "the pious will sleep a sweet sleep" (100:5). "The wise among men" who "will see the truth" in the next verse appear to be more precisely the wise among the righteous and holy and pious. That is, the latter are a larger group among whom "the wise" have special knowledge and a special role. What Nickelsburg's translation labels as "An Oath to the Wise" (98:1–3) appears to be an aside addressed directly to "the wise," who receive special knowledge. Further, the rich sinners are addressed as "fools" precisely because they "do not listen to the wise," that is, their scribal opponents (98:9), whereas "all who listen to the words of the wise" are blessed (99:10). Apparently, the wise enjoyed the special role vis-a-vis the larger circles of the righteous. The Epistle of Enoch thus appears to be a scribe/sage addressing a circle of other scribes/sages, pronouncing woes of destruction in the divine judgment against the "rich/sinners" for oppressing the righteous/pious, who will be vindicated and rewarded in the divine judgment.

When we then examine the pronounced woes and blessings for a more precise determination of the relationship between the sinners and righteous, between the rich and those they oppress, there is no separation between what modern Westerners distinguish as "religious" and "political-economic" matters. As suggested by the above analysis of Ben

Sira's speeches about social relations and roles in ancient Judean society, the wealthy were those who held political or political-religious power. The rulers used their positions to increase their wealth and thus to consolidate their power further. This is precisely what is found in the woes of the Epistle of Enoch, It is the "mighty" or powerful who gain great riches and an easy and luxurious lifestyle by their oppression and destruction of the righteous (96:8; 97:2). The political-economic-religious structure is similar to that evident in Amos 6:4–6, whose mockery of the idle rich "drinking wine from the krater/bowl" may be alluded to in *1 Enoch* 96:5–6. That is, those who are indulging themselves in a luxurious lifestyle at the expense of the poor are the ruling families in Zion and Samaria (Amos 6:1).

In what ways have they oppressed the lowly righteous? Many of the indictments of the rich sinners are allusive and still vague. The hypothetical lament of the lowly over what has been done to them in 103:9–15, however, contains clearer indications of the oppressive relationship into which they were maneuvered.

> In the days of our tribulation, we toiled laboriously;
> We toiled and labored and were not masters of our labor;
> we became the food of the sinners.
> And the lawless weighed down their yoke upon us;
> our enemies were our masters,
> and they goaded and penned us in,
> and to our enemies we bowed our necks,
> and they had no mercy on us. (103:9, 11–12)

Following the pattern of how the future reward for the righteous matches their suffering in the present, they are reassured that they will receive much good "in the place of [their] labors" (103:3). Closely related is the assertion that "it was not ordained [for man] to be a slave [or] for a woman to be a handmaid" (98:4). These passages suggest clearly that, against the norms of the society (the Mosaic law), the righteous had been subjected to some equivalent of forced labor, perhaps debt-slavery or other labor for the wealthy, who had gained the power to determine how their labor would be deployed. In this connection, the repeated charge that the wealthy sinners "build their houses with sin" and "build their houses not with their own labors, [but] make the whole house of the stones and bricks of sin" (94:6–7; 99:13) suddenly makes sense. The wealthy rulers were unlikely to have manipulated the scribes into the physical labor of building; but they could easily have deployed those who came under their power in the building of their own houses. That this was contrary to traditional norms and expectations can be discerned by analogy to Jeremiah's objections to the way Jehoiakim rebuilt his palace with forced labor (and the objections by the Israelites to Solomon's forced labor to build the original temple [1 Kings 12]).

If the command that the powerful wealthy had over the labor of the lowly was rooted in the peasants' indebtedness or even debt-slavery, as in the crisis recounted by Nehemiah (Neh 5:1–12), then some other accusations against the sinners also make sense. The rich sinners rejoice over the troubles of the righteous (98:13). They "lie awake to devise evil" (100:8). An indictment of the powerful wealthy of his time by the prophet Micah (2:1–2) may provide the key to these charges.

> Woe to those who devise wickedness and evil deeds upon their beds!
> When the morning dawns they perform it, because it is in their power.
> They covet fields, and seize them; houses, and take them away;
> they oppress the householder and house, people and their inheritance.

Peasants, who are always marginal economically—partly because of dues to the rulers in the form of taxes, tithes, and tribute—come easily into desperate circumstances, needing to borrow to feed their families (as in Neh 5:1–5). The rulers and their officers, who have access to stores of staple goods such as grain and oil, are only too ready to make loans—at high rates of interest. These rates were 25 percent and 100 percent on grain and oil, respectively, in one of the parables of Jesus (Luke 16:1–9), which matches figures from other traditional agrarian societies. Such exorbitant interest was contrary to the Mosaic covenantal tradition (Exod 22:25; Lev 25:36–38), but it was standard practice (again as in the account in Neh 5:1–12). Rulers could thus take advantage of "the troubles of the righteous" by maneuvering them into indebtedness, and then by "foreclosing" on their ancestral inheritance, that is, their fields and houses, or by forcing family members into debt-slavery, or by forcing whole families effectively into the position of sharecroppers on their own land. Perhaps the "lying awake to devise evil" was a standing image, rooted in prophetic tradition since Micah, for the way the powerful and wealthy would scheme against vulnerable peasant families, in violation of the covenantal principle against "coveting the neighbor's house." When the powerful took action, they then also violated the covenantal principle against "stealing," as in the charge against them that by maneuvering peasants into debt they "plunder and sin and steal and get wealth" (102:9).

Another apparently typical means by which the wealthy exploited their desperate debtors was by manipulating the weights used to measure the grain or oil that they were borrowing. This is what Amos castigates in the charge that "they sell the righteous for silver" (2:6). The complaint against the rich sinners that they "weigh out injustice" (*1 Enoch* 95:6) may well be an allusion to this fraudulent practice. In this same connection, it is tempting to take the charge that they also "write lying words and words of error" as deceitful dealings in debt or labor contracts that they forced upon the vulnerable peasants.

Another standard indictment that the classical prophets made against the rulers and their officers was that they manipulated the courts. One could take several lines in the Epistle of Enoch precisely as allusions to such (ab)use of the courts: they "acquire gold and silver in judgment/unjustly" (94:7; 97:8; 97:10). Closely related to the way in which the wealthy and powerful could use the courts to their advantage is the lament of the righteous that when they had complained "to the rulers," to the high priest himself, or to the highest officers of the high priesthood (presumably the only court of appeal), the latter sided with their wealthy oppressors—others who were in the closed circle of the powerful and wealthy elite (103:14–15). All of these oppressive practices, of course, were blatant violations of Mosaic covenantal principles, which is pointedly articulated at several points in this section of *1 Enoch* (e.g., 97:6; 98:4, 7–8, 12; 99:2).

The Epistle of Enoch may provide an important indication of the wider imperial dimension of the overall structure of political-economic-religious relations, depending on how the text of the key passage is reconstructed from the Ethiopia and Greek manuscripts. It has often been assumed that the wealthy sinners are accused of idolatry in 99:6–9. The Greek version (which Nickelsburg follows in his translation), however, apparently makes clearer than the Ethiopic version a distinction between "you sinners . . . who will be destroyed" in 99:6, 9, on the one hand, and "those who worship stones, and carve images of silver . . . and stone . . ." in 99:7, on the other. The latter are clearly the idolaters. Confirming the distinction, the sinners are warned at the end of 99:7: "No help will you find from them," that is, the foreign idolaters. "Those who worship stones and demons" were presumably foreigners, and the warning that the sinners would receive "no help" from them suggests that they were the imperial patrons of the powerful and wealthy sinners. It is perhaps impossible to project just what the original (Aramaic) text had in mind, but the Greek translator presents a subtle ironic play on words, comparing the sinners' exploitation of their people by building houses of stone and by gaining gold and silver (cf. 94:6–7; 97:8–9; 99:13) with their imperial patrons' idolatrous worship of images of stone, gold, and silver—false gods of power and wealth. If this reconstruction of the text and its meaning is reasonable, then it provides a window onto the determining imperial dimension of the overall structure of political-economic-religious power relations.

The social relations evident in the Epistle of Enoch thus appear parallel to those articulated by Ben Sira.[16] A scribal author (Ben Sira) addresses other scribes/sages and focuses, in part, on the relations between the powerful and wealthy (rulers) and the peasants that they rule, from whom they receive dues, and whom they oppress in various ways. The "speakers" and their addressees see themselves as socially and/or culturally superior to the poor peasants. Nevertheless they are concerned about the ways in which the poor are abused by the powerful and wealthy, assuming that it is part of their responsibility to address or even to do something about such oppression. In both cases, this sense of responsibility is rooted in their personal commitment to the Mosaic covenantal tradition, the principles of which supposedly protected the rights of ordinary Israelites/Judeans. Particularly striking is how Ben Sira and the woes of "Enoch" share the same rhetoric in charging the elite with "murder," with so oppressing the people that they are taking away the very life of their neighbors, in effect violating the covenantal commandment "you shall not kill" (99:15; 103:13; Sir 34:25–27).

The differences between this "Enoch" text and Ben Sira's book are also considerable. Ben Sira occasionally criticizes the wealthy and (potentially) oppressive rulers, whereas the Epistle of Enoch is completely devoted to a condemnation of them. While Ben Sira discusses the issues in a more detached and reflective manner, the Epistle of Enoch calls down divine judgment on the sinners in several series of prophetic woes. And while Ben Sira delivers his reflections and admonitions with-

---

16. For more general comparison of *1 Enoch* and Sirach on key themes, see Argall, *1 Enoch and Sirach*.

out much of a wider framing, the Epistle of Enoch finds considerable satisfaction in anticipating the future divine judgment in which the oppressive sinners will be destroyed and the righteous rewarded with what the sinners deprived them of. The wise themselves, moreover, will be vindicated in their knowledge and commitment to the law.

We should not think that *1 Enoch* 91–104 is the product of a movement or group any more than we would understand the text of Sirach as evidence of Ben Sira heading a social movement. In both cases they see themselves as having a role integral to the operation of the whole society. In both cases that role is situated between the rulers and the peasantry. Whereas Ben Sira is on such good terms with the incumbent high priest and his "brothers" that he proclaimed the glories of the high priesthood and the incumbent high priest (Sirach 44–50), the producers and audience of the Epistle of Enoch were sharply opposed to the incumbent rulers (and any other wealthy). They declared God's punitive judgment against the wealthy and powerful (94–104) and appear to have rejected the legitimacy of the temple-state itself (93:9). But in this section of *1 Enoch* we find indications neither of a separate community nor of alternative incumbents for the temple-state, as in some of the Dead Sea Scrolls; nor do we find evidence of a resistance movement, in contrast with Daniel 10–12 and the "Animal Vision" (*1 Enoch* 85–90). At most, it would seem, we can imagine a relatively small circle or clique, a circle of extremely dissident scribes. "The chosen ones . . . to whom will be given sevenfold wisdom and knowledge" and who "will uproot the foundations of violence" in the seventh week of the "Ten-Week Vision" (93:10 + 91:11) would appear to be self-references to this circle of scribes/sages. Also judging from the "Ten-Week Vision" (91:11–17), the scribes responsible for this text envisaged—after the eighth week, in which the righteous would "execute righteous judgment on all the wicked (presumably on the perverse, violent, and deceitful generation of the second-temple period)—a future age of righteousness under a "new heaven" in which "all humankind will look to the path of eternal righteousness." That is, they imagined, somewhat vaguely, a future societal life without sin, without oppression by the wealthy and powerful.

6

4 Ezra: Anti-Apocalyptic Apocalypse

INTRODUCTION

IN THIS ESSAY I investigate *4 Ezra*'s use of apocalypse, a use reminiscent both of earlier apocalypses and earlier wisdom traditions.[1] The text of *4 Ezra*, or *2 Esdras*, is Ezra's account of seven visions. In these visions Ezra either raises problems relating to theodicy and receives various answers or receives allegorical visions about the end of time. In each case the problem is closely related to the Roman's recent and heart-breaking conquest and destruction of Judea. Most of the answers have to do with the judgment, the coming of the Messiah, and the nearness of the end of the age. Notable among the visions are the vision of a woman in mourning for her only son and her transformation into the glorious city of Zion (9:26—10:59), and the historical vision of an eagle rising from the sea which represents the Roman Empire (11:1—12:39).

The original Judean apocalypse (chapters 3–14) is usually supposed to have been composed around 100 CE.[2] This is based partly on the first verse of the text which states, "In the thirtieth year after the destruction of our city [. . .]" Although the city spoken of in the text is Babylon, the text is probably a cryptic reference to the destruction of Jerusalem in 70 CE. The original number "thirtieth", however, could have been used in imitation of Ezek 1:1, "In the thirtieth year, in the fourth month on the

---

1. For a convenient introduction to *4 Ezra*, see Metzger, "Fourth Book of Ezra," 516–59; or Nickelsburg, *Jewish Literature*, 287–94. All quotations from *4 Ezra* are taken from the NRSV. Quotations from *2 Baruch* are taken from Klijin, "2 Baruch," 621–52.

2. Stone, *Fourth Ezra*, 9–10.

fifth day, while I was among the exiles by the Kebar River, the heavens were opened and I saw visions of God." Since *4 Ezra* seems clearly to refer to the destruction of the Temple and since it is clearly quoted in Clement of Alexandria, *Stromata* 3:16 (quoting 4 Ezra 5:35), it must have been written after 70 CE and before the end of the second century. If the common identification of the three heads of the eagle with Vespasian, Titus, and Domitian is accepted, the book must have been written during the reign of Domitian (81–96 CE). Finally, Michael Stone cites two Hebrews expressions (עולם and אחרון קץ), assumed to have been used in ways which seem to fall midway between the usage of the Dead Sea Scrolls and that of Mishnaic Hebrew.[3]

Translation errors and the existence of Greek quotations of the text point to Greek as the language of the common *Vorlage* of the extant versions (Latin, Syriac, Ethiopic, Arabic, Georgian, and Armenian).[4] Most scholars, however, suppose that the original language was either Hebrew, or, less likely, Aramaic on account of semiticisms.[5] The book was later expanded through the addition of a Christian framework consisting of chapters 1–2 (the call of Ezra and his vision of a multitude of Gentiles on Mount Zion, receiving a crown from the "Son of God") and chapters 15–16 (woes against the nations and warnings of impending tribulation; preserved only in Latin).

LITERARY GENRE

The genre of the work is clearly that of apocalypse.[6] It is a narrative about visionary revelations of future and heavenly realities delivered or interpreted in part by the angel Uriel[7] (although Uriel is not, strictly speaking, an *angelus interpres*).[8] It includes a symbolic, visionary review

---

3. Stone, *Features*, 10–11, 179–80.
4. Ibid., 1–2.
5. Ibid., 10–11.
6. Various source theories have been proposed, but none are generally accepted. The main evidence is the sudden appearance in 4:1 of "the angel that had been sent to me, whose name was Uriel" and of the lack of preparation for the first vision. Possibly some material has been lost from the end of chapter 3. There is also an unexplained reference to Ezra's being "taken up" in 8:19. Other anomalies could also be noted.
7. See the widely accepted definition of apocalypse in Collins, "Morphology," 9.
8. According to Brandenburger, *Die Verborgenheit Gottes*, "Er trägt vielmehr in vielem die Züge einer himmlischen Offenbarerfigur, die den Offenbarungsempfänger im Gesamtgeschehen begleitet und die Stationen des Weges bestimmt" (He bares rather

of history that begins in the past and extends into the future (11–12).⁹ Its function, like that of the first, fourth, and fifth books of *1 Enoch* is in part to provide answers to questions of evil and theodicy. As the works now collected in *1 Enoch* were driven by the desire to come to terms with the seemingly unnatural events that were happening in and around Jerusalem, so the writer of *4 Ezra* writes to respond to the destruction of the Jerusalem Temple by the Romans. He provides encouragement to remain faithful and hopeful and assurance that wisdom, understanding, and knowledge are still accessible (14:47).

Although *4 Ezra* is undoubtedly an apocalypse in form, its apocalyptic heart has been torn out. It is often said about apocalypses that they represent a pessimistic view. While that is true, it is equally true that in the "big picture" they are quite optimistic. The present world, with its cosmological, political, economic, social, religious order is condemned and doomed to final judgment. But this world is viewed from a transcendent perspective gained by heavenly visions and angelic guides. In *4 Ezra*, however, all optimism has faded; the work does not understand the present, aberrant, earthly realities from the perspective of heavenly realities. It is for *4 Ezra* impossible to understand heavenly realities, and indeed, Ezra makes little attempt to understand earthly realities. Instead assurance is given that things are the way they must be, that God loves his creation, that the end is near, and that the final judgment will bring life to those who have been faithful to God and God's law. The text of *4 Ezra* represents an apocalyptic concession to the failure of an apocalyptic worldview. This can be seen most clearly in its view of the limits of human understanding and in the subject matter of its speculative discussions. The concession is also apparent in the book's final narrative of the rewriting of the ninety-four books, and its symbolic treatment of history. Like Job, in the end Pseudo-Ezra can only affirm God's goodness and justice, but he cannot understand it; he leaves his readers unsatisfied.

---

in many respects the features of a heavenly revealer who accompanies the recipient of revelation throughout the whole event and determines the stops along the way). The distinction between an interpreting angel and a revealing angel is not significant for generic classification

9. The book also begins a review of history (3:4–27). But it is entirely historical and not revelatory.

THE LIMITS OF HUMAN UNDERSTANDING

One might expect to find some discussion of cosmology, astronomy, meteorology, ouranology, or angelology in an apocalyptic text. This is especially true of *4 Ezra* since the angelic interpreter is Uriel, who, according to the Astronomical Book of *1 Enoch*, revealed the astronomical secrets of the sun, moon, and stars to Enoch on his tours of the cosmos in chapters 17–36 of the Book of the Watchers. But *4 Ezra* has none of these elements. Stone has analyzed what he calls "lists of revealed things" that occur in apocalypses and in a different form in much of the wisdom literature.[10] Stone analyzes lists found in *2 Bar.* 59:5–11; *1 Enoch* 41:1–7; 60:11–22; 93:11–14; *2 Enoch* 23:1; 40:1–13; *4 Ezra* 14:5, 7; and Pseudo-Philo, *Liber Antiquitatem Biblicarum* 19:10; Job 28:25–27; 38; Sirach 43; and others. These lists occur in one of three forms: (1) a list of things revealed to the seer; (2) a list of divine secrets; and (3) a list of rhetorical questions designed to demonstrate the unbridgeable distance between divine and human understanding. Stone, following von Rad in part, traces the origin of these forms partly to earlier wisdom traditions.

Especially interesting for our purposes are the recurring questions about the measurements of fire, wind, rain, the abyss, paradise, and the future. In Ezra's first vision, after he complains about the "evil heart" inherited from Adam and the unfavorable treatment of Israel in comparison with Babylon, and after he asserts his ability "to comprehend the way of the Most High," he receives God's answer through Uriel.

> And he said to me, "Go, weigh for me the *weight of fire*, or measure for me a *measure of wind*, or call back for me the day that is past." I answered and said, "Who of those that have been born can do this, that you ask me concerning these things.?" And he said to me, "If I had asked you, 'How many dwellings are in the heart of the sea, or how many streams are at the source of the deep, or how many streams are above the firmament, or which are the *exits of Hades*, or which are the entrances of paradise?' perhaps you would have said to me, 'I never went down into the deep, nor as yet into hell, neither did I ever ascend into heaven.'" (*4 Ezra* 14:5–7)

Similarly, in the list of things revealed to Moses in *2 Bar.* 59:5–11, we have the following items:

---

10. Stone, *Lists*, 414–52.

> ... *the measures of fire,* the depths of the abyss, the *weight of the winds,* the number of the raindrops, ... the height of the air, the greatness of Paradise, the end of the periods, ...the worlds which have not yet come, the *mouth of hell,* ... the multitude of the angels which cannot be counted, the powers of the flame, the splendor of lightning, the voice of the thunders, the orders of the archangels, the treasuries of the light ...

The almost exact correspondence of the underlined phrases, their reoccurrence elsewhere, and the similarity of other phrases indicate that we are dealing with lists which are at least partly determined by their traditional usage. Pseudo-Ezra's use of this list, however, is not only an innocuous adaptation of older wisdom lists, but also a self-conscious rejection of the typical apocalyptic use. Pseudo-Baruch, on the other hand, embraces the older apocalyptic view. In 48:3–4, along with the admission that "you do not reveal your secrets to many," he prays, "You make known the multitude of the fire, and you weigh the lightness of the wind." The striking difference between the views expressed in *4 Ezra* and *2 Baruch* seems significant.

Stone suggests two possibilities for understanding the significance of these lists in apocalyptic literature. They may be merely "formulaic, traditional lists" that had only partial overlap "with the actual concerns of the apocalyptic authors."[11] But Stone prefers an alternate explanation of their "common function." "They all occur at the high point of a revelation, where a brief statement of its contents is desired, or else as a summary of what is revealed to the seer. It seems likely, therefore, that by examining in detail the information which the lists claim to have been revealed to the seers, a view can be reached of what the writers of the apocalypses thought to lie at the heart of apocalyptic revelation itself."[12] This explanation would be consistent with the origins of Enochic traditions in astronomical, angelological, and cosmological speculations. If true, then *4 Ezra* represents the use of the apocalyptic genre by a writer who does not share the theoretical underpinnings of apocalypticism. If, however, the lists are merely formulaic and not representative of the actual speculative concerns of apocalyptic writers, then *4 Ezra* still represents a rejection of the form traditional in apocalyptic literature in favor of the form characteristic of wisdom literature.

11. Ibid., 419.
12. Ibid., 418.

For *1* and *2 Enoch* and *2 Baruch* these are things that are revealed either to Moses or to Enoch, but for *4 Ezra*, as for Job, the items are mentioned in the form of rhetorical questions that ask about the protagonist's knowledge. Neither Job nor Ezra is able to answer questions about these mysteries. Especially interesting in contrast is *1 Enoch* 93:11–14. The form of this passage, like the passages in Job and *4 Ezra*, is that of the rhetorical question. Whereas in Job and *4 Ezra* the answer to be supplied by the reader is "I do not know about these things," in *1 Enoch* the reader is expected to understand that Enoch knows precisely these things. As Enoch confidently says in *2 Enoch* 40:1, "I know everything."

In *4 Ezra*, Uriel and Ezra agree that heavenly knowledge is inaccessible to human beings. Ezra goes so far as to wish that all knowledge and understanding were withheld from humans, since it only makes them miserable (4:22; 7:63). This conviction, however, is not simply representative of traditional Israelite wisdom traditions, but goes beyond such traditions in its pessimism concerning any kind of understanding. *Fourth Ezra* denies the possibility of receiving information by revelation, which is the standard subject of revelation in other apocalypses. In reference to *4 Ezra* 5:36–37, Stone concludes, "When seen in this light, the passage receives its full dramatic dimension. It is a denial, daring, perhaps even polemical, of the availability of certain types of special knowledge, a denial therefore of a specific part of apocalyptic tradition."[13] What is confidently asserted in other apocalypses as the basis for understanding the natural world and its implications for human society is rejected in *4 Ezra*. The optimistic view that it is possible to come to terms with human experience, no matter how overcome by evil, is simply rejected. The only understanding of interest to Ezra is the understanding of what is on the earth (*4 Ezra* 4:21). In *4 Ezra*, the form of apocalypse is used to deny the possibility of apocalypse.

SPECULATIVE INTERESTS

While *4 Ezra* denies the possibility of knowing the traditional objects of speculative investigation, it has its own speculative interests. The only cosmological speculation in *4 Ezra* is the claim that one-seventh of the earth is water and the rest dry land (6:42). There are, however, other kinds of speculation. Note the tradition that the ancient monster

---

13. Stone, *Lists*, 420.

Behemoth lives in the mountains, Leviathan lives in the water, and both will be eaten at a time and by people of God's choice. This may refer to some kind of messianic banquet. There is also a rather lengthy discussion of the state of the dead before the last judgment. The souls of the unrighteous dead, *4 Ezra* states, will immediately (after seven days of observation) enter torment, but the souls of the righteous will immediately enjoy rest after the same seven day period (7:75–101). There is also speculation about the appearance and nature of the Messianic period (7:26–31); the timing and signs of the end; the efficacy of prayer for the ungodly (7:102–15); and the attributes of God (7:132–40). Other similar speculations may be found, but cosmological speculations are absent. More significant is that these speculations have almost no practical implications. The author is keenly interested in signs of the end of the age and other eschatological issues, but the only significance seems to be that this information illustrates the ways of God. This information is useful for accepting the notion of the justice and goodness of God, but there do not seem to be many moral or other behavioral consequences.

MEANING OF HISTORY

In the fifth vision of the eagle, *4 Ezra* includes a visionary review of a brief bit of Roman history, but there is no attempt to explain the meaning of the history. Nor is there implicit theodicy in the symbols of the vision. Nothing in the vision prepares the reader to find meaning in life under Rome's jurisdiction. The vision serves only to identify a period in Roman history as the time when the Messiah would arise to destroy the wicked and to deliver the saved remnant of his people.

There is no attempt to make sense of the present predicament; only assurance that it will soon be over. In fact, Pseudo-Ezra is advised not to "be quick to think vain thoughts concerning the former things, lest you be hasty concerning the last times" (6:34). The bulk of the first three visions consists of the assertion that it is impossible to understand the meaning of the past or the reasons for God's actions; only the future is certain and even that is obscure in its details. This is contrary to some of the older apocalypses (Daniel; Animal Vision; Ten-Week Vision) that review history in the form of *vaticinium ex eventu*. In those cases the purpose is not only to establish the competence of the pseudepigraphic seer, but also to explain the significance of past events. But *4 Ezra* knows of no such significance.

SCRIPTURE

Instead of the revelation of heavenly secrets by way of heavenly tablets (as in *1 Enoch* and *Jubilees*), Ezra is permitted to rewrite the twenty-four books of the Scriptures along with seventy other books that are to be reserved only for "the wise among your people" (14:46). Seen in the light of the previous discussion, this takes on new meaning. No doubt the seventy books to be secretly delivered to the wise are full of esoteric wisdom. Indeed, even in 12:37–39, Ezra was instructed to write the eagle vision (and presumably its interpretation) in a book, which was also to be delivered secretly to the wise. In this final episode, Ezra functions precisely as a scribe, but not quite as a sage. Ezra increased in wisdom and understanding, but most notably in memory-retention. There are a few hints as to the contents of these seventy books. First, we may assume that the eagle vision was included among them, given the parallels with 12:37–39. Second, Ezra's prescribed preparation is to put away human thoughts, burdens, and nature. If one may assume that the doubts and intellectual struggles described in the first three visions represent such thoughts and burdens, then one may also assume that the seventy secret books do not go any further than the rest of *4 Ezra* in answering those thoughts. Third God's directions to Ezra in 14:17–18 and Ezra's instructions to the people in 14:34–36 concern the future: the final ages of human history and the final judgment. It seems likely then, that the esoteric wisdom contained in the seventy books should be presumed to be the same sort of wisdom as that promoted in the rest of *4 Ezra*: faithful resignation and acceptance of God's justice and wisdom.

The significance of Ezra's rewriting scripture cannot be overstated. This episode focuses the reader on the revelation of the past. It is the preservation and remembrance of past revelation that eventually brings meaning to Ezra's quest for understanding. New revelation, such as that contained in *4 Ezra* brings assurance, but not new understanding.

CONCLUSIONS

Pseudo-Ezra is no longer able to make sense of this world in the light of heavenly and future realities. The most compelling part of *4 Ezra* is the depth of Ezra's despair at ever finding answers to his questions about evil and the sufferings of God's people. According to Stone (1989), the apparent lack of correspondence between the rationally ordered questions posed in the first part of the book and the eschatological answers in the second part of the book is due to "the author . . . not really thinking in 'logical' terms, not interested in reaching an answer to his questions by means of reasoned, propositional argument."[14] Nevertheless, the urgency and forcefulness of Ezra's questions and complaints in the first three visions leads the reader to look for an equally forceful and satisfying answer.

Revelations about wicked or good angels, the cosmos, the divine throne room, or the future are unable to satisfy the author's intense desire to understand. Like Job, in the end Pseudo-Ezra can only affirm God's goodness and justice, but he cannot understand it; thus he leaves his readers unsatisfied.[15] Only by accepting Pseudo-Ezra's transformation of his queries into eschatological questions for which answers are forthcoming, can the reader gain a sense of satisfaction. This satisfaction, however, is not based on the feeling that life makes sense, but on the feeling that, in the end everything will be alright and that, in the meantime, the evils are necessary incomprehensible evils.

Ezra's movement from dispute and doubt in the first three visions to acceptance, it is often noted, culminates the elevation of Ezra into a second Moses. Indeed *4 Ezra* shares the common apocalyptic conviction that earthly troubles can be resolved by reference to heavenly wisdom. What is new is the conviction that this wisdom is inaccessible to human understanding, and must simply be accepted on the basis of written tradition. No new revelation is meaningful; the focus on the scriptures of Israel provides meaning.

---

14. Stone, *Features*, 25.

15. Brandenburger asserts that *4 Ezra* solves the dual problems of the way of God and of the evil heart by rejecting earthly wisdom and accepting heavenly wisdom (*Die Verborgenheit Gottes*, 200). The heavenly wisdom as revealed forces earthly wisdom out of the recipient, resulting in the experience of the way of God. Even in this explanation, however, the reader is asked to suspend rational judgment (which leads only to despair) and not simply to accept the rightness of the way of God.

7

Late-Twentieth-Century Scribes' Study of Late Second-Temple Scribes[1]

CLOSE ANALYSIS OF TEXTS during the last generation by George Nickelsburg and others has transformed the study of second-temple Judean literature from where it remained after the foundations were laid by R. H. Charles and his contemporaries. This close examination, particularly of texts usually classified as "apocalyptic," has challenged and changed the field in several significant respects. The results of this close study (along with new research and recognition on related issues), however, have left unresolved issues and led to new ones that will be prominent in the agenda of further research and reflection on second-temple Judean literature and related fields of study.

With no pretence of covering even the majority of these issues, I will focus on three interrelated aspects of the research and debates of the last generation: (1) how Nickelsburg's and others' close examination of texts has led to fuller appreciation of them as literature with particular patterns and forms; (2) how such close attention to texts led to questioning and revision of what had become standard interpretive constructs and concepts; and (3) how their more precise understanding of texts led

---

1. This essay was originally written at the invitation of the editors of *The Review of Rabbinic Judaism* as a review of the two-volume "Ongoing Dialogue of Learning," consisting of the collected articles of George Nickelsburg with responses from many other scholars (*George Nickelsburg in Perspective*, ed. Neusner and Avery-Peck). While Nickelsburg's magisterial oeuvre remain central, I have somewhat broadened and updated the scope of the review of the "quantum leap" that Nickelsburg and others the last generation of scholars has made in our understanding of second-temple Judean texts and their contexts.

to interest in the social context of texts. Their research on second-temple Judean literature, moreover, often had implications for the interpretation of the Gospels and other "New Testament" literature. In each of the interrelated sections below, I focus first on the quantum advance in the study of late second-temple Judean texts over its elementary previous stage, and then explore possible future research agenda arising out of the work of the last generation.

MORE PRECISE ANALYSIS OF LITERARY FORMS

Only a few decades ago canonical books of the "Old" and "New" Testaments were treated as sources of proof-texts for Christian theological doctrines. Correspondingly the "intertestamental" books were treated as sources of proof-texts for "Jewish expectations" and "Jewish background" that set up their supposed fulfillment in Jesus, Paul, and early "Christianity." Far from being assigned to read complete books such as Sirach, *1 Enoch*, or the *Psalms of Solomon*, even graduate students were sent to handy selections of text-fragments chosen to illustrate key components of that "Jewish background" in what was basically a schematic world of motifs and ideas. Nickelsburg and some of the rest of us, however, took the liberty of reading such books all the way through, even attending to the shape of whole documents. In a precursor of narrative criticism or plot-analysis, for example, Nickelsburg delineated a sequence of motifs that are paralleled in various pieces of literature from Judea and the Judean Diaspora that has been suggestive for others working on the same documents or on the Gospels' "passion narratives."[2]

Literary analysis of plots and patterns in biblical and related texts has grown considerably in sophistication in the last generation. This has often involved anachronistic application of concepts derived from study of modern authorial narrative composition (e.g., developed characterization). The scholars who were working with ancient Judean texts extant in Ethiopic and/or Aramaic and/or Greek and/or Latin, however, focused directly on the distinctive character of the documents they were dealing with. Following upon their pioneering efforts, we are still struggling to discern the patterns inherent in these previously under-examined documents. The reviews of Nickelsburg's magisterial com-

---

2. Nickelsburg, "Genre."

mentary on three early texts included in *1 Enoch* suggest that this will be a continuing focus of scholarly analysis and debate.³

A prominent concept from modern literary criticism that scholars of Judean literatures have applied to their texts and text-fragments is that of *genre*. On the one hand, inquiry into the genres of second-temple Judean literature has led to far more precise analysis and interpretation than before. On the other hand, close attention to the particular patterns they discern in texts led probative scholars such as Nickelsburg not to acquiesce too quickly in what other scholars thought they had established as consensus definitions. Most influential for the literature still categorized as "apocalyptic" by Nickelsburg and others is the genre constructed from and applied to documents such as sections of Daniel and sections of *1 Enoch* by John Collins and others in the journal *Semeia*, vol. 14. This scholarly definition has taken on such "canonical" status for some that they cannot understand how Nickelsburg could not have included "apocalypse" among the genres of *1 Enoch*. His own analysis of the sections of *1 Enoch* on which he focused vol. 1 of his commentary led him to claim that the genre of those texts was "testament." Reviewers of the commentary such as Collins and VanderKam allow that the Epistle of Enoch looks like a testament, but that the Book of Watchers and the Book of Dream-Visions do not, and are not held together (in the collection known as *1 Enoch*) by the macro-genre of testament. On the other hand, while Collins views *1 Enoch* as a collection of different writings held together mainly by association with Enoch and some common themes, he reimposes "apocalypse" as the more determinative genre on the grounds that "Enoch's" ascent and visions are the prototype for a long tradition of such ascents "commonly called apocalypses." He insists especially that the Animal Vision is a paradigm of "the historical type of apocalypse" found in the visions of Daniel. Collins himself, however, admits that there were really two different genres of "apocalypse:" "historical apocalypses" such as "Enoch's" Animal Vision and those in Daniel 7, 8, and 10–12, respectively, and (the generally later) "otherworldly journeys" such as *2 Enoch*.

Other scholars, however, have questioned and qualified the quest for the definitive genre of a text. They recognize, for example, that different genres could be found in the same text,⁴ or that a text might display a

3. Reviews by Collins, Tiller, and VanderKam.
4. Doran, "Wise Apocalypticist," 255.

mixture of genres. Such observations suggest that genre criticism cannot be used as the basis for determining literary sources. Most significant for future research is that, since features that Collins and others saw as typical of (or even distinctive to) "apocalypses" function prominently in texts that are framed as testaments, as Nickelsburg laid out, genre was not all that clearly delineated and was not all that determinative of meaning.

Another feature of Nickelsburg's scholarship on early Enoch texts that, in my view, undermines the claim to one or more distinctive genres of "apocalypse" is his close attention to prophetic and other forms and the continuity of their function from earlier texts to those commonly classified as "apocalyptic." A salient example is his delineation of how the bulk of the Epistle of Enoch consists of a series of sets of "woes" that indict and pronounce sentence upon the wealthy and powerful for oppression of the righteous. This form is prominent in prophetic books such as Amos, Isaiah, and Habakkuk. Even some recent interpreters tend to miss or underplay the continuity of prophetic forms and concerns into later Judean texts classified as "apocalyptic."[5]

I find this especially important perhaps mainly for its potential influence on New Testament scholars. Because many are not well-acquainted with the traditional forms of the Israelite prophets and other traditional forms that are standard in Hebrew Biblical literature, they tend to miss the continuation of these forms, especially in Gospel materials. For example, scholars of the "source" ("Q") of the parallel speeches of Jesus in Matthew and Luke (but not in Mark) have tended to ignore the relevance of the sets of woes (indictments + sentence) in the Israelite prophets for interpretation of Jesus' woes against the Pharisees and scribes (Q/Luke 11:37-52; cf. Matthew 23).[6]

For further study of Gospel materials and the "teachings" of Jesus in particular, Nickelsburg's and others' recognition that "apocalyptic" writings have literary forms far broader than the individual verses defined by modern translators has decisive implications. Many scholars of Jesus' teaching and of Gospel materials such as Q still focus on individual sayings that they classify as either "sapiential" or "apocalyptic." That forms the basis on which debates have raged recently over whether Jesus

---

5. This is illustrated by the failure of the reviews of Nickelsburg's commentary on *1 Enoch* to mention his close attention to traditional prophetic forms in Enoch texts. Discussion of such forms in Horsley, *Scribes, Visionaries*, chaps. 8-9.

6. Explored in Horsley with Draper, *Whoever Hears You Hears Me*, 285-91.

was an "apocalyptic" prophet proclaiming "the end time" or a sensitive sage inviting select individuals to a countercultural lifestyle. In contrast to his later followers, however, even the grandfather of form criticism, Rudolf Bultmann, could list only a handful of examples under his category of "apocalyptic sayings." The closer study of apocalyptic literature by Nickelsburg and his scholarly generation have recognized that (the scholarly construct of) "apocalyptic *sayings*" did not comprise the units of composition, communication, and meaning in apocalyptic literature.

The scholarly labors of the last generation have thus brought appreciation of whole documents, closer analysis of forms, and a deepening maturity of literary criticism to the interpretation of second-temple Judean texts. In what is perhaps also a mark of the effectiveness of their labors, however, it is becoming evident (1) that heavy emphasis on genre may be as problematic as it is illuminating, (2) that "wisdom" literature has not been as closely analyzed as apocalyptic literature, and (3) that scholarship remains embedded in the assumptions of modern print culture that are inappropriate to the culture of ancient Judea.

First, the debate about the genre(s) of the sections of *1 Enoch* between Nickelsburg and others, along with the work of Lawrence Wills and others on other second-temple Judean literature, only points up the fact that staking so much on genre is almost surely problematic. The very concept of genre, as well as the definitions of "apocalypse" and "testament" (and "aretalogy," *logoi sophon*, and "revelation discourse") as genres, are modern scholarly constructs. Perhaps genre is not as much of a key to unlock insight and interpretation of this literature as thought by this last generation that has done such pioneering work. It is surely imagining too much to claim that a particular genre, such as "apocalypse," carries or articulates a particular worldview.

It seems highly likely that what modern scholars see as genres change with new circumstances, that new forms are created out of old, that distinctive cultural patterns are used in different types of literary works. Perhaps the next generation of interpreters might want to reconsider certain concepts and foci as they formulate their research agenda and strategy. Also, since much of the focus on genre has been rather "formal," they might want to broaden into analysis of the function of various forms.[7]

---

7. Function was included in the original agenda of form criticism.

Second, while Nickelsburg and his generation have pioneered closer analysis of texts classified as "apocalyptic," their genres, component forms, motifs, and agenda, little corresponding work has been done on what is usually called "wisdom" literature.[8] Collins and others have delineated and, in a limited way, explored several distinct broad types of wisdom: proverbial, theological, natural, mantic, and revelatory. While proverbial wisdom, particularly in its micro-forms such as maxim, has received extensive study, and mantic wisdom has been probed somewhat,[9] there has been little by way of compelling analysis of the broader forms, functions, motifs and agenda of these different types of wisdom. Most discussion of "wisdom" still proceeds as if "wisdom" consisted (primarily) of wisdom sayings/proverbial wisdom, with no further refinement of such vague categories. The result is that "wisdom," "sapiential," and "wisdom literature" are perpetuated as extremely vague and all-encompassing scholarly constructs.

It is possible, however, on the basis of several Judean texts, particularly Proverbs, Sirach, Daniel, and the texts included in *1 Enoch*, to delineate more appropriately and precisely the different kinds of wisdom that Judean scribes/sages cultivated and some of the typical forms they took.[10] While (temporally) earlier sections of the book of Proverbs have the form of "wisdom sayings" such as proverbs, the later sections (e.g., Proverbs 1–9) and much of the book of Sirach consist of short speeches of *instructional wisdom* on various topics given by a parent/senior scribe-sage to a "child"/scribe-in-training. Scribes/sages also cultivated *reflection on wisdom*, as illustrated by the poems in Proverbs 8 and Sirach 24. They further cultivated *cosmological wisdom*, which often took hymnic form, as in Sirach but was also more elaborately articulated in the more systematic topical form evident in the Book of Luminaries included in *1 Enoch* (chaps 72–82). What Collins calls "revelatory" wisdom appears to have been influenced by *mantic wisdom*, which took the form of dream-visions-and-interpretation.[11] According to the introductory first chapter of the book of Daniel, Daniel and the other young Judean

---

8. As pointed out by Tanzer, "Response to 'Wisdom and Apocalypticism,'" 290–94.

9. VanderKam, *Enoch and an Apocalyptic Tradition*.

10. Collins, "Wisdom, Apocalypticism," 168, delineates five types; Horsley, *Scribes, Visionaries*, 126–28, discusses four types, with textual references.

11. With strong Babylonian influence, as emphasized by VanderKam, *Enoch and an Apocalyptic Tradition*.

scribes/sages serving in the Babylonian court were trained in all of these kinds of wisdom. In the tales as well as the dreams-and-interpretations in chaps 7–12, of course, Daniel himself specialized in mantic wisdom, as appropriate to the difficult circumstances in which he – and the latter day visionaries of the second century BCE who actually produced the dreams-and-interpretations—was caught. It remains for the next generation to study more closely and carefully these distinctively different kinds of wisdom and their forms, which are evident in Judean texts but thus far remain relatively unexplored.

Third, in what may offer the greatest challenge for the next steps in study of second-temple Judean literature as well as other ancient literatures, scholars have only begun to recognize that written texts in the ancient world were floating on a sea of oral communication. The composition and cultivation of texts, moreover, were closely interrelated with oral performance. Modern scholars devoted to the study of written texts, especially those dedicated to study of sacred texts, "scriptures," are (not surprisingly) deeply rooted in the assumptions of print-culture. As Nickelsburg's contribution to the field illustrate, particularly his commentary on *1 Enoch,* the staring point, the basis of all other criticism, is to "establish the text" by working from ancient manuscripts in whatever languages they survive. Yet as Enoch literature itself says explicitly, what was written down on parchment scrolls was heard aurally, often from a divine voice (e.g., *1 Enoch* 81:1–6; 82:1–2; 85:2; 91:2, 18–19). "Enoch" was the "scribe" who received and wrote down for his "children" the message that was spoken. Even more striking, in "wisdom" literature, are the repeated references to speaking and hearing: "Listen, O children."[12] And the "children" are being instructed in how to speak, especially in a deliberative assembly. Biblical scholarship has so far resisted recognizing that communication in scribal circles as well as in ancient societies in general was largely oral. In recent years, however, well-researched book-length studies have explained both that literacy was limited to the ruling elite and their staff[13] and that even among the elite literacy had limited functions.[14] Even when "texts" were written down, the "texts"

---

12. Crenshaw, "The Primacy of Listening in Ben Sira's Pedagogy"; Fox, "Wisdom and the Self-Presentation of Wisdom Literature."

13. On limited literacy in Roman Empire generally, Harris, *Ancient Literacy* ; on limited literacy in Roman Palestine, Hezser, *Jewish Literacy in Roman Palestine.*

14. Carr, *Writing on the Tablet of the Heart*; Horsley, *Scribes, Visionaries,* chap 5.

were still performed orally, even among literate circles. Passages that we have translated with "reading" meant in effect "reciting."[15] A telling illustration can be taken from the Qumran Community Rule (1 QS 6:6–8), in the procedure for meetings of ten members, where I have made the appropriate changes in the translation by Vermes (1997):

> And the many shall watch in community for a third of every night of the year,
> to recite the writing (*lqrw' bspr*)
> and to search the justice-ruling (*ldrws mspt*)
> and to offer communal blessings (*lbrk byhd*).

As Martin Jaffee has suggested, the "text" was inscribed as much or more on the memory of the reciter as on the scroll.[16] And as William Scott Green has explained, the rabbis knew very well the difference between "what was read" and "what was written."[17]

The implications of what we have grown accustomed to thinking of as written texts having been embedded in an oral communication environment are considerable, with potential to challenge many of the most basic assumptions with which we work. To start with, as Doran illustrates with the six copies of Tobit found at Qumran, one in Hebrew, five in Aramaic, the variations are typical of an oral culture, where each telling of the tale varies somewhat.[18] In a society where different textual traditions represent different oral performance traditions, there may never have been an "original" text. We may have to come to grips with ancient texts having been multiform.[19] Composition, perhaps of "wisdom" literature such as Sirach, was not by a single "author" in writing, but in the course of multiple performances, and what our manuscripts provide us with are transcripts of more or less standardized performance traditions. That is, in extant manuscripts of Sirach or Tobit or Enoch texts, we may be looking something like what Jacob Neusner has been saying about the Mishnah, Tosefta, and Talmuds: the written crystallization of transmissions of orally-performed "texts" or traditions. This is what some of us are beginning to think also, e.g., about the Gospel

---

15. Boyarin, "Placing Reading."
16. Jaffee, *Torah in the Mouth*.
17. Green, "Writing with Scripture."
18. Doran, "Wise Apocalypicist," 258–60.
19. Ulrich, *The Scrolls and the Origins of the Bible*.

of Mark and the speeches of Jesus paralleled in Matthew and Luke, the speeches of Q.[20] Further study of the close relation of literacy and orality in "biblical" and other second-temple literature will almost certainly require serious attention to creative exploration of the relation of oral performance and written manuscripts of "texts" in other cultures and the nascent theorizing of these issues.[21]

CHALLENGING STANDARD INTERPRETIVE CONSTRUCTS AND CATEGORIES

A second major result of this last generation's study of late second-temple Judean texts is the problematizing and challenging of interpretive concepts and categories that had become standard in biblical studies and related fields. As Sarah Tanzer and Nickelsburg point out, we have a tendency to confuse scholarly constructs with the realities of the ancient cultural world which we are studying.[22] After more critical examination of the texts, however, studies of second-temple Judean and later rabbinic literature have been challenging and adapting the received concepts of interpretation. Of four key illustrations, one underwent serious change a few decades ago, two have been under discussion for decades without much resolution, and the fourth is only beginning to be discussed.

Messiah

Stimulated by the brief article by Marianus de Jonge,[23] Krister Stendahl led a graduate seminar in 1965 that examined closely the very limited occurrences of the term *messiah* in second-temple texts. The seminar reached the (now obvious) conclusion that not only was there no standardized "Jewish expectation" of "the Messiah" at the time of Jesus. Rather the limited and diverse use of the term *messiah* suggested that different texts and/or groups had different conceptions of one or more anointed figures or no interest in an "anointed" figure at all. The concept of "the Messiah," however, remained central in Christian New

---

20. Dewey, "A Really Good Oral Story"; Horsley with Draper, *Whoever Hears You Hears Me*; Wire, *Mark Composed in Performance*; and several of the essays in Weissenrieder and Coote, eds., *Interface of Orality and Writing*.
21. Foley, *Singer of Tales in Performance*.
22. Nickelsburg, "Wisdom and Apocalypticism," 285; Tanzer, "Response," 289.
23. De Jonge, "Use of the Word 'Anointed.'"

Testament studies and related fields such as Jewish history. It was another twenty years and many critical books and articles later before an international scholarly conference was organized (1987 at Princeton) to survey the wreckage of the old concept of the "Jewish expectation" of "the Messiah,"[24] and attempts to put adapted concepts in its place, such as the 1987 volume of essays on *Judaisms and Their Messiahs*.[25]

Nickelsburg's contributions to the discussion illustrate both the scholarly recognition that the old synthetic concept had become problematic and the difficulty of moving beyond a concept that had long been standard in the discourse of biblical studies. On the one hand, his essay in *Judaisms and Their Messiahs*,[26] on agents of "salvation" in Enoch texts, is a model of "cutting through" the standardized constructs that had been imposed in interpretation of ancient texts. He is scrupulous in refusing to use inappropriate concepts such as "messiah" and "title" and "messianic," as he examines terms and images and traditions in *Enoch* and other literature. Yet he still allows that the few brief references in other Judean texts testify to (the vague concept of) a "live messianic hope in the two centuries B.C.E."[27]

Three decades of scholarly skepticism about the highly synthetic old construct of expectations of "the Messiah" led to recognition that different texts attested different discrete figures, including a "suffering servant," a returning Elijah, a prophet like Moses, an anointed priestly and a lay messiah in tandem, and various construals of "(one like) a son of man." But it was impossible any longer to claim that "the anointed one, son of David," virtually distinctive to *Psalm of Solomon* 17, was some sort of standard expectation of "the Messiah" at the time of Jesus. In addition, it was recognized that at the non-literate popular level there were several concrete figures whom their followers acclaimed as "kings" or believed to be prophets like Moses or Joshua.[28] Nevertheless John Collins marshaled various terms and images from various Qumran texts to rehabilitate the standard synthetic messianic construct, attempting, as

---

24. Collected papers in Charlesworth, *The Messiah*.
25. Neusner and Green, eds., *Judaisms and Their Messiahs*.
26. Nickelsburg, "Salvation Without and With a Messiah."
27. Ibid., 79.
28. Horsley, "Popular Messianic Movements"; Horsley, "'Like One of the Prophets of Old'"; and Horsley, "'Messianic' Figures and Movements."

it were, to "put Humpty-Dumpty together again."²⁹ It seems likely that there will continue to be a collegial disagreement between those who will press to more consistently and completely analyze and interpret ancient texts independent of standard scholarly constructs, on the one hand, and those who seek to maintain more continuity with traditional Jewish and/or Christian theological concepts, on the other.

Apocalypticism and Wisdom

Closer study of late second-temple Judean texts during the last generation has also resulted in repeated questioning of what had become standardized scholarly constructs of "apocalyptic/ apocalypticism" and "wisdom" and their dichotomization, particularly in theologically-oriented Christian biblical interpretation. This was expressed sometimes in direct challenges to the standard synthetic constructs,³⁰ sometimes in attempts to refine the conceptualization (e.g., separating analysis of genre from that of worldview),³¹ and mostly in simply no longer using the standard concepts. Scholars focused on other issues who have not paid attention to the questioning of the standard synthetic constructs of "apocalyptic" and "wisdom" and their dichotomization have simply perpetuated them. Scholarly debate continues unabated, for example, on whether the historical Jesus was an "apocalyptic" visionary proclaiming an imminent "cosmic catastrophe"³² or a sober sage teaching about individual lifestyle,³³ with both sides still assuming the standard synthetic scholarly construct of "apocalyptic" and focused on individual sayings classified as "apocalyptic" or "sapiential." Yet there seem to be at least three principal ways in which the standard constructs of "apocalyptic" and "wisdom" and their dichotomization are being challenged.

First, upon closer examination of the texts some scholars cannot help but be struck by the astounding lack of fit between the essentialist scholarly constructs and particularities of the ancient Judean texts. No particular text classified as "apocalyptic" exhibits even the majority of the features supposedly typical of "apocalyptic"—unless it be *4 Ezra*,

---

29. Collins, *Scepter and the Star*.
30. Klaus Koch, *Ratlos vor der Apokalyptic* (*Rediscovery of Apocalyptic*).
31. Collins, ed., *Apocalypse: Morphology of a Genre*.
32. E.g., Allison, "Eschatology of Jesus."
33. E.g., Crossan, *Historical Jesus*.

composed in despair over not only the devastation of Judea and Judeans but also the decimation of previous "apocalyptic" hopes for judgment of the dominant imperial rule and renewal of the people. Does the *Epistle of Enoch* have any features that would justify its classification as an "apocalypse," in either of Collins' two types? As suggested perhaps in the above discussion of the forms evident in Proverbs 1–9 and Sirach, if wisdom consists of observations about nature in simple proverbial sayings, then what do we do with the speeches about social relations and professional scribal life that constitute most of the material in Sirach and the reflection on wisdom and the cosmological wisdom that take the form of hymns in Sirach?

Second, closer reading of particular texts strongly suggests that the modern scholarly dichotomy between "wisdom" and "apocalyptic" is inappropriate. The prototypical "apocalyptic" visionaries, "Daniel" and "Enoch," are trained as learned scribes. Sections of the book of Daniel and *Enoch* texts show knowledge of the same or similar cosmological wisdom that Ben Sira knows, albeit deployed in different forms. Ben Sira knows of mantic or revealed wisdom, but chooses not to cultivate it. If anything, the late second-temple texts that have been classified as "apocalyptic" appear to be a development of a particular kind of wisdom (mantic-revelatory) in creative combination with prophetic forms of heavenly vision. Gerhard von Rad argued that apocalyptic developed from wisdom. Frank Cross and his student Paul Hanson insisted that apocalyptic developed from late prophecy.[34] But these cannot be seen as mutually exclusive alternatives, for as Ben Sira clearly indicates wise scribes saw themselves as the heirs of the prophetic tradition and actively cultivated it as well as Mosaic torah and various kinds of wisdom (Sir 39:1–4).

Third, claims that "apocalyptic" texts express an apocalyptic worldview seem to have dwindled. Recent treatment of the book of Daniel and Enoch texts find only vestiges of the worldview previously claimed for such literature and, on that basis, even Judean society in general. Nickelsburg still sees various dualisms in *Enoch* texts.[35] But, Koch, who was one of the early critics of the standard synthetic construct of *Apokalyptik*, questions whether even the milder dualisms are attested

---

34. Cross, "New Directions"; Hanson, *Dawn of Apocalyptic*.
35. Nickelsburg, *1 Enoch*.

Late-Twentieth-Century Scribes' Study of Late Second-Temple Scribes 153

in the texts.[36] He focuses instead on people, suggesting that interpreters must allow for "poetic exaggerations" in expressions previously read, some literally, in terms of cosmology and theology. Amos Wilder, always literarily sensitive, was pressing a similar point over fifty years ago,[37] but few theologically-oriented scholars seemed to "get it." Collins continues to find an "otherworldly" orientation in Daniel and other texts.[38] Both concepts, "otherworldly" and cosmological "dualism," however, seem somehow inappropriate to the view of the world articulated in prophetic as well as "apocalyptic" texts that understood historical affairs as governed ultimately by God and other heavenly forces (*bene-elohim*/"watchers"/"holy ones"/"angels").[39]

Interpreters of "apocalyptic" literature might well attend to interpreters of other Judean texts who have rediscovered rhetoric and ideology, i.e., that texts are composed to persuade people and use language in non-cognitive ways such as metaphor, hyperbole, and allegory. Specialists might consider the imagery, rhetoric, and ideology of "apocalyptic" texts in relation to their agenda, which is, like that of late prophetic texts, focused on the judgment of foreign rulers and the renewal of the people.

(Early) Judaism and (Early) Christianity

The most fundamental standard synthetic concept being rethought, as a result of the last generation's analysis of texts, is surely that of ancient (early) *Judaism*, along with its "spin-off" counterpart, (early) *Christianity*. Partly if not largely because of the modern western separation of religion from politics and economics, the concept *Judaism* tended to reduce the realities of life of ancient Judeans to religion. Close attention to Judean texts in the last generation led quickly to the recognition of the diversity of their viewpoints. One response, particularly after the discovery of the Dead Sea Scrolls and the dissident Qumran community, was to speak primarily of "sectarian Judaism," recognizing the differences between Pharisees, Sadducees, Essenes/ Qumran, and other "sects," a term derived from study of the separation of "sects" from the state "churches"

---

36. Koch, "Response to 'The Apocalyptic Construction of Reality.'"
37. Wilder, "Apocalyptic Imagery and Earthly Circumstance."
38. Collins, "From Prophecy to Apocalypticism."
39. Horsley, *Scribes, Visionaries*, 204–5.

in early modern Europe. Another important response, emphasizing the religious/ cultural/ideological dimension, was to speak of Judaisms (plural).

It is difficult to read Judean texts closely, however, and not discern that the "diversity" involved divisions. Ben Sira instructs his students to beware of their superiors who have power over them as well as to aid the poor in a society where the rich prey on the poor. The *maskilim* who produced the historical vision-and-interpretation in Daniel 10–12 are being martyred by the imperial regime of Antiochus Epiphanes, who is allied with their fellow Judeans whom they consider to have broken the sacred covenant. The wise "Enoch" scribes who produced the Epistle of Enoch pronounced several series of woes on the wealthy and powerful who were exploiting the righteous poor. It may be necessary to read Nehemiah, Josephus' histories, and the Gospels as well as Ben Sira's speeches to recognize that ancient Judea was a society with a particular political-economic-religious structure, more particularly an agrarian society of numerous farming villages ruled by a temple-state subject to an empire. Once such recognition is gained, however, it is difficult not to see that Judean society involved two significant and continuing divisions. Not only did the wealthy (high priestly) rulers control and economically exploit the villagers, who were poor, as can be seen in Ben Sira, Josephus, and the Gospels. But the various circles of scribes who produced the "apocalyptic" texts and the Dead Sea Scrolls opposed, sometimes actively, the incumbent high priestly regimes in Jerusalem as well as the imperial regimes who backed them.

Recognition of the divisions as well as the diversity in late second-temple Judean society also facilitates the recognition that the concept "(early) Christian" is misleading when applied to certain texts that were later included in the New Testament.[40] The Gospels of Mark and Matthew and the Apocalypse to John stand in direct continuity with Israelite tradition. Such texts have no sense of any separation from Israel. Rather they articulate an agenda of a renewed and an expansive Israel. Far from breaking with the Law, Mark (esp. 10:2–45) and Matthew (esp. chaps 5–7) articulate a renewal of Mosaic covenantal community, parallel in many ways to the Community Rule and the Damascus Rule from Qumran. They stand with or parallel to other Judean literature against the Roman rulers and the incumbent high priestly rulers in Jerusalem.

---

40. Chesnutt, "Nickelsburg's *Jewish Literature*," 352.

They are, however, sharply critical also of "the scribes and Pharisees" as representatives of the Jerusalem "chief priests." And in this they parallel those Judeans who opposed the "provisional government" of high priestly figures and leading Pharisees in 66–67.

(The Hebrew) Bible / The Law and the Prophets / Scripture

An emerging focus of research and discussion that is seriously challenging basic concepts previously taken as secure knowledge is the relation between second-temple Judean "books" that were later included in the Hebrew Bible and other second-temple Judean texts. "The Bible" will perhaps be the concept most difficult to rethink. It has simply been assumed that in late second-temple times the five books of the Torah and the books of the Prophets already existed in standardized form and wording as "scripture" widely known, read, and shared by all "Jews." It has simply been assumed, on the basis of Sirach 44–49 that Ben Sira, in the early second century BCE, already knew the books of the Pentateuch, the Prophets, and (at least some of) the Writings. It has simply been assumed that Mark, Q, and Matthew were quoting standardized texts of "the law and the prophets." And even Jesus, who was assumed to be literate on the basis of the account of his "reading" from a scroll in Luke 4, was supposedly "quoting" the "Old Testament." It has been standard practice, therefore, to refer to these books as "biblical" in discussion of other late second-temple texts that were later grouped into the Apocrypha and the Pseudepigrapha. These other books were taken as supplementary or complementary, but in any case of secondary importance. Texts that covered (some of) the same events and figures (e.g., *Jubilees*) as those covered in the Pentateuch were more recently classified as "rewritten scripture/Bible/Torah," on the assumption that they were already the standard (and only) account of such events and figures.[41] Certain Qumran texts have been classified similarly (e.g., the Temple Scroll, Genesis Apocryphon, 4QMMT).[42]

More recent research, however, is indicating that again in the case of "the Bible/ biblical" we have been confusing scholarly constructs with the realities of the ancient cultural world that we are studying. Ithamar Gruenwald comments that we know little about "scripturehood" before

---

41. Vermes, *Scripture and Tradition*.
42. Tov, "Biblical Texts as Reworked"; White Crawford, "Rewritten Pentateuch."

the second century BCE.[43] Recently published analysis of the scrolls of books that were later included in the Hebrew Bible, however, suggests that "scripturehood" must have been rather fluid and diverse until the end of the Second Temple, or even until around 200 CE. As Eugene Ulrich explains after a career of detailed poring over the manuscripts, there coexisted at Qumran two or three different textual traditions of the books of the Pentateuch, all of which were still undergoing development.[44] This suggests that—insofar as the Hebrew Bible had not yet been defined and the texts of books later included were still developing—*Jubilees*, Pseudo-Philo's *Biblical Antiquities*, the *Temple Scroll*, and 4QMMT were not "rewritten Pentateuch/Bible" but alternative versions of Torah. The on-going close study of such texts suggests that there must have been multiple and perhaps competing traditions of Israelite tradition and torah.[45] We must thus reckon with considerable diversity and fluidity of "Torah" and "scripture" through the end of the second-temple period and beyond. Nickelburg demonstrates that Enoch literature in effect ignores or "leapfrogs" Mosaic Torah in its concentration of revealed knowledge.[46] Recognizing this situation, compounded by the recognition that written texts were closely interrelated with oral performance, requires some crucial rethinking of how we approach our texts in the first place, as well as how we interpret them.

SOCIAL CONTEXT AND HISTORICAL REFERENCES

I remember thinking, while reading Nickelsburg's *Jewish Literature* (1st ed., 1981) and Collins' *Apocalyptic Imagination* (1984), that in the precision with which they dealt with the component parts of books such as *1 Enoch*, Daniel, and the *Testament of Moses*, they had brought the analysis of second-temple Judean texts right to the threshold of historical social context. "Social world" analysis, particularly in terms of 1960s studies of millenarianism applied to "early Christianity" in the 1970s and 1980s, did not gain much traction in study of the "groups" that supposedly produced apocalyptic texts.[47]

43. Gruenwald, "Commentary on 1 Enoch," 398.
44. Ulrich, *Scrolls and Origins of the Bible*.
45. Gruenwald, "Commentary on Enoch," 400.
46. Tiller, "George Nickelsburg's 1 Enoch," 369–70.
47. Although Ploeger's thesis of "conventicles" (in *Theocracy and Eschatology*) was influential for a time.

Nickelsburg explored some of the "social aspects" of early apocalyptic literature and Philip Davies probed the social context of Daniel and other books.[48] Several scholars have explored the Qumran community in terms of sociology of religion analysis of "sects."[49] Davies also led a Group in the SBL that explored mainly sociology of literature analysis of second-temple texts. None of these initiatives, however, ventured more fully into broader sociological analysis. Historical social context includes both a narrower sense of the social location in which a text was produced and a broader sense of the historical situation it presupposes and perhaps addresses. And to approach either or both, more comprehensive sociological analysis is necessary.

With regard to the broader historical context, Nickelsburg took the unusual step of suggesting that at particular points apocalyptic literature was making references to historical figures and circumstances such as the Hellenistic imperial rule of Judea. Early on he suggested that the myth of the giants in *1 Enoch* 6–11 was a parody of the claims of divine generation by the Diadochi of Alexander the Great and that the oracles against the watchers in *1 Enoch* 12–16 referred to the defiled Jerusalem high priesthood at the time.[50] More recently he ventured that royal messianic expectations in late second-temple texts such as *Psalm of Solomon* 17 are set against Roman imperial rule.[51] Some colleagues are skeptical. Gruen insists that what might seem to be historical references are rather literary displays of a sense of humor.[52] VanderKam requires more specifics to be convinced.[53] Nickelsburg responds persuasively that apocalyptic literature trades in allusive language, and that there must have been some historical provocation for the revisionary retelling of the traditional giants legend.[54]

As suggested, perhaps, by vagueness of the current discussion of "sectarianism" and the dialogue partners' skittish reserve about political

---

48. Nickelsburg, "Social Aspects"; Davies, "Social World"; and "Reading Daniel Sociologically."

49. Baumgarten, *Flourishing of Jewish Sects*; Jokiranta, "Sectarianism of the Qumran 'Sect'"; Newsom, "Sectually Explicit Literature from Qumran."

50. Nickelsburg, *Jewish Literature*, 52.

51. Nickelsburg, "Response to Wiard Popkes," 102–3.

52. Gruen, *Heritage and Hellenism*.

53. VanderKam, "Response to Nickelsburg, 1 Enoch," 385–86.

54. Nickelsburg, "Response on the Commentary," 411–12.

references, investigation into the social-context and political engagement of second-temple Judean literature remains at a very elementary stage of development. Now that it has begun, however, it will almost certainly gather momentum and will play an important role in the future interpretation of texts. The discussion so far points to further development in three connections.

First, the sociology of religion concept of "sect" and "sectarian" is problematic with respect to second-temple Judean society. It was developed by Ernst Troeltsch and others a century ago with reference to the differences between the established state church(es) in western European countries and the religious groups that split off in the Reformation and after. The concept "sect" and its counterpart "church" presupposed a separation between religion and political economy in early modern Europe that is anachronistic in application to ancient Judea. The discussion between Newsom and Nickelsburg notwithstanding, the concept would be remotely applicable only to the Qumran community as reconstructed by certain scholars, and seems quite inappropriate to any other identifiable second-temple Judean group. Furthermore, adaptation and application of the intricate abstract sociology of religion typology of "religious sects" constructed from Western religious groups by Bryan Wilson in the 1960s and then applied to social-religious movements in the "undeveloped" world[55] is unlikely to be attractive to scholars focused on interpretation of texts and reconstruction of ancient Judean history. It has proven to have little explanatory value for ancient materials and movements, since each concrete ancient group turns out to be a mishmash of several of Wilson's different types of sect. It will certainly be of little help in relating texts to groups. The concept of "sectarian Judaism" is perhaps even more problematic than the construct of "Jewish apocalypticism." One useful principle to be drawn from the discussion so far is that an exclusivist-sounding text does not necessarily imply a separate or separatist group. The Qumran community apparently had in its possession texts from other groups as well as many produced earlier in support of the Jerusalem temple-state.

Second, while some (usually theologically-oriented) scholars view second-temple literature as religious, separate from political affairs, others (including Israeli historians) find that these texts not only make

---

55. Wilson, *Magic and Millennium*.

historical references, but have particular political agendas.[56] The second and first centuries BCE during which much of this literature is dated were rife with political conflicts. These ranged from the levels of imperial wars and civil war wars between rival high priestly factions to the levels of conflicts between rival scribal and priestly circles and popular revolts against the high priestly regime in Jerusalem. It would be difficult to claim that Qumran literature is not politically engaged when we find documents in which "the smooth interpreters" are attacked for their legal rulings, the "Wicked Priest" is cursed and the faithful remnant is rehearsing holy war against "the Kittim" (code term for the Romans). The *Psalms of Solomon* articulate rather sharp criticism of both the Hasmonean regime and the Roman conquerors of Judea, and anticipate that the (rather scribal) anointed Son of David will slay the imperial rulers with the sword of his mouth. And as noted above, the *maskilim* who produced the visions of Daniel stood steadfastly against their high priestly rulers who were collaborating with the Seleucid imperial rulers, some of them having been martyred for their resistance. If anything it would appear that Nickelsburg was rather timid and limited in his suggestions of political references. Certainly Enoch texts were not alone in being politically unengaged.[57]

Third, it would appear that second-temple texts and their producers are just waiting for fuller historical social analysis, both for their social location and for their broader historical political engagement. It has long since been recognized that in second-temple Judea we are dealing with a whole society. It had a religious dimension surely, but one that cannot be abstracted from the political-economic institutions and patterns with which it was embedded and inseparable. Ancient Judea had a particular political-economic-religious structure that resembles that of other traditional agrarian societies studied by historical sociologists. Rather than simply apply a sociological model constructed by comparative historical sociologists, however, it seems more appropriate as historical method—and probably more convincing to textual scholars—to examine second-temple Judean texts themselves for the evidence they may contain for political-economic structure, power-relations, and social location. Ben Sira is a particularly rich source of information. Tiller and I have taken some initial steps in this regard and hope that they will

---

56. For example, Mendels, *Land of Israel*; Eshel, *Dead Sea Scrolls*.
57. Horsley, *Scribes, Visionaries*; and *Revolt of the Scribes*.

result in fruitful further discussions with colleagues who engage primarily in critical literary analysis. As evident in Sirach and confirmed by other documents, the basic structure of second-temple Judea consisted of the high-priestly aristocracy, assisted by scribal and other "retainers" and served by artisans, in control of and economically supported by the vast majority of people living in villages and working the land.[58]

When we then juxtapose the recent recognition that literacy was limited to the ruling elite and their scribal retainers, it seems fairly clear that the only candidates for the production of texts were scribal circles or groups formed by dissident scribes and priests, such as the Qumran community. Scribes who served the incumbent high priests would understandably take positive, supportive attitudes toward their patrons or even compose literature to support their regime. Ben Sira's support for the Oniads has frequently been noted, and *Jubilees* as well as 1 Maccabees have been seen as sponsored by or propaganda for the Hasmoneans, Simon in particular. On the other hand, scribal circles who became disaffected with high priestly incumbents or who lost out in the power-struggles between different high priestly factions were quite capable of articulating their criticism, either directly, as in the Epistle of Enoch and some texts from Qumran, or indirectly, as in leaving a new temple conspicuously absent from the future restoration of the people in "Enoch's" Animal Vision and the Ten-Week Vision linked with the Epistle of Enoch and the alternative torah of the Temple Scroll. This is the approach we have taken in chapter one above.[59] Such an approach should enable interpreters of second-temple texts to discern the social-political relations of the scribal authors, who were in or out of favor with the incumbent high priests, and their social-political agenda in connection with particular historical situations.

This last generation of scholars has greatly advanced our appreciation of second-temple Judean texts, particularly in drawing attention to whole texts, their mix of forms, and their historical social context. As a result of their stimulating and well-grounded learning, their successors will be working on a solid foundation and their agenda will be complex and challenging.

---

58. See chap. 1 above.

59. And applied to particular texts in chaps. 2–5 above. See further Horsley, *Scribes, Visionaries*.

PART THREE

Questioning the Categories as Applied to the Gospels and James

8

Questions about Wisdom and Apocalypticism in Q

THE MODERN SCHOLARLY CONSTRUCTS of wisdom and apocalypticism have become prominent and often dominant in interpretation of Jesus and the Gospels. Wisdom and apocalypticism have also become dichotomized as paradigmatic literary forms, theologies, and worldviews according to which New Testament texts and figures are categorized and interpreted. During the 1970's and 1980s the dichotomy between wisdom and apocalypticism became prominent in the American discussion of Jesus' teachings paralleled in Matthew and Luke, commonly called the synoptic sayings source, "Q" (short for *Quelle*, the German term for "source"). Indeed, American specialists on Q thought the differences between wisdom and apocalyptic sayings and motifs so clear that they could distinguish two distinctive strata in the hypothetical document Q: a formative sapiential layer and a secondary apocalyptic layer. In a closely related development, during the 1990s, the critical liberal scholars of the Jesus Seminar made the distinction they found between sapiential sayings and apocalyptic or judgmental sayings the basis for the construction of Jesus as a serene teacher of wisdom, as opposed to the apocalyptic preacher of the end of the world that Schweitzer had imagined at the turn of the twentieth century and Bultmann still presupposed in the next generation.

This classification of individual sayings of Jesus as sapiential versus apocalyptic and the separation of sapiential and apocalyptic layers of Q, however, were part of a broader scheme of early Jewish and early "Christian" literature that became prominent a generation ago: the assumption of a dichotomy between wisdom and apocalyptic at every level, from individual sayings to the genres of texts to theology and christology to worldview. This is evident in the highly influential schematic work Helmut Koester and James M. Robinson who, directly or indirectly, were mentors to many in the field. It can be seen in a key paragraph by Koester.

> The primary problem in the assessment of the Synoptic Sayings Source is the difficulty which arises when one tries to determine its literary genre (Robinson, "LOGOI SOPHON"). On the one hand, wisdom materials are obvious. In addition to proverbs and rules for right conduct, there are I-sayings in which Jesus speaks in the first person with the voice of Wisdom (Matt 11:25–30) and even a quotation from wisdom material (Luke 11:49–51). On the basis of such materials, the Synoptic Sayings Source would have to be identified as a wisdom book, comparable to such works as the Wisdom of Solomon. On the other hand, a number of sayings reveal a very different theological orientation that is more clearly evident in the sayings about the coming Son of Man (Luke 17:22–32). This eschatological expectation has its ultimate origin in the Book of Daniel. It appropriately dominates the Synoptic Apocalypse (Mark 13). Among the wisdom sayings of the Synoptic Sayings Source, it is a foreign element. If the genre of the wisdom book was the catalyst for the composition of sayings of Jesus into a "gospel," and if the christological concept of Jesus as the teacher of wisdom and as the presence of heavenly Wisdom dominated its creation, the apocalyptic orientation of the Synoptic Sayings Source with its christology of the coming Son of man is due to a secondary redaction of an older wisdom book.[1]

Ironically, this schematic dichotomy between wisdom and apocalyptic has developed during a time when an increasing number of scholars have been engaged in close study of ancient Jewish texts. Ever closer examination of what are classified as "wisdom" and "apocalyptic" texts in the last several decades has led to more precise appreciation of those texts in ways that raise serious questions about the dichotomization of Gospel materials and their interpretation. As specialization among biblical scholars has increased, it has become ever more difficult for inter-

---

1. Koester, "Apocryphal and Canonical Gospels," 112; cf. his more nuanced subsequent interpretation of Q that qualifies the dichotomy between sapiential and apocalyptic in *Ancient Christian Gospels*.

preters of the Gospels and Jesus to keep up with research and discussion in late second-temple Judean texts. Some interpreters engaged directly in study of wisdom and apocalyptic texts have responded specifically to the hypothesis of different layers in Q, on which we will focus here.[2] Problems raised by the application of the dichotomy to Q, however, should be placed in the broader context of more general questions, rooted on fuller and more precise knowledge of particular apocalyptic and wisdom texts, posed the imposition of the wide-ranging dichotomy between wisdom and apocalyptic onto Gospel materials (exemplified in the quoted paragraph from Koester).

The genre "sayings of the wise" delineated by Robinson has become understood as the catalyst for the composition of the sayings of Jesus into a "gospel."[3] This statement begs the question of what a Gospel is, whether it is not more than a mere collection of sayings, as suggested by the examples Robinson cites of "sayings of the wise." It also begs the question of composition, whether a collection of sayings involves any composition beyond merely compiling one saying after another, as in Prov 10:1—22:16, in contrast to the short speeches or discourses in Prov 22:17—24:34 (also entitled "words of the wise") and the longer instructional speeches in Proverbs 1–9 and the instructional speeches that make up most of the book of Sirach.[4]

One senses that a written literary model of genre underlies the discussion of "words of the wise" as the catalyst of composition, despite Robinson's implication that the genre functioned in an oral milieu.[5] It will require much fuller understanding of the function or oral modes of communication and their relation to written texts, however, before we can attribute such "generative" importance to a written literary genre in a predominantly oral communication environment such as that in ancient Roman Palestine.[6]

---

2. A. Y. Collins, "The Son of Man in the Sayings Source"; J. J. Collins, "Wisdom, Apocalypticism"; Horsley, "Questions about Redactional Strata."

3. Robinson, "LOGOI SOPHON"; Kloppenborg, *Formation of Q*, 30.

4. See Kirk, *The Composition of the Sayings Source*; Horsley, *Scribes, Visionaries*, chap 7.

5. Robinson, "LOGOI SOPHON," 102–3.

6. See now Horsley with Draper, *Whoever Hears You Hears Me*; Horsley, *Scribes, Visionaries*, chaps 5–6.

That the Wisdom of Solomon is used to illustrate the theological orientation as well as the literary form of a wisdom book raises the question of how wide a range of "wisdom" literature and "wisdom" genres are to be included in the synthetic concept of wisdom with reference to which the formative layer of Q is to be interpreted. Koester seems to have in mind primarily "proverbs and rules for right conduct," which is what most biblical scholars think of under the concept wisdom, a collection of which can be found in Prov 10:1—22:16. Wisdom of Solomon, however, is comprised of three sections and different kinds of wisdom, the poetic reflection on the persecuted righteous one rewarded with immortality in chaps 1–5 (a mystical individualistic development of the persecuted righteous in Isaiah 52–53), the devotional mystical meditation on the personified etherealized heavenly figure of Wisdom in chaps 6-9 (clearly influenced by Platonic philosophy in a Hellenistic philosophical milieu), and the long poetic meditation on how Israel received benefit through the very things by which their enemies ("Egyptians") were punished in chaps 11–19. Other books of wisdom are also composites of different kinds of wisdom. Do all of these various kinds of wisdom articulate the same worldview? Certainly the "otherworldly" individual mysticism of Wisdom of Solomon 6-9 seems to come from a different "world" from the Jerusalem scribal ethos of the instructional speeches that make up most of Sirach. It seems ironic, if not contradictory, that the quotation of "Wisdom" in Q 11:49–51 is a judgmental declaration that would be classified under "apocalyptic/judgmental" in the governing dichotomy of sayings.

The book of Daniel, the illustration of a "very different theological orientation," is indeed the prototypical "apocalyptic" text, by widespread consensus, although it is also a composite document of tales and visions-plus-interpretations. But in chapter 1 Daniel and his friends are represented as trained and skilled in all kinds of wisdom (in order to serve at court) and the *maskilim* who produced the visions-and-interpretations in chaps (7, 8, 9) 10–12 are portrayed as "making many wise" (11:33–35). If "apocalyptic" texts featured and were produced by sages knowledgeable in all kinds of wisdom, then what might account for the supposedly different theologies or worldviews of apocalypticism and wisdom? Does a vision-and-interpretation that we classify as "apocalyptic" (the term is not used in Daniel) or does instructional wisdom express a distinctive theology or worldview, as recent discussion of layers in Q seems to suggest?

Making a sharp dichotomy between Judean wisdom and apocalyptic literature surely makes little sense sociologically. In a traditional agrarian society such as ancient Judea in the second-temple period the principal people who were literate and capable of or inclined to produce written texts were those who served as scholarly "retainers" for the ruling aristocracy.[7] One of the responsibilities of these sages-teachers-lawyers in the second-temple era was apparently to cultivate and interpret the Torah as the constitution and law code for the temple-state ruled by the high priesthood. And covenantal torah had come to be understood as synonymous with wisdom. Given the imperial situation that prevailed in Hellenistic times after about 200 BCE, however, these sages-teachers-lawyers periodically came into sharp disagreement or even conflict with the rulers they ostensibly worked for. That is, insofar as the ruling high priestly families pursued policies of assimilation into Hellenistic culture and politics, the "retainers" whose whole raison d'être was to preserve and interpret the distinctive Judean way of life would have been both threatened and alienated. It seems abundantly clear, sociologically speaking, that the people who produced apocalyptic literature such as the various sections of *1 Enoch* or the book of Daniel were some of the same people who taught wisdom and Torah. The mixture of "apocalyptic" and "sapiential" materials in the same text can be observed quite clearly in *1 Enoch*. What was produced depended on the times and circumstances, but both apocalyptic and wisdom literature stemmed from the same, numerically quite small, social stratum. The differences between texts we classify as apocalyptic and those we classify as wisdom (of various kinds) may have to do with the different forms of knowledge cultivated by professional scribes/sages and with the historical circumstances addressed in particular texts.[8]

QUESTIONS ABOUT HYPOTHETICAL LAYERS IN Q

John Kloppenborg laid out an elaborate hypothesis of formative and secondary strata in Q that became virtually "canonical" among many

---

7. Discussion of the political-economic structure of Roman Judea in Horsley, *Jesus and the Spiral of Violence*, 15–19; more extensive discussion in Saldarini, *Pharisees, Scribes*. More fully developed subsequently in Horsley and Tiller, "Ben Sira and the Sociology," reprinted as chap. 1 above.

8. More fully explored subsequently in chap. 2 above. See now Horsley, *Scribes, Visionaries*.

American Q scholars.[9] He and others, moreover, proceeded to construct the "social history" of the Q tradents on the basis of these hypothetical strata.[10]

Kloppenborg assigns five complexes of Q sayings—3:7-9, 16-17; 7:1-10, 18-35; 11:14-26, 29-32, 39-52; 12:39-59 and 17:23-35—to the same secondary redactional stratum on the basis of "several common features" revealed by his analysis of the composition and redactional history of the sayings and units within these complexes.[11] The common features he has discovered involve a projected audience, form, and motifs. The *projected audience* "consists of the impenitent and the opponents of community preaching ... The target group of the final form of the Q woes and the five speeches as a whole ... includes all of Israel." The *form* typical of this stratum of Q is that of chriae which criticize the response of "this generation" to the preaching of the kingdom, and which encapsulate the *prophetic judgment and apocalyptic words* typical of this stratum. Correspondingly, preponderant in this stratum are *motifs* related to the theme of judgment, such as imminence, the *parousia*, with Israel obstinately rejecting John, Jesus and the Q preachers while the Gentiles respond positively, thus highlighting Israel's unfaithfulness.

These same "common features" function prominently throughout Kloppenborg's analysis of particular texts as the substantive criteria according to which this all-important redactional stratum is determined. Thus Q appears to have a "polemic against Israel's lack of recognition," and "Israel is guilty of rejecting God's envoys," etc.,[12] while certain texts "speak of *actual Gentile belief*," and "the theme of Gentile response and faith occurs in Q" with "frequency," such that Q can be seen to have an "interpretation of Gentile faith as an *Unheilszeichen* for Israel."[13] Certain sayings are found to be "apocalyptic predictions" of "apocalyptic judgment" or "eschatological" events.[14] Similarly, Kloppenborg finds in this stratum of Q apocalyptic *topoi* such as "war" and the "division

---

9. Kloppenborg, *Formation of Q*.

10. Kloppenborg, "Social History of the Q People"; Mack, "Kingdom that Didn't Come."

11. Kloppenborg, *Formation of Q*, 166-70.

12. Ibid., 120, 147; see also 119, 125, 127, 236-37, 238.

13. Ibid., 236, 119-20; see also 193, 196, 226.

14. Ibid., 102-3, 108, 128, etc.

of families" and motifs such as "nearness of the end," the *parousia*, and "impending catastrophe."[15]

When one examines the actual complexes of Q sayings assigned to this redactional stratum, however, it is difficult to find the "common features" that Kloppenborg used as the substantive criteria. Little of the material in those five complexes in fact appears to be "directed at the 'out-group'" of the impenitent and the opponents. The majority of the material in these five complexes consists of rationalizations, exhortations, and particularly sanctions directed at the "in-group" of Jesus' followers themselves (7:18–23, 24–28; 12:39–46, 51–53, 57–59; 17:23–35) or is not particularly threatening in the first place (11:14–26). The only texts that can easily be understood as rationalizations of the rejection and persecution encountered by Q preachers are 11:29–32 and possibly 7:31–35. But there is no reason internal to these texts to think that "this generation" refers to "Israel" in contrast with "Gentiles." The only occurrence of "Israel" is in 7:1–10. Here in Luke's version a Gentile is indeed responding to Jesus with faith. But the point of the story is not to exemplify a mission to Gentiles,[16] but to challenge (or embarrass) Jews/Israel into fuller response. Beyond 7:1–10, moreover, there is no indication in Q of "actual Gentile belief." Q 11:31–32 cites the historical cases of the Queen of the South's response to Solomon's wisdom and the Ninevites' response to Jonah's preaching, respectively, as contrasts to the response of "this generation" to "something greater," but not as Gentile response to Jesus or preaching of the kingdom. Q 10:13–15 does not in fact "predict Gentile faith" but offers a hypothetical contrast to the lack of repentance in two particular towns (and not "Israel"). And 13:28–29 speaks of the future ingathering of Israel (again to challenge the "sons of the kingdom"), not "an actual Gentile mission."[17] There is simply no basis in Q for "Gentile faith" as a significant theme, let alone its interpretation as an *Unheilszeichen* for Israel.

As for the "common feature" of *form*, only one of the chriae listed (11:29 + 31–32) actually criticizes the response of 'this generation' to the preaching of the kingdom. Moreover, of the sayings that these chriae "encapsulate," none of them appear to be "apocalyptic words," but are

---

15. Ibid., *topoi*, 151; nearness of the end, 152, 155, 166; *parousia*, 102, 150, 152, 157, 163, 165; catastrophe, 152–53, 164.

16. As Kloppenborg admits; ibid., 119.

17. Cf. ibid., 119–20, 236.

"prophetic sayings," and of the other sayings that supposedly articulate a threat, only three of the nine listed could intelligibly be interpreted that way (i.e., possibly 12:39, 54-55; and 17:37b; but not 11:20, 23, 24-26, 33, 34-36; and 12:57-58).

The failure of the "common features" to appear in Q texts becomes even more acute for the "motifs." The assumption that Q speaks of the *parousia* is probably rooted in a Pauline understanding of Christ's return. But "(the day of) the son of man" in Luke 12:40; 17:24, 26, 30 is merely a symbol for the judgment, and not a reference to an individual figure of redemption or judgment (see further below). Moreover, judgment is not particularly "imminent" in Q, except perhaps in John's. Both 12:51-53 and 54-56, for example, refer to the present crisis. Finally, only in 11:29-32 and 49-51 (and not in 7:31-35; 11:19-20, 24-26, 33-36; 12:57-59) does lack of response to John, Jesus, or Q preachers constitute grounds for condemnation. As with the projected audience, so with the motifs, there is little or no basis for the claim that Q has a polemic against "Israel" in contrast to the positive response of the Gentiles.

Strictly speaking, only two texts (11:29-32 and 11:49-51) actually attest the three common features used as criteria for the secondary, judgmental layer, and then not quite in the distinctive ways Kloppenborg has characterized them: i.e., they are prophetic sayings (but not apocalyptic sayings) in form, they contain the motif of rejection of Jesus' preaching as a basis for condemnation (but no apocalyptic traits), and they also focus on "this generation" (but not "Israel") as the projected audience. It hardly seems justified to assign five whole complexes of sayings to a particular "redactional stratum" on the basis of only two sayings that actually manifest the "common features" used as criteria.

Is it possible that the stated criteria of assignment of Q material into redactional strata come not so much from the texts as from the interpretive concepts of modern New Testament scholarship? It is precisely because of ever more precise and sophisticated analysis of texts such as that by Kloppenborg that we are realizing just how diverse were the communities of Jesus' followers and their understandings of Jesus; yet we have not adjusted our conceptual apparatus to accord with that diversity. Thus it may be that we are still applying to Q material concepts which are derived from an earlier, more synthetic scholarly understanding of "early Christianity" but which may not be expressed in Q itself. An especially critical eye should be focused on scholarly concepts that have been heavily influenced by Christian theology and christology, such as "apocalyptic" or "eschatological" motifs and concepts, the *parousia*, and what are often taken as "christological titles," such as "the son of man." My argument is thus not with Kloppenborg, who is simply continuing the standard scholarly categories utilized in recent treatments of Q,[18] but with the conceptual apparatus of our field.

Both Kloppenborg and Mack have stressed that Q is far less "apocalyptic" than previously imagined. In fact the observation that "much of the specialized vocabulary of apocalypticism and even some of its central presuppositions are absent from large portions of Q"[19] does not go nearly far enough. As noted already, in assigning certain material to the judgmental stratum, Kloppenborg finds plenty of elements that have been labeled as "apocalyptic" for which he uses the stereotypical scholarly phrases.[20] But it is not at all clear to the critical eye that "the catastrophic destruction of the world" by fire or flood is visualized in 3:9, 17; 12:49; 17:29; and 17:27, or that "historical determinism" and "eschatological events" are implicit in 10:23–24.[21] There is nothing in the text of 12:54–56 itself or in the immediate or larger context of Q that suggests "signs of the end" or "the impending catastrophe."[22] 12:54–56 refers rather to a present crisis. The division of families in 12:51–53 is not an "apocalyptic *topos*" (whatever some of the handbooks may suggest), but a prophetic motif, particularly from Micah 7:6.[23] Further, the apocalyptic sense of the "nearness of the end" (*Naherwartung*) is difficult to find in Q, particularly in 17:23–37, which stresses the suddenness, not the imminence, of the judgment. Only the prophetic words of the Baptist in 3:9 imply an immediacy of judgment. Finally, it should not seem surprising that in Q there is "only passing reference to the motifs of cosmic transformation," because such motifs do not in fact occur with "high frequency" in Jewish apocalypses, especially not in those prior to

---

18. Particularly by German scholarship such as Lührmann, *Redaktion der Logienquelle*; and Schultz, *Q: Spruchquelle der Evangelisten*.

19. Kloppenborg, "Symbolic Eschatology," 292.

20. Mack, "Kingdom that Didn't Come," 613, finds an "overbearing presence" of "apocalyptic idiom" in Q2.

21. Kloppenborg, "Symbolic Eschatology," 296.

22. Kloppenborg, *Formation of Q*, 152.

23. Kloppenborg "Symbolic Eschatology," 299; *Formation of Q*, 151.

time of Q.²⁴ To state the matter more precisely, it is difficult to find much of anything in Q that is typical of Judean apocalyptic literature.

The idiom "the son of man" and "the day of the son of man" are special cases that require some critical review of both texts and scholarly concepts. "Son of man christology" and the closely related concept of the *parousia* appear to have been read into Q along with a number of "apocalyptic" elements. It is confidently asserted in a variety of contexts that "Son of Man" christology was important and perhaps even distinctive to Q and the Q community.²⁵ "'Son of Man' is the only christological title found in Q and was both fundamental to the community's confession of Jesus and the cause of its persecution."²⁶ "The Son of Man christology originated, flourished, and, for the most part, died within what can be called the 'Q Community.'"²⁷ Ironically, just when it is being recognized that there is no basis in contemporary Judean texts for the modern concept of "the apocalyptic Son of Man," something similar is still being read into Q texts. That is, it is still assumed that the phrase "the son of man" refers to a figure coming in eschatological judgment, and that Q texts think of that figure as the risen and exalted Jesus in his *parousia*. This image of Jesus returning as the eschatological judge is then also placed in the broader context of the twentieth century scholarly composite scenario replete with "the delay of the *parousia*," the "nearness of the end," and "the impending catastrophe."²⁸

There appears to be little basis in Q itself either for these generalizations regarding Q's "christology" or for there being any expectation of a *parousia* in Q. The "son of man" sayings in Q are basically of two sorts. In the one, Jesus uses the phrase to refer to himself in various connections. Whatever one's conclusion about the scholarly debate concerning whether the generic use of the phrase *bar (e)nash(a)* ("a human being" or "anyone/someone") provides a basis for a circumlocution for the speaker's self reference ("I/me"), "the son of man" would appear to be used in the latter sense in Luke 6:22; 7:34; 9:58; and 11:30. In the other

---

24. Vs. "Symbolic Eschatology," 299–300, 306.

25. Surely influential in this connection have been Tödt, *Son of Man in the Synoptic Tradition*, 232–74, esp. 269; and Hoffmann, *Studien zur Logienquelle*, 82–158.

26. Boring, *Sayings of the Risen Jesus*, 141.

27. Walker, "Son of Man"; see further the review of Q scholarship on this subject in Neirynck, "Recent Developments in the Study of Q," 69–74.

28. Kloppenborg, *Formation of Q*, esp. 152–53, 162–64.

sort, "the son of man" is used in reference to divine judgment, most often in the stereotyped phrase "the day(s) of the son of man," and is not identified with Jesus (Luke 12:8–9, 40; 17:24, 26, 30). In none of these references does the phrase "coming in the clouds" occur, so they offer no basis for finding a reference to "one like the son of man" in Dan 7:13. In Daniel 7, the "human-like" figure is interpreted to symbolize 'the people of the holy ones of the Most High," that is the people of Judea/ Israel, to whom is given the kingdom. By contrast in Q, "the son of man" in 12:8–9 is an advocate or accuser before the angels of God in the court of judgment. In 17:24, 26, 30, "the day(s) of the son of man" refers to the time of judgment; the focus is not on "the son of man" as the agent of judgment or deliverance. Similarly, "the son of man" in 12:40, standing in analogy to the uncertain time that a thief might break in, refers to the uncertain time of the judgment. Thus it would seem inappropriate to import into these Q texts the Christian theological overtones now resonant in the term *parousia* that Matthew substituted for "the days of" and "the Son of Man" as the eschatological judge.

Finally, there is no indication in Q that the one sort of 'son of man' sayings is connected in any way with the other. The key text in this respect is 11:30: if "the son of man" here had been a reference to the judgment and not a self-reference by Jesus, then it would have been better coordinated with its context (Luke 11:29–32) in which both the queen of the south and the men of Nineveh are mentioned as arising "at the judgment" as accusers. Thus it is clear in the Q texts that when Jesus is referring to himself with "the son of man" he is not referring-to the judgment, and when he uses "the son of man" in connection with the judgment, he is not referring to himself. In neither case is "the son of man" a title, much less a "christological title."

It is thus unclear how Q could be said to have either a "Son of Man christology" or an expectation of the *parousia*. Not only is there "no indication of a kerygmatic interpretation of Jesus' death in Q,"[29] but there are also "no indications that Q represented itself to its intended audience as oracles of the Exalted Lord."[30] Thus there would appear to be no basis whatever for positing the concept of "the *parousia*" in Q, let alone for believing that two whole sections of Q (12:39–59; 17:23–37) deal with it.[31]

29. Mack, "Kingdom that Didn't Come," 618.
30. Kloppenborg, *Formation of Q*, 322.
31. Ibid., 102, 150, 152, 153, 157, 163, 165.

OF TAXONOMY AND GENRE: NOT A COLLECTION OF SAYINGS BUT A SERIES OF DISCOURSES

It is also thus evident that the genre of Q cannot be established by determining the types of sayings according to the broad general categories of "sapiential" and "apocalyptic" for a several basic reasons. (a) *Very few of the sayings can be classified as "apocalyptic" according to the standard criteria of form criticism.* Clearly the term has been used loosely and the characterization of several of the Q sayings as apocalyptic has involved reading motifs from the scholarly construct of "apocalypticism" into Q (as explained just above).[32] Recognizing this Kloppenborg now agrees that the "apocalyptic" character of the supposed redactional stratum cannot be stressed.[33] With that admission, however, the dichotomy with regard to the types of sayings in supposed Q strata would seem to disappear. Admittedly, of the five supposedly "sapiential" speeches, the bulk of material in two of them (Q 10:2-16 on mission and Q 11:2-4, 9-13 on prayer) was not typically sapiential at all. And it was admitted that the material in the formative stratum is not sapiential "with respect to traditional forms of conventional wisdom," but appears "sapiential" only by comparison with the "apocalyptic" secondary layer.[34]

(b) *The categorization according to the dichotomized concepts "sapiential" and "apocalyptic" simply does not fit certain key sayings, as noted above.* That the figure Wisdom appears in an "apocalyptic" (prophetic) saying while "sapiential" sayings use "apocalyptic" language against the sages suggests that these scholarly categories do not elucidate Q's medium and message. Those same sayings indicate that there is a relationship, apparently an important and particular one, between wisdom and revelation in Q (one which cannot be captured by our scholarly dichotomy). Those Q sayings claim vindication by Wisdom for the poor, the persecuted, the babes, the prophets, to whom the kingdom has been "revealed," over against "the sages," the professionals who cultivate wisdom.

(c) *As was clearly understood in earlier form criticism, it does not take us very far to categorize sayings by purely formal features.* Analysis of the *function* of sayings in social context was integral to earlier form criti-

---

32. Similarly Collins, "Son of Man in the Sayings Source"; Jacobson, "Apocalyptic and ... Q."

33. Kloppenborg, "Formation of Q Revisited," 208.

34. Mack, "Kingdom that Didn't Come," 613.

cism. In many cases in Q, the function of a saying is not clear without reference to at least the immediate literary context.

Recognition of genre as a factor in meaning has also pointed toward the importance of both literary context and social context for understanding the sayings of Jesus. The genre of Q, however, would have to be determined from the structure and contours and function of the text as a whole and/or its component "clusters" or discourses, the combination of sayings as means of communication, rather than from the classifications of individual sayings. This also is the clear implication of Kloppenborg's "compositional" analysis of the Q speeches. Much of the scholarly analysis of Q and other sources of the sayings of Jesus has assumed, in effect, that "in the beginning was the aphorism," the separate individual saying. Indeed, to extricate the teachings of Jesus from later narrative and other literary contexts which overlaid the supposedly early form of those sayings, we have struggled precisely to isolate those nuggets of Jesus' wisdom. But not only does meaning depend upon context, suggesting that the current literary context of Jesus sayings would have to be the starting point of analysis;[35] it may well be that individual sayings were not the basic medium of communication but components of larger units which were that basic medium of communication.

In generic terms, the Synoptic Sayings Source is not a collection of sayings, but a series of discourses or speeches focused on several related topics/concerns, as I proposed in 1991, if somewhat provisionally and without fuller argument from comparative materials and social context.[36] In recent American discussion of Q it has been assigned to the broad general genre of "words of the wise," of which the *Gospel of Thomas* supposedly represents a stage in the generic development antecedent to the final form of Q. However, comparison of Q and the *Gospel of Thomas* in terms not of individual sayings but of the contours of whole documents suggests they are strikingly different. The *Gospel of Thomas* is indeed a collection of sayings, the point of which is to provide individual or coupled sayings for focused individual meditation and interpretation (stated at the very outset in logion 1; cf. 3). Q, however, is a series of discourses, each focused on a particular issue or concern of communities of a movement, although the number and shape of those

35. See further Horsley, "Q and Jesus."

36. "Q and Jesus." Further developed in Horsley with Draper, *Whoever Hears You Hears Me*.

discourses cannot always be discerned through the use made of them by Matthew and Luke.

Many of these discourses can be seen to have an internal structure as well as a focal topic or theme, and a function for a concern of a community. In some the functions are readily apparent, such as the instructions for "mission" in 9:57–62 + 10:1–16 (+ 21–24?), or the instructions on prayer in 11:2–4,9–13, or woes against the Pharisees in 11:39–52, or the exhortation on preparedness in 17:23–37. The function of others may not be all that difficult to discern. The "sermon" in 6:20–49, with its opening blessings (and "curses"), closing sanctions (6:46–49), and covenantal instruction on social-economic relations within the community (not religious teaching to individuals; 6:27–38), is evidently a paradigmatic renewal of covenant for the Q communities/movement.[37] Some of these discourses can even be seen to have a function in the "document" as a whole. For example, the covenantal discourse could be foundational for the whole (community as well as "document" itself). The exhortation on preparedness in 17:23–37 could be the sanction on all of the preceding exhortations. The preaching of John in 3:7–9, 16–17 on the crisis of impending judgment and salvation ("Spirit and fire") and Jesus' reassuring declaration in 22:28–30 on the liberation (effective justice for, not judgment) of Israel function respectively as the opening and closing of the whole series of discourses. The unifying theme of the whole document is clearly "the kingdom of God," which appears prominently at key points in most (nine) of the discourses (6:20; 7:28; 10:9,11; 11:2; 11:20; 12:31; 13:18–21; 13:28–29; 22:28–30).

Integral to appreciating the function of the series of speeches that comprise Q would be to take into account the oral communication environment in which the speeches were repeatedly performed in communities of Q people. The effects of the standard scholarly assumptions of print culture and its literary models criticized by Kelber persist in our discussions of Q and related materials.[38] We are only beginning to learn where to look for guidance in understanding the forms of oral communication. If Q is not simply a collection of sayings but a series of discourses—that is, if some internal structure can be discerned in Q—and if those discourses can be seen to have had a function in a community,

---

37. See Horsley, *Jesus and the Spiral of Violence*, 255–73; "Q and Jesus," 184–86; further developed in Horsley with Draper, *Whoever Hears You Hears Me*, chap 9.

38. Kelber, *Oral and Written Gospel*.

then it may be easier to imagine the relationship between the situation or oral communication in which the material remained alive and the formation of a document that was available for use by Matthew and Luke.[39] Other implications of Q being a series of discourses, however, should be noted. What took the form discerned through Matthew and Luke had been functioning as discourses, however they may have been related, and would presumably have been changing and developing as used in an oral communication environment. The parallel discourses in Mark to the mission speech, the exhortation to fearless persistence under repression, and the Beelzebul controversy, along with several shorter Markan parallels, provide a few windows onto such uses and parallel or divergent development of discourses. That means, however, that for most of the discourses we have little "control" on the use of the material prior to Q. But behind Q stands a well-rehearsed and frequently performed standard repertoire of the principal spokespersons of a movement, of which we have no "transcript" other than the speech material parallel in Matthew and Luke.

THE PROPHETIC ORIENTATION OF Q— IN COMPARISON WITH SAPIENTIAL AND APOCALYPTIC

If we consider the function along with the form of sayings and discourses and consider the substantive message as well as the medium of the document, the speeches in Q have prophetic characteristics rather than sapiential or apocalyptic. If function is taken into account along with form, most of the Q discourses could be described as prophetic. This includes not just material in the supposedly secondary stratum, much of which is clearly prophetic (and not apocalyptic) in form and substance, but much of the material assigned to the "sapiential" layer. The "beatitudes" that open the covenant renewal "sermon" are not sapiential makarisms, but prophetic declarations of blessings (and woes; 6:20–26). In this and other speeches, Q's "Jesus" speaks in the voice of a prophet (like Moses), not as a scribal teacher of wisdom. The admonitions that follow the prophetic declarations of blessing ("love your enemies, . . . do good and lend, etc.") are renewed Mosaic covenantal demands, not instructional advice from a parental teacher to a scribal protégé, as prominent in

---

39. See further Horsley with Draper, *Whoever Hears You Hears Me*.

Sirach and Proverbs 1–9. The covenantal speech in Q 6:20–49 addresses communities about social-economic interaction, as do the prophets, not individual students, as in instructional wisdom. The introduction to the mission discourse alludes to Elijah's call of Elisha, whereupon the speech commissions a prophet's protégés to extend his mission, as Elisha had Elijah's.

Another prominent prophetic feature of Q is the portrayal of Jesus, John, and even the Q people themselves as prophets and/or in the great line of the prophets. Again, this is not simply in the clusters assigned to the supposed redactional stratum (7:18–35; 11:20; 11:29–30; 11:39–52; 12:49?, 51–53; 13:34–35), but in the so-called "sapiential" speeches as well, with the prophetic announcement of renewed covenantal teaching and the introduction of the mission discourse with allusion to Elijah's commissioning of Elisha (6:20–23, 27–49; 9:57–62 + 10:2–16).

Moreover, the general eschatological orientation of Q, while it cannot be characterized as "apocalyptic," is associated with the prophetic forms, features, and roles in the discourses. This can be seen by comparison with the general eschatology of Daniel. While the eschatology of Q and Daniel may seem similar insofar as both are clearly collective-historical, in contrast to the individual-immortality of Wisdom of Solomon, they display significant differences. Daniel presents revelations about the future judgment of foreign imperial oppressors, the future restoration of Israel, and (briefly) the future vindication of the martyred wise ones. Q, on the other hand, presents a prophetic oracle and lament of judgment against the Jerusalem rulers and their scribal representatives, as well as prophetic speeches about the renewal of Israel newly underway, and statements of assurance about the vindication of martyred prophets (including John and Jesus). Whereas in Daniel the judgment of rulers and restoration of the people will be in the not too distant future, in Q the renewal of Israel has already begun, while the sanctioning judgment will be utterly unexpected in the future (see esp. Q 6:20–21; 7:18–35; 10:1–16; 11:14–22; 11:39–52; 13:28–29,34–35; 14:16–24; 22:28–30).

SOCIAL CONTEXT AND SOCIAL RELATIONS INDICATED IN Q

Interpreters of Q have argued that the "sapiential" stratum taught a "radical ethic and lifestyle," "visible and overt social radicalism," a "mildly counturcultural lifestyle," a "countercultural and inversionary gospel," or a "mildly subversive" lifestyle.[40] Judging from available instructional literature in general and Judean wisdom texts in particular, it is difficult to imagine that any sapiential literature would espouse "visible and overt social radicalism." Similarly, based on what we know of retainers in general and of scribes, Pharisees, and other retainers in the Judean temple-state in particular, it is difficult to believe that such people who were so dependent on the rulers could really "imagine a radical alternative to the present system." Even the scribal-priestly Qumran community that was so "radically" alienated from the incumbent Judean high priestly aristocracy apparently imagined their own exodus to the wilderness and new covenant community as a temporary situation, evidently until they could take control of the temple-state themselves. Not the instructional speeches in Sirach but the Animal Vision of the "Enoch" scribes envisaged a restored "house of God" without its "tower," that is the restored people without a temple-state. In the cities of the Roman empire, one might use the term "countercultural" to describe the Cynics, vagabonds who dropped out of the system they were criticizing, but generated no vision of an alternative society.

The principal problem with the vague characterizations of the teaching of the "sapiential" layer of Q as "countercultural" or "mildly subversive," however, is that we must know more precisely "counter" to which culture (courtly, scribal, or village) or "subversive" of which social forms (control by the Tetrarchal regime of Antipas or the temple regime of the high priests, or local village customs and interfamilial relations. Clearly we need a more concrete and precise sense of the historical social situation in Roman Palestine than we have heretofore been working with in New Testament studies. Whether or not we are aware of it, of course, we are all working with some image or another of ancient social realities, even when we are only engaged in literary analysis. Language is by definition social and communicative, and both we and the texts we are interpreting presuppose some particular network of social relations. Thus it makes sense, when pursuing historical analysis and interpretation, to begin with a critically reconstructed view of the historical situation.[41]

---

40. Kloppenborg, *Formation of Q*, 240; Kloppenborg, "Social History in Q," 11, 14, 15; Mack, "Kingdom that Didn't Come," 611, 612, 613, 614, 624.

41. Fuller sketch of the historical context of Jesus and the Gospel tradition in

Most important in this regard surely is to realize that "society" is a modern abstraction. The concept may even be of questionable application to ancient social realities. Some social scientists argue that any traditional "bureaucratic empire" consisted of several different societies, the rulers being ethnically and culturally different from most of the ruled peoples, who were usually diverse. Obviously that applies to the Roman empire as a whole. But even if we think about such a small area as Palestine, it is significant to remember that whatever common heritage the Galileans may have shared with the ruling high priestly families and the temple apparatus in Jerusalem, Galilee had been brought under Jerusalem rule little more than a century before Jesus by the Hasmonean High Priests. The inherent historical and structural conflict was manifested periodically in concrete events. Large numbers of Galileans resisted the imposition of Herodian rule and even larger numbers apparently burst out in rebellion when Herod died. During the lifetime of Jesus the city of Sepphoris was rebuilt as a Hellenistic city and the city of Tiberias was founded by Herod Antipas as his new capital from which men with Roman or Hellenistic names governed his Tetrarchy. During the great revolt of 66–70 CE against Roman, Herodian, and Jerusalem high priestly rule a generation after Jesus' death, the Galilean country people were eager to attack the pro-Roman Sepphoris and Agrippa II's officials in Tiberias.

Whatever the level of tension or hostility from time to time, Roman Palestine was divided between the ruling cities such as Jerusalem and Sepphoris or Tiberias, on the one hand, and numerous villages and towns where the vast majority of people lived, on the other. As long as the people paid their tithes and other dues to the Temple and priesthood, their taxes to Herod or Antipas, and the tribute demanded by Rome, the villages and towns were left relatively alone as semi-independent communities. Such local communities had forms of self-government such as local assemblies and groups of elders. Indeed, what the Gospel of Mark refers to as "synagogues" appear to be just such local assemblies.

It is not difficult to imagine what the role of the "scribes and Pharisees" was in this situation on the basis of comparative sociological studies of such traditional agrarian societies. They were the "retainers" of the rulers who carried out functions such as scholars, teachers,

---

Horsley, *Sociology and the Jesus Movement*, chaps. 4–5. See now the more extensive discussion in Horsley, *Galilee*.

lawyers.[42] They were not "religious sects," on the analogy of the "free churches" in modern European history, but the guardians, interpreters, and administrators of the Torah as the "constitution" and "law book" of the temple-state, in the service of the priestly aristocracy. Although non-literate, villagers were by no means ignorant of Israelite traditions. They cultivated what anthropologists have called their own "little tradition" in oral form that usually parallels and interacts in some degree with the "great" or "official tradition" maintained in written form by the scribes, which helped provide legitimation of the temple-state and its taxation and control of the people.

Recognition of this political-economic-religious structure in Roman Palestine and its culture(s) means that we can no longer assume a monolithic entity such as "Judaism" or "Jewish society," over against which some people could be "countercultural"/"radical" or "resist conventional wisdom" or even advocate some "non-societal ethos." In ancient history the only people who were literate and left literary remains were in the tiny scribal stratum. It is thus not warranted to generalize about either the ordinary people or the ruling families on the basis of the literary expression of the literate, who had their own particular roles, interests, and views within a larger situation that often involved considerable tension or conflict. The historical social-cultural situation was further complicated, moreover, by the recent establishment in lower Galilee of two urban centers of Hellenistic-Roman culture. Thus we must seek to establish more precisely in relation to whom or what the Q material might have been "radical" or "mildly subversive."

A number of characterizations have been made about the social ethos of the Q people that have little basis in Q material. The most influential of these is surely that the sayings tradition was carried by and articulated an ethos of itinerant charismatics. Moreover, the most influential statement of that hypothesis, that of Theissen, is probably the least substantiated from the texts.[43] A certain literalism prevents him from appreciating the subtlety or nuances of some sayings, and he repeatedly applies only to his wandering charismatics a number of sayings that clearly were addressed to a broader audience (e.g., Luke 12:22–32). A number of passages he simply misconstrues. The only two texts that re-

---

42. See Saldarini, *Pharisees, Scribes*.

43. See further the extensive and detailed critique of Theissen's sociological reconstruction in Horsley, *Sociology and the Jesus Movement*, chaps. 1–3.

ally support his contentions are "mission" passages, Luke 10:4 and Mark 1:16, 20—to which he appeals repeatedly for successive "analytical conclusions" regarding "homelessness," "lack of family," and "lack of possessions." Itinerants there may well have been, but there is certainly little or no evidence that the Jesus movement consisted primarily of them. Even Theissen himself had to make clear that there were communities of "supporters," in a nod to the importance of the concrete forms of life that even highly abstract sociology must recognize. It is perhaps a telling commentary on the inadequacy of the itinerancy hypothesis that both Kloppenborg and Mack question it when they move into discussion of social context.[44]

It may be a carry-over from the view that Q, understood as a Sayings Source, was linked particularly with itinerants that it is still argued that Q placed a high "religious and symbolic value" on poverty, and that this poverty was voluntary.[45] The vast majority of people in any traditional agrarian society, of course, were farmers or fishers who lived near the subsistence level. That is, most of them would have been poor and many of them would have been indebted or even dispossessed. So there are very few candidates in such a historical situation who would have responded to some ideal of voluntary poverty. Moreover, the texts usually cited to attest that Q's Jesus advocated this ideal indicate no such thing. Luke 12:13–14 (which is questionably part of Q in the first place) and 16:13 have nothing to do with poverty, let alone voluntary poverty, and Luke 12:33 articulates a typically Lucan theme not present in the Matthean parallel, which is surely closer to Q. The "poor" who are pronounced blessed in 6:20b are parallel to the hungry and mournful in the other beatitudes, and such terms indicate the general concrete condition of the people to whom the kingdom, including, finally, enough to eat (in the Lord's Prayer), is being offered. Q 11:3, 9–13, and 12:22b-31 do not say that "the necessities of life" should "be left to divine care." Rather 11:3, 9–13 articulate a petition for sufficient food (and with forgiveness of debts!) along with assurance that the Father will surely respond to such requests. Q 12:22–31 exhorts people not to be anxious about food and clothing, about which they are apparently genuinely concerned and which they will surely receive if they single-mindedly "seek first the kingdom." There appears to be no saying in Q that suggests poverty as an

---

44. Kloppenborg, "Social History"; and Mack, "Kingdom that Didn't Come."
45. Kloppenborg, *Formation of Q*, 240–41.

ideal. And there is similarly no saying that suggests voluntary poverty, unless it would be 10:4 taken utterly out of the context of the mission discourse. But 10:2–16 is dedicated mission instruction, the point of the saying is not an ideal of voluntary poverty, but how the envoys of the movement are to proceed on their mission in which they would be fed and housed by receptive households.

Yet another carry-over from the image of the Q people as itinerants is the sense that discipleship for Q involved a radical "separation from family and rejection of the norms of macro-society."[46] But this requires reading Luke 9:59–60, 61–62, and 14:26 more or less literally, when they are surely intended as hyperbole to convey the seriousness of the commitment required.

Instead of pursuing such aspects of the hypothetical *ethos* of the Q people, it may take us further to examine the social relations that are indicated in Q material. As noted, Q speeches give no indication of rejecting Israel in general. But two prophecies in Q in particular pronounce condemnation of the Jerusalem rulers and the series of woes in Q indict and pronounce sentence on the scribes and Pharisees for their role in the oppression of the people. The prophetic lament in 13:34–35a in effect pronounces judgment against the Jerusalem ruling house, the high priestly rulers based in the Temple, precisely because it has rejected the prophets and now Jesus, who climaxed the historical series of prophets (e.g., Luke 3:16–17; 7:24–28). The priestly aristocracy, who take pride in their high lineage, may be the ones implicated also in two other sharply judgmental passages, against presuming on one's position of privilege as "children of Abraham" or "sons of the kingdom," Luke 3:7–9; 13:28–29.

The woes against the scribes and Pharisees in 11:39–52 deliver sharp indictments for their role in economic exploitation of the people. The standard assumption in Christian biblical studies of "Judaism" as a religion focused or obsessed with legalism and ritual, of which the Pharisees were the leading figures, led to the reading of these woes as criticism of the Pharisees for their obsession with the Law, especially the purity codes. Once we recognize that the religious and political-economic aspects of life were inseparable in antiquity and that the scribes/lawyers and Pharisees were retainers in service of the Judean temple-state, we can dispense with the old theologically determined picture of the Pharisees as leaders of a legalistic "Judaism."

46. Ibid., 241.

Some of the woes do indeed mock the Pharisees rhetorically for their obsession with purity and scrupulous tithing (11:39–40, 42).

Underneath the rhetorical mocking, however, the woes indict the scribes and Pharisees for one after another of their practices as representatives of the temple-state. The woe in Matt 23:25–26/Luke 11:39–40 mocks their concerns about ritual cleanliness, but the point is condemnation of their "extortion and rapacity"—which their concerns for cleanliness apparently veils or distracts attention from. Tithes, in 11:42, were hardly simply a matter of ceremonial law, but taxes. The indictment that the Pharisees were concerned even about the minor crops such as mint and herbs serves to indicate how rigorous they were about the more substantive products such as grain. And if the Pharisees, as representatives of Jerusalem, were still insisting on payment of tithes in addition to the taxes that Galilean peasants were paying to Antipas or Agrippa and the tribute they were rending to Caesar, they were indeed neglecting justice and compassion! The "heavy burdens" in 11:46/Matt 23:4, are surely not the multiplication of rules to keep by scribal interpretation, but the burdens of tithing and other dues—with the reference to not moving them with their finger probably an allusion to how such retainers or lawyers responsible for application of the Torah could help alleviate the burden through their scribal role, if only they would.

As for the tombs of the prophets, 11:47–48, the custodians of such memorials to dissident figures of a previous age, who had been taken up into the "great tradition," would have been precisely those whose responsibility it was to cultivate and apply that tradition. In the "popular tradition," however, those same prophets were surely remembered as sharp critics of power and privilege. The indictment in 11:43 might seem mild by comparison with the others. But for the people whose shoulders perpetually bore the "heavy burdens" it would have been particularly galling to be expected to honor and defer to the Pharisees and other retainers who helped keep those burdens squarely in place. The final woe, 11:52, is the most comprehensive regarding the role of the lawyers, scribes, or Pharisees. Shutting "the kingdom of heaven" (Matt 23:13) and taking away "the key of knowledge" are parallel or even synonymous expressions. As in key biblical passages, "knowledge" must be "covenant keeping" (see, e.g., Isa 1:2–3), the possibility of which is now opened with the advent of the kingdom. But these whose role it is supposedly to foster and interpret that covenantal Torah are standing in the way, barring entrance into the kingdom. Sharpened in judgmental attack by the insertion of 11:49–51, all of these sayings in 11:39–52 pronounce woes on Pharisees or lawyers because of some way in which they are contributing to the exploitation of the people and/or are helping legitimate the established order, including their own positions of privilege.

Corresponding to the condemnation of the Jerusalem ruling house and its representatives, the Q speeches and Q people seem unconcerned about either priestly ritual action or the official Torah of the temple-state. Q gives no attention to priestly (ritual or purification) activities. Similarly, the Torah does not appear to function at all as sacred writ or law. Rather aspects of traditional Mosaic covenantal teaching, probably derived from popular Israelite tradition, can be discerned behind the renewed covenantal principles in 6:27–35. The only scriptural "quotation" is from Mal 3:1 in the attempt to clarify the prophetic role of John in Q/Luke 7:27. Q/Luke 7:22 alludes to the tradition behind prophetic passages such as Isa 35:5–6 and 61:1, but is not a "quotation" of either of those Isaiah passages. Such allusions, along with all of the references to the persons of or events associated with Abraham, Isaac, Jacob, the prophets, Solomon, Noah, Jonah and the Ninevites, Lot, the queen of the south, appear to come out of common popular tradition and not learned interpretation of scripture.

However, as indicated by the abundant allusions to figures and events in Israelite historical tradition, particularly as groundings for responses to or rejection of Jesus, the Q people identify with and see themselves as the continuation, indeed the fulfillment of the hopes, of Israel. "Many prophets and kings desired to see what you see..." (10:24). "Israel" is being restored according to its "twelve tribes," with the disciples in the role of "liberating/establishing justice for" the people (Matt 19:28 / Luke 22:28–30). The "Israel" that is being renewed under the coming or presence of "the kingdom of God" is not concerned about maintaining boundaries over against other peoples, but is open to them, on the one hand. On the other hand, the "Israel" of the Q people is defined over against Jerusalem and the representatives of the temple-state and its official traditions. Participation in the renewed Israel is based not on one's proper lineage as children of Abraham but on repentance and action according to the teachings of Jesus (3:7–9; 6:46–49; etc.). In particular the Q people understand John and Jesus as the climactic prophets in the long line of the prophets who spoke against and were killed by the ruling institutions and their representatives (7:18–35; 11:47–51; 13:34–35).

Judging from certain Q material addressed to the in-group, the social location or setting in which the renewal of the people/Israel was taking place appears to have been local communities, villages and towns. It is assumed that the hearers of the sayings are involved in families and village communities, with neighbors, children, and marriages on which there are pressures (11:9–13; 14:26; 16:18). They are also acquainted with very large households, with several servants and run by a steward (Luke 12:35–38, 42–46); but they themselves do not appear to be members of or servants in such households. The most direct instructions in Q, however, concern local social-economic relationships among individuals or ordinary households, such as periodic mutual borrowing and assistance, the conflicts that could emerge from one person being indebted to another, the importance of mutual aid despite reluctance and tensions, and the mitigation and resolution of tensions and conflicts (6:27–31, 37–38, 41–42; 17:1–2, 3–4).

The difference between the Q speeches' direct engagement with the difficult circumstances of the people in village communities and the more detached reflection of sapiential instruction comes to the fore in their respective treatment of the same covenantal commands to give loans to the needy. This is clearly evident from a comparison of sapiential instruction on covenantal commands in the discourse in Sir 29:1–13 with the prophetic renewal of covenantal commands in Q 6:20–49, especially 6:27–36. The respective discourses also display the difference between sapiential instruction on covenantal commands and Q's prophetic renewal of covenantal commands. At the outset Sir 29:1–13 connects mercy closely with the exhortation to lend, just as Q 6:27–36 uses the command to be merciful in imitation of God's mercy as the clinching command. The stance of the sapiential teaching, however, is somewhat detached from and reflective about the concrete situation of the needy, and the motives mentioned are mainly those of obligation to the commandments (in general/ the abstract) and prudential self-interest ("profit") in relation to the Most High, not concern for the needy themselves. In addition to the general opening statement, the reflective reservations (complaints!) about the ungrateful "many" reneging on their loans (29:4–7) have the effect or undermining the exhortation to "lend to your neighbor" (29:2—a standard traditional covenantal exhortation;

cf. Deut 15:7–8; and without interest, Exod 22:25–27). "Nevertheless," urges the learned scribe, with a touch of *noblesse oblige*, "be patient with someone in humble circumstances, . . . help the poor for the commandment's sake" (29:8–11). The social location of the wise/scribes was a step above that of immediate involvement in the local social-economic push-and-shove of hungry and mutually indebted villagers (Q 11:2–4) who were at each others' throats in their desperate circumstances. And Jesus ben Sira's sapiential discourse offers nothing comparable to the opening declaration of blessings that Jesus bar Maryam pronounced as the basis on which the quarreling villagers could renew their commitments to covenantal cooperation and mutual assistance (6:20–26).

COMMUNITIES, LEADERSHIP, AND COMPOSITION

Biblical studies, like other modern western academic fields, has developed on the assumptions and approaches not just of literate culture but specifically of print culture. Even more than other academic fields, because focused on Scripture, the *written* text whose very words are sacred and authoritative (the word of God), the text that is "established" on the printed page, Biblical studies is deeply embedded in and committed to the assumptions of print culture.

It is understandable, therefore, that biblical scholars project concepts from modern print-culture onto ancient communication and cultural practices. Even though Robinson allowed that the genre "words of the wise" functioned in orally performed texts as well as written texts, Koester and Kloppenborg assumed and discussed (the formative layer of) Q as a text composed in writing. Also following the modern western cultural assumptions according to which Biblical studies has developed, they understood the composition of Q as carried out by a literate (scribal) "author" or "authors." Starting with the conclusion that the determinative genre of the formative "sapiential" layer of Q was "words of the wise," more specifically this genre known from Jewish and other instructional texts, it seemed clear that some scribal authors "selected a relatively learned and characteristically scribal genre by which to convey sayings of Jesus."[47] And it follows that "to account for the origin and transmission of the Q instructions" one would look not to non-literate

---

47. Kloppenborg, "Social Setting," 85.

peasants but to a group of "'petit bourgeois' in the lower administrative sector of the cities and villages" of Galilee and Syria.

After the analyses in the preceding discussions, however, it should be clear that these assumptions and this approach are problematic. As Kloppenborg has stated, much of the material in the supposedly "sapiential" clusters of Q is not typical of instructional wisdom and does not exhibit a high level of self-conscious and studied composition. As Robinson indicated, the "origin and transmission" of Jesus sayings, as of other "words of the wise" (or "words of the prophets"), was not necessarily through writing. Even today people do not need writing to remember and transmit proverbs, maxims, aphorisms. People do not need writing to know and recite, for example, the Lord's Prayer or stanzas of poetry or songs. Although interpreters of Q seldom notice, most of the speeches in Q, which are mostly short, are in poetic form, even in Greek, hence easily memorable and, if the authoritative words of a revered teacher or prophet, important to recite regularly. Judging from the short poetic instructional speeches that comprise much of the book of Sirach, it seems likely that those speeches were originally delivered orally by a revered learned scribe to his student protégés. Moreover, we have no references in sources for Syria-Palestine of "village scribes"—only Josephus' account of Herod's two younger sons of caustic comment that they would make two of their half-brothers into "village scribes" (the lowest or the low local administrators of the state in Egypt), a sarcastic allusion to the elaborate Hellenistic education they had received (*War* 1.479; *Ant.* 16.203). The various "elders, heads-of-assemblies, collectors, servants, etc." mentioned in late inscriptions in Syrian villages and Jewish rabbinic texts are references to local village officers, not (supposedly literate) lower level state administrators in cities or villages. References to "village scribes" in papyri from Egypt suggest that they barely possessed the "craft literacy" to record local payment of taxes and had learned no "instructional wisdom," much less the ability to compose instructional speeches, whether orally or in writing.[48] In most areas of the Roman empire, however, rulers and other wealthy and powerful figures in the cities were not involved in "administering" the agrarians resident in villages except for the collection of taxes and rents. Otherwise many village communities were more or less self-governing through their local assemblies ("synagogues") and their elders and other leaders.

48. Youtie, "*Aggramatos*"; "*Hypografeus*."

Our investigation of the form and content of the speeches in Q, moreover, has shown that the dichotomy of modern scholarly categories "sapiential" and "apocalyptic" do not fit. The speeches are those of a prophet, in the line of Israel's prophets, addressing communities of ordinary people living evidently in villages. The prominence of agrarian images and concerns suggests that the material originated from and was addressed to villagers. And communication was oral in village communities. The assumption of all the work done in form criticism of the Synoptic tradition was that Jesus materials in various forms were cultivated orally and that the stories and short combinations of sayings were not just transmitted but had functions in communities of Jesus' followers. This is just what we noticed about the speeches that comprise Q. These are short poetic discourses about some issue or concern of a community that were easily memorable and repeatable. As indicated by several of the speeches that have parallels in Mark, such as the Beelzebul discourse, the mission speech, the speech about persistence in the face of arrest and trial, and even the longer covenant renewal speech. Some of the same concerns were being addressed by parallel speeches in the communities of different but parallel Jesus movements. Some of these topics or concerns were traditional in Israelite tradition. Prophets spoke in such forms as laments or a series of woes that combined indictments and declaration of sentence. The Mosaic covenant and covenant renewal had distinctive forms that persisted over centuries (Exodus 20; Joshua 24; 1QS; Matthew 5–7; Q/Luke 6:20–49). It seems necessary, for understanding the composition of the speeches in Q, to question the applicability of the modern print-cultural concept of author. In the composition, or perhaps rather the composition-in-performance of the speeches in Q—in the shaping and reshaping of speeches—there may never have been any conscious, "authorial" decision about literary genre in a formal sense. The forms appropriate to the topic or issue were given in the Israelite tradition that was shared by Jesus, his followers, and those who performed Jesus-speeches in communities of his followers.

Thus we are probably not looking for a number of "relatively learned and scribal" people who could possibly have comprised the community that supposedly comes to expression in Q as, supposedly, a "relatively learned and scribal genre." Rather, we should be considering the likelihood that Jesus movements developed their own leadership, just as other popular movements did, and that some of those leaders were spokespersons who developed and regularly performed the speeches of Jesus on issues of concern to their communities. The construction of "Judaism" standard in the field focuses heavily on the "sects" or what Josephus calls the "philosophies," who were among the literate cultural elite of retainers of the temple-state, albeit some of them dissidents. In our study of "early Christianity," moreover, we give much attention to Saul/Paul, who also had education of some sort (even if not elite Hellenistic), who pushed his way into the leadership of a movement among ordinary people. The accounts of Josephus, however, tell of many popular movements that generated their own leadership. Among them were a shepherd and his brothers, the son of a brigand chieftain, a former royal servant, "a crude peasant." There is no reason why other figures, like John the Baptist, Jesus of Nazareth, Simon and Andrew, Mary Magdalene, but never so important or well-known, could not have developed, composed, and performed the speeches of Q. Even after they may have been written down by some scribe, they would still have been performed orally. We know of them, of course, only because *both* the Gospel of Matthew and the Gospel of Luke incorporated some or much of them into the frame of their narrative Gospels.

9

Sayings of the Sages or Speeches of the Prophets

Reflections on the Genre of Q

IN INFLUENTIAL ARTICLES WRITTEN during the 1960s Helmut Koester argued that the *Gospel of Thomas* is a development from an early stage of a "wisdom gospel,"[1] in the genre of *logoi sophōn*, as expounded by his friend James M. Robinson.[2] The gnostic proclivities of the genre, he argued, were blocked by the inclusion of the apocalyptic Son of Man sayings in Q. The "wisdom gospel" can thus be seen as a secondary redaction of an older collection of wisdom sayings. This suggestion of Koester became the crucial step leading to the distinction of a formative, "sapiential" stratum from a redactional, "apocalyptic" layer in Q by John Kloppenborg.[3]

THE QUESTION OF APOCALYPTIC AND SAPIENTIAL STRATA IN Q

Kloppenborg's imaginative reconstruction of the formation of Q, while very suggestive with regard to the composition of Q in "clusters of sayings" or discourses (speeches) of various lengths, seems questionable in its hypothesis of a formative "sapiential" layer and a secondary "apocalyptic" or judgmental layer.[4] The discernment of these two strata may

---

1. Koester, "GNOMAI DIAPHOROI."
2. Robinson, "LOGOI SOPHŌN."
3. Kloppenborg, *The Formation of Q*, 32–33.
4. Ibid. The following analysis is heavily dependent on the work of Kloppenborg.

be rooted more in the conceptual apparatus of modern New Testament scholarship than in the text of Q.[5] Ironically, it is precisely the sophisticated analyses of texts like those by Koester and Kloppenborg that make it possible—and necessary—to call into question the very conceptual apparatus with which we have been working.

Kloppenborg assigns five complexes of sayings in Q (3:7-9, 16-17; 7:1-10, 18-35; 11:14-52; 12:39-59; 17:23-37) to a secondary redaction on the basis of three common features discerned in those complexes—projected audience, form, and motifs. But those common features are not consistently present in the five complexes of sayings. First, only one of the five clusters of sayings, Luke 11:14-26, 29-32, 39-52, appears to be clearly directed at the "out-group" of "this γενεά," or impenitent opponents, as the ostensive or implied audience. All or most of the sets of sayings in the other four complexes are addressed directly to the Q people themselves. Moreover, there is no reason internal to the sayings in these complexes to think that ταύτη γενεά (usually translated "this generation") refers to "Israel" as opposed to "Gentiles," no indication of a mission to Gentiles, and no indication outside of Luke 7:1-9 of Gentile faith—hence, little evidence that "Gentile faith" is a significant theme, let alone that it functions as an *Unheilszeichen* for Israel.[6] Second, while many of the sayings in these complexes are clearly prophetic, it is difficult to find many that are arguably "apocalyptic words." Third, it is difficult to find in these five complexes motifs that could be identified as apocalyptic. Kloppenborg and Burton Mack have both pointed out that Q is much less apocalyptic than previously imagined.[7] But we can press

---

He has been a generous and patient mentor in my attempt to enter the complex world of Q scholarship. It seems only fair that, if I am to question his hypothesis regarding the stratigraphy of Q, I should suggest some alternative hypothesis regarding the development, composition, and function of the document.

5. These points, among others, were more fully laid out in chap. 8, and were further developed in Horsley, "Q and Jesus"; and Horsley with Draper, *Whoever Hears You Hears Me*, chap. 4.

6. Given that Koester, Kloppenborg and others place so much weight on (their reading of) *taute genea*, it should be noted that "this generation" may not even be an appropriate translation. Immediate literary context is surely the key. Thus, in reference to the scribes/lawyers and Pharisees, "this kind/type/group" may be the more appropriate translation in Luke 11:49-51 (and probably in 11:29-31 in the same "complex" of sayings), as can be seen from the comparison with Mark 9:19, where *genea* refers to the disciples, or Mark 8:12, where it refers to the Pharisees, in contrast to Mark 8:38 and 13:30, where the reference is something broader, like "this generation" or "era."

7. Kloppenborg, "Symbolic Eschatology and the Apocalypticism of Q"; Mack, "Kingdom That Didn't Come," for example, 614.

that critical realization far more sharply: there are virtually no apocalyptic motifs in the supposedly apocalyptic stratum of Q. For example, Luke 12:54–56 does not suggest "signs of the end" or "the impending catastrophe" but refers to a present crisis, and the division of families in 12:51–53 would be more appropriately called a prophetic, not an apocalyptic, motif (see Mic 7:6). It is difficult to find "the catastrophic destruction of the world" by fire or flood in Luke 3:9, 17; 12:49; 17:27, 29. Luke 12:40, 42–46 and 17:23–37 indicate the suddenness of judgment, but hardly an apocalyptic *Naherwartung*.[8]

Indeed, by strict analysis, only two sets of sayings, both in the same complex (11:29–32 and 11:49–51), actually contain the three common features used as criteria for differentiating the supposedly secondary "apocalyptic" or "judgmental" layer, and even then not quite in the distinctive ways Kloppenborg has characterized them. That is, they are prophetic (but not apocalyptic) sayings in form; they contain the motif of rejection of Jesus' preaching as a basis for condemnation (but no apocalyptic traits); and they also focus on "this generation" (but not "Israel") as the projected audience (in fact six of the seven occurrences of "this generation" occur in these two brief passages!). This would not appear to be a sufficient basis for assigning five whole clusters of sayings to a particular redactional stratum.

There are similar difficulties with the purported common features of the supposedly formative "sapiential" stratum.[9] First, this stratum cannot be differentiated from the judgmental stratum on the basis of "implied audience" since: (a) (as just noted) most of the latter is also addressed directly to the members of the community; and (b) at least two clusters in the "formative" stratum include material ostensibly directed at outsiders, which must then be dismissed as later redactional insertions (e.g., Luke 10:13–15; 13:28–30, 34–35; 14:16–24). But that same argument could be made for materials in the supposedly secondary clusters (e.g., that Luke 7:31–35, ostensibly directed at outsiders, is a redactional addition to 7:18–28, which is addressed directly to the community). Second, the argument from characteristic forms is particularly weak. In order to purify the stratum it must be purged of prophetic sayings,

---

8. Pace Kloppenborg, *Formation of Q*, e.g., 151–52; "Symbolic Eschatology," 296, 299–300, 308.

9. The following observations respond to Kloppenborg's summary in *Formation of Q*, 238–43.

which are dismissed as later insertions. But even the material left is not particularly sapiential "with respect to traditional forms of conventional wisdom," and appears "sapiential" only by comparison with materials in the "apocalyptic" secondary stratum.[10] Since the supposedly secondary layer is not particularly apocalyptic, this ostensible distinction between the strata would appear to collapse. And since the supposedly formative layer contains "some rather specialized instructions which go beyond what is usually understood as sapiential admonitions," such as sayings regarding mission, discipleship, and the Holy Spirit,[11] there appears even less basis for its characterization as distinctively and consistently "sapiential." Third, the motifs claimed as characteristic for the supposedly formative stratum do not run through all of the component "clusters," and it is questionable whether the texts cited actually illustrate the motifs listed. Fourth, the references provided as evidence for characteristic structural features throughout this stratum are not convincing, in some cases (12:13–14; 12:33a) not even clearly part of Q.

Thus it appears, upon closer examination, that the criteria used to differentiate the supposedly secondary, apocalyptic stratum from the supposedly formative, sapiential stratum in Q—that is, the different sets of common features in each stratum—are either difficult to find in the actual Q clusters or are not distinctive to one stratum or the other.

These problems of characterizing and distinguishing strata are compounded by generic considerations. Kloppenborg claims that "the formative stratum has the strongest generic contacts with the genre of 'instruction.'"[12] Yet the "two notable departures from the typical form of instruction" would appear to be decisive. In contrast to the instructional genre, the "sapiential" speeches in Q do not take the form of parental instruction. Even more important, "in contrast to the generally conservative comportment of the [scribal] instruction, Q presents an ethic of radical discipleship which reverses many of the conventions which allow a society to operate. . . ."[13] The explanation? "Q has moved towards the form of gnomologium." And "although Q infuses the form with new content, and although it shifts from a presupposition of this-worldly order to eschatological order, the basic hermeneutic of the instruction

---

10. Mack, "Kingdom That Didn't Come," 613.
11. Kloppenborg, *Formation of Q*, 239–40.
12. Ibid., 317.
13. Ibid., 318–19.

is preserved."[14] Yet Kloppenborg himself, besides drawing attention explicitly to how different Q's hermeneutic is from that of "instructional" literature, has set up our discernment that Q's hermeneutic matches none of the three hermeneutical modes of gnomological literature.[15] That of "penetration and research" surely fits the *Gospel of Thomas*, but not Q. "Fittingness" fits Q even less. Kloppenborg seems to be suggesting that the supposedly formative sapiential speeches of Q presuppose the gnomological hermeneutic of "obedience and assimilation." But whereas such gnomologia require study, reflection, and interpretation toward the attainment of a perfect and untroubled condition of the soul (again the *Gospel of Thomas* might fit!), Q requires obedience in the sense of response to a new social order of troubled social interaction and conflict ("love your enemies"; being sent out "as sheep in the midst of wolves"; "Do not fear those who (only) kill the body") in an ethos concerned about the basic human necessities of food and shelter (see Luke 6:20–21; 6:27–36; 10:5–8; Q/Matt 6:11–12; Luke 12:22–31). The new wine of the kingdom would appear to have burst the old wineskins of instruction and gnomologia. The hermeneutic of the formative layer of Q, some of which is not sapiential instruction anyhow, is simply not that of an assimilation of a wisdom ethos—not in 6:20–49, concerned with community interaction; nor in 10:1–16, concerned with mission; nor in 11:2–4, 9–13, concerned with prayer; nor in 12:2–12, concerned with struggle; nor in 12:22–31, concerned with anxiety.

If, therefore, the "apocalyptic" stratum of Q is not particularly apocalyptic in form or motif, and the "sapiential" layer is not particularly sapiential in substance or hermeneutic, perhaps another look at the formation and genre of Q would be in order.

CHARACTERISTICS OF Q COMPLEXES

Kloppenborg and others have relied on Koester's analysis of the *Gospel of Thomas* as the basis for the claim that "as far as Gattungsgeschichte is concerned, the *Gospel Thomas* reflects a stage antecedent to the final form of Q."[16] With that claim as an operative assumption, the first step

---

14. Ibid., 319, 321.
15. Ibid., 301–6.
16. Ibid., 33.

would appear to be a critical review of the characteristics of the *Gospel of Thomas* and the tradition behind it.

Although he accepted Robinson's view that both the *Gospel of Thomas* and Q belong to the genre of *logoi sophōn*,[17] Koester also drew attention to the prominence of prophetic and apocalyptic sayings in *Gospel of Thomas*.[18] Indeed, the materials that Koester classified as prophetic materials in *Gospel of Thomas*, including the "kingdom" sayings and parables and the other, largely prophetic parables taken together constitute nearly half (50 +) of the 114 logia. They are far more prominent in the *Gospel of Thomas* than proverbs and other wisdom sayings (roughly 15–20 in various judgments), which have roughly the same frequency as the I-sayings and what were apparently "community rules" in the pre-Thomas traditions and which are less prominent than the apparently "gnostic" material. Of the prophetic materials that dominate the collection, there are several that are "apocalyptic" in motif or could be classified as "apocalyptic" sayings, even if we are careful to follow Bultmann's more restrictive usage of that category (as opposed to the rather loose use of the synthetic concept often encountered in scholarly discourse).[19] This includes even a few that are reminiscent of motifs otherwise more distinctive to "apocalyptic" literature proper, concerning the heavens passing away or being rolled up (11, 111), speculation about the end or fate of the dead and the new world (e.g., 18, 51; cf. 19 and 85), and elements known mainly through Paul (17; cf. 1 Cor 2:8-9). Far more prominent and typical of *Gospel of Thomas* are prophetic sayings, particularly those that have parallels in Q, and a remarkable number of parables, particularly parables of the kingdom and/or with parallels in Mark. The hermeneutic of the *Gospel of Thomas*, however, can be discerned more clearly in the "gnostic" materials located in a score of logia scattered throughout the collection, materials that have few parallels in the Synoptic Gospels.

The implications of this review of Koester's analysis of materials in the *Gospel of Thomas* for assessment of Q appear to lead in a direction different from that taken in recent discussions of stratigraphy in Q. First, although the absence of "apocalyptic Son of Man sayings" in the *Gospel of Thomas* is striking in comparison with Q, there are far more

---

17. Robinson, "LOGOI SOPHŌN."
18. Koester, "One Jesus," 166–85.
19. Bultmann, *History of the Synoptic Tradition*, 120–25.

"apocalyptic" (and much more vividly "apocalyptic") materials in the *Gospel of Thomas* than in Q. Thus the difference between (the tradition of sayings leading to and/or reflected in) the *Gospel of Thomas* and (the final version of) Q cannot depend on the absence or presence of "apocalyptic" sayings or motifs generally. But this eliminates the basis on which Kloppenborg and others posited a stage of a sayings genre antecedent to the final form of Q that was basically sapiential and distinguishable from a redactional apocalyptic layer in the final form of Q.[20]

Second, although there are indeed many "sapiential" sayings in the *Gospel of Thomas* (along with several "apocalyptic" sayings), the most striking impression received from Koester's (form-critical) analysis of logia in the *Gospel of Thomas* is the dominance of prophetic sayings and kingdom parables.[21] Rather than call into question Robinson's thesis that the *Gospel of Thomas* (and supposed proto-Thomas collections) belonged to the broad general genre of *logoi*, this merely presses us toward greater specificity and precision about the kind of *logoi*. Robinson made it quite clear that the literary label or self-designation *logoi* was used far more broadly than for collections of "wisdom" sayings. In fact, particularly when he focused on early "Christian" literature, *logos/logoi* referred to prophetic (even apocalyptic) "words of the Lord," often understood prophetically and sometimes understood explicitly as transmitted through the Lord's as prophets, as is clear in literature from Paul to Justin.[22] The designation *logoi* is very general and fluid. If we are to take our cue from the type of material dominant in the *Gospel of*

---

20. That the *Gospel of Thomas* as we have it may (re-)interpret apocalyptic sayings does not change the situation, because what are categorized as apocalyptic sayings and motifs were thus still contained in the tradition of sayings that led to or was reflected in the *Gospel of Thomas*. It may be indicative of the gospel's hermeneutics that what appears to be a typical apocalyptic motif of the end resembling the beginning (#18) and a statement of seemingly "realized eschatology" (#51) and a saying that rejects apocalyptic-style calculations (#113//Luke 17:20-21) can stand, as it were, side-by-side.

21. A related impression is that there are fewer changes in the wisdom sayings in the *Gospel of Thomas* compared with their parallels in the Synoptic tradition, while many of the prophetic sayings have been adapted with specific changes, twists, and additions. As Koester notes, "we can see in it a distinctive reinterpretation of originally eschatological sayings and their terminology" ("GNOMAI DIAPHOROI," 137). This suggests that the wisdom sayings were more susceptible of understanding according to the special hermeneutic presupposed in the *Gospel of Thomas*, whereas the prophetic sayings required explicit adaptation and interpretation.

22. Robinson, "LOGOI SOPHŌN," 95–103.

Thomas, then *logoi prophētōn* would appear to be a more appropriate specification than *logoi sophōn*.

Rather than focus the argument on the most suitable label for the apparent genre, however, it may be more fruitful to compare the *Gospel of Thomas* and Q for ways in which the *Gospel of Thomas* may reflect a stage antecedent to the final form of Q in terms of generic development. If we think in compositional terms rather than types of sayings, a major difference between the *Gospel of Thomas* and Q is immediately evident. Whereas Q is composed as a series of coherent discourses or speeches, in the *Gospel of Thomas* most of the material stands in much smaller units, usually as single, double, or triple "sayings" or parables. Certain materials (e.g., logia 14, 21, or 47) appear in combinations similar to the fuller "clusters" found in Q. A useful comparison can be focused on Luke 12:49 (50), 51–53, 54–56 (which some view as part of a still larger complex in Q): *Gos. Thom.* 16 joins the same two sayings that comprise Q/Luke 12:51–53, but the parallel to Luke 12:49 is isolated in *Gos. Thom.* 10 and that to Luke 12:56 is the answer to a question of Jesus' identity in *Gos. Thom.* 91. Clusters of sayings, such as those in logia 14, 16, or 47, are rare in the *Gospel of Thomas*. However they dominate in Q and indeed give it an internal structure lacking in the *Gospel of Thomas*.

This suggests an approach to understanding the character and composition (perhaps even the genre) of Q as a whole document quite different from (and no longer dependent on) the attempt to characterize Q as a whole on the basis of the forms and motifs of individual sayings and sets of sayings. In this connection much of Kloppenborg's compositional analysis and reconstruction can be accepted quite apart from the stratigraphical hypothesis and the sets of questionable common features on which it is based.[23] That is, if Q is composed almost entirely as larger or shorter speeches, then the composition, character, and function of those speeches may be the key to understanding Q as a whole. Outlines and divisions of Q have been proposed with increasing specificity.[24] But they have been basically topical or thematic labels or sequential indi-

---

23. Although much critical analysis remains to be done on the composition of "clusters" (discourses or speeches), building on such investigations as the chapter "Aphoristic Cluster" in Crossan, *In Fragments*; and Sellew, "Early Collections of Jesus' Words."

24. From Manson, *Sayings of Jesus* (1937) to Schenk, *Synopse zur Redenquelle der Evangelien* (1981).

cators. We may get further by looking for the functions, the possible purposes and/or likely effects of the various discourses or speeches.

In a few cases the functions appear immediately evident. Q/Luke 10:2–16 (one of those supposedly sapiential speeches that goes beyond what is usually understood as sapiential admonitions, as Kloppenborg noted) is instruction regarding mission. Q/Luke 11:2–4, 9–13 is instruction specifically on prayer. The Q material underlying Luke 17:23–37, the contents of which are exhortation on preparedness in the face of the suddenness of judgment, appears to have functioned as the sanction on the whole of Q (somewhat analogously to the way in which Q/Luke 6:46–49 is the sanction on the exhortations in 6:27–45).

The functions of other complexes may not be far to seek. Q/Luke 6:20-49 is, to be sure, Jesus' "inaugural sermon." In addition, it is a set of opening admonitions that corresponds to the set of sanctions that closes the document in Q/Luke 17:23–37. But, more precisely, as can be discerned from the contents of such admonitions as Q/Luke 6:27–38, it appears intended as instruction on covenantal social-economic relations within the community, and not merely religious teaching to individuals. More than that, the speech has a fairly clear structure or sequence: the initial blessings set the stage for the exhortations regarding local social-economic interaction, which are followed by sanctional sayings that reinforce motivation to observe the preceding injunctions. Q/Luke 7:18–35 deals not simply with Jesus, John, and "this generation" but with the significance of what is happening with John and Jesus, that is, the fulfillment of expectations and prophecies of salvation. Q/Luke 11:39–52 (and possibly the whole of 11:14–52) condemns the principal opponents of the Q community and/or of the people with whom the Q people identify. The Q material in Luke 13:28–30, 34–35; 14:16–24, similarly, appears to be another cluster or discourse directed against opponents, in this case the rulers in Jerusalem. The fragments of Q utilized in Luke 14:26–27, 34–35; 15:4–7; 16:13, 17, 18; and 17:1–6 apparently formed a cluster of stringent demands on discipleship and community discipline with the appropriate encouragement (although this material could also be viewed as two shorter clusters divided on either side of 16:13). Also not too far to seek, the sayings by John in Q/Luke 3:7–9, 16–17 on the crisis of impending judgment and salvation and that by Jesus in Q/Luke 22:28–30 on the restoration or liberation of Israel function respectively as the opening and closing sayings of the whole collection.

Less evident but nevertheless intelligible are the division, coherence, and functions of the remaining materials, largely in Luke 12. Q/Luke 12:2–12, apparently following immediately after the complex that condemned the community's principal opponents, exhorts Jesus' followers to be confident and bold in their witness, with the specter of heavenly judgment as sanction. Q/Luke 12:22–31(33–34) addresses the (Q) people's anxieties about necessities of life, which will take care of themselves if they are single-minded in pursuit of the kingdom. Luke 12:39–40, 42–46 could be sanctions on the previous exhortation or part of a larger complex of sanctions addressed to the Q cornmunity. Q/Luke 12:49–56 (57–59) proclaims the disruptive, conflictual effect of Jesus' practice or movement, with a challenge to those who do not respond to the crisis. Q/Luke 13:18–21 are simply two parables indicating the amazing expansion of the kingdom (of the Q/Jesus movement?).

The dominant, unifying theme of the whole document is clearly the kingdom of God. Featured prominently at crucial points in most of the speeches (6:20; 7:28; 10:9, 11; 11:2; 11:20; 12:31; 13:18–21; 13:28–29; 16:16?; 22:28–30), the kingdom of God is virtually assumed or "taken for granted" as the focus of the Q discourses as well as the comprehensive agenda of preaching, practice, and purpose in Q. The kingdom of God, moreover, is double-edged, having positive, salvific benefits for those who respond to its presence, but negative, judgmental implications for those who do not (see esp. 10:9 and 11; 11:20; 13:28–29).

In fact, by focusing on the kingdom theme, we can discern how the various complexes cohere as a whole document. Q/Luke 3:9–11, 16–17 and 22:28–30 provide, respectively, a threatening as well as promising opening and a highly positive, anticipatory ending, in which the kingdom clearly means the renewal of Israel. The opening discourse in 6:20–49, after announcing the kingdom for the poor, etc., presents fundamental commandments for interaction in the kingdom community(ies) and is followed by a discourse in 7:18–35 that affirms the fulfillment of longings now happening with Jesus and the kingdom. After these more programmatic opening speeches come successive discourses on the mission of spreading the kingdom (10:2–16), on petitioning God boldly for the kingdom (11:2–4, 9–13), on confidence in confession and no anxiety in pursuit of the kingdom (12:2–12), and then sayings on the crisis constituted by Jesus' ministry (12:49–59), which is in turn followed by two encouraging parables of growth of the kingdom (13:18–21). Between the exhortation on boldly petitioning God and the other encouraging exhortations directed to the community and just following the latter are two clusters of sayings in which Jesus stands in conflict with or condemns the Pharisees (11:39–52) and the ruling house/families in Jerusalem (13:28–29, 34–35), for both of whom, in their presumption of their own salvation, the kingdom means condemnation.

Throughout the sequence of speeches, the types of sayings and motifs correspond to the function of the speeches. As Kloppenborg admits, the materials in the covenantal speech (6:20–49), the mission discourse (10:2–16), instruction on prayer (11:2–4, 9–13) and the discourse on seeking the kingdom (12:22–31) do not correspond to conventional forms of instructional wisdom. Prophetic forms come to the fore in the discourses directed to the community as sanctions (the Q materials behind Luke 12 and 17:23–37) as well as in the clusters of sayings against the Pharisees and Jerusalem rulers—again not surprising considering the traditional function of prophetic woes, laments, etc. Not surprisingly, the motif of the killing of the prophets occurs in the two prophetic clusters ostensibly addressed to the opponents (11:47–51; 13:34–35), and the (at one point overlapping) polemic against "this *genea*" is almost exclusively concentrated in one of those clusters, that directed against the Pharisees/lawyers (11:29–32, 49–51).

There are kingdom sayings or parables also scattered through the *Gospel of Thomas*. But they do not play the same role in providing the unifying theme, because the *Gospel of Thomas* is a collection of various sayings without any (as yet clear) internal structure and sequencing corresponding to that provided by the clusters that constitute Q. The speeches with their distinctive functions would appear to be the key to understanding Q, to what makes Q different from that earlier stage in the vague genre of sayings collection behind the *Gospel of Thomas*.

It is in this connection that the presence of the "apocalyptic" son of man sayings may be a key to Q in comparison with the *Gospel of Thomas*. We must be careful not to continue to project the modern synthetic concept of "the Son of Man" onto Q texts in this regard. It seems clear that when "son of man" is a self-reference by Jesus in Q it does not refer to judgment, and when "(the day of) the son of man" refers to judgment, it does not refer to Jesus. Thus, "son of man" is not a christological title and apparently does not even refer to an individual agent of redemption in Q/Luke 12:8–9; 12:40; 17:24, 26, 30. Rather, "son of man" in 12:8–9 is an advocate figure in the divine court of judgment and "(the day of) the son of man" in 17:24, 26, 30 may simply be an image of the divine judgment (i.e., so standardized that no reference to the text of Daniel 7 is involved), without emphasis on an individual heavenly figure. Moreover, it is not clear at all that these "(day of) the son of man" sayings in Q evoke a particularly apocalyptic scenario of "the last judgment" with attendant signs and cosmic disturbances. In fact, the references to "the day(s) of the son of man" in Q/Luke 17:23–30 are almost anti-apocalyptic in their explicit rejection of watching for signs and emphasis on the suddenness of judgment.[25] In every case, of course, these "son of man" sayings function as sanctions on the community's or members' discipline and courage, positively in 12:8–9 and negatively as a threat in 12:40 and 17:23–30. Thus these sayings do not lend Q an apocalyptic orientation, but they do provide a sanction of the suddenness of judgment for a community caught in the midst of a struggle.

It would seem an obvious next step, following up Koester's observation about the absence of these "apocalyptic" son of man sayings in the *Gospel of Thomas*, to look for other materials that function importantly in Q but are absent in the *Gospel of Thomas*. Significantly, the latter has no parallels to the series of woes against the Pharisees (a parallel only to Q/Luke 12:52 in logion 39; cf. 102) or to the prophetic sayings directed against the rulers in Q/Luke 13:28–29 and 34–35 (contrast the guarding against the "world" in logion 21). Nor does the *Gospel of Thomas* have parallels to the sayings that involve or suggest a community in struggle, such as Q/Luke 7:31–35; 11:14–20; and 12:3–9 (only the general saying 12:2 is paralleled, in logia 5–6). It is also significant that many of the prophetic sayings in the *Gospel of Thomas* have been explicitly adapted or interpreted in an individualizing and/or gnosticizing direction, as can be seen by comparison with some counterparts in Q, which still have a social thrust. The effect becomes clear, however, particularly when we consider the discourse composition in Q in contrast to relatively isolated sayings in the *Gospel of Thomas*. The discourses provide a social context in which the sayings have significance in Q, whereas in the *Gospel of Thomas* we are left without much of any context for interpretation of

---

25. Similarly Kloppenborg ("Symbolic Eschatology," 301–3)—although terms such as "the parousia" and "events prior to the end" and "universal destruction" appear to be derived from the synthetic modern scholarly construct of apocalypticism rather than from the Q text.

individual sayings. For example, in logion 73 the saying about sending out workers into the harvest has no particular connotations of mission, whereas in Q/Luke 10 it functions as the keynote to the mission of spreading the kingdom, which evokes sharp social conflict. In *Gos. Thom.* 35 the saying about binding the strong man and plundering his house has no connotations of the struggle against Satan's rule that not only has been engaged but is being won, as suggested by the complex of sayings in Q/Luke 11:14–23. "Cleansing the outside of the cup" and the Pharisees' hiding the key to knowledge in *Gos. Thom.* 89 and 39, respectively, have no religious-political context at all because they are not part of a series of woes against the Pharisees, as in Q. What is hidden becoming revealed in *Gos. Thom.* 5 and 6 gives no sense of encouragement or vindication in the face of acute social conflict that it has in Q because it is part of 12:2–9.

The clusters and their functions thus also appear to be the key to the hermeneutic implicit in Q, in contrast to that in the *Gospel of Thomas*. The latter is a matter of "penetration and research" basically of particular sayings toward the goal of individual enlightenment, with no concern for a social group and no social conflict in view. Q, by contrast, is concerned not with a "radical mode of existence" for individuals but with a new or renewed social order, which entails social conflict as well, and is structured into a series of speeches focused on particular aspects of that social renewal and social conflict.

Q AS PROPHETIC COMMUNITY INSTRUCTION

Once we recognize that Q has been composed as a series of discourses or speeches, we should be comparing Q not only with the *Gospel of Thomas* but with other texts that are composed as series of discourses as well. The most obvious case might be the *Didache*. Indeed, there are some striking similarities between Q and the *Didache* in the function or focus of their respective discourses, and even in their sequence.

The *Didache* opens with traditional "two-way" teaching in chapters 1–5 (closely related to that in *Barnabas* 18–20).[26] The first major section then happens to be a discourse with close affinities to Q/Luke 6:27–35/ Matt 5:38–48 (as part of Q/Luke 6:20–49), and continues with exhortations in the form "Do not . . . ," and in the form of "parental instruction."

26. See Kraft, *Didache and Barnabas*.

More to the point here, however, the overall complex is covenantal in substance (decalogue and related prohibitions and admonitions) and is concerned with social-economic interaction within a community. *Did.* 1.3b–6 in context, like the more explicit covenantal structuring of Q material in Matthew 5, further confirms that Q/Luke 6:20–49 is discourse concerned with social relations in a community and not with individual ethical admonition. Thus in function the opening discourse in the *Didache* corresponds to "Jesus' inaugural sermon" in Q, both in itself and in its position at the beginning of the series of speeches.

The *Didache* ends with what has been termed "eschatological admonition." Substantively it has more affinities with Mark 13 and Matthew 24 than with Q (e.g., Luke 12:35, 40), is replete with what are usually classified as "apocalyptic" motifs (such as "the world-deceiver," "signs spread out in heaven," etc., and "the Lord coming on the clouds of heaven") that are utterly lacking in Q. But the function of *Didache* 16 is parallel to that of the discourse in Q/Luke 17:23–37 regarding the suddenness of judgment. That is, it is a sanction on the other discourses in the text as a series of speeches.

In between these opening and closing discourses of *logoi* (*Did.* 1.3a) are several speeches on various topics. Q has no parallels to the brief sections concerning food, baptism, and fasts or to the longer section on the Eucharist. But it does have a parallel instruction on the Lord's Prayer (*Did.* 8.2–3; Luke 11:2–4) and a parallel to the brief section on community discipline placed immediately before the closing judgmental sanction (*Did.* 15.3–4; Luke 17:1–4). Considering the later stage in the development of the early "Christian" movement represented by the *Didache*—and assuming that Q is dated much earlier in the "mission" of Jesus' followers—the lengthy discussion concerning the support and treatment of itinerant apostles and prophets (*Did.* 11–13) is a complex of teachings that corresponds to the mission discourse in Q (Luke 10:2–16). Thus we have parallels to five of the Q complexes in the *Didache* that exhibit the same or similar function and the same sequence.

These parallels do not suggest, however, that Q is merely a proto-*Didache*, an early form of "community rule" for a nascent Jesus movement in Palestine-Syria. That is clearly an important aspect of its composition and apparent function, but it has the form of *logoi* of Jesus. And the bulk of the *logoi* organized in respective complexes are exhortations of promise and encouragement as well as of crisis and warning directed to the community(ies) of his followers: Q/Luke 7:18–35 about the fulfillment at hand, 12:2–12 about fearless confession, 12:22–31 on not being anxious, 12:49–59 on the crisis at hand, and 11:39–52, 13:28–29, 34–35, condemning the rulers and their retainers. The keynotes with which the series of discourses in Q apparently begins and ends, moreover, are prophetic threat and promise: the "stronger one who is coming" will baptize "with holy spirit" as well as fire and "gather the grain" as well as burn the chaff (Q/Luke 3:16–17, and (once we translate terms more appropriately) the twelve are to be "liberating/ making justice for" (not negatively "judging") the twelve tribes of Israel (Q/Luke 22:28–30). Finally, in these speeches Jesus is clearly understood as a prophet—indeed (along with John) as the culminating prophet in a long line of prophets (3:16–17; 7:18–28; 11:49–50; 13:34).

Although comparison with the similarly functioning sequence of discourses in the *Didache* enables us to discern that Q is a document concerned with community life, it is also clearly a perpetuation of the prophetic preaching of Jesus (and John). This prophetic preaching announces the presence of the kingdom, which means fulfillment of longings and renewal of community life in Israel for those who respond, and indicts the "Pharisees" and Jerusalem rulers who have been oppressing the people. But if Q is more than a *Didache*-like "rule" for community order, it is much more than "instruction" addressed to individual disciples in the tradition of "parental" instructional wisdom evident in literature such as Sirach. The sayings tradition that culminates in the *Gospel of Thomas* does indeed focus individual penetration and interpretation of particular sayings of Jesus—and in pursuit of its hermeneutic must adapt and alter the dominant prophetic components of that tradition. Q, on the other hand, is concerned not with instruction of individuals but with the social life and conflicts of a movement. Q consists of speeches focused on the principal concerns of communities of a Jesus movement, such as covenantal social-economic relations within the community, mission, economic subsistence, group discipline and solidarity in the face of repression. Several of the speeches take traditional prophetic forms of woes and laments announcing God's judgment on the rulers and their scribal representatives, as well as prophetic sanctions on the community's own group discipline and solidarity. Among the latter are the threatening "(day of) the son of man" sayings—lacking in the *Gospel of Thomas*, as Koester noted. Their function in Q, however, is not to block Gnostic proclivities in what is otherwise a "wisdom gospel," but to support discipline and solidarity in communities of a Jesus movement, especially in the penultimate speech that sanctions the preceding discourses (17:23–37).

It is conceivable that determination of the precise literary genre of Q is not of crucial importance for understanding its composition and function. Robinson's survey of literature designated as *logoi* turned up a great variety, some of it sections of larger wholes, some of it "sapiential" in character, some of it "prophetic." It is difficult to understand how, when we find hermeneutics as widely variant as those of Q and the *Gospel of Thomas*, the classification of both under *logoi sophōn* helps to elucidate either. Assuming that some term of reference to genre may be appropriate in dealing with literature, however, we should focus on the composition of Q in a series of speeches with particular functions for the community to which it was addressed, and not on the types of sayings included in those complexes. Moreover, if the authority (and founder?) of the Q community(ies) is understood as a prophet in a series of prophets including John, then an appropriate specification of the document of the clusters of his and John's sayings would appear to be *logoi prophētōn*. Q is not a "wisdom gospel" overlaid by "apocalyptic" sayings, but a series of prophetic speeches addressed to communities of a movement of Jesus' followers.

10

Apocalypticism and Wisdom

Missing in Mark

IN THE STANDARD WISDOM of New Testament scholarship, not only does the Gospel of Mark have an apocalypse—the "Synoptic Apocalypse" of Mark 13—but it is itself apocalyptic. Since Johannes Weiss and Albert Schweitzer, not only Jesus but Mark as well has been understood as presupposing and articulating an apocalyptic view of the world. This has been argued or dealt with in somewhat different ways, nearly all of which now seem problematic.

The standard basis for categorizing Mark or any other piece of early Christian literature as apocalyptic has been the presence of features typical of what is understood as apocalypticism. We are increasingly recognizing this as a questionable approach. But it is instructive to note what motifs and language classified as apocalyptic are present or absent and, when present, whether they are functional and/or qualified in Mark.[1]

Present are both the motif of resurrection and the figure of "the son of man." However, the occurrences of the term "the son of man" in Mark are diverse, with only a few referring to the future or "apocalyptic son of man" and even those differing significantly in function. Moreover, "resurrection" in Mark refers basically only to Jesus "rising again" in the three predictions in the middle section of the Gospel along with the empty tomb at the very end. Otherwise there is only the academic

---

1. In the writing of this essay, published in 1993, I had developed only a nascent sense of the discrepancy between the modern scholarly concept of apocalypticism and Judean apocalyptic texts, hence I tacitly accepted some of the classification of certain motifs, concepts, and images as "apocalyptic" (or "sapiential"). Now I would begin by describing the discrepancy and disputing the classification, as in chap. 11 below.

discussion of the implication of the laws of levirate marriage for belief in the resurrection initiated by the Sadducees, in 12:18–27. In striking contrast to Paul, Mark makes nothing of the general resurrection (of believers) or of Jesus' resurrection as its firstfruits.

Also present in Mark are a reference to "mysteries"[2] and plenty of "unclean spirits." However, the mysteries disclosed in the parables in Mark 4 do not appear comparable with the apocalyptic plan of God for the resolution of the major historical crisis, as in Daniel 2 (or the "wisdom in a mystery" of 1 Cor 2:6–7). And, besides not being distinctive to apocalyptic literature, the demons and Satan are not part of a more complete mythical or metaphysical scheme of spatial and temporal dualism supposed to be inherent in apocalypticism. Mark has no transcendent world inhabited by angels, no angel-interpreter appears, no semidivine forces explain mysteries or assist a helpless humanity. Nor is there a temporal dualism. "This age" and "the age to come" appear in passing in 10:30, but the emphasis is explicitly on manifold social-economic restoration "now in this age." Mark simply does not trade in concepts or symbols such as the end time, the eschaton, or a new world of some sort. It is even difficult to claim a last judgment for Mark. The term "the son of man" appears in an apparent judgment scenario twice. But, as we shall see below, one of those sayings functions as a sanction on the disciples' readiness to suffer martyrdom for the cause (8:38), and the other functions as apparent vindication for Jesus as he is about to be turned over to the Roman governor to be sentenced to death (14:62). Mark includes plenty of judgment, but in the form of Jesus' prophetic pronouncements and demonstration against the rulers and ruling institutions (11:12–23; 12:1–9, 38–40; 13:1–2). Furthermore, Mark gives no indications of pessimism, historical determinism, cosmic disorder, social anomie, or impending cosmic catastrophe. One might doubt that the mere presence of mysteries, demons, a rising Jesus, and a future "son of man" make Mark apocalyptic.

The results are similarly negative when we measure Mark 13 and/or Mark as a whole against one of the standard synthetic lists of apoca-

---

2. In establishing the text of Mark, we must always keep in mind the possibility that the "common agreements" of Matthew and Luke against Mark may be rooted in an earlier version of Mark than the one behind our best manuscript evidence. See the compelling recent arguments for an Urmarkus in Koester, *Ancient Christian Gospels*, 275–86.

lyptic motifs.³ (1) The imminent end of the world or earthly conditions is expressed neither in Mark 13 nor in Mark as a whole. (2) The end as a cosmic catastrophe is not present, even in 13:24–25. (3) The determinism or predetermined periods of history is absent; events that occur are not to be seen as signs (13:7) and there is no point in seeking revelation about the climactic event of deliverance (13:32). (4) Although the appearance of "unclean spirits" is evoked by Jesus' presence at points in the narrative of Mark 1–9, armies of angels and demons do not appear in Mark. (5) New paradisal salvation appears nowhere in Mark (Mark 10:2–9 simply appeals to the original divine intention for marriage at the creation). (6) Action from the throne of God to bring manifestation of the kingdom of God does not appear in Mark; rather Jesus preaches the presence of the kingdom of God, as in 1:15, anticipating that it will eventually come "with power." (7) A mediator with royal functions does not appear in Mark, who clearly downplays Jesus as the Messiah; the son of man appears in 13:26 to gather in the people from afar and is anticipated in 14:62 to vindicate Jesus, in but neither instance as a royal figure. (8) "Glory" appears in passing, 13:26, but the emphasis in Mark's story is on suffering. Jesus' preaching of "the kingdom of God" and a seriously qualified and deemphasized "messiah" hardly seem to be a sufficient basis for classifying the Gospel of Mark as apocalyptic.

Redaction critics have found more sophisticated ways of arguing that Mark is apocalyptic. In an important study of the kingdom of God in Mark, Werner Kelber makes the case not so much on the appearance of several apocalyptic motifs as on the basic scheme that Mark presupposes and presents.⁴ He finds Mark's overall agenda to be the progressive revelation of the kingdom. He understands this as unfolding in terms of Christian apocalyptic eschatology: the kingdom, only partially realized and hidden during the ministry of Jesus, reaches its climactic events in the crucifixion and resurrection, but will finally be fully revealed only with the παρουσία of Jesus as the son of man. Reading Mark 8:38—9:10 according to this scheme, Kelber finds the basic components in particular terms or symbols taken from the immediate framing or contents of the transfiguration story. Thus, for example, 8:38 turns out to be "the first explicit announcement of the *parousia*"; then the transfiguration itself is

3. That in Koch, *Rediscovery of Apocalyptic*.
4. Kelber, *Kingdom in Mark*.

"a *parousia* epiphany."[5] The other two "future son of man sayings" (13:26; 14:62) also turn out to be references to the παρουσία. The result of such redaction criticism of Mark is an attractively compact eschatological-christological scheme. "This apocalyptic function of the *parousia* is of a piece with Mark's theology of the Kingdom. As the Kingdom arrived with Jesus, is hidden at present, but will be seen shortly *en dynamei* (9:1), so also did the Son of Man walk on earth with authority, is absent at present (2:20; 13:34; 14:25), but will be seen *meta dynameos polles* (13:26)."[6]

This scheme might well be documented from Paul or Matthew, who do indeed write of the παρουσία. Once we appreciate the Gospel of Mark as a sustained story, however, as Kelber has pioneered in his subsequent work,[7] the references to the future "son of man" in 8:38; 13:26; and 14:62 do not appear to be announcements of or references to the *parousia*. Read in narrative context, 8:38, inseparable from 8:34–37, sanctions "taking up the cross and following" Jesus. Without the Matthean transformation of this and particularly other "future son of man sayings" it is difficult to find any παρουσία in Mark.

Those who have been embarrassed by the apparent presence of apocalyptic elements or worldview in Mark have pursued one or another of two strategies. Some have attempted to deny or discount the apocalyptic motifs and perspective in Mark, assigning these to Synoptic traditions or more likely Jewish traditions that Mark used but reworked and mitigated. Others, most recently and critically Burton Mack,[8] accepting the standard judgment that Mark is apocalyptic in one way or another, have argued that the apocalyptic elements and/or ideology were developed by the Markan community or the author of the Gospel—thus freeing Jesus and/or the earliest followers of Jesus from features distasteful to modern sensibilities.

PROBLEMATIC CONCEPTS AND PROCEDURES

There are a number of problems with our standard assumptions, concepts, and procedures, however, when it comes to "apocalyptic." All of the above approaches are caught within and/or struggling against a

---

5. Ibid., 74, 76.
6. Ibid., 123.
7. Starting with *Mark's Story of Jesus*.
8. Mack, *Myth of Innocence*.

synthetic modern scholarly construct of apocalyptic. "Apocalyptic" and related concepts were constructed in highly synthetic fashion at the turn of the century by a theologically oriented scholarship that drew the components from ancient Jewish apocalyptic literature in various languages and ranging over a millennium in dates of origin. From this literature, read as descriptive and theological rather than as symbolic or visionary language, a particular "apocalyptic" worldview was constructed. Then that view of the world was found in a particular document or even fragment of literature when certain component motifs or terms were present.

Some of the problems with this would appear to be obvious. (1) Some of the language labeled "apocalyptic" may have been simply common cultural coin and not distinctive to apocalyptic literature: hell/hades, angels, demons, divine judgment, and so on. Such terms appear in popular or prophetic discourse as well as in apocalyptic texts. (2) With the synthetic modern construct in place, the tendency is to take particular passages or motifs out of their original literary context and to place them instead into the modern conceptual context. (3) The use of such an abstract synthetic construct means that a particular piece of literature such as Mark is being compared with a worldview that never existed in any particular document or community. It is unclear what might be learned from comparison with such a vague and wide-ranging cultural reification. (4) The misreading of visionary or other metaphorical or hyperbolic imagery as descriptive or metaphysical means that modern misconceptions (such as "cosmic catastrophe" or "antihistorical" or "end time") are imposed onto ancient Jewish and Christian literature and its communities. For most of this century standard scholarly handbooks have insisted that Jewish apocalyptic literature was an unfortunate and unprecedented departure from biblical traditions and orientation.[9] The differences found, however, appear to have been merely differences constructed.

More critical analysis of the literary sources on which the synthetic modern construct was ostensibly based has only made the old conceptual apparatus seem all the more problematic. The more we try to formulate a general definition of the *genre* of "Jewish apocalypses"

---

9. See the brief critique in Horsley, *Jesus and the Spiral of Violence*, 131–40; several critical and critically reconstructive articles by Elisabeth Schüssler Fiorenza, George Nickelsburg, and others in *Apocalypticism in the Mediterranean World*; and the earlier critique of Koch, *Rediscovery of Apocalyptic*.

that spanned several centuries (as did the SBL "Genre of Apocalypse" group),[10] the less satisfactory our points of comparison for dealing with the earliest "Christian" literature. Virtually no Judean apocalypses other than the *Similitudes of Enoch* and an updated *Testament of Moses* are extant from the generations just prior to the time of Jesus and Mark. The *Psalms of Solomon* and *Testaments of the Twelve Patriarchs* do not qualify substantively or generically; most Qumran literature does not qualify generically; and *2 Baruch* and *4 Ezra* are later. We are left with Daniel and the Enoch literature usually dated to two centuries earlier.

Many of the same observations are appropriate to the assessment of "wisdom" in Mark. It is ironic, and a source of considerable divergence of scholarly energy, that wisdom and apocalyptic became separated so dramatically into different worlds and worldviews in New Testament scholarship. Hebrew Bible/Old Testament scholarship does not necessarily divide the two. Indeed, the line of interpretation associated with Gerhard von Rad finds that the wisdom tradition, more broadly understood, was the matrix from which apocalyptic literature originated.[11] A major part of the problem is that wisdom is usually understood mainly as proverbs and other wise sayings. A closer examination of Judean "wisdom" books, however, finds that the ancient sages cultivated different kinds of wisdom, only one of which was comprised of proverbs and brief discourses. In addition to this instructional wisdom, the scribal sages cultivated cosmological wisdom, speculative or theological wisdom, and mantic wisdom.[12]

This simultaneously more comprehensive and more precise understanding of wisdom in its different types makes credible the possibility that texts classified by modern scholars as apocalyptic may very well have developed out of mantic wisdom. Just such a development may be evident in the book of Daniel (see the dream interpretation opening onto the "mystery" according to which God has planned the resolution of historical crisis in Daniel 2 and the parallel dream in Daniel 7) and in Enoch's Animal Vision (*1 Enoch* 85–90). Scholars who work on both "sapiential" and "apocalyptic" literature have been pointing to the presence

---

10. See *Semeia* 14 (1979); and Collins, *The Apocalyptic Imagination*, chap. 1. In retrospect it seems ironic that scholarly definition of genre is based so exclusively on form when it comes to literature that was so deliberately functional for crises of history and/or faith.

11. See von Rad, *Old Testament Theology*, 2:301–15.

12. Outlined by Collins, "Wisdom, Apocalypticism, 166–69.

of wisdom sayings in apocalyptic literature and of apocalyptic elements in ostensibly sapiential literature.[13] Thus it makes no sense to maintain the wedge driven between the categories "sapiential" and "apocalyptic" according to which interpreters jump from the form of sayings both to separate literary genres and to whole different worldviews or orientations to life supposedly expressed in those respective types of sayings. Given the complex relationship between ostensibly "sapiential" and "apocalyptic" literature, the recent separation of the synoptic "sayings source" Q into separate sapiential and apocalyptic layers seems questionable.[14] Nevertheless, we must deal with the clear difference between a Sirach and a Daniel, between a composite collection of different kinds of wisdom from a scribe-sage who also interprets dreams, on the one hand, and a collection of dream-visions with attendant interpretations for those undergoing the historical trauma to which they pertain, on the other.

THE PROBLEM OF DIFFERENT "SOCIAL LOCATIONS"

Considerations of the different social locations of Judean apocalyptic and sapiential literature and the Gospel of Mark further complicates the question of wisdom and apocalyptic elements in Mark. Both apocalyptic and sapiential texts were almost certainly produced by and directed to intellectual strata, circles of scribes or sages. The Gospel of Mark and the Jesus traditions it includes were evidently of popular provenance and were orally performed and cultivated in communities of ordinary people, not in Jerusalem scribal circles. The Gospel, moreover, would have been performed (read aloud) in those popular communities. There is probably also an important regional difference between Mark and Judean apocalyptic literature. Mark evidently has origins in the Galilean or Syrian periphery—which of course it views as the center of significant action—while apocalyptic (and sapiential) literature is focused on the ruling city of Jerusalem, even when it is hostile to the rulers there.

Recent analyses of apocalyptic literature in historical context have laid the basis for a far more adequate understanding of that literature

---

13. J. J. Collins, *Apocalyptic Imagination*; Nickelsburg, *Jewish Literature*; and Nickelsburg, "Wisdom and Apocalypticism in Early Judaism," 18–20.

14. See the critique of the use of these categories as a basis for claiming different strata in Q in chap. 8; see the parallel critique in Collins, "Wisdom, Apocalypticism," 165–66, 181–85.

and the situations and people addressed.[15] The question then is the way in which Jewish scribal apocalyptic texts may be used for comparisons with and elucidation of the Gospel of Mark, which derived from communities of ordinary people. Certain comparisons and elucidations may be possible because, as I have noted in another context, the scribes who produced apocalyptic literature had come to experience a situation somewhat similar to that of the common people under alien imperial rule in late Hellenistic and early Roman Palestine.[16] Yet the relation of apocalyptic literature to a popular text such as the Gospel of Mark was at best very indirect. Further consideration of the social role and location of the scribes who produced both apocalyptic literature and sapiential literature may elucidate their differences as well as their common provenance.

We begin with two apparent and determinative realities in ancient Near Eastern societies such as Judea: few people could write, and the social structure was relatively simple. Basically the only people who were literate and who produced literature were the scribes, and their role was, in subordination to and dependence on the Judean aristocracy, to assist them in governing the society. Ben Sira lays out a rather illuminating description of the fundamental social structure in 38:24—39:11. As long as the scribes and sages could serve under rulers who were either independent or were subject to Persian imperial sponsorship of local cultural and legal traditions, they could simply, as Ben Sira says (39:1-4), "study the law of the Most High, . . . preserve the discourse of notable men, and seek out the hidden meanings of proverbs," while serving "among great men and . . . rulers." But once the Judean aristocracy compromised too much with an imperial situation politically and culturally or even assimilated to the dominant politics and culture, weakening or even abandoning the ancestral laws and customs, they also threatened or even eliminated the role and function of the scribes/sages. It is precisely from the point at which the Judean rulers seriously assimilated to the dominant Hellenistic imperial political culture that apocalyptic texts such as the sections of *1 Enoch* and Daniel appear, in protest against political and cultural domination by alien imperial forces. The composers of these apocalyptic visions and interpretations were precisely the

---

15. See especially Collins, *Apocalyptic Imagination*; and Nickelsburg, *Jewish Literature*.

16. See further Horsley, *Jesus and the Spiral of Violence*, chap. 5.

scribes and sages, the teachers and the wise (*maskilim*, etc.) who had to struggle for their lives as well as the rights to continue to obey the covenantal torah as well as to "preserve proverbs and penetrate parables." It is only to be expected that sapiential admonitions would appear in apocalyptic literature. The book of Daniel does indeed articulate a different view of the world from the book of Sirach, because the world had changed. The scribes and sages produced different texts in response to different situations. But rather than reify two different worlds of wisdom and apocalyptic on the basis of different types of wisdom, interpreters can more appropriately attend to the historical circumstances that particular pieces of literature addressed—instead of pulling motifs and "aphorisms" out of their literary as well as historical context.

Discernment that both instructional wisdom and apocalyptic wisdom come from people of the same social location and role—that is, scribes and sages who ordinarily served as "retainers" to the Judean rulers—means that for both we have the same problems of comparison with and relevance to popular texts such as Mark. Thus with both extant apocalyptic texts and extant instructional literature there are problems of both temporal and regional distance with regard to Mark. Like Daniel and most sections of *1 Enoch*, Sirach is over two hundred years earlier. And given that Galilee had been separated politically from Judea for centuries before the Hasmoneans conquered the area about a hundred years before Jesus, we might expect some regional variation.

MARK'S PLOTTING: WHAT THE GOSPEL IS ABOUT

After the pioneering recognition of the Gospel of Mark as a sustained narrative, a whole story, we can hardly pretend that it is a mere collection of pericopes and read them for their "theology," as was done by redaction criticism.[17] Mark's story, moreover, is indeed about the kingdom of God, but in a concrete political, or rather political-religious, sense. Jesus preaches the kingdom and heals people in the villages of Galilee and the surrounding areas. He never goes into the ruling cities of Galilee or the surrounding areas. And his activity and preaching in Jerusalem comprise one aggressive prophetic condemnation after another against the ruling institutions of Temple and high priesthood. Meanwhile, his

---

17. See especially Kelber, *Mark's Story of* Jesus; Myers, *Binding the Strong Man*; and Moore, *Gospels and Literary Criticism*.

preaching and manifestation of the kingdom in Galilean and other villages are unmistakably portrayed as a renewal of Israel. This is signaled clearly in the appointment of the Twelve as symbolic of the whole people of Israel. It is continued then more substantively in the two chains of miracle stories (chapters 4–8) that clearly repeat the key facets of the founding and renewal of Israel under Moses and Elijah, in stories of sea crossings and wilderness feedings, healings and exorcisms.[18] The renewal of the people Israel is also consistently portrayed—in the alternative cures and forgiveness Jesus offers the people—as a challenge to the established political-religious system centered in Jerusalem, and Jesus is regularly challenged in turn by the representatives of the established system, who are already plotting "how to destroy him" by 3:6. The advent of the kingdom (or should we translate the "politics"?) of God as the renewal of the people of Israel is then further concretized in the renewal of local (covenantal) community. Chapters 8–10 may well be focused on "discipleship," but it is not the individualistic discipleship of much modern exegesis. If it is not already evident in the announcement of new "familial" community in 3:31-35, then the succession of passages (in Mark 10) dealing with the fundamental forms and dimensions of local community, marriage/family, membership, use of economic resources, the manifold restoration of "houses, families, and fields, now in this age," and finally the egalitarian policy of leadership makes abundantly clear just how concrete the kingdom of God announced by Jesus is to be. These teachings about the concrete shape of the renewed community are juxtaposed with and sanctioned by precisely the predictions of the passion and resurrection. Meanwhile, in the pronouncement stories, or more particularly the controversies with the Pharisees and scribes, Mark has Jesus defend local prerogatives, customs, and claim to economic resources over against the representatives of the established system centered in Jerusalem and its efforts to supervise local life and extract economic resources for support of the Temple and priesthood.

Closely linked with the main plotting of the preaching and manifestation of the kingdom of God is the role played by Jesus the proclaimer and healer-exorcist. Mark represents Jesus as a prophet like Moses and Elijah, engaged in the renewal of Israel. Mark fleshes out his special understanding of the prophet's role and agenda not only with miracle

---

18. See Mack, *Myth of Innocence*, chap 8, for critical elucidation of the miracle chains and their function in Mark.

chains and controversy stories but also with announcements of the necessity of "the son of man" suffering and dying for the cause and then being raised in vindication. Only at three points, beginning, middle, and end, does the story give any suggestion of Jesus as the messiah or Son of God. Indeed, in narrative sequence, Peter's confession of Jesus as the messiah is followed immediately by Jesus' first announcement of his suffering, execution, and rising and his rebuke of Peter for objecting.

MARK'S USE OF APOCALYPTIC MOTIFS

With some sense of the basic narrative or plotting of the Gospel, it may be possible to discern how features of Mark identified as apocalyptic are used or adapted. The place to start is surely at the end. It is not only a fearsome ending, but an open one, inviting the readers/hearers to make a new beginning. After thrice announcing his suffering, death, and rising again in the middle of the Gospel, Jesus then says pointedly, in Gethsemane after the Last Supper, "But after I am raised up, I will go before you to Galilee." Then, in the next to the last statement of the Gospel, the "young man" says not only "he has been raised" but (again) "he is going ahead of you to Galilee." Can there be any doubt that Mark, among all the Gospels, with no actual portrayal of the resurrection or appearances, means that the resurrection is Jesus going back to Galilee and leading his disciples (including the women!) to get back to the business of the kingdom that the whole Gospel has just been about? No standing around waiting for ascension, enthronement, Pentecost, or the general resurrection in Mark! Jesus' resurrection in Mark sends people right back to community renewal in Galilee.

What about the *parousia*? Far from being a Pauline crucifixion-resurrection kerygma with a long introduction, Mark may not even have known the Pauline gospel. Or if he did, he does not seem to have picked up the concept of *parousia*. The proof texts previously claimed for the *parousia* in Mark, as noted above, are "the apocalyptic son of man" sayings. The occurrence at three points in Q of "son of man" sayings classified as "apocalyptic" has been the principal basis for claiming a secondary redactional layer in Q. Even so, the occurrence at three points of similarly classified "son of man" sayings continues to be a principal basis for the apocalyptic reading of Mark.

Most of the "son of man" sayings in Mark, of course, have nothing to do with judgment or gathering the elect or influence of visionary imagery from Daniel 7. They are rather the three announcements of the suffering, death, and raising of Jesus (8:31; 9:31; 10:33–34) and four or five other references to Jesus' death or raising that appear to be Markan compositions related to those three formulaic sayings (9:9, 12; 14:21, 41; and possibly 10:45 as well). The sayings about the authority of "the son of man" in 2:10 and "the son of man" as lord of the Sabbath in 2:28 similarly pertain to Jesus' life or ministry—and perhaps also still have the general sense of humankind/people having authority to forgive/over the Sabbath. Thus it is only the other three "son of man" sayings that have provided a basis for the apocalyptic reading of Mark in general and the *parousia* motif in particular.

Although they are usually classified together somewhat vaguely as "future" or "apocalyptic," the formulations and the functions of the three sayings are rather different. In 8:38, a variation on the saying also found in Q/Luke 12:8–9, the "son of man" appears to be an advocate at the divine judgment in the attending company of the angels, and neither saves nor condemns people himself. Mark 13:26–27 alludes to the "coming with the clouds" known also from Dan 7:13. In contrast with the "human-like one" of Daniel 7, however, which symbolized the people who are to be delivered, the "son of man" in Mark 13:26–27 presides over the deliverance, the gathering, of the elect. In Mark 14:62, because of the apparent allusion to "coming with the clouds of heaven" in Dan 7:13 (along with the allusion to "seated at the right hand" in Ps 110:1), it is difficult to tell whether "the son of man" is the divine agent of judgment, ready to condemn the high-priestly court and vindicate Jesus, or perhaps rather a figure symbolizing (or agent of) the restoration of the people (as in Daniel 7).

In none of these sayings in Mark is Jesus identified with "the son of man." Indeed, in Mark 8:38 and 14:62 in particular, Jesus refers to a figure different from himself, in the latter text, perhaps a figure who will vindicate him. One could imagine that if Mark had wanted to identify clearly the "son of man" who is Jesus with the future "son of man" as advocate, agent of deliverance (or judge), he would have added a fourth step to the predictions: that is, "the son of man" would suffer, die, rise, and save (or judge). We can surmise that the relationship between the two types of "son of man" is so unclear and indefinite in Mark because

Mark is at pains to identify the prophet of renewal with the suffering "son of man" (= Jesus), and/or because Mark is the first in the tradition in which he stands to imply that the two types of "son of man" were the same person. But even the three "future son of man" sayings in Mark are so different from one another that it is difficult to find a consistent image or to imagine that Mark intends them all as the same "title" of a clearly defined redeemer figure. Scholarly specialists on apocalyptic texts have warned that "the son of man" in the (first century CE) Similitudes of Enoch (*1 Enoch* 37–69) is not a title of an eschatological agent of judgment. And besides the absence of the term *parousia*, there is no indication in these sayings that Mark had some sort of *parousia* in mind. Jesus had already "gone before them to Galilee." No *parousia* was to be expected in Mark.

Because there simply is no "end" or *parousia* in Mark, there is not even the possibility of the Gospel coordinating or juxtaposing such with the defeat of the demonic forces. Satan and numerous "unclean spirits" play a key role in Mark's drama. But they are already being "bound" or driven out by Jesus and disappear from the narrative before the climactic political confrontation of Jesus with the rulers in Jerusalem. Moreover, even though Satan appears as the tempter of Jesus himself and the adversary of the word early in the Gospel (1:13; 4:15), the dominant conflict even there is the religious-political one with the rulers and their scribal/Pharisaic retainers (see esp. 1:21–28; 2:1–12; 3:1–6; 4:30–32). This subordinate role and decisive defeat of Satan and the unclean spirits in Mark contrast sharply with the programmatic visualization in the scribal-priestly Community Rule from Qumran (1QS 4:18–25), where the destruction of Falsehood/the Angel of Darkness is coordinated with the final intervention or "visitation" by God.

In fact, Mark's portrayal of the struggle between Jesus and the demonic forces contrasts with that in the Dead Sea Scrolls in a more general way, despite their similarities. Mark and the ethos from which Mark and the pre-Markan materials come share with the Qumran community the view that life as they know it is caught in a struggle between two superhuman forces; such is the assumption behind the "Beelzebul controversy" in Mark 3:22–27. And in both Mark and the Dead Sea Scrolls the "unclean spirits" or "Spirit of Falsehood/Angel of Darkness" (1QS 3–4; cf. "Prince of the Kingdom of Wickedness" in 1QM 17) symbolize the struggle of superhuman or divine forces that helps explain how social-political life could be so completely beyond comprehension in terms of ordinary human causation.[19] Moreover, in both the demonic forces are clearly reflections, as well as explanations, of the control of their lives by the Roman imperial forces; hence the defeat of the demonic forces has more or less direct political implications.[20] In the War Scroll from Qumran the defeat of the Prince of the Kingdom of Wickedness is simultaneously the defeat of the Roman imperial forces, and in Mark 5:1–20 the "unclean spirit(s)" are named "Legion" and are driven into the sea to their destruction. In Mark, however, the "unclean spirits" appear to function in an ad hoc manner, possessing particular persons while being more or less "at large" as an ominous presence over the land. That Mark and pre-Markan materials simply reflect a common popular belief in demons and Satan is indicated by the scribes' accusation, in which they exploit the common belief to charge Jesus with witchcraft (3:22). The intellectuals at Qumran, on the other hand, had articulated a systematic demonology that helped explain all matters of life under the struggle between the two superhuman "spirits." Mark, originating in and addressed to a popular movement, does not appear to have assimilated much by way of the more systematic reflection cultivated among the scribal circles that produced the extant apocalyptic literature.

A "SYNOPTIC APOCALYPSE"?

But would not the presence of a "little apocalypse" or "the Synoptic Apocalypse" in Mark 13 make Mark apocalyptic? With all due respect to traditional scholarly labels, the use in this case may constitute, as it were, an academic self-fulfilling prophecy. Many of the standard topics of scholarly debate may simply be generated by the standard synthetic construct of "apocalyptic" presupposed when discussing the contents of Mark 13. Assuming that "Jews" and "early Christians" believed in something such as "the end," modern scholars find it in the phrase "he who endures to the end" in 13:13. Assuming that ancient Jews and

---

19. On the function of such symbols/images in an imperial situation, see further my preliminary reflections in Horsley, *Jesus and the Spiral of Violence*, 129–45, and Horsley, *Sociology and the Jesus Movement*, 96–99; and further reflections in Horsley, *Revolt of the Scribes*.

20. See further Horsley, *Jesus and the Spiral of Violence*, 184–90; and Myers, *Binding the Strong Man*, who suggests that Mark has even identified the demonic forces with the Jewish rulers and ruling system.

Christians believed in a special period of time before "the end," scholars find it in the editorial phrase that the gospel must be preached first in 13:10. Assuming that ancient Jews and Jewish-Christians believed that Jerusalem was to be connected in some way with "the end," and finding in "the desolating sacrilege" of 13:14 a reference to the Roman desecration of the Temple and/or the destruction of Jerusalem in 70 CE, modern scholars conclude that Mark 13 is in some way struggling with the relation of the end of Jerusalem and the end in the larger sense. Or, assuming that ancient Christians believed in a sequence of "eschatological" events in which the *parousia* would happen in connection with the end, modern scholars find the whole scenario where they detect hints of parts of it.

In order to use the label "apocalyptic" for any motif or symbol in Mark 13, however, we would have to compare each particular motif with attention to its respective literary and historical contexts. Because we are still so heavily under the influence of the old synthetic construct, even the careful search for fundamental schemes on a less grandiose scale, as pursued by Lars Hartman, is problematic; as he himself warned, one rarely finds a whole scheme in a single text.[21]

That we may be reading schemes into ancient texts rather than out of them should make us skeptical about attempts to identify a pre-Markan "apocalypse" behind Mark 13. Debates continue on the extent and character of an apocalyptic "flier" or other *Vorlage* possibly used by Mark. A very careful analysis found that what appears in 13:7–8, 14–20, 24–27 was written by a Jewish-Christian prophet during the revolt of 66–70 CE to interpret Daniel's "desolating sacrilege" as the coming destruction of the Temple.[22] It is clearly impossible to engage that debate in a short article. But the whole procedure may be questionable for another reason. Isolating a pre-Markan *Vorlage* has meant taking Mark 13 out of the literary context of Mark as a whole, and then the *Vorlage* out of the context of Mark 13—and ironically then interpreting Mark 13 and even Mark as a whole on the basis of the isolated *Vorlage*. But this procedure leaves no literary context on the basis of which to make judgments about historical context and the possible references in Mark 13 to particular situations and events. If anything we should proceed in the opposite

---

21. Hartman, *Prophecy Interpreted*, 236.
22. Brandenburger, *Markus 13 and die Apokalyptik*.

manner, beginning with Mark and Mark 13 as a whole precisely in attempting to discern such references to historical situations.

In fact, in treating Mark 13 we should consider not only that it is an integral part of the Gospel, but also that images or motifs may well have been utilized previously or in other ways than in apocalyptic literature, and that there was escalating social conflict throughout the middle of the first century, from the time of Jesus' death through the outbreak of the great revolt against Roman and Judean high-priestly rule.

It just so happens that the severe political-economic-religious conflict portrayed by Mark as a whole closely matches the structural social conflict in Roman Palestine known through other sources, such as Josephus. That conflict erupted into widespread revolt both a generation before and a generation after the mission of Jesus, and it was manifested in numerous protests, social unrest, resistance movements, and official measures of repression during (the period of) the formation of pre-Markan traditions.[23] Much of the previous treatment of Mark 13 seems to assume that, somehow in contrast to the idyllic scene of Jesus' ministry in Galilee, Mark 13 suddenly addresses a situation of conflict for Jesus' followers, and it assumes that the Roman devastation of Galilee and Judea was utterly unanticipated. In Mark's portrayal, however, the mission of Jesus was a sharp and escalating struggle against the repressive rulers and their retainers, with basically a similar struggle apparently continuing for Jesus' followers (e.g., 8:34-38). Thus the situation of class and regional conflict in Palestine exacerbated by the overall imperial situation was continuous. And that is the general situation of continuing structural social conflict that we must take into account when probing phrases in Mark 13 for possible references to particular events.

Insofar as there then appear to be several references to specific events in Mark 13, we are in the advantageous position of knowing of a number of major and minor conflicts or movements that occurred between 30 and 70 CE. But we may find it impossible to reach any degree of precision in relating particular possible references to particular possible events. For example, some find in 13:7 a reference to Gaius's order to erect his bust in the Temple. Others suggest that the "desolating sacrilege" in 13:14 is a reference to that same event. Still others claim that the "desolating sacrilege" refers to the final destruction of Jerusalem, or

---

23. Sketched briefly in Horsley, *Sociology and the Jesus Movement*, chaps. 4-5. A fuller analysis in Horsley, *Jesus and the Spiral of Violence*, chaps. 2-4.

to the impending attack on the Temple by Titus. In relation to 13:21–22, there were a number of "prophets" active in Palestine roughly at mid-century, while certain "messianic pretenders" emerged at the beginning and during the midst of the great revolt of 66–70 CE.

If attempts to read Mark 13 as somewhat analogous to the rehearsal of past history in order to "set up" reassurance about a present crisis have any validity, then the discernment of 13:14 as the shift from past to present-and-future provides some criteria for the identification of references. On such a basis the "rumors of war" and "famine" of 13:7–8 could be references to the impact of Gaius's order to erect his bust in the Temple and the disastrous effects of the severe drought in the late 40s. But that would not mean that the reference of 13:14–20 was necessarily to either the Jewish War of 66–70 CE or the Roman destruction of Jerusalem and the Temple. Social conflict was escalating steadily during the 50s and 60s, and at several points the Roman governors sent out the military to suppress popular unrest. Moreover, people in Palestine had long experience—periodically from 63 to 37 BCE and again in 4 BCE—with how the Romans reacted to actual or perceived resistance with severe repressive measures, including "scorched earth" and "search and destroy" tactics in (re)conquering a people. Anytime after the dramatic events touched off by Gaius's order, a discerning prophet could have anticipated a scenario so suddenly devastating for the people that "one in the field must not turn back to get a coat." A prophet would not need to have experienced the Roman reconquest of Galilee or northern Judea in 67–68 CE to have composed the sayings in Mark 13:14b–18. Thus arguments that situate Mark prior to or during the actual revolt of 66 CE and the imminent destruction of the Temple and Jerusalem are more persuasive than those that read Mark 13 as prophecy after the fact. Were Mark 13 *vaticinium ex eventu* ("prophecy after the fact"), then we would expect to find in the text a more precise reflection of the way in which the Temple was actually destroyed. Moreover, if Jerusalem were already in ruins, then there would have been no longer a problem with potential false prophecy and false messiahs.

Thus, with regard to the possible particular references of the statements usually listed as "apocalyptic" or ascribed to a pre-Markan "apocalypse," reasoning is necessarily somewhat circular. In order even to consider whether the phrases in 13:7–8 or the sayings in 13:14–20 refer to particular events or people, we must have some possibilities in mind. The phrases in 13:7-8 were apparently already stereotyped and could be simply apocalyptic rhetoric (*4 Ezra* 9:3; 13:31; *2 Bar.* 27; 70:8), and that in turn may even have been rooted in prophetic rhetoric (Isa 8:21; 13:13; 14:30; 19:2; Ezek 5:12; see any number of commentaries, articles, or monographs). On the other hand, in Palestine during the decades after Jesus' death, there was indeed a disastrous famine following a serious drought in the late 40s, and besides the rumors of war (e.g., in the wake of Gaius's mania), the Roman governors frequently sent out the army against any popular unrest, from banditry to would-be new Joshuas at Jericho or the Jordan. Whether particular references are intended, Mark's point is clear at the end of 13:7: such events must be expected and should not provoke any unusual excitement.

The sayings in 13:14b-18 appear to have far more specific reference, most likely to current events prior to or during the revolt and Roman reconquest. But they have no particular apocalyptic traits (unless it be "in those days" of 13:17). Even though not apparently written from the perspective of Jerusalem or even of Judea, they seem to have anticipated events in Judea in mind, events that threaten the lives of ordinary people with sudden disaster (i.e., apparently a Roman reconquest of the land). The scope of the firestorm, however, seems ominous from the sobering yet reassuring comments in 13:19-20. The style and substance of assurance here have more of an apocalyptic tone (cf. Dan 12:1). The puzzle of this section is what the βδέλυγμα might refer to. In his historicizing transformation looking back on the Roman siege of Jerusalem, Luke has simply wiped out the term (21:20). Matthew makes explicit reference not only to Daniel but to the Temple. Matthew's rewriting makes the vague simplicity of the Markan statement all the more striking. Nothing in the saying or immediate literary context suggests Jerusalem or the Temple. And the masculine participle is as weak a basis for finding here a reference to Titus as it is for finding one to Satan. The "parenthetical" phrase "let the reader understand" should perhaps be a clue to us that the reader must possess much more understanding of the cultural lore of ancient Palestine than we do to "get" this one. We can certainly reason that referring the desolating sacrilege to (the threat of) the Roman destruction of the Temple does not make sense for a community or Gospel so opposed to the Temple.

The imagery in 13:24-25, often labeled "cosmic" and even read as reference to "cosmic catastrophe," is derived ultimately from traditional prophetic imagery of the appearance of God in deliverance and is standard symbolization of "the day of Yahweh," usually with connotations of God's judgment against foreign regimes (e.g., Isa 13:10; 34:4; Ezek 32:7–8; Joel 2:10). A few apocalyptic texts simply continued the prophetic use of such prophetic imagery (*As. Mos.* 10:3–5). Thus it is not distinctively apocalyptic. And it is clearly symbolic language, hyperbole dramatizing just how ominous God's judgment would be. The two-step scene presented in Mark 13:24–25, 26–27 is reminiscent of Daniel 7 quite aside from the allusion to the "coming with the clouds" from Dan 7:13 in Mark 13:26. But we may doubt just how directly and explicitly Daniel 7 was in mind here, because in Daniel the "human-like one" symbolized the elect to be gathered, while in Mark "the son of man" presides over the gathering. The gathering of the elect from the four winds may come from Zech 2:6, not from Daniel, and the image of gathering the scattered people of Israel from the nations or ends of the world is fairly common in prophetic traditions.

All of these prophetic (and not distinctively apocalyptic) predictions, however, are framed, balanced, and interpreted by the parenesis in 13:5–6, 9–13, and 28–37, particularly by the carefully positioned and repeated "watch" (βλέπετε) in 13:5, 9, 23, 33 (cf. γρεγορεῖτε, 13:35, 37). The main point of the parenesis, and thus of the material framed by the parenesis, seems to be, "Do not be diverted from the struggle by the difficulties attendant upon the struggle." The first main section of parenesis, 13:9–13, partly paralleled by similar exhortations elsewhere in the Synoptic tradition (Q/Luke 12:2–12; 12:51–53) as well as sayings earlier in Mark (8:34–38), focuses on the trials the movement is undergoing, internal dissension as well as external persecutions by rulers and local enemies. Far from being distracted by wars and famines (13:7–8), the members of the movement are to heed this advice: "Watch! Expect repressions, but do not worry! Expect to be hated by all, but endure!" These are not vague apocalyptic predictions, but realistic prophetic exhortation.

The second main section of parenesis follows up the prophecy of sudden devastation for those in Judea and the promise of judgment and gathering of the elect in two steps. First are statements that the positive resolution of the crisis is near and that Jesus' words are sure, utterly credible (13:28–31). But neither here nor elsewhere does Mark appear to be emphasizing or giving special weight to "nearness." The only comparable saying, that the kingdom of God will come with power soon, also serves as a reassurance or sanction on remaining focused on the cause in a similar sequence (8:34–9:1). Then, after those words of reassurance, and as the final word in the section, comes the concluding point that no one, including the angels or "the son" himself, knows when the crisis will be resolved, hence: "Watch! Keep alert! Keep awake!"

There thus appears to be no "little apocalypse" in Mark 13. Is the discourse in Mark 13, perhaps along with that in Mark 4, to be understood as esoteric apocalyptic teaching? Many of the motifs taken as evidence for an apocalypse here seem to disappear once we both abandon the old synthetic construct of "apocalyptic" and examine the motifs more critically. Mark 13 appears rather to be somewhat analogous to 1 Corinthians 13, where Paul is borrowing a certain style and a few associated motifs in order to turn the subject matter of esoteric spiritual wisdom on its head. Mark appears to be utilizing some motifs that modern scholars classify as apocalyptic in order to caution the audience against jumping to conclusions about the historical crisis in which they are living. In Mark 13 the "apocalyptic" motifs serve two parenetic purposes: "rumors of war, famine," and so on characterize the current difficulties that are not to divert members of the movement from the struggle, and the impending coming of "the son of man" to gather the elect provides hope and reassurance that "summer is near," the crisis will not last forever. Mark 13, like the rest of the Gospel, is focused clearly on the historical struggle. Even in the context of a German theology focused on "the problem of history" thirty-five years ago, it was clear that Mark 13 "is not primarily concerned with speculating about the end (vv. 14–27), but rather with the struggles of the present time (vv. 5–13), the help of the Spirit (v. 11), and the exhortation to watch (vv. 28–37)."[24]

Because Mark's and the other Synoptic Gospels' statements ostensibly about the destruction of Jerusalem and the Temple have played such an important role in Christian ideology as well as biblical scholarship, we should at least clarify what Mark does not say in chap. 13, even if it may be impossible to discern exactly what Mark does say. There can be no question but that Mark sharply condemns the Temple and high priesthood. Moreover, the prophecy of the destruction of Jerusalem in 13:2 follows immediately upon Jesus' prophetic demonstration and pronouncements in chaps. 11–12, and then the double question of 13:3–4

---

24. Robinson, *Problem of History in Mark*, 50.

("When will these things be and what will be the sign . . . ?") appears to link what ensues in the rest of chap. 13 with the prophesied destruction of the Temple and high priests. Yet nothing in the rest of chap. 13 implies that the events prophesied have anything to do with Jerusalem. Judging from 13:14, these paragraphs must be composed from a viewpoint outside of both Jerusalem and Judea (fleeing to the mountains in Judea would mean fleeing toward Jerusalem). Even if we were to read these sayings as pertaining to events that included Jerusalem, the author's main message is to refuse to be distracted by ostensibly earth-shaking events from the concerns of the movement. But the concerns of the movement were renewal of Israel centered in Galilee, with a rejection of Temple and high priests as exploitative and unfaithful stewards. Hence, Mark is not rejecting Jerusalem rulers and ruling institutions because they had already been destroyed by Rome. Nor is Mark proclaiming God's judgment of Jerusalem and Jewish rulers in a vindictive way because they had killed Jesus. Rather, the conflict involving Jesus and the Jesus movement in Mark is rooted in and mirrors the structural social conflict in Roman dominated Judea and Galilee.

WISDOM IN MARK

With regard to instructional wisdom and torah-rulings in Mark, most striking is that the point of only the second story Mark tells at the opening of Jesus' ministry is to draw a sharp contrast between Jesus' teaching and that of the scribes. In distinction from the supposedly authoritative official teachers, Jesus teaches with ἐξουσία, that is, authority/power that is efficacious for and resonates with the people. In one of the major subplots of the Gospel, moreover, Mark further portrays Jesus as repeatedly challenging the authoritative wisdom of the scribes and Pharisees in several controversies in which Jesus appears to be building on traditional popular understandings or customs (e.g., 2:23–28; 7:1–23; 10:2–9). Mark thus provides us a clear sense of the structural social conflict in the context of which we must assess the presence or influence of instructional wisdom and torah-rulings in the Gospel.

Of the various types of wisdom mentioned above, there is simply no trace of speculative or cosmological or mantic wisdom in Mark. The deciphering of parables in Mark 4:10–20 might well be compared with one of the traditional functions of scribes (see Sir 39:1–3), assuming that the earliest establishable text of Mark read "mysteries" in 4:11, with each of the parables representing or containing a mystery. Only if the original text read "mystery" in the singular, virtually a technical term for the revealed plan of God, would we be inclined to view Mark 4 as a discourse in which Jesus was revealing an esoteric apocalyptic mystery. The relation of Jesus' parables to wisdom and their function in Mark has been dealt with extensively and critically in recent studies.[25]

Besides the parables, there is a handful of proverbs in Mark. Nearly every one of these appears to be from popular lore rather than from the learned scribal circles—certainly those about the unshrunk cloth on an old garment and new wine in old wineskins and that about a lamp under a bushel, and probably also the proverb about prophets not without honor except in their hometown (2:21–22; 4:21; 6:4). Most of these sayings do not stand alone, but have been used in formation of "pronouncement stories" or "controversy stories": for example, "the well have no need of a physician" climaxing 2:15–17; the "unshrunk cloth" and "new wine" attached to 2:18–20; and the proverb/parable about first binding the strong man before plundering his house as the climax of the Beelzebul controversy (3:22–27). How these sayings have been developed into or linked with chreiae or pronouncement stories in the pre-Markan tradition and Mark is evident by contrast with their standing as isolated sayings or in a series of similar sayings in the *Gospel of Thomas* (e.g., 31b; 104; 47e; 47d; 35; 31a, respectively). Insofar as these very controversy stories, along with several others, are directed against the Pharisees and/or scribes, popular-wisdom is utilized in Mark in a distinctive polemical argument against the officially sanctioned wisdom of the professional sages. Little influence of traditional professionally transmitted wisdom appears in Mark except in the negative sense: Mark's Jesus attacks it.

One suspects that the "apocalyptic" motifs in Mark, like the wisdom sayings, were simply common cultural coin. The presence of alien demonic forces that "possessed" particular people as well as provided an explanation for extreme social distress; the belief in resurrection as vindication of those martyred; the symbol of "the son of man" as an advocate or judgmental figure in the divine judgment—these were more than likely all standard features of Galilean culture, the latter two only very indirectly connected with Daniel 7 and 12. Mark, like the tradition upon which he drew, used both common popular wisdom sayings and common beliefs in his portrayal of the political-religious struggle to bring

---

25. See esp. Scott, *Hear Then the Parable*.

renewal in concrete social terms to the people (Israel). Mark portrayed Jesus as having already "bound the strong man" and exorcized unclean spirits as part of the establishment of the kingdom of God among the people. He used the symbol of "the (future) son of man" in sayings of sanction on discipline and reassurance of vindication for those in the movement, and perhaps most originally Mark used the resurrection of Jesus to point the movement back to Jesus' agenda of concrete social renewal in Galilee.

11

Apocalypticism in Gospels?
The Kingdom of God and the Renewal of Israel [1]

SINCE THE BEGINNING OF the twentieth century, Jesus and the Gospels have been interpreted as "apocalyptic," even as direct expressions of Jewish apocalypticism.[2] In his classic presentation of the apocalyptic Jesus, Albert Schweitzer thought that the Gospels of Mark and Matthew, along with the apostle Paul, could be used alongside other Jewish texts as sources for the apocalypticism that he and others believed pervaded Judaism at the time.[3] Critical liberal scholars have recently attempted to rescue a Jesus more compatible with modern rational sensibilities, a Jesus who did not proclaim the imminent end of the world.[4] As a way of isolating a non-apocalyptic Jesus they ascribe the apocalyptic elements in the Gospel tradition to John the Baptist and the interpretation of Jesus by his followers that found expression in the Gospels. In reaction, others scholars have strongly reasserted Schweitzer's view that Jesus, as attested

---

1. Only just before I came to writing the article for the *Encyclopedia of Apocalypticism* had I begun to gain greater clarity about the discrepancy between the standard scholarly construct of "apocalypticism" and what I found in reading through the texts themselves. At that time it seemed inappropriate for a contribution to a collaborative textbook on this important subject to raise questions about the standard construct that informed many of the other articles in the volume. For this collection of essays, however, I briefly sketch the discrepancy, and compare the Gospels and Gospel materials mainly with particular Judean apocalyptic texts, with only occasional comparisons with the standard construct as well. Accordingly the essay presented here is a considerably revised version of the original.

2. Schweitzer, *Quest*, 350–97; Bultmann, *New Testament Theology*, 1.1–4.

3. Schweitzer, *Quest*, 367.

4. For example, Crossan, *Historical Jesus*.

in the Synoptic Gospels, shared and preached the apocalyptic scenario that they believe was widely shared in his society at the time.[5] Both sides in the debate over the apocalyptic Jesus thus believe that the Gospel sources were apocalyptic. Any disagreements revolve only around the degree and the ways in which the Gospel tradition and the Gospels were apocalyptic.[6]

Ironically, many of those debates may have more to do with modern theology than with ancient Judean scribal texts and the Gospels produced by early Jesus movements. The concept of apocalyptic(ism) that dominates much of this discussion was developed over a century ago, when many of the texts classified as "apocalyptic" were (re-)discovered. It is a synthetic construct of typical features abstracted from a variety of Jewish "revelatory" literature ranging over several centuries, from the third century BCE to late antiquity. This construct was developed, moreover, during a time when scholars read the language of revelatory texts somewhat literally, without taking into account the way in which given images may have been used. For example, ancient Jewish apocalypticism supposedly involved the expectation of the imminent end of historical, earthly conditions in a "cosmic catastrophe"; historical life, meanwhile, was determined by "supernatural" forces, and apocalyptically minded people were "alienated from history" and oriented to an "otherworldly" existence. This highly synthetic construct was then found in a given text such as the Gospel of Mark on the basis of the presence of particular features classified as "apocalyptic." Even individual sayings in the Gospels were categorized as "apocalyptic" on the basis of the occurrence of one of the typical motifs or images, such as judgment or imminence.

This synthetic construct of "apocalypticism" or "apocalyptic eschatology" that dominated discussion of Jesus and the Gospels through much of the twentieth century centered on an "apocalyptic scenario" of the end of the world. In Schweitzer's presentation of Jesus (and in recent reassertions by neo-Schweitzerians), the imminent Jewish apocalyptic end-of-the-world scenario supposedly preached by Jesus and evident in the Gospels consisted of four main events or themes: the unprecedented suffering of the Great Tribulation, the eschatological Last Judgment, to be brought about by the Parousia of the Son of Man as the eschatological Judge, and accompanied or followed by the Resurrection of the dead.

5. For example, Allison, "The Eschatology of Jesus"; Allison, *Jesus of Nazareth*.
6. For example, Beasley-Murray, *Jesus and the Last Days*; Mack, *Myth of Innocence*.

During the last four decades, however, more critical analysis has resulted in a far more subtle and sophisticated understanding of particular Judean apocalyptic texts and the scribal circles that produced them.[7] Close scrutiny of key passages in Daniel 7 and the Similitudes of Enoch, made it increasingly clear that "the son of man" was not a title of the eschatological agent of judgment at the time of Jesus. It is difficult to find specialists on apocalyptic texts discussing "the Great Tribulation" in recent decades; they simply do not find it in the texts.

There is still considerable continuity, however, in the standard scholarly sketch of apocalypticism nearly a century after Schweitzer. In his pivotal essay in *The Encyclopedia of Apocalypticism*, John Collins, one of the most knowledgeable and influential scholars of Jewish apocalypticism, still presents Judean apocalyptic texts and the (presumed) apocalyptic worldview as centered on the end of the world, the final judgment, and the resurrection of the (individual) dead to a life of eternal glory (with the angels).[8] Perhaps because scholars tend to focus on text-fragments rather than complete texts, however, there is a considerable discrepancy or mismatch between the scholarly construction of apocalypticism and what the apocalyptic texts are about, not least on these supposedly key "events" or "themes." This can be illustrated briefly from Collins's essay, which seems to be a representative statement of the continuing interpretation of Judean apocalyptic texts in terms of the standard construct of apocalypticism.

The thesis stated at the outset of the article is that prophetic images of the end as involving a catastrophe of cosmic proportions was developed in apocalyptic texts into the notion of the end of the world.[9] Those images of the earth shaken and the heavenly bodies darkened, however, were standard prophetic language portraying the historical intervention of Yahweh to defeat the imperial enemies of Israel and to restore the people on their land (Isaiah 13; 24–27; Joel). The two brief passages in second-temple apocalyptic texts that mention the shaking of the earth or mountains and the darkening of the heavenly bodies (*1 Enoch* 1:4–7; *T. Mos.* 10:3–7, neither of which are cited) merely continue this standard prophetic portrayal of God's coming in judgment.[10] Earlier scholars evi-

---

7. Collins, *Apocalyptic Imagination*, is an influential example.
8. Collins, "From Prophecy to Apocalypticism."
9. Ibid., 129–45.
10. The only two brief passages that Collins cites (pp. 140 and 145, respectively) as envisaging "the end of the world in a literal sense" are problematic. That "the world will

dently tended to take the language a bit literally. But these images are hyperbole. Far from speaking of the catastrophic end of the world, they present God coming in judgment on the oppressive imperial rulers. Far from speaking of the end of the world, in fact, Judean apocalyptic texts look forward to a life of peace and justice on a renewed earth under a restored heavenly governance (for example, *1 Enoch* 10:4–8; 10:16—11:2; 24–25; 45:4–6; 48:10; 51:4–5; *T. Mos.* 10:1).

Judgment is indeed an important theme in apocalyptic texts in passing references and/or as an event in the resolution of the historical crisis on which the texts are focused. Judgment, of course, was already prominent in Israelite tradition, particularly in the tradition of prophetic oracles, and is hardly distinctive to apocalyptic texts. The subject of the judgment varies from text to text, moreover, as does the issue to which it is the resolution. And almost never is it very imminent.[11] Most of what Collins designates as "historical apocalypses" (perhaps better called historical visions-and-interpretations), focused on the emperor Antiochus IV Epiphanes' attacks on Jerusalem in 169–167 BCE, and conclude with a (usually brief) oracle or vision of the divine judgment of the invading oppressive and repressive king (Dan 7:11–12; 12:1a; the Animal Vision, *1 Enoch* 90:20–25; *T. Mos.* 10:3–7). Enoch's Animal Vision also includes the unfaithful Judeans in the judgment ("blinded sheep," 90:26–27), and the "Ten-Week Vision" has both a historical judgment of the wicked by the righteous and a divine judgment of the rebel heavenly watchers (*1 Enoch* 91:12, 15). In none of the historical visions-and-interpretations, however, is the judgment "on a cosmic scale" in a cataclysmic end of the world. It is rather the anticipated end of the particular imperial domination and exploitation in recent history by Antiochus Epiphanes (and the collaborating Judean "reformers"). Similarly, the first century CE

---

be written down for destruction" (*1 Enoch* 91:14) is based an older reconstruction of the text from one of the variants, which he seems to take literally. George Nickelsburg's more recent reconstruction of the text and translation gives almost the opposite sense of the text, as the end of injustice and the universal spread of justice in keeping of the law (*1 Enoch 1*, pp. 434, 437). Similarly there is nothing in Dan 12:1-3, which Collins takes as referring to what will happen "at the end of days" (Dan 12:13), that suggests the end of the world.

11. In the Book of Watchers (*1 Enoch* 1–36) judgment has already been implemented against the rebel heavenly "watchers" who had generated the race of giants who originated imperial war and exploitation, and is already prepared for the spirits of the giants who still perpetrate violence and desolation (15:8—16:1).

Similitudes of Enoch (*1 Enoch* 37–69) are all about judgment of the imperial "kings and mighty ones," but again the judgment is not "cosmic."[12]

The resurrection of the dead is a vague synthetic concept in the standard construction of apocalypticism. Many of the passages from earlier texts that have been taken as attesting the concept, however, speak rather of the restoration of the people (e.g., Ezekiel 37; even Isaiah 26:16–19). It is unclear how the gathering of the destroyed and dispersed "sheep" into the "new house" (*1 Enoch* 90:33) can be read as a figure for the resurrection when we have no attestation of the concept in an earlier text.[13] The gathering of the sheep is clearly part of a longer vision of the restored Israel at the conclusion of the Animal Vision. Evidence for belief in "the resurrection of the dead" at the time of Jesus comes mainly from three brief references: Daniel 12:2; *Pss. Sol.* 3:12; and the standard reading of Josephus' account of the beliefs of the Pharisees. This suggests that the resurrection was not a distinctively apocalyptic expectation. In Dan 12:2 it occurs as part of the restoration of the Judean people (12:1–3), which is not "the end of the world." Collins finds special importance in the judgment of the individual and "the hope of the individual for eternal glory with the angels" in "the new and distinctive worldview" of apocalypticism.[14] He is thus combining the reference to resurrection in Dan 12:2 with the vindication of "the wise" (*maskilim*) who, having been martyred for their resistance to the attacks by Antiochus Epiphanes, "will shine like the stars forever" in Dan 12:3. This is an image separate from the resurrection, however, as indicated in its application to the vindication of the righteous (at the judgment) in the Epistle of Enoch (*1 Enoch* 104:2) and to the restoration/ exaltation of the whole people in *T. Mos.* 10:8–9. In the context of Dan 12:1–3 (and the rest of Daniel 7–12), both the resurrection of the dead in 12:2 and the vindication of the martyrs

---

12. In *4 Ezra* and *2 Baruch*, which are desperately attempting to understand the disastrous devastation of Judah and Jerusalem by the Roman legions in 70 CE, judgment is closely linked with attempts to find an alternative to the now highly problematic Deuteronomic theology of reward and punishment for keeping or violating the covenant law. In his sketches of the "apocalyptic worldview" Collins ("From Prophecy to Apocalypticism," 147, 157) is unclear about where judgment focuses. For the second-century BCE texts, he emphasizes the judgment of individual human beings (which is, however, difficult to find in any of these texts); in his final sketch he focuses on "judgment of all nations on a cosmic scale" (again difficult to find in any apocalyptic text).

13. Collins, "From Prophecy to Apocalypticism," 141.

14. Ibid., 147.

in Dan 12:3 would appear to be particular (subordinate) aspects of the restoration of the people in 12:1.[15]

Even more striking than the paucity of attestation in second-temple Judean texts for the principal events in the apocalyptic scenario constructed by modern scholars is the scholars' lack of attention to the bulk of the content of these apocalyptic texts. As we shall see further below, the "historical apocalypses" focus their attention on the violent oppression and repression of the Judeans by imperial rulers, particularly Antiochus Epiphanes and in the brief concluding sections the restoration of the people/Israel, not the resurrection of the dead, is usually paired with the divine judgment of the imperial ruler(s).

There seems to be little point, therefore, in rehearsing the debates about Jesus and the Gospels carried on in terms of the standard synthetic construct of apocalypticism. What was being discerned as present, for example, in the Gospel of Mark or in a given saying of Jesus, were features in the modern concept of apocalypticism, and not the agenda and concerns of particular Judean texts.[16]

THE PRINCIPAL CONCERNS OF JUDEAN APOCALYPTIC TEXTS

Two results of recent research on second-temple apocalyptic texts, however, may provide a more appropriate basis for assessment of the Gospels in relation to them. Better-informed scholarly work on the manuscripts of texts that have produced more appropriate translations of the texts have enabled us to have a more comprehensive and critical grasp of their overall contents, agenda, and concerns.[17] And we now have a clearer sense of the general historical situation of the people who produced Judean apocalyptic texts as well as of those who produced the Gospels.

---

15. References to the resurrection of the dead are rare even in the late *4 Ezra* and *2 Baruch*. In the only discussion in 4 Ezra (7:32, 37, etc) it is "the nations" raised for judgment, not the individual raised in order to be glorified with the angels. Only in *2 Bar.* 50–51 (and 1 Corinthians 15) are the resurrection and glorification combined as part of the transformation from the old age/world to the new age/world—but that is on a renewed earth (*2 Bar.* 57:2; 73). As Collins suggests, however, the discussion in *2 Baruch* is yet another aspect of a Deuteronomic discussion, in this case of the respective rewards of the righteous and the wicked.

16. For example, by Perrin, *New Testament*; Mack, *Myth of Innocence*.

17. For example, Nickelsburg, *1 Enoch 1*; Tiller, *Commentary*; J. J. Collins, *Daniel*.

Generally speaking, Judean apocalyptic texts were the product of and were addressed to crises that emerged from the imperial rule of Judea by the Hellenistic and Roman empires.[18] Following the Babylonian destruction of Jerusalem and deportation of the Judean ruling class in 587 BCE. Judea was under the control of one empire after another. Whereas the Persian imperial regime had sponsored the return of the Judean ruling class to Jerusalem to rebuild the Temple and consolidate Judea's cultural and legal traditions, the "Western" empires, beginning with Alexander the Great, fostered a cultural as well as political-economic imperialism. The Hellenistic and Roman empires encouraged the ruling classes of the ancient Near East in particular to assimilate to the dominant Greek cultural as well as political forms.

That policy placed Judean scribes, who aided the high priestly families in governing the Judean temple-state, in a difficult situation. Scribes were the professional guardians and interpreters of the traditional Judean way of life, including the torah of Moses. When the Judean high priestly rulers in Jerusalem collaborated too closely with the Hellenistic and Roman imperial rulers and even adopted some of the dominant cultural and political forms, some scribes felt their own position as well as the traditional way of life threatened. In the escalating crisis that led up to the Maccabean Revolt, for example, the high priestly families appeared to "sell out" completely to the empire in an attempt to transform Jerusalem in to a Greek type of government along with its attendant culture. Evidently several circles of scribes steadfastly resisted this Hellenizing "reform." They began to receive "revelations" in the form of dreams that now appear in Daniel 7–12, the Animal Vision and the Ten-Week Vision (*1 Enoch* 85–90 and 93:1–10 + 91:11–17, respectively), and *T. Mos.* 1–5, 8–10. These visions and their interpretations not only explained how history had come to such an extreme crisis, but also reassured the faithful that God was still in control and would eventually take action to deliver them from the intolerable situation.

What comprised the bulk of the visions-and-interpretations was a revelatory review of history that led up to the historical crisis. The reviews in Daniel 7 and 10–12 focus on the succession of imperial rulers that dominated Judea during second-temple times, particularly the

---

18. The following paragraphs are a summary of the fuller discussion in chaps. 1–4 above; see further Horsley, *Scribes, Visionaries*, chaps 8–9; and Horsley, *Revolt of the Scribes*.

unprecedented violence of Antiochus Epiphanes' invasion and persecution. The Animal Vision and the *Testament of Moses* take a broader view of the history of Israel and Judea, indeed beginning with primordial history, but focus especially on the heightened exploitation and violence under imperial rule in the second-temple period and the persecution by Antiochus. The Ten-Week Vision is concerned with the "reform" but with less emphasis on imperial rule. In all of these texts except Daniel 8, the usually brief concluding sections focus on a two-fold resolution to the historical crisis: the divine judgment of oppressive imperial rule and the restoration of the people (the Judeans/ Israel). As part of the restoration two texts include a vindication of the martyrs who had resisted the imperial violence (Dan 12:3; *Testament of Moses* 9–10).

Judean apocalyptic literature displays both continuities and innovations in comparison with late prophetic literature in the Hebrew Bible. The principal innovation, which received little attention in the standard earlier construction of apocalypticism, is the review of history. It is difficult, in fact, to discern what might have been the precedent for such review in the Israelite cultural repertoire cultivated in second-temple scribal circles. The principal continuity lies in the resolution of the historical crisis in the judgment of foreign rulers and the restoration of the people. The portrayal of the vision of the divine court in judgment (Dan 7:9–12), of the coming of God in judgment (that entails the shaking of the earth and darkening of the heavenly bodies; *T. Mos.* 10:3–7), and of the judgment of oppressive rulers are continuations from Israelite prophetic tradition. Such portrayals stand in continuity with prophetic representations of "the day of the Yahweh and the divine warrior's action against the oppressors of Israel (e.g., Judg 5:4–5; Isaiah 13; 24–27; Joel). Portrayal of the restoration of the people in hyperbolic images is also a continuation of prophetic tradition (e.g., as in the fantastic imagery of a "new heaven and new earth" in Isa 65:17 and the idyllic conditions represented in Isa 65:19–25).

The representation of the divine/heavenly governance of the world, including earthly affairs and international relations, also stands in continuity with Israelite tradition, particularly the prophets and their oracles. Prophets received their oracles from apparent ascents to heaven in which they witnessed deliberations and decisions in the divine court where Yahweh presided over the "children of the gods" (e.g., 1 Kings 22; Isa 40:1–13). Certain of the heavenly figures were believed to be attached to or defenders of certain kingdoms ("nations," as in Deut 32:8). The visionaries who produced apocalyptic texts simply developed this into a more elaborate picture of the divine governance of historical affairs. Michael and Gabriel and a host of "the holy ones of the Most High" had particular responsibility to care for and defend Judeans (e.g., against the [divine] "prince of Persia" and the invasion of Antiochus Epiphanes; e.g., Daniel 7; 8; 10–12). It must have been difficult for Judean scribes dedicated to the maintenance of Judean tradition to understand how God could have been responsible for the Judeans' prolonged and intense experiences of suffering and oppression under one empire after another. Thus, perhaps not surprisingly, in somewhat of an innovative shift from earlier prophetic representations, Enoch texts appear to picture the Most High as a remote heavenly emperor who had delegated governance of historical affairs in second-temple times to "seventy [heavenly] shepherds" who had jurisdiction over imperial regimes, who in turn had jurisdiction over subject peoples such as the Judeans (*1 Enoch* 89:59–90:19). Similarly, it must have been difficult for those who were striving mightily to maintain the traditional way of life under circumstances of oppression or persecution to believe that their suffering was due only to their own sins. Again it was scribes who produced the Enoch texts who concluded that the imperial violence and exploitation were the result of a rebellion by some of the heavenly agents ("watchers"/"stars") against the divine commands and the "giants" (imperial regimes) they had generated on earth (e.g., *1 Enoch* 5–11; 86:1—87:1).[19]

It would thus be difficult to argue that the portrayal of the judgment of foreign rulers and the restoration of the people is distinctively "apocalyptic." It is rather a continuation of the prophetic tradition. It is also difficult to discern that apocalyptic texts display a distinctively new "worldview." Their portrayal of the divine governance of earthly affairs is an elaboration of long cultural tradition. As noted above, moreover, the

---

19. Modern interpreters have viewed these superhuman heavenly forces anachronistically as "supernatural" and they found here an unprecedented and distinctively "dualistic" apocalyptic worldview (for example, Collins, "From Prophecy to Apocalypticism," 147, 157). These heavenly figures are rather an elaboration of the Israelite, Judean, and general ancient Near Eastern worldview of the heavenly governance of earthly affairs. One of the types of "wisdom" that professional scribes cultivated was cosmological knowledge of just this divine governance, exemplified in the Enoch text, the Book of Heavenly Luminaries (*1 Enoch* 72–82). See further Horsley, *Scribes, Visionaries*, 127, 161–62; Stone, "Lists of Revealed Things."

resurrection of the dead (mentioned only in Dan 12:2, briefly) was not a distinctively apocalyptic expectation. What is new in these texts is the broad perspective on history that comes to crisis under the most recent imperial ruler. This comprises the majority of their contents. They then articulate their expectation of the divine termination of the oppressive empire and the restoration of the people sometime in the not too distant (but not imminent) future, the resolution to the historical crisis that they address.

Before proceeding to the Gospels, however, we should raise an important issue seldom addressed in study of Jesus and the Gospels. Generally it is simply assumed that Judean texts from around the time of Jesus provide evidence for a common Jewish culture or "Judaism" shared by most people in the society, except perhaps for the high priests and Herodian rulers. This assumption, however, does not take into account clear differences in social location. Apocalyptic texts were composed and written down by the literate cultural elite. Jesus and his followers, among whom the Synoptic Gospel tradition originated, were non-literate ordinary people who cultivated their own Israelite tradition in village communities.

A distinction made by anthropologists may help us understand the possible relationship between the literary products of the scribal elite and the traditions and ideas of the villagers. In many societies like that in ancient Judea and Galilee, two parallel traditions operate at different social levels. The elite cultivate a "great" or official tradition, usually oral but often also in written form. Meanwhile, villagers cultivate a "little" or popular tradition, completely in oral form, according to which life in local communities is conducted. There is often interaction between the two parallel traditions. Yet because of the differences in social location and interests, there is often considerable difference, even conflict, between the two. A good example of such conflict appears in Mark 7:1–13. There Jesus defends the Galilean villagers' concern for retaining their economic produce in order to feed their families, according to the basic "commandment of God" ("Honor your father and mother"), against the scribal "traditions of the elders" that, in this instance, encouraged the villagers to "devote" some of their economic resources to support of the Temple.

Judean apocalyptic texts, therefore, may not provide good evidence for the views and attitudes of ordinary Galileans and Judeans. In periods of crisis under imperial rule, such as the attacks by Antiochus Epiphanes or (re-)conquests by Roman legions, scribes may well have come to experience the kind of humiliation and oppression to which villagers were regularly subjected by their rulers. But the scribal composers of apocalyptic texts were working out of a long tradition of scribal forms and lore. We would not expect distinctively scribal lore and reflection to appear in popular movements or communities. On the other hand, the scribal producers of apocalyptic texts were heirs of the Israelite prophetic tradition, which they shared in some ways with Judean and Galilean villagers. This shared prophetic tradition, however, points to what may be more appropriate comparative material for Jesus movements and the development of the Synoptic Gospel tradition into Gospel texts.

The scribal circles who produced apocalyptic texts were not the only ones longing for the renewal of Israel and, in certain circumstances, ready to mount resistance to the rulers. Brief accounts in Josephus' histories offer windows onto two kinds of popular movements right around the time of Jesus and early Jesus movements. Both a generation earlier and a generation later, large numbers of villagers, acclaiming one or another of their leaders as "king" (messiah), managed to revolt and maintain their independence from their rulers for up to three years. In the decades immediately after Jesus's mission, prophets such as Theudas, the "Samaritan," and the "Egyptian," posing as the new Moses and/or Joshua, led popular movements in which they anticipated God's new act of deliverance of the people. Both types of movements were those of renewal of the people in resistance to the rulers, with a sense that they were participating in decisive events of the termination of their rulers' control of their lives. In that sense they had moved a decisive step beyond the scribes who produced apocalyptic texts who, while suffering martyrdom in their resistance to imperial rule, were reassuring themselves that at some point in the future, hopefully soon, God would reassert control of history and enact the judgment of empire and the restoration of the people. The difference was less a matter of the degree of imminence than of whether the renewal and judgment were already underway.

In another respect, however, apocalyptic texts and the popular prophetic and messianic movements are parallel in their *historical* understanding of their situation. Both exhibit a strong *memory* of God's previous acts of deliverance (and discipline) of the people, memory that then informs their *imagination* or creative vision of a life of independence and justice for the people in the present or future. The combination of this memory and the imagination of a new, different future made possible a critical *demystification* of the present situation of imperial rule through the client high priesthood and/or Herodian kings. The emperors were not divine and the high priests were not sacrosanct. God willed a different life, one of independence and justice. The Judean scribes who produced apocalyptic texts and the Judean and Galilean villagers who participated in the popular messianic and prophetic movements shared this vision, deeply rooted in the Israelite prophetic tradition.

THE SERIES OF JESUS-SPEECHES IN Q: THE PROPHETIC RENEWAL OF ISRAEL

The standard understanding of the relationship among the Synoptic Gospels —Matthew, Mark, and Luke—is that Mark was composed first and that Matthew and Luke followed Mark's narrative, while inserting a great deal of additional material. The large amount of non-Markan material in both Matthew and Luke, much of it identical in wording, must have come (it is believed) from a common source known as "Q." This is hypothesized to be the earliest text from among Jesus movements.

This earliest of the "gospels" texts consists of a series of Jesus speeches, with little or no narrative. It makes no mention of Jesus' crucifixion and resurrection and has no concern for Jesus' identity as the Messiah/Christ. Those "omissions" were not found to be particularly significant so long as Q was understood to be basically "catechetical" (teaching) material supplementary to the fundamental "gospel" proclaimed in Mark and followed by Matthew and Luke. Once Q was viewed as an independent gospel text, however, it also appeared to be the product of and to provide evidence for a Jesus movement different from the one from and for which Mark originated.

Until recently "Q" was understood merely as a collection of sayings. The discovery of the *Gospel of Thomas* early last century seemed to provide another example of the same literary genre. Among those who have studied Q closely, opinions are sharply divided over the degree to which it displays "apocalyptic" features. A generation ago prominent scholars in the U.S. understood Q, like the Gospel of Mark, as an expression of "apocalyptic Christianity."[20] More recently, North American scholars

20. Perrin, *New Testament*.

have claimed that "apocalyptic" material in Q belongs to a secondary layer, as opposed to the supposedly original document, which consisted mainly of wisdom sayings. One motive in this effort has been the desire to free Jesus as a wisdom teacher acceptable to late-twentieth-century liberal sensibilities from the eschatological visionary who predicted a "cosmic catastrophe," as envisioned earlier in the twentieth century by Albert Schweitzer and Rudolf Bultmann.

One particular division of Q into a formative "sapiential" layer and a secondary "apocalyptic" layer became highly influential among members of the "Q Seminar" of the Society of Biblical Literature.[21] Five clusters of Q sayings (3:7–9, 16–17; 7:1–10, 18–35; 11:14–26, 29–32, 37–52; 12:39–59; and 17:23–35) are assigned to a later "apocalyptic" layer on the basis of three common features. The projected audience supposedly consists of the impenitent opponents of the Q people, all the other people of Israel. The literary form of "prophetic judgment" and "apocalyptic" sayings, it is claimed, dominate these clusters. And supposedly preponderant in these five clusters are motifs related to the theme of judgment, such as imminence and the *parousia*, with "Israel" obstinately rejecting Jesus and the Q preachers while "the Gentiles" respond positively. When one examines these five clusters of sayings, however, it is difficult to find these hypothesized "common features." The vast majority of material in these clusters is directed to the "in- group" of Jesus' followers themselves (3:16–17; 7:18–35; 11:14–26; 12:39–59; 17:23–35). Part of one cluster is ostensibly directed against the "scribes and Pharisees" (11:37–52). Yet there is no reason to think that "this generation" accused in 11:29–32 refers to "Israel" as opposed to "Gentiles." Moreover, in form virtually none of the sayings in these clusters can be classified as "apocalyptic." Rather, many would more legitimately be classified as "prophetic," raising questions about why the label "apocalyptic" should be used for this supposed layer in Q in the first place. The motifs that dominate these "clusters" of sayings, finally, are not particularly "apocalyptic." For example, judgment is not particularly "imminent," and the expectation of the *parousia* is not found in Q itself but is introduced in Matthew's resetting of certain sayings. We shall find that Q expresses the same basic concerns as apocalyptic texts and the earlier prophetic texts (the renewal of the people and the judgment of the rulers). Yet since it lacks many of

---

21. The following is a summary of Kloppenborg, *Formation of Q*. Fuller discussion in chap. 8 above.

Apocalypticism in Gospels? 243

the key forms and motifs typical of apocalyptic literature, attempts to distinguish an apocalyptic literary stratum are not persuasive.

What has come out of the sharp debate about the hypothetical "apocalyptic" and "wisdom" layers in Q has been the growing recognition that Q is not merely a collection of sayings like the *Gospel of Thomas*. Whereas the sayings in the *Gospel of Thomas* appear separately or in pairs, most of the sayings in Q appear in speeches focused on particular issues. It is now increasingly being recognized that Q is a series of discourses, each focused on some particular issue such as instructions for mission or exhortation to fearless confession when on trial. Q is more like the *Didache* (Teaching of the Twelve Apostles), a sort of handbook providing instruction on basic issues for early "Christian" communities in Syria. To a degree the issues dealt with in Q come in the same sequence as the same issues in the *Didache*. Q can thus be read as a coherent set of discourses addressing key concerns of an early Jesus movement.[22]

The series of speeches in Q even has a dominant connecting theme. Sayings about the "kingdom of God" occur prominently at crucial points in most of the discourses. In Jesus' first words to his followers he offers the kingdom to the poor (6:20); the envoys Jesus sends out are to announce that in the healing of the sick "the kingdom of God has come near" (10:9). Indeed, in his exorcisms the kingdom of God has "come upon you" (11:14–20). If those anxious about food and clothing will earnestly "seek the kingdom of God," then they need not worry about subsistence food and shelter (12:22–31). The reality, nearness, or presence of the kingdom is accompanied by a sense of experiencing something utterly new, unprecedented in the history of Israel, a fulfillment of age-old longings and expectations. Now that the kingdom is coming, the hungry will be filled, those who weep will laugh (6:21; 11:2–4). In the practice and preaching of Jesus the blind now see, the lame walk, the deaf hear, and the poor receive good news, in fulfillment of well-known prophecies in the book of Isaiah (7:22; cf. Isa 35:5–6; 61:1). While the greatest figure in history is John the Baptist, "the least in the kingdom is greater than he" (7:28). Those who experienced Jesus' ministry are seeing what many prophets and kings desired to see (10:24). This is something greater than the famous wisdom of Solomon or the preaching of Jonah (11:31–32).

---

22. The following discussion of the Q speeches is based on Horsley, "Q and Jesus"; fuller subsequent analysis in Horsley with Draper, *Whoever Hears You Hears Me*.

An intense sense of a new historical time, a fulfillment of age-old longings, of renewal of personal and community life, dominates Q.

The unprecedented situation created by Jesus' preaching and practice is in fact a historical crisis with a sense of fulfillment of deep-seated longings. John announced that the coming one would baptize with both "Holy Spirit and fire," that he would "burn the chaff with unquenchable fire" as well as "gather the wheat into his granary." This is exactly what the Q discourses portray as underway. As indicated in the instructions for the "workers in the harvest," the kingdom of God is being manifested in the healings of the sick, but it also comes near in the judgmental mode for those who reject the movement, its message, and its workers (10:8–11, 12–16). Those who think they can rely on their aristocratic genealogy or those who presume upon their wealth and privilege will find themselves cast out when all Israel gathers for the glorious feast of fulfillment (13:28–29). Those who do not respond now will be accused and condemned in "the judgment" (11:31–32). Holy Spirit and fire, grain gathered into the granary and chaff burned with fire.

Given the prominence of both fulfillment and judgment running through its discourses, it may not be surprising that earlier interpreters found "apocalyptic Christianity" in Q. Parallel to the scribal dream-vision in Daniel 7 that envisaged God's return of sovereignty (the kingdom) to the "people of the saints of the Most High," the prophetic discourses in Q proclaimed the benefits of God's kingdom already under way for the desperate villagers of Israel. Parallel to anticipation of judgment against the wealthy and powerful rulers in Jerusalem in the Animal Vision and the Epistle of Enoch, in Q the prophets John and Jesus pronounced judgment against the ruling house of Jerusalem and its representatives (13:34–35; 11:37–52). It is striking, however, that it is difficult to find the features of the modern scholarly construct of apocalypticism in the Q discourses. In fact, particular expressions in the Q discourses also rarely resemble the images and motifs found in particular Judean apocalyptic texts. The Q discourses display little or nothing that resembles scribal lore. The parallels are rather in the fundamental agenda that they share with the prophetic tradition in focusing on the renewal of Israel and the judgment of the rulers.

John the Baptist's preaching of repentance and prophecy of a stronger one coming after him who would "baptize in Holy Spirit and fire" (Luke 3:7–9, 16–17//Matt 3:7–12) would appear to have opened the series of discourses in Q. The images of "the wrath to come" as a harvest-time winnowing of wheat from chaff and a burning of unfruitful trees drew on both familiar experiences in an agrarian society and a long Israelite prophetic tradition of impending divine judgment. John sets his call for repentance and renewal of the Mosaic covenant directly over against the upper-class Jerusalemite trust in the unconditional Abrahamic promise and their cultivation of proper genealogies (Q/Luke 3:7–9, 16–17; cf. 13:28–29). In the context of Q, the "stronger one" coming with "Spirit and fire" is Jesus, who is about to proclaim and manifest the kingdom of God. In subsequent discourses Jesus performs in his ministry what John prophesies (see especially Q/Luke 7:18–28). In that respect (despite the obvious differences in social location) Q seems similar to key texts from the Qumran community, where the new exodus and new (Mosaic) covenant community are already under way (see especially the opening "covenant renewal" sections of the *Community Rule* and the *Damascus Document*). The long-awaited renewal of Israel is already happening in the communities' very foundation, and the communities live in intense anticipation of fuller realization of their now-intensified hopes and expectations. None of the imagery used by the Baptist, however, suggests an imminent "last judgment," let alone "cosmic catastrophe."

Next comes the only extended narrative in Q, the story of Jesus' temptation by the devil. This section of Q does not seem to fit well with (the rest of) the series of discourses. Especially interesting is the opposition of the devil and the Spirit, which leads Jesus into "forty days in the wilderness," the period of preparation for a Moses-like or Elijah-like prophetic mission. The same opposition between the devil/Satan and Jesus in the power of the Spirit (or "finger") of God appears later in the Beelzebul discourse (Q/Luke 11:14–26). This resembles the struggle between the Spirit of Light and the Spirit of Darkness (= Belial) in the *Community Rule* from Qumran. But the opposition in Q is nowhere near as all-encompassing and determinative of human affairs in general, nor is it as systematically developed as in the scribal reflection evident in the Qumran texts.

The Q "sermon" (Q/Luke 6:20–49) presents a renewed Mosaic covenant, with many similarities to the renewed covenant in the opening columns of the *Community Rule* from Qumran. As interpreters of the Mosaic covenant in Exodus 20 and the covenant renewal in Joshua 24 have explained, the covenant that served as Israel's basic form of governance under the direct rule of God had three interrelated parts. God's great acts of deliverance (from Egyptian slavery, etc.) were recited first; then the principles of exclusive loyalty to God and the principles of social-economic relations (the Decalogue) were presented; and finally sanctions such as "blessings and curses" were declared as motivation for the people's compliance. The same basic pattern is evident in the Q sermon, although the blessings and curses seem displaced from the end to the beginning. The set of sayings about "love your enemies, do good, and lend" and "turn the other cheek" in Q/Luke 6:27–38(–42), which closely resemble traditional covenantal exhortations (e.g., Leviticus 19), constitute the principles of social-economic relations, in this case renewed reciprocity and mutual care in the (village) communities. The sayings about good and bad trees and the double parable about building one's house on rock versus sand in Q/Luke 6:43–49 serve as sanctions on maintaining the renewed covenantal relations.

Consideration of the historical social context addressed may help clarify the seeming displacement of the blessings and curses to the beginning of the renewed covenant in Q.[23] As in most agrarian societies, the Galilean and Judean peasantry were economically marginal at best. Compounding the people's burdens of tribute to Rome and tithes and offerings to Temple and high priesthood, Herod the Great and Herod Antipas had intensified economic exploitation of their subjects to fund their massive building projects. Given the Mosaic covenantal scheme, however, the struggling people would presumably have understood their worsening conditions of poverty and hunger as God's curses for their having violated the commandments. In the opening of the Q covenant renewal speech, Jesus directly addresses this debilitating self-blame of the "poor" and "hungry" people. God's bringing of the kingdom is the new act of deliverance on the basis of which the people can now renew the covenantal care and cooperation of their community life. Once we are aware of Israelite covenantal traditions and the historical social context it is possible to discern that the "beatitudes" of the renewed covenant in Q are yet another indication of the renewal of Israel underway in Jesus' prophetic preaching.

The next major discourse, Q/Luke 7:18–35 confirms this intense sense of fulfillment as already underway. The age-old longings of the

---

23. See Horsley, *Jesus and the Spiral of Violence*, 246–73; further developed in Horsley with Draper, *Whoever Hears You Hears Me*, chap 9.

people are now being fulfilled in the good news Jesus is preaching and the healing and liberation he is practicing (7:22; cf. Isa. 35:5–6; 61:1). Not only is John the Baptist's work set over against the Herodian rulers (against whom he prophesied, according to Mark 6 and Josephus), but he is held up as the greatest figure of history, in comparison with whom even the least in the kingdom of God is greater! This discourse intensifies the sense of unprecedented renewal now happening, a sense of fulfillment that goes well beyond that expressed in Qumran literature. It also indicates that the prophetic pronouncements and the work of John and Jesus have provoked sharp criticism and accusations (7:31–35).

The "mission" discourse in Q/Luke 9:57—10:16 makes unavoidably clear that Q is the document of a movement, not a mere collection of Jesus' pithy sayings addressed to individuals. The introduction to the mission instructions alludes to the well-known stories of the prophet Elijah's calling of his successor Elisha, who carried on his prophetic project of renewing an Israel suffering under alien and exploitative rule. The harvest imagery is now completely positive, in contrast with the double-edged imagery of John's preaching: the huge harvest requires sending out workers. The village-by-village preaching and healing by the workers, however, vividly illustrate the dual impact and effect of the kingdom now at hand: healing for the receptive, but proleptic judgment for those who reject the offer. Jesus' woes consigning the unreceptive villages to judgment cite "Sodom," the standard "historical" example of God's destructive punishment in Israelite prophetic tradition, as well as Tyre and Sidon, standard foils in earlier prophetic oracles, as well as nearby alien and wealthy cities. The kingdom of God is already effective in anticipation of its nearness and the rhetoric of rejection intense, but judgment does not seem particularly imminent.

The most "revelatory" language in Q comes in the next sayings, Q/Luke 10:21–24, the contours of whose discourse cannot be fully discerned from Matthew's and Luke's editing. Jesus gives thanks to the Father that he has "revealed" ("apocalypsed") all these things to "babes," that is, the ordinary people, and in fact hidden them from the sapiential elite, the professional scribes and sages who cultivated and, on occasion, received "revelations." This indicates explicitly that the Q discourses were products of a popular movement and not the political elite of kings and high priests or the cultural elite of the scribes and Pharisees. Apocalyptic texts such as the sections of *1 Enoch* were produced by dissident scribal circles also opposed to the high priestly rulers of Judea. Q, however, was "revelation" specifically for a popular movement of renewal, self-consciously set over against scribes as well as rulers. We should thus not expect in these discourses the kind of scribal lore, reflection, and speculation that we find in apocalyptic literature.

The content of the following section in Q, which contains the Lord's Prayer, was shifted into a more distinctively religious mode by Luke, then variously spiritualized through generations of Christian recitation. While Luke has surely retained the shorter form more original to the Q prayer for the kingdom, Luke 11:2–4, Matthew has probably preserved more of the wording of particular phrases in Q. The third petition in particular, Matt 6:12//Luke 11:4, enables us to discern just how concrete and down-to-earth the kingdom of God was understood to be among the Q people. The most serious problems for Galilean as for any peasants would have been chronic hunger and the spiral of indebtedness into which they were forced by their obligation of taxes, tithes, and tribute, leaving less than enough to feed hungry families. In the prayer for the kingdom, Jesus taught the people to petition the Father in heaven for subsistence bread and for cancellation of debts! The concrete economic meaning of the "kingdom of God" in Q is reminiscent of the concrete economic meaning of the "new heaven and new earth" prophecy in Isa 65:17–22. In severe circumstances prophetic vision resorts to extreme hyperbole in its symbolization of longings for a simple life free of war, oppression, and exploitation. The prayer in Q/Luke 11:2–4 is also consistent with the covenantal exhortations in the Q sermon, which admonish the people to reciprocal cooperation and sharing (Q/Luke 6:27–36). Those who petition for cancellation of their debts are reciprocally therewith forgiving the debts of their neighbors.

The matter-of-fact language about demons in the Beelzebul discourse in Q/Luke 11:14–26 suggests that the Q people lived in a world in which demons and demon possession were familiar. It would appear that in Judean and Galilean society in the second-temple period, particularly under the highly intrusive Seleucid and Roman imperial rule, the traditional covenantal explanation of suffering as punishment for sin was no longer adequate. Surely God could not be responsible for the extreme suffering of his people. Surely superhuman forces were at work. Like colonized peoples in modern times who dare not focus directly on imperial violence as the cause of their malaise, the ancient Judean and

Apocalypticism in Gospels? 249

Galileans understood various forms of their personal and social disorder in terms of possession by alien spirits. Indeed, such colonial situations seem to be caught in a struggle between two superhuman/divine forces.

The Qumran community developed a systematic and comprehensive scheme whereby all history was understood as caught in a struggle between the Spirit of Light and the Spirit of Darkness, created at the beginning by God. By contrast with the *Community Rule* and the *War Scroll* from Qumran, the struggle between Holy Spirit and Satan in Q is relatively undeveloped. It is nowhere nearly as pervasive and comprehensive in Q as among that scribal- priestly community. It may also be noteworthy that this opposition is introduced into the discussion ostensibly by Jesus' opponents who accuse him of working in cahoots with Satan. Comparative materials such as the sixteenth- and seventeenth-century western European witch-hunts suggest that the intellectual and/or political elite of a society can press a comprehensive dualistic ideology on a population precisely in order to eliminate "deviants." The Beelzebul discourse appears to be cleverly formulated. Opponents (evidently scribal) representing a systematic ideology of opposing spiritual forces ascribe Jesus' remarkable influence over demons to the Satanic side of the struggle. This provides Jesus with the occasion to demonstrate (logically) that even on the establishment's own terms Satan's rule is collapsing, as manifested in his own exorcisms, hence the kingdom of God has come upon the people. Thus also Q's Beelzebul discourse represents God's final victory over Satan as already under way (Q/Luke 11:17–22), whereas the Qumran community was still awaiting "the time of his visitation."

The short (fragmentary) speech in Q/Luke 11:29–32 juxtaposes a blunt rejection of "this generation seeking a sign" with a vivid portrayal of "this generation's" condemnation at "the judgment." Q/Luke 11:32 indicates that "the preaching of Jonah" was the "sign of Jonah" for the Ninevites (who repented!). Thus, in the analogy drawn with "the sign of Jonah" in 11:30, the "son of man" must be a self-reference by Jesus, somewhat like "son of man" in the fourth Q beatitude (Luke 6:22; cf. Matt 5:11) and the introduction to the mission discourse (Q/Luke 9:58), and not a reference to the judgment, which is mentioned explicitly in 11:31–32. The "son of man" in 11:30, moreover, stands parallel to "something greater than Solomon . . . [and] Jonah" that "is here" in 11:31–32. Thus, besides excoriating "this generation" for its lack of response, these charges parallel the point made in earlier Q discourses (especially Q/ Luke 7:18–28; 10:23–24), that in Jesus' preaching and healing something long-awaited but historically unprecedented is happening. "The judgment," however, does not seem particularly imminent. Also noteworthy is the matter-of-fact way that the statements assume the resurrection of earlier generations to appear as accusers at the judgment. These are not simply literary motifs. Resurrection and judgment have become integral parts of the prevailing cultural "symbol system" or "symbolic universe" that Q and the Q community presuppose.

The series of woes against the Pharisees and scribes, Q/Luke 11:37–52, mocks their concerns for purity and indicts them for the debilitating effect of their role as retainers of the temple-state on the people, for example, when they urge the people to pay the full levy of tithes and other (economic) "burdens." The corresponding pronouncement of "sentence" in 11:49–51 indicates that the Q people understand the hero-founder of their movement to stand in a long line of Israelite prophets killed by the elite, (by implication) the rulers as well as their scribal retainers. The Q discourses portray Jesus, like John the Baptist, in a prophetic role in both his preaching and healing, with reminiscences of Moses (6:20–49) and Elijah (9:57–62). Jesus himself is evidently the greatest and final prophet in that line, since the kingdom of God is clearly under way in his ministry.

That "hidden" things are "revealed," at least to the elect, is a prominent theme in Judean apocalyptic texts. The "hidden . . . revealed" in Q/ Luke 12:2–12, however, refers not to what a scribal visionary has received from an interpreter-angel, but to the eventual public triumph of the mission of the Q people that is currently pursued surreptitiously because of the threat of repression by the authorities (12:3, 11). In the further statements of assurance given in 12:4–5, Gehenna, the ravine south of Jerusalem that had become a symbol for the fiery punishment upon condemnation in "the judgment," seems to be another component in the basic "symbolic universe" presupposed in Q. Similarly standard in the symbol system that Q presupposes is the picture in 12:8–9 of the judgment as carried out before "the angels of heaven," a traditional picture of the divine court. The "son of man" figure in 12:8 probably not another self-reference by Jesus (as in 6:22; 9:57; and 11:30), but a (prophetic) "correlative" to Jesus as a witness or advocate/accuser before the divine court (somewhat like the Ninevites or the Queen of the South in 11:31–32). Contrary to earlier assumptions, the "son of man" figure here is not the agent of judgment.

Another saying referring to the "son of man," in Q/Luke 12:(39–)40 appears to go together with and to be interpreted by 12:41–46. This (difficult to delineate) discourse would appear to be an admonition to the members (or leadership?) of the movement to maintain rigorous discipline, sanctioned by judgment that will occur at an unexpected time. The emphasis is clearly on the unexpectedness of judgment, as indicated by the very imperfect analogy between "the thief" and "the son of man"—who again in this Q statement is hardly an agent of judgment, and does not appear to be a self-reference by Jesus.

The discourse in Q/Luke 12:49–56 refers to the crisis in families and local communities provoked by Jesus' mission and movement. Jesus uses the ominous hyperboles of fire, flood, and war, and cites the traditional prophetic (not distinctively "apocalyptic") scenario of generational division in households (12:49–51, 52–53; cf. Mic 7:6). He then draws the analogy from interpreting the appearance of earth and sky to interpreting historical events of the present, meaning apparently the significance of the movement under way, in which the kingdom of God is finally present. It is unclear if the parables of the kingdom in Q/Luke 13:18–21 belonged to a larger discourse. In any case, the comparisons they make parallel the discourses in Q/Luke 12:2–12; 12:22–31; and 12:49–56. They suggest that Jesus' mission and movement (in which the kingdom is now coming or is about to come), while seemingly insignificant at the outset, will grow dramatically, having a transforming effect on society.

The prophetic oracle and prophetic lament in Q/Luke 13:28–29 and 13:34–35 have often been interpreted according to a certain Christian paradigm of salvation history that has seriously skewed the reading of Q generally. It has been assumed that in the Gospels as well as in Paul, the new, universal religion Christianity was replacing the old, particularist religion Judaism. According to this scheme, "the sons of the kingdom" in Matt 8:12 and "Jerusalem" in Luke 13:34//Matt 23:37 are taken as symbols of a monolithic "Judaism," and these sayings appear to be prophetic condemnations of "all Israel" or "Judaism." It is difficult to discern the possible contours of the one-time Q discourse of which these prophetic statements may have been components. Yet read against the background of a more precise understanding of the Judean temple-state, they can now be understood as prophetic condemnations of the ruling house in

Jerusalem, not "all Israel." The parallel references from earlier prophetic literature to the "pilgrimage" from east and west into the banquet of fulfillment in 13:29, moreover, refer not to "Gentiles" but to dispersed Israelites. These sayings thus express the same basic opposition between rulers and ruled within "Israel" that prevailed at the time in the political-economic-religious structure of the Judean temple-state, including ideological conflict over the form that "Israel" should take. Q/Luke 13:28–29 is thus a prophetic vision of the finally restored Israel banqueting with its founding ancestors, but significantly without the rulers who presumed on their ancestry (cf. John's words in 3:7–9). Q/Luke 13:34–35— which is paralleled strikingly thirty years later by the woes on Jerusalem by another rustic prophet, Jesus son of Hananiah—is a prophetic lament over the Jerusalem ruling house, which has repeatedly blocked God's attempts at renewal of Israel through the messages of the prophets.

What is perhaps the next to the last discourse in Q, Q/Luke 17:23–24, 26–30, 33–34, 37, focusing on the suddenness of "the day of the son of man," is probably a sanction on all of the exhortation in the preceding Q discourses. This speech is the locus of most of the so-called "future Son of Man sayings," which have been claimed as proof texts for the "apocalyptic" character of Q in general and/or for the secondary "apocalyptic" layer in Q.[24] "Logia apocalypse" is an inappropriate designation, since it lacks any narrative presentation of final events ("and then . . . ," etc.). The concept of the "coming" (παρουσία) is Matthew's contribution (24:27, 37, 39). Within the discourse there is nothing even to suggest that "the son of man" is Jesus, although that meaning may carry over from Jesus' self-references in earlier discourses in Q. The series of parallel sayings in Q/Luke 17, with the analogies of "the days of Noah" and "the days of Lot" simply emphasize the suddenness of judgment symbolized in "the day of the son of man." Judging from references in various texts, such as Ezekiel, *Jubilees*, and *Testaments of the Twelve Patriarchs*, use of references to Noah and/or the destruction of Noah's generation and to "Sodom (and Gomorrah)" and/or the escape of Lot were quite varied as examples of judgment and/or deliverance in Judean and wider Jewish culture (and is not distinctively "apocalyptic"). But nothing in this Q discourse comes close either to "cosmic destruction" or to the portrayal of the present generation as so wicked that it, like that of Noah,

---

24. Collins, "The Son of Man in the Sayings Source"; Jacobson, "Apocalyptic and the Sayings Source Q."

needed to be utterly destroyed. "The days of Noah and those of Lot in Q/Luke17:26–27, 28 serve simply as analogies for the future judgment and how sudden and unexpected it will be. The Q discourse does not appear to be directed against apocalyptic-style calculation or prediction of "signs," but against the Q people becoming distracted by any other movements or leaders (Q/Luke 17:23). This discourse could even be reassuring to the Q people, on whose behavior it is a sanction, insofar as the prophetic correlatives indicate how the suddenness took the others unawares, while the heroes Noah and Lot were delivered.

It seems likely that Luke 22:30//Matt 19:28 was (part of) Jesus' final speech in Q. This saying, read, like Q/Luke 13:28–29 and 34–35, through a Christian paradigm of salvation history, has been taken to mean that the Twelve are to be (negatively) "judging" Israel. This reading involves a misleading translation of the Greek verb κρίνειν, which clearly carries the positive meaning of "doing justice for" or even "delivering" in the Greek translation of the Hebrew Bible (the Septuagint)—as when God "defends" the widow, the orphan, and the poor in the Psalms and elsewhere.[25] Matthew's interjection of "the Son of Man sitting on his glorious throne" may have contributed to the skewed Christian reading of the saying. But the term "renewal" (παλιγγενεσία) in Matt 19:28, used by the Judean historian Josephus for the restoration of Israel on its land (*Ant.* 10.66, 107), suggests what "kingdom" in Q/Luke 22:30 means. Indeed, the whole series of discourses known as Q, consistently focused on the theme of the kingdom of God, constitutes a sustained presentation of various aspects of the renewal of Israel.

The symbol of "twelve tribes of Israel" makes this meaning unavoidable. The Q people (or the leadership, symbolically also "twelve," as in Matthew's version) are to be establishing justice for or delivering the twelve tribes of Israel. This concept is paralleled in Jewish literature of that time such as the (non-apocalyptic) *Psalms of Solomon* (17:28–32) and the *Community Rule* from Qumran (1QS 8:1–4). In the latter, "the council of the community," consisting of twelve men and three priests, is to effect "righteousness, justice, loving-kindness, and humility, . . . preserve faith in the land, . . . and atone for sin by the practice of justice." Thus, Q does not end with Jesus' setting up the Twelve to condemn Israel at the last judgment. Like the scribal-priestly community at Qumran, the peasant movement that produced the Q discourses was engaged in a

---

25. Horsley, *Jesus and the Spiral of Violence*, 201–8.

renewal of Israel. The Q movement aimed at renewal of Israel, however, did not withdraw from the rest of society, either as a community in the wilderness or as a bunch of "wandering charismatics," but focused on revitalization of the village communities, the fundamental social form in which Israel was constituted.

There thus appears to be little basis for classifying the discourse "gospel" Q as "apocalyptic" in the older sense that has dominated the field of New Testament studies. No imminent cosmic catastrophe looms. The imagery of harvest or fire upon the earth or allusion to historical destructions (in Q/Luke 3:9, 17; 12:49; 17:27) does not point to any sort of "catastrophic destruction of the world."[26] There is no feeling of "historical determinism." References to "the judgment" abound, but it is not particularly imminent. Contrary to much recent scholarly discussion, Jesus does not appear to be identified with a heavenly judge or redeemer with the title "the Son of Man." When "the son of man" refers to Jesus, he is not playing the role of an eschatological judge or redeemer, and when "the day of the son of man" refers to the time of judgment, it does not appear to be identified with Jesus. The most prominent image of the future fulfillment of the people's longings is that of a banquet in the kingdom of God, known in the Israelite prophetic tradition from Jeremiah. References to heaven and the divine court; to hell, Hades, and Gehenna; to resurrection; and even to the Holy Spirit and Satan/demons appear to be components of the standard "symbolic universe" of late second-temple society under foreign imperial rule. Certainly Q does not fit the synthetic modern concept of "apocalyptic" constructed by biblical scholarship more than a century ago.

On the other hand, the series of speeches in Q does parallel the two principal concerns of apocalyptic literature, the judgment of oppressive rulers and the renewal of Israel, as well as the vindication of martyrs that appear at least in Daniel 11–12. The images in which the Q speeches present these themes, however, are less elaborate, derived from the basic covenantal and prophetic traditions of Israel. And the anticipated fulfillment in the Q speeches is much further advanced than in the scribal apocalyptic texts. Daniel 7 looks forward to God's restoration of the people to sovereignty; Q presents the kingdom as already under way in Jesus' ministry and movement. The hopes and expectations of the common people are being wondrously fulfilled in the message and

26. Kloppenborg, *Formation of Q*, 296.

actions of Jesus and continue in the mission of the movement, if the people remain single-mindedly focused on "seeking first the kingdom of God." As in the scribal-priestly community at Qumran, the program of the renewal of society now under way in the Q communities is a renewal of the Mosaic covenant. But it lacks the elaboration of new *mishpatim* of the *Community Rule* from Qumran. Like Dan 12:3, the Q speeches also promise vindication for those who are persecuted or killed for the kingdom's/Jesus' sake (Q/Luke 6:23; 7:35; 11:49–51; 12:2–12). Yet the Q people anticipate nothing as fantastic as the martyred scribes "shining like the stars."

Perhaps because of its emphasis on the renewal of Israel already under way in the preaching and manifestation of the kingdom of God, Q has no portrayal of a future intervention by God accompanied by disturbances in the cosmic order, as in the deployment of traditional prophetic language of God's coming in judgment in the *Testament of Moses* 10. The future judgment in Q functions more as a sanction on the discipline of the Q community itself than it does as a condemnation of its opponents. The most striking differences between Q and scribal apocalyptic literature are Q's lack of scribal apocalyptic lore and the kind of schemes that resulted from more systematic scribal reflection.

THE GOSPEL OF MARK

Mark's Gospel portrays Jesus engaged in a programmatic renewal of Israel, over against the Jerusalem rulers and Temple, according to a basically prophetic "script" that is overlaid with a radically transformed understanding of the role of a Messiah.[27] More programmatically but less prominently than in the discourse gospel Q, "the kingdom of God" forms the theme of the Gospel. At the outset of his mission in Galilee, Jesus summarizes the "good news" he proclaims as the imminence of the kingdom of God in the time of fulfillment: "The time is fulfilled, and the kingdom of God has come near; turn your lives around, and trust in the good news" (Mark 1:15). The kingdom, the plan of which has been communicated in private to the disciples and other followers, like seeds that grow secretly and eventually produce an abundant harvest or large bushes, is already "planted" and "growing" (4:11, 26–32). In the near

---

27. This understanding of the Gospel of Mark is now more fully discussed in Horsley, *Hearing the Whole Story*.

future it will "come with power" (8:34—9:1). Meanwhile, Jesus warns that "whoever does not receive the kingdom of God as a little child will never enter it" (10:14-15). Indeed, for wealthy people (who have gained their wealth only by defrauding others) it will be virtually impossible (10:17-25). "It is easier for a camel to go through the eye of a needle than for someone who is rich to enter the kingdom of God." At his last meal with his disciples, at which he institutes the Lord's Supper with his followers, he declares that in the future he will once again "drink the fruit of the vine . . . new in the kingdom of God" (14:25). Daniel 7 and *Testament of Moses* 10 looked for God to implement his/the people's kingdom as the deliverance from the historical crisis under imperial repression. Mark, like Q, however, portrays the kingdom of God as already underway in Jesus' ministry, although it will "come with power" only in the imminent future (9:1).

The "kingdom of God" theme is just one among many ways in which Mark indicates that fulfillment of long-standing expectations and prophecies of the renewal of Israel was set in motion first by John the Baptist's preaching and then especially by Jesus' preaching and practice. John was God's messenger "preparing the way of the Lord" (1:2-3; cf. Mal 3:1; Isa 40:3). Jesus himself was a Moses- and Elijah-like figure engaged in the restoration of Israel, in sea crossings, exorcisms, healings, wilderness feedings (4:35—8:26; 9:2-8), and in appointing the Twelve as representatives of and envoys to the people now undergoing renewal (3:13-19; 6:7-13). In his instruction on marriage Jesus even restored the conditions of God's original creation and in his economic exhortation renewed the original egalitarian reciprocity of the Mosaic covenant (10:2-9, 17-31).

In the course of his programmatic preaching and practice of the renewal of Israel, Jesus comes into conflict with the scribes and Pharisees, authorities who have "come down from Jerusalem," and (like John) with Herod Antipas and his representatives, "the Herodians." In contrast to the former, Jesus teaches "with authority/power" (1:22-27). The Pharisees keep him under surveillance (2:1–3:5; 7:1-5) and, with the Herodians, conspire to destroy him (3:6). In a story that prefigures Jesus' martyrdom, Herod Antipas imprisons and beheads the prophet John (6:17-29). More ominous than the Pharisaic-Herodian conspiracy, moreover, Jesus engages the demonic forces in battle. Right from the outset of his manifestation of the kingdom of God, Jesus casts out "unclean spirits" from demon-possessed people and restores them to productive lives among the people (1:21–28, 32–34, 39; 3:11–12, 15). Indeed, it is the "unclean spirits" who know who he really is, "the holy one of God" (1:24; 3:11–12; 5:7). It is clear at points that these "unclean spirits" represent the political as well as cultural-spiritual dimension of the imperial forces under which the people live: "My name is Legion" (that is, Roman troops). Although they beg Jesus not to "send them out of the country," the demonic forces named "Legion," pointedly self-destruct by drowning in the "Sea (5:10–13).

As in the discourse gospel Q, Jesus takes the occasion of the scribes' accusation that he is working in cahoots with "Beelzebul, the ruler of the demons," to point to the deliverance already accomplished precisely in his exorcisms (3:22–27). The Gospel of Mark is not permeated throughout with a sense that all actions are determined by the struggle between "the Prince of Light" and "Belial," as in the priestly-scribal Qumran literature. Perhaps one reason for this can be seen precisely in Jesus' argument in the "Beelzebul controversy." Jesus ostensibly accepts the assumption of the scribal accusation, that all actions are determined either by "Satan" or God. But if indeed Satan's house is divided, it will fall and surely Satan is not so foolish as to be divided against himself. Thus, since "the strong man's" house is clearly being "plundered" in the exorcisms, then Satan must have been "tied up" (by Jesus or God). Again, as in the Legion story, the political implications are evident precisely on the assumption of the scribal demonology, such as that articulated in Qumran literature. According to this demonology, which Mark as well as Q shared with the Qumran scribal literature, oppressive rulers such as the Romans ("Kittim," or the Jerusalem high priests, the "Wicked Priest") are under the control of superhuman forces headed by Belial, the "Prince of Darkness/Lies." But if Satan has been "tied up," the oppressive rulers' days must be numbered.[28]

Indeed, as the demonological language disappears in the second half of the Gospel of Mark, the conflict becomes much more explicitly and ominously political. Mark has Jesus sharply reject the role of a popular messiah/ king who would lead the people in active revolt against Jerusalem and Roman rule. If Mark's Jesus is a messiah, then it is only in the transformation of the role into martyrdom and vindication. "It is necessary for 'the son of man'" to be condemned by the high priestly

---

28. More fully discussed in Horsley, *Jesus and the Spiral of Violence*, 184–90.

and scribal rulers, to be killed, and after three days to rise (8:31; 9:31; 10:33). Mark portrays Jesus basically as a prophet heading the renewal of Israel against the rulers. He enters the capital city in a noisy messianic demonstration and then carries out a dramatic prophetic demonstration against the Temple, the sacred center of political-economic power (11:1–10, 15–19). In a sequence of further stories, Jesus embarrasses the high priestly rulers, indeed tells a prophetic parable declaring their condemnation by God as rebellious "tenants" of God's vineyard (Israel), and prophesies the destruction of the Temple (11:27—13:2). Accordingly, Jesus is apprehended by an armed posse, tried and condemned for his prophecy against the Temple, and handed over to the Roman governor for crucifixion as an insurrectionary against the imperial order (14–15).

In contrast with the modern scholarly construct of "apocalypticism," Mark has no fantastic imagery of "the end of the world." It is difficult to discern any "last judgment" in Mark. "This age" and "the age to come" appear in passing in 10:30, but emphasis there falls explicitly on manifold social-economic restoration "now in this age." Even Jesus' battle with "unclean spirits" fades as the action escalates into direct political confrontation in Jerusalem. In contrast with the scholarly construct of apocalypticism, Mark pursues a basically prophetic "script" rooted in popular Israelite prophetic traditions of Moses and Elijah.

On the other hand, like the Q speeches, the Gospel of Mark does parallel the dominant concerns of prophetic and apocalyptic texts: a focus on the present historical crisis, divine judgment of oppressive rulers, and the renewal of Israel. Yet whereas apocalyptic texts review a wide sweep of prior imperial rule, Mark focuses closely on the mission of the prophet Jesus as the fulfillment of Israel's hopes and expectations. In contrast with Enoch texts, Mark has little concern with the divine heavenly governance of earthly affairs. While apocalyptic texts expected the restoration of Israel in the future, Mark presents the renewal of Israel as already underway in the proclamation and actions of Jesus. In contrast with Daniel 7, 8, 10–11, "Enoch's" Animal Vision, and the *Testament of Moses*, which focus divine judgment on the oppressive empire, Mark has judgment focused on the Jerusalem rulers. Renewal of Israel and judgment against Jerusalem rulers in Mark follow distinctive prophetic traditions and patterns, with Jesus portrayed primarily as a new Moses and new Elijah in chapters 1–10, to which reminiscences of Isaiah and Jeremiah are added in the Jerusalem climax. Mark limits messianic motifs to Jesus's baptism at the beginning, Peter's (problematic) confession at the middle, and the high priestly trial and the crucifixion toward the end.

As it becomes clear that a prophetic "script" dominates the narrative in Mark, we should give special attention to three of the principal reasons that Mark has previously been described as "apocalyptic" in tone and character. First, since the renewal of Israel is already under way in Jesus' mission of preaching and healing and the kingdom of God is "at hand," a tone or urgency and excitement permeates the Gospel. The vindication of the martyred prophet evident from the empty tomb serves to further intensify this sense of fulfillment in Mark. Second, the lengthy discourse of Jesus in Mark 13 includes several motifs that were often classified as "apocalyptic" according to the standard scholarly construct, some taken as direct references to the book of Daniel. The heavy concentration of motifs categorized as apocalyptic in Mark 13 has led many to posit a "Synoptic" or "Little Apocalypse" of Jewish or Jewish-Christian origin that Mark adapted to form this discourse. Third is the claim that what have been labeled the "apocalyptic (or future) son of man sayings" have been taken to give the Gospel an orientation toward an imminent "end time" or even "end of the world." Upon closer examination, none of these constitute a basis on which Mark can be understood as "apocalyptic."

First, the announced resurrection of Jesus, confirmed by the empty tomb story, which forms the open ending of the Gospel, adds appreciably to the sense of fulfillment already under way and excitement over imminent completion. Jesus was martyred, but has also been vindicated. The rising again implied in the empty tomb intensifies the sense of fulfillment and renewal that continues in the Jesus movement which Mark expresses and addresses. Significantly, however, Mark makes no reference to the vindicated Jesus "shining like the stars of heaven" (in contrast to Dan 12:3) or to Jesus' enthronement in glory (cf. Phil 2:9–11; 3:20–21). Mark rather directs Jesus' followers back to Galilee (whence Jesus has gone before them), presumably to resume the renewal of Israel he had begun. The excitement and urgency about fulfillment are thus more intense in Mark than in Jewish apocalyptic texts. Whereas Jewish scribal literature looks for eventual vindication in the future, Mark's Gospel assumes and articulates vindication accomplished in the case of the martyred prophet Jesus. And that confirms and reinforces both the conviction that God's judgment on the rulers is certain and the sense that renewal of Israel is already under way—as well as the motivation to expand and solidify the movement Jesus started.

Second, the concentration of "apocalyptic" motifs in Mark 13 is the most important basis on which Mark as a whole has been viewed as "apocalyptic." It also provides the material for numerous reconstructions of a "Little Apocalypse" supposedly adapted here in Mark. Such theories of a Jewish or Jewish-Christian apocalypse behind Mark 13 are questionable on a number of grounds.[29] They began in the nineteenth century as defensive attempts to explain that Jews or Jesus' followers, and not Jesus himself, were responsible for the mistaken prediction that the end was imminent (cf. 13:30). Attempts to distinguish apocalyptic narrative units from parenetic (exhortative) units falter because prophecy and parenesis are combined at key points, such as 13:7 and 14–20. Previous scholarly interpretation found that Mark 13 features some of the key motifs typical of Jewish apocalypticism.[30] It is even supposedly organized in terms of "birth pangs" (13:5–8), "sufferings" (13:14–23), and finally the eventual restoration of the people (13:24–27). But those "birth pangs" and "sufferings" of the supposed "Great Tribulation" in the scholarly "apocalyptic scenario" are not evident in second-temple Judean apocalyptic texts (except perhaps briefly in Dan 12:1). In the list of wars, nation against nation, earthquakes, and famines (13:7–8), Mark uses traditional prophetic rhetoric (Isa 8:21; 13:13; 14:30; 19:2; Ezek 5:12). These motifs are not particularly apocalyptic prior to the time of Jesus; they appear only in later apocalyptic literature (*4 Ezra* 9:3; 13:31; *2 Bar.* 27; 70:8). The supposed reference in 13:14 to the "desolating sacrilege" in Dan 9:27; 11:31; 12:11 does not seem to have the same reference to a desecration of the Temple as in Daniel. With its sharp condemnation of the Temple and its focus on Galilee, the Gospel of Mark seems to have a very different orientation from that of the Judean "wise" who wrote Daniel.

We must also be careful not to read Mark 13 in terms of later Christian theories of salvation history, according to which Jerusalem was destroyed by the Romans as a direct result of the crucifixion of Jesus. As noted above, Mark portrays Jesus engaged in a renewal of Israel cen-

---

29. Beasley-Murray, *Jesus and the Last Days*; A. Y. Collins, *Beginning of the Gospel*, chap. 3.

30. Beasley-Murray, *Jesus and the Last Days*.

tered in Galilee and in opposition to the rulers in Jerusalem. Nothing in the Gospel of Mark itself suggests a "Christian" community separated from "Judaism" or "Israel." Matthew and Luke, written after the Roman destruction of Jerusalem, assume that the discourse in Mark 13 refers to those events. But Jesus' prophecy in Mark 13:2 of the destruction of the Temple, which provides the occasion of the discourse in Mark 13, is not sufficiently specific to be read as a "prophecy after the fact." While the "abomination that desolates" in Daniel (9:27; 11:31; 12:11) referred to the profanation of the Temple by the Seleucid emperor Antiochus Epiphanes, nothing in the immediate literary context in Mark 13 indicates that "the desolating sacrilege" in Mark 13:14 refers to the Romans' destruction of the Temple in 70 (contrast Matt 24:15 and Luke 21:20–21). Although Jesus' prophecy about the Temple provides the ostensible occasion for the discourse, it is formulated from a perspective apparently outside Jerusalem and Judea (13:14) and evidently prior to the Roman destruction of Jerusalem.

The historical context of Mark 13, as of the rest of the Gospel, was the intense social conflict that was escalating throughout the middle of the first century.[31] That conflict had erupted in widespread revolt at the time of Herod's death (and Jesus' birth) in 4 BCE and erupted again in the great revolt of 66–70 CE. The Synoptic Gospel traditions included in Mark developed during decades of extensive social unrest, periodic protests, resistance movements, and violent repression by Roman military actions. While the many "prophecies" and warnings in Mark 13:5–27 appear to refer to future events, it has previously been assumed that they refer to the events of the great revolt in 66–70, either from a position during the revolt or in retrospect on it. But this may be because scholars have been unfamiliar with earlier events that resembled those in the revolt itself. It may be impossible to reach any degree of precision regarding particular events to which the discourse in Mark 13 refers. It is thus more difficult to discern in Mark 13 the break between past or present and future than in the rehearsal of events in Judean apocalyptic texts (for example, Daniel 10–12; *1 Enoch* 85–90; *Testament of Moses*).

For example, the wars and rumors of wars" in 13:7 could refer to the crisis caused by the emperor Caligula's order to install his statue in the Temple (in 40 CE). "Nation will rise against nation" could refer to the

---

31. A. Y. Collins, *Beginning of the Gospel*; Horsley with Hanson, *Bandits, Prophets, and Messiahs*; Horsley, *Jesus and the Spiral of Violence*, 26–58, 90–120.

great revolt, already begun, and the extreme distress described in 13:14–20—far from being a reference to the "Great Tribulation" of the scholarly "apocalyptic scenario—could well refer to the people's suffering under the "search and destroy" tactics of the Roman reconquest of northwest Judea in 67–68. Yet these could also be prophecies delivered at any time in the decades leading up to the great revolt, informed by knowledge of common Roman practices. The "scorched earth" practices of the Roman military were still fresh in people's memories from the reconquest led by Varus in 4 BCE. And at several points during the escalating conflicts of the 50s and 60s the Roman governors reacted to actual or perceived popular unrest with severely repressive military violence. Especially after the crisis touched off by Caligula's madness, no clairvoyance was necessary to prophesy an imminent major crisis and to describe how the Romans would treat people such as pregnant or nursing women who remained in their villages.[32] A prophet or an evangelist would not need to have experienced the Roman reconquest of Galilee or northwestern Judea in 67–68 to have articulated Mark 13:14b–18.

Similarly, after the disastrous effects of the severe drought of the late 40s, the possibility of further famines in the near future would have been on everyone's mind. The "false messiahs" and "false prophets" of 13:6 and 21–22 could be the ones who appeared in the middle of the great revolt. Yet, as we know from Josephus, popular prophets had been active since shortly after Jesus' death, and memories were alive of the popular messiahs who arose at the death of Herod. Like the warnings and exhortations about trials before councils, governors, and kings in 13:9–13, the warnings, prophecies, and exhortations of 13:5–9 and 14–23 refer to what appears as future escalation of the severe conflicts that the Judean and Galilean people were already undergoing during the mid-first century.

What struck earlier interpreters as the most apocalyptic-sounding part of Mark 13 were the apparent references to "cosmic disturbances" suggesting "the end of the world" in 13:24–25 and "the Son of Man coming on the clouds" in 13:26–27 taken as a reference to the Parousia of Christ as the eschatological judge. As noted above, however, the disturbances in the heavenly bodies were standard images in the older prophetic tradition of God coming to judge foreign rulers and to deliver Israel (e.g., Isaiah 13; 34; Ezekiel 32; Joel 2). Mark's use of the imagery

---

32. See Horsley, *Jesus and the Spiral of Violence*, 28–49, 116–20.

here is indeed somewhat parallel to that in the concluding oracle of *Testament of Moses* 10. Mark 13:24–27, however, focuses solely on the ingathering of the people (of Israel), with the barest if any allusion to judgment of Rome. Moreover, not God but, "the son of man coming in clouds with great power and glory" carries out the deliverance by sending out the angels. The "son of man" here, moreover, is not the agent of judgment. And we may also wonder just how explicitly or directly Mark has Dan 7:13 in mind. In Daniel the "human one" symbolized the people who were about to be delivered, whereas Mark has "the son of man" preside over the deliverance.

Striking throughout Mark 13 is how the references to traumatic events are framed, balanced, and interpreted by the exhortations in 13:5–6, 9–13, and 18–37, particularly by the carefully positioned and repeated "watch" (13:5, 9, 23, 33) and "keep awake" (13:35, 37). The main point of the exhortations in Mark 13, and thus of the prophecies and warnings framed by them, seems to be "Do not be diverted from the struggle by the difficulties attendant upon the struggle." The first main section of exhortation (13:9–13) focuses on the movement's persecutions by rulers. Far from being distracted by wars and famines, members of the movement are to "Watch! Expect repression, but do not worry." The climactic prophecy of deliverance reassures the readers that God is ultimately in control. The second main section of exhortation (13:28–37) follows up this prophecy of divine deliverance in two steps. First comes assurance of both the imminence of deliverance and the veracity of Jesus' words (13:28–31). It is worth noting that the only comparable saying in Mark, that the kingdom of God will come with power soon, also functions as a reassurance to Jesus' followers to remain focused on their cause in similar circumstances of persecution and repression ("take up the cross...," 8:34–9:1). Second, and the concluding point in the discourse, is the insistence that, since no one knows precisely when deliverance will come, the people are to "keep awake" and focused on the work of building the movement—to which they are directed by the open-ended conclusion of the Gospel in 16:8. In sum, the purpose of the discourse in Mark 13 seems to be to reassure Jesus' followers that the renewal of Israel already inaugurated in Jesus' preaching and practice will finally be completed despite the crisis they are living through in the period just before or during the great revolt.

The third reason Mark has appeared apocalyptic is because of the "apocalyptic/ coming Son of Man" sayings in 8:38, 13:26-27, and 14:62, which have usually been understood as references to the eschatological agent of judgment as well as references or allusions to Dan 7:13. As noted just above, 'the son of man" figure in 13:26-27 is not an eschatological agent of judgment, but the agent of the ingathering of Israel, and that in contrast with "the human one" of Dan 7:13, who is interpreted in Daniel 7 as a symbol of the people' restoration, as they receive the kingdom. This should give us pause regarding the significance of the figure in 14:62. It is evidently a figure different from Jesus himself, a figure coming to vindicate Jesus, who is on trial before the council of the high priest, and thus again not the eschatological judge. If the "coming with the clouds" is indeed an allusion to Dan 7:13, then "the son of man" may be rather, like that in Daniel 7, a symbol of the restoration/renewal of the people/ Israel at the judgment (which would include the vindication of Jesus). Again in 8:38, "the son of man" figure is not explicitly represented as the agent of eschatological judgment. The portrayal of the scene of judgment in Mark 8:38 is still close enough to the parallel in Q/Luke 12:8-9 that "the son of man" seems like more of an accuser or advocate than a judge.

In none of these sayings is Jesus explicitly identified with "the son of man. But by using the same phrase "son of man" both for Jesus as the martyred prophet and for a future accuser/deliverer/judge, Mark may have been the first in the Synoptic Gospel tradition to suggest that the two were the same person. Mark has thus taken an important step toward the more elaborate Christian apocalyptic scenario of the *parousia* ("[second] coming") of Jesus as heavenly Lord, as we find in Paul, in Matthew, and in later Christian doctrine. As can be seen in the open ending of the empty tomb with Jesus "gone before them into Galilee," however, Mark's emphasis was not on the resurrected and exalted Lord who was coming again but on the continuation of Jesus' mission of the renewal of Israel.

THE GOSPEL OF MATTHEW

Matthew's Gospel presents simultaneously a less intense feeling of the fulfillment of longings for the renewal of Israel and an eschatological expectation elaborated in "apocalyptic" terms. As in both Mark and Q, which Matthew has appropriated, the kingdom is the central theme of Jesus' teaching. Also as in Mark and Q, Jesus' and his disciples' preaching and activities focus on the renewal of Israel. Matthew's "kingdom of heaven" is simply a circumlocution to avoid uttering the divine name, not an indication of an otherworldly orientation. Reading Matthew, however, one does not have the same feeling as in reading Mark of being caught up in the struggle of the kingdom's manifestation in Jesus' and his envoys' preaching and practice. Matthew organizes the gospel traditions received from Mark, Q, and elsewhere more systematically into five major sections, each consisting of both narrative and discourse. For example, in constructing the famous Sermon on the Mount, he dramatically expands the covenant renewal discourse from Q into an unavoidably explicit new covenant charter for the movement. The communities of the movement seem more settled. Peter is named as the rock on which Jesus founds the "assembly" (Greek ἐκκλεσία, 16:17–19). And Matthew establishes procedures for community discipline (18:15–20). In many ways Matthew's Gospel resembles the *Community Rule* from the scribal-priestly renewal movement that had seemingly settled into an indefinite period of waiting for the final divine intervention into history that would complete the provisional fulfillment that they already embodied. And since the intensity of fulfillment in the present has subsided somewhat, more is pushed off into the future, to the more distant "end of the age" (not "the end of the world").

One major reason that Matthew displays both a less intense tone and a more elaborate scenario of future judgment than Mark is surely the sequence of events that intervened between their respective composition. Mark appears to address the situation in Palestine and Syria before or during the great revolt. Matthew addresses communities fifteen or twenty years after the Roman destruction of Jerusalem. He alludes to it in the parable of the wedding feast (22:1–14, especially 22:7). When the Romans destroyed Jerusalem, they also destroyed the Judean high priestly regime based in the Temple, leaving no centralized Jewish political-religious institution with authority over the Jewish communities of Palestine and Syria. The nascent rabbinic movement located initially at Yavneh on the Judean coast and later in the cities of Galilee did not come into prominence until several generations later. A currently prominent interpretation views Matthew's Gospel as addressed to communities that understood themselves as a renewal movement of Israel that broadened its mission to include other peoples as well.[33] Matthew declared repeatedly in the "formula quotations" that Jesus' ministry is the fulfillment of what Israel's prophets had prophesied, then at the very end extends the fulfillment of the hopes of Israel to all peoples.

The decline of intensity compared with Mark may not be evident in the first sections of Matthew's Gospel. Indeed Matthew's combination and elaboration of the Markan and Q mission discourses make the movement's struggle against opposing forces all the more ominous. Efforts of Jesus' disciples to expand his program of renewal in Israel will only further exacerbate the social conflict already rife in society: "I have come not to bring peace, but a sword!" (10:34–36). Their continuation of his mission can only be expected to bring divisions between the younger and older generations, in fulfillment of a standard prophetic tradition of "a man against his father, and a daughter against her mother, and so on" (e.g., Mic 7:6). Jesus demands unwavering commitment to the cause (10:37–39). And he reassures the envoys that through the Spirit they will know how to speak when hauled before governors and kings, that God is watching out for them, and that people in the movement will welcome them in their prophetic mission (10:20, 29–31, 40–42). Yet in Matthew, as in Mark, Jesus does not speak of anything as fantastic as the vindication held out for the wise scribes in Daniel, that they would "shine like the stars" (11:33–35; 12:2).

Into, this expanded mission discourse Matthew inserts a statement that loomed central in Schweitzer's insistence that Jesus thought the end of the world was imminent: "For truly I tell you, you will not have gone through all the towns of Israel before the Son of Man comes"(10:23). Given Matthew's indications elsewhere in the Gospel of the prolonged period of time during which the renewal movement begun by Jesus will continue before "the end of the age," it is highly unlikely that this was meant to be taken at face value. Yet it indicates the urgency of the original mission, some degree of which carried over into Matthew's own time, partly by the repeated readings or performances of just such a discourse in the Gospel. The lower level of intensity of the mission in Matthew may be indicated in the last set of sayings in the discourse: "Whoever welcomes a prophet in the name of a prophet will receive a prophet's reward" (10:40–42).

---

33. Saldarini, *Matthew's Jewish-Christian Community*.

In his third major discourse Matthew articulates an expanded perspective on the continuing effects of Jesus' message of the kingdom, evidently in the communities of the Jesus movement that the Gospel is addressing. Among the several "parables of the kingdom" that he adds to those in Mark 4 is the parable of the weeds (13:24–30). The interpretation of this parable given privately to the disciples (13:36–43) lays out a scenario of how to understand what is happening in the movement Matthew addresses, which understands itself not only within Israel but as the renewal of Israel.

It is easy to understand how this parable and its explanation, taken out of the literary and historical context indicated in the Gospel of Matthew, could have been read in terms of the supposed Jewish "apocalyptic scenario," particularly focused on "the last judgment." Here is the image of "the harvest" that Schweitzer seized upon, a seeming dualism of God/the Son of Man and the Devil, of good and evil, the angels gathering in "the children of evil/ evildoers" at "the end of the age" and casting them into "the furnace of fire" and the righteous shining like the sun in the heavenly kingdom. Moreover, some claim to see a similar image of the harvest in "Jewish apocalyptic literature" in the late text, 4 Ezra 4:26–32.

Read more carefully in context, however, the explanation of the parable of the weeds focuses on what is happening in the movement in Israel in the world. Whereas "the seed" in the explanation of the parable of the sower (13:18–23) is the word of the kingdom, here it is the people who have born fruit, "the children of the kingdom." The seeds of the kingdom are still growing. But they have not reached fulfillment; there are also weeds among them, sown by the devil. The obstacles (indicated in 13:41) are all the stumbling blocks (σκάνδαλα), the occasions or causes of sinning, and those who do lawless deeds (not "evildoers" as in NRSV, but "doers of lawlessness," presumably those who do not faithfully keep the [renewed] covenant; cf. Matt 24:12). The "weeds," however, are not to be "weeded out" (expelled from the movement?). Judgment is to be deferred to the time of fulfillment ("end of the age," and presumably the beginning of the new age), when the divine judgment will deal with them.

The (seed-field-)harvest as a metaphor for the future judgment in 4 Ezra 4:26–32, which is about the only occurrence in any text classified as apocalyptic, is applied quite differently and from a sweeping perspective.

The problematic seed is the inclination to sinning sown in Adam's heart, which results in the sadness and infirmities of this age. The good seed that has been sown, however, cannot come to fruition (presumably in the new age) until after the time of threshing. The significant difference of the Gospels from this late apocalyptic text is clear. In contrast with the latter, the Gospel of Matthew, like that of Mark, understands the fulfillment, the renewal of Israel, as already underway in the mission of Jesus and the spread of his movement of renewal. Matthew's image of "the righteous" in the kingdom "shining like the sun" seems similar to, although not as elaborate as, the glorification of the righteous in *2 Baruch* 51. Both are collective and both use heavenly imagery. But they do not involve any "cosmic catastrophe" of "the end of the world." Matthew's passing representation of "the Son of Man" as the apparent title of the figure who presides over the future judgment moves well beyond anything in Judean apocalyptic texts or in Mark. And Matthew's evident identification of "the Son of Man" with Jesus at the beginning of the explanation of this parable moves well beyond anything in the Gospel of Mark.

Matthew's elaboration on the fulfillment of history thus corresponds to a decline in the intensity with which the fulfillment was experienced. Matthew's communities must wait until the indefinite end of the age. During that patient period of waiting, what is required is community discipline (including mediation of conflict and mutual forgiveness), to which Matthew devotes the fourth major discourse (chap. 18).

In the fifth and final discourse (chaps 24–25) Matthew has Jesus deliver an elaborate discussion of what to expect at "the end of the age," with focus on the Son of Man coming in judgment. He sets the stage in earlier references to the Son of Man in statements that provide sanctions on the disciples' (and the communities Matthew addresses) persistence in continuing his mission until the kingdom is finally fully established (10:23; 16:27–28; 19:28–29). The statements in 10:23 and 16:27–28 make the coming of the Son of Man sound imminent, but are hardly to be taken literally in modern chronological terms (contra Schweitzer). In both cases, the point (in context) is to offer assurance and sanction in circumstances in which the disciples would find themselves persecuted and perhaps even executed, as Jesus was. The reference to the enthronement of the Son of Man in Matt 19:28–29 has been standardly mistranslated and misinterpreted.³⁴ It is not about judgment or his role in it, and is an important corrective to the standard narrowing of the role of the Son of Man in Matthew's Gospel to judgment. This statement indicates that in Matthew the coming Son of Man symbolizes more broadly the full realization of the kingdom in the future, as evident in a more adequate translation of 19:28: "At the restoration [of Israel], when the Son of Man is seated on the throne of glory, you who have followed me will also sit on twelve thrones, establishing justice for the twelve tribes of Israel." The juxtaposition of the exaggerated ("hundred-fold") restoration of houses and families with "eternal life" in 19:29 confirms that the enthronement of the Son of Man goes together with the restoration of Israel.

The παρουσία—popularly thought of as the "second coming"—of Christ is really Matthew's construction, at least in Gospel literature. The effect of Mark's narrative was to identify Jesus with the Son of Man coming with the clouds, even if the Gospel never stated this identification in so many words. The term παρουσία, however, occurs only in Matthew 24, where it is the focus of the whole discourse about the coming of the Son of Man in final judgment at the end of the age in Matthew 24–25. This discourse is the source of the standard picture of the last judgment in subsequent Christian art, architecture, and literature. Such representations of the last judgment and the second coming of Christ, however, miss the thrust of this last, "apocalyptic" discourse in the Gospel of Matthew.

---

34. The misunderstanding of two terms in 19:28-29 both reflects and has reinforced the modern scholarly construction of a supposedly standard Jewish apocalyptic scenario of the end of the world, including the last judgment. In what Christian scholars have taken to be (Matthew's) Jesus' adaptation of the scenario, "the Jews" have tragically as well as ironically been implicated. NRSV translates the term παλιγγενεσία as "the renewal of all things" (cf. RVS "new world," as if the current world is about to end), evidently along the lines of the Stoic doctrine of the regeneration of the world. As noted above on Q/Luke 22:28–30, however, this term is what Josephus uses for the restoration of Israel. Reinforcing the misunderstanding, NRSV (like RSV and the New Jerusalem Bible) still translates the term κρίνειν with "judging," which has clear negative connotations in English (as does *richten* in German translations). The implication drawn by many interpreters, following this translation, has been that the disciples will be "sitting on twelve thrones (negatively) judging the twelve tribes of Israel" (i.e., "the Jews")—which is further reinforced by reading 21:43 in terms of the kingdom being taken from the Jews and given to the Gentiles. In Israelite cultural tradition, however, the term κρίνειν (and the corresponding term in Hebrew), was used in the sense of God "delivering/ liberating/ doing justice for Israel or the widow, orphan, etc., as in the Psalms. See further Horsley, *Jesus and the Spiral of Violence*, 200–208.

This final discourse of Jesus in Matthew 24–25 is ostensibly addressed to the disciples just before his arrest, trial, and crucifixion. Yet it was actually composed in and addressed to a situation some sixty years (two generations) later, fifteen or twenty years after the Roman destruction of Jerusalem. Far more than Jesus' final discourse in Mark, Jesus' final speech to his disciples in Matthew is a review of history up to the situation of the readers, similar to that in Daniel 7, 10–12. Matthew's final discourse is nearly three times as long as Mark's, incorporating several long parables in addition to material from Q. As indicated in the introductory questions of the disciples, Matthew's concerns run well beyond the events covered in Mark 13:5–23 (–27), the rather vague "these things." In contrast to Mark, Matthew really does focus (ostensibly) on "the end," on "last things": "what will be the sign of *your coming* and of *the close of the age*." Like the παρουσία, "the close of the age" is distinctive to Matthew among the Gospels, figuring prominently in the explanations of the parables of the weeds and the dragnet, as well as here and at the very end of the Gospel (13:39, 40, 49; 24:3; 28:20).

In fact, while the Roman destruction of Jerusalem figures prominently in the Gospel, Matthew's concerns focus on the situation of the movement in the new circumstances created by that destruction. Matthew had already implied the destruction of Jerusalem and its high priestly rulers in the parable of the wedding feast: when those invited to the feast killed his servant messengers, the enraged king "sent his troops, destroyed those murderers, and burned their city" (22:1–7; cf. taking away the vineyard from the tenants in 21:43). By concluding the woes on the scribes and Pharisees with Jesus' prophetic lament on the Jerusalem ruling house in 23:37–38, Matthew ties the destruction of Jerusalem closely with the discourse that follows in chapters 24–25. The destruction of Jerusalem and the Temple, however, is by no means the crucial point reviewed in the narrative of events. Matthew (24:15) does indicate, in a way that Mark (13:14) does not, that the "desolating sacrilege" would be "standing in the holy place," surely referring to the Temple. The ensuing travails of war taken from Mark, however, do not constitute "all things" that Jesus has "told [them] beforehand" (which Matthew, in 24:25, significantly deletes from Mark 13:23).

Although Matthew does not focus on the destruction of Jerusalem, that event and the vacuum of central institutionalized authority for Judea and Jewish communities in Syria created a completely new situation for a renewal movement in Israel such as the one Matthew addressed.[35] Suddenly the authorities that had exercised some check on the movement (if we place any trust in key sections of the book of Acts) had disappeared from the historical stage and no centralized leadership in Jewish Palestine had emerged or been appointed by the Romans. The fact that the capital and symbolic center of "Israel" was now in ruins, moreover, might well have led the renewal movement behind Matthew to turn outward. The destruction of Jerusalem would almost certainly have provided a major impetus in expanding the movement's mission to include all peoples in a more programmatic way than the earlier outreach to "Gentiles" in Antioch and elsewhere. This is exactly the program delineated at the very end of Matthew's Gospel: "Go therefore and make disciples of all nations (peoples), baptizing them . . . and teaching them to obey everything that I have commanded you" (28:19-20a). In the revelatory narrative of Jesus' final discourse in Matthew 24–25 the point at which the mission to the peoples is announced (for the first time in the Gospel) is as the destruction of Jerusalem is pending: "And this gospel of the kingdom [which Jesus had preached before in Galilee] will be preached throughout the whole world, as a testimony to all nations (peoples)" (24:14a). The period of this new mission, moreover, is the present to which the discourse is addressed. Only after that program of evangelizing all the peoples, only "then," would the end come (24:14b). Meanwhile, the exalted Jesus to whom "all authority in heaven and on earth had been given" would be with them "every day" (literally "all the days"), "to the end of the age" (28:18, 20b).

The importance of the time during which the wider mission of Jesus' kingdom-movement takes place for Matthew helps us understand why the apparent climax of the revelatory narrative in 24:30-31 is only the apparent climax. The discourse is a response to the disciples' question, "What will be the sign of your *parousia* and the end of the age" (24:36). The answer is given apparently in 24:29-31: "immediately after the suffering of those days" (the violence and chaos of the Roman reconquest of Judea [24:16-28]), accompanied by the standard prophetic images of the cosmic disturbances when God comes to judge the empire and deliver Israel, "then the sign of the Son of Man will appear in heaven." Matthew even enhances the Markan coming of the Son of Man on the clouds of heaven and sending out of the angels to gather in the elect with

---

35. Saldarini, *Matthew's Jewish-Christian Community*.

"a loud trumpet call" (24:30–31; cf. 1 Cor 15:52). There ensues a lengthy delay in the narrative of the παρουσία to explain the implications of "the delay of the parousia" itself (delay mentioned explicitly in 24:48; 25:5, 19). Matthew devotes more than half of the discourse, including repeated exhortations and three long didactic parables (24:37—25:30), to the importance of behavior and relationships in the communities of the movement during the "delay."

After reproducing the Markan point about "all these things" (24:32–35), Matthew then uses the next point from Mark, that the day and hour are unknown (24:36), to launch his lengthy exhortation on watchfulness and responsibility. As in the rehearsals of past history by seers in apocalyptic literature such as Daniel 7 and 10-12, the preceding predictions in Matt 24:5-28 lend credibility to the prophecy of the *parousia* of the Son of Man in fulfillment of the renewal of Israel (now with other peoples?). Matthew combines this certainty of the Son of Man coming in fulfillment with the uncertainty and suddenness of the timing in 24:36-44 (including the analogy from Q with "the days of Noah"). Matthew then uses the certainty and suddenness of the coming of the Son of Man in fulfillment looming in the future to insist upon discipline and responsible relations within the communities of the movement. A principal function of apocalyptic literature was to reinforce the solidarity of dissident scribal circles in a threatening situation by assuring them that God would act soon and/or that judgment was sure. Matthew does not appear to be in the urgent situation of Daniel 10-12 or *Testament of Moses* 9-10—although the Roman reconquest of Judea and the destruction of Jerusalem must have sent shock waves through any and all Jewish groups and movements. Matthew rather addresses communities settling in for prolonged periods of further building and solidification of the movement. Thus, the point of the exhortative analogies as well as all these parables in 24:37—25:30 is not simply passive watching but active service. As he proceeds in the discourse Matthew embellishes the parables with "Christian" apocalyptic motifs such as the "cry" and the summons "to meet" the bridegroom in the parable of the maidens (25:6; cf. 1 Thess 4:16-17).

In the climactic scene of the discourse, Matthew portrays the peoples gathered before the Son of Man on his glorious throne for judgment. If it had not become clear from the preceding exhortations and didactic parables, then it becomes clear in this judgment scene that the real "crisis" (Greek κρίσις means "judgment") lies in people's behavior in the present, not in the *parousia* of the Son of Man at the end of the age. The assumption within the discourse is that, since the end would not come before the gospel of the kingdom was preached to the peoples, the peoples gathered for judgment have been evangelized. The judgment scene is therefore directed basically to the communities of the movement itself. And the criteria for the ostensibly future judgment, which are repeated four times, direct attention "back" to the present of the readers. Only insofar as they have fed the hungry, clothed the naked, visited the imprisoned, and so on among the least of the Son of Man's brothers and sisters have they done it to him and thus become eligible to inherit the kingdom prepared from the foundation of the world. The Son of Man, who will appear on his glorious throne, is hidden in, or rather is identical with, the brothers and sisters of the movement. The obvious clue earlier in the Gospel, of course, was the suffering and crucified Son of Man, who both had authority to forgive sins and over the sabbath and had nowhere to lay his head. The final "judgment" scene in Matthew's last discourse thus comes back around to a main principle in the first section of the first discourse. The "kingdom" movement inaugurated by Jesus focuses on active love (lovingkindness or mercy as action, not attitude) toward others, particularly the needy. In Matthew this renewal of mutual care and reciprocity in community life is motivated by the fulfillment manifested in Jesus' ministry but also by the final judgment. But more than in Mark or Q it is motivated also by the promise/threat that one's fate in the judgment at the end of the age is determined by present actions.

The Son of Man coming in judgment is what Schweitzer saw as the center of the eschatological scenario of the Jewish apocalypticism that he believed Jesus was not only preaching but acting out. Specialists have been warning that it would be difficult to argue that "the son of man" is a title of the eschatological judge, even in the first-century CE Similitudes of Enoch. It might be tempting to argue, on the basis of Matthew 24–25, that followers of Jesus had developed an "apocalyptic scenario" of the future centered on the παρουσία of "the Son of Man." But in Matthew 24 (as in Mark 13), "the Son of Man" is not coming as the eschatological judge, but coming to gather the elect in the fulfillment of the renewal of Israel begun by Jesus, whom Matthew identifies as the Son of Man. The last scene in Matthew 25, moreover, when "the Son of Man" does become the judge of the peoples in the last step of implementation of the kingdom, places the focus on how people in the present are treating Jesus' "brothers and sisters" who are in need or in special difficulties. If Matthew presupposes and/or presents some sort of "apocalyptic" scenario, it has nothing to do with "the end of the world" in a "cosmic catastrophe." It rather functions to focus attention on, to offer reassurance to, and to sanction the practice of love and justice in the communities of the movement Matthew addresses.

Finally, we should note the embellishments that Matthew makes to Mark's portrayal of Jesus' arrest and crucifixion and the empty tomb. In the arrest scene (26:47–56), Matthew has Jesus declare to his brash follower who drew his sword that if he wanted he could appeal to the Father to send more than twelve legions of angels to the rescue. That God commanded heavenly armies was a long-standing tradition from as far back as early Israel. It is difficult to find any references in apocalyptic texts, although Josephus' account of popular fantasies during the Roman siege of Jerusalem may attest the continuing belief among ordinary people (*War* 6:296–99). At the moment of Jesus' death and at his resurrection (27:50–53; 28:2) Matthew adds to the tearing of the curtain in the Temple that there was an earthquake and the resurrection of many dead saints who appeared to many in Jerusalem. Although, as noted above, expectation of the future resurrection of the dead is not widely attested, and is rarely attested in second-temple apocalyptic texts, it was evidently current in Judean and Galilean society. The point here in Matthew is that Jesus' death and resurrection were the beginning of the general resurrection; what was previously expected in the future was happening in the present. This is the most ominous indication that in his mission and death and resurrection the fulfillment of (Israel's) history was now underway. Finally, in the concluding scene in the Gospel story, when the disciples meet him back in Galilee on the mountain, he declares that "all authority in heaven and earth has been given to [him]." Second-temple apocalyptic texts have no human persons assuming positions of extraordinary authority. In that statement Matthew also makes a claim far above and beyond what is said in the sixth vision-and-explanation in the late, "postapocalyptic" Jewish text, *4 Ezra*,[36] of the Son that the Most

---

36. On *4 Ezra* as having moved beyond the "apocalyptic" genre, see Tiller's discussion in chap. 6 above.

THE GOSPEL OF LUKE

Like Matthew, Luke also follows Mark's narrative and assimilates the prophetic discourses of Q. Far more noticeably than Matthew, however, Luke tones down many of the overtones he finds in his sources.[37] With a few deft deletions of words from Mark's narrative, he effectively tones down the sense of imminence. As Jesus begins his ministry in Galilee in 4:15, Luke deletes completely Mark's summary of Jesus' preaching as "the kingdom of God is at hand." In 9:23–27 Luke retains Mark's reference to "the son of man" coming in glory. But in 9:27 he tones down the imminence in Mark 9:1, "some standing here will not taste death before they see the kingdom of God," by deleting "come with power." In rewriting the discourse in Mark 13, Luke minimizes the sense of imminence in Mark 13:30 by deleting "these things," in Luke 21:32. He also suppresses some of the motifs previously labeled "apocalyptic." He deletes "to the end" in connection with "enduring" in 21:19 (cf. Mark 13:13b) and the allusion to Dan 12:1 (in Mark 13:19) in 21:23b and the reference to the angels gathering the elect (in Mark 13:27) in 21:27 (but what does 21:28 mean?). Any sense of an imminent coming of the kingdom or an imminent appearance of "the son of man" is merely a carryover from the Markan materials Luke has assimilated.

The Gospel of Luke reconfigures in matter-of-fact historical terms what Mark and Matthew expressed in more prophetic terms. The longings and prophecies of Israel have indeed been fulfilled, in part, in the mission of Jesus. "Luke," however, narrates the history not only of Jesus but of the movement that he founded that has spread from Galilee and Jerusalem to the imperial metropolis, Rome. The Roman destruction of Jerusalem, moreover, is not simply a past event but a major turning point in the history of fulfillment. That history has taken a different course from what was expected (in Jewish prophetic circles) because of Jerusalem's resistance to Jesus as the Messiah who was to have restored Israel. The most telling example of Luke's matter-of-fact historical treatment of events is his substitution for Mark's allusive "desolating sacri-

---

37. Tannehill, *Narrative Unity of Luke-Acts*.

lege" (in Mark 13:14) of "when you see Jerusalem surrounded by armies, then know that its desolation has come near" in 21:20.

The disciples' ostensible misunderstanding plays an important role in Luke's presentation of the unexpected turn of history on account of Jerusalem's rejection of Jesus. They are not completely mistaken in their supposition "that the kingdom of God was to appear immediately" when Jesus went to the city (19:11) or in their hope that this "prophet mighty in deed and word before God and all the people" was "the one to redeem Israel" (24:19, 21). Indeed, the disciples' acclamation of Jesus as "the king who comes in the name of the Lord!" indicated precisely what was happening in the "triumphal entry" into the city. The Jerusalem rulers and their Pharisaic retainers, however, did not recognize "the time of their visitation from God." Luke has Jesus articulate the historical result of Jerusalem's rejection: "Your enemies will surround you . . . and crush you to the ground . . ." (19:41–44; cf. 13:34–35).

Even more than Mark 13 and the Q discourse concerning "the day of the son of man," Luke warns against a sort of jumping to conclusions with regard to current events and the struggles in which the movement is engaged. In 17:20–21 Jesus warns that "the kingdom of God is not coming with things that can be observed . . . for the kingdom of God is among you." To the statements in Q about the unpredictable timing and suddenness of "the day of the son of man" Luke adds a warning against yearning for it, for first Jesus must suffer and be rejected (17:22, 25). Luke's revision of the discourse in Mark 13 is similar. The disciples should not heed false teachers who claim that "the time is near" because they themselves must first endure rejection and persecution (21:8, 9–19).

For all his deletion and downplaying of the excitement of fulfillment of hope now underway, however, Luke is not devoid of prophetic motifs that evoke a sense of fulfillment and crisis. That Jesus has come "to cast fire upon the earth," has "a baptism with which to be baptized," and has come to bring not peace but division (12:49–53, probably from Q) lends Luke's narrative a sense of crisis and of straining forward to completion. Besides integrating the Q prophetic saying about the banquet of fulfillment as a future judgmental sanction on discipline necessary for the kingdom in 13:28–29, Luke frames the "great supper" parable from Q with the traditional prophetic motif of the future banquet of fulfillment in 14:15. In those and many other discourses used by Luke, "the day of the Son of Man" as a symbol of future judgment (and/or the future return in judgment by the Lord) plays an important role in exhortation, as in 12:35–48; 17:20–37; 21:34–36. That day may appear suddenly, so Jesus' followers must both keep awake and maintain ethical discipline in the movement.

CONCLUSION

More comprehensive and precise analysis of Judean apocalyptic texts and their historical social context have made possible a more critical perspective on their relation to the Synoptic Gospels and the Jesus-movements that produced them. The significant discrepancies between the contents and concerns of the second-temple Judean apocalyptic texts and the standard scholarly construct of Jewish apocalypticism as articulated by influential interpreters such as Schweitzer and Bultmann suggested that it would be anachronistic to look primarily for the key events or themes of the supposed Jewish "apocalyptic scenario" of the end of the world in the Gospels. The more appropriate historical approach is to consider the contents and concerns of particular Gospel texts while checking for similarities to and differences from those of particular Judean apocalyptic texts.

Second-temple Judean apocalyptic texts were Jerusalem scribal circles' creative responses to the Hellenistic and Roman imperial pressures and military attacks on the traditional way of life, of which they were the professional interpreters and guardians. How could the Most High God, who headed the heavenly governance of the universe and had delivered them in the past, allow continued domination by one empire after another and even apostasy and oppression by their own high priestly rulers? Through the dream-visions of legendary wise men of the past such as Daniel and Enoch, interpreted by heavenly messengers, the "Daniel" and "Enoch" scribes received revelations that helped explain imperial violence and reassured them that the Most High would soon take decisive action to reassert control of the heavenly governance of the world. Like the most fearsome beasts, a series of empires had ferociously attacked and devoured subject people such as the Judeans; renegade heavenly forces, rebelling against God's orders, had generated imperial military violence and economic exploitation. Soon, however, in the heavenly court of judgment, God would condemn and punish the violent and oppressive imperial rulers, along with the rebellious heavenly forces, and would restore the people to a life of peace and justice on a renewed earth. Second-temple Judean apocalyptic texts thus have the same basic agenda as do prophetic texts such as in Isaiah, Jeremiah, and Joel: the judgment of oppressive imperial rule and the restoration of the people/ Israel. One of the revelatory texts included, albeit briefly, the resurrection of the dead and the vindication of the martyred wise scribes as part of the restoration of the people (Dan 12:1–3).

Somewhat parallel to the circles of dissident scribes who produced apocalyptic texts, movements of resistance to imperial domination and/ or oppressive domestic rulers, more closely contemporary with Jesus and his followers, arose among the ordinary people living in the villages of Judea and Galilee. These follow either a prophetic "script" or a messianic "script" embedded in Israelite popular tradition cultivated in village communities. That is, they are informed by and patterned after either the great acts of deliverance led by Moses and Joshua or those led by Saul and David. Because of the different social locations of Jerusalem scribal circles and Judean and Galilean villagers, and the limitation of literacy to the scribal circles, we would not expect that the villagers shared the key images and views of the scribal apocalyptic literature. It is simply not possible to use scribal texts as direct sources for the attitudes and idea of the ordinary people (including Jesus and his followers). It is clear, however, that the dissident scribes who produced apocalyptic texts and the villagers who formed popular movements were responding to parallel experiences of domination by imperial rulers and their local clients. And in the basic concerns are also parallel: they look to God's action to judge the oppressive imperial rulers and to restore or renew the people of Israel.

Because the Gospels function primarily as scripture for Christian churches, it is easy to lose sight of the fact that the communities from which they arose were originally movements of renewal of Israel and resistance to Roman imperial rule. Whereas the apocalyptic texts were produced by circles of Jerusalem scribes, however, the Gospels originated from movements of ordinary people, told the story and/or presented the speeches of a popular prophet who, in preaching and action, catalyzed a movement among villagers in Galilee. While the scribal visions-and-interpretations survey a broad sweep of history in a succession of empires climaxing in Antiochus Epiphanes' invasion of Jerusalem, the Gospels focus on the mission of Jesus in the renewal of Israel as the fulfillment of Israelite tradition, in opposition to and by the rulers of Israel. While the apocalyptic texts consist of visions, vision-interpretation, and learned lore familiar from other Judean and ancient Near Eastern scribal repertoires, the Gospels consist of oracles and actions of a prophetic figure influenced by and patterned after previous prophetic leaders of the people against their oppressive rulers, such as Moses and Elijah. The Gospels see revelation as having come to the ordinary people in the message and practices of Jesus, and pointedly not to "the wise" scribes and their patrons, the rulers who actively oppose him. What the Gospels share with the apocalyptic texts is a concern for the restoration or renewal of the people Israel, but at a different social level and in a more concrete form of renewal of mutually supportive covenantal community(ies).

In addition to their differences in social location, the Gospels, particularly Mark and Q, proclaim that God's saving action, the fulfillment of the people's longings, is already happening in Jesus' preaching and practice of the kingdom of God. This emphasis on the fulfillment that is already under way in Jesus shifts the focus to the present, to the renewal of Israel embodied in the Jesus movement itself. In Mark, followed by Matthew and Luke, the sense of fulfillment already accomplished is confirmed by the empty tomb or resurrection of Jesus himself, which constitutes the vindication of his cause, the validation of his preaching and practice, including his prophetic oracles and demonstrations against the rulers and ruling institutions. Correspondingly, the future judgment in the Gospels has a function somewhat different from that in Judean apocalyptic literature. In the latter, God's judgment will focus primarily on the rulers. In the Gospels, the judgment functions more as a sanction on the movement's own discipline than as vengeance on the rulers, who have already been decisively condemned by Jesus' prophetic pronouncements. In its representation of "the παρουσία of the Son of Man" (but more in the ingathering of the saints to complete the fulfillment in the kingdom than in judgment), the Gospel of Matthew articulates what some would consider a kind of Christian apocalypticism. The point of these scenes in Matthew 24–25, however, is to direct the faithful followers of Jesus to acts of justice and mercy in solidarity with "the least of these," his brothers and sisters in the communities of the movement.

12

The Rich and Poor in James
An Apocalyptic Ethic

INTRODUCTION

IN A PREVIOUS MEETING of the "Wisdom and Apocalyptic" Consultation of the Society of Biblical Literature, Patrick Hartin[1] and Matt Jackson-McCabe[2] wrote about wisdom, apocalyptic, and eschatology in the Letter of James. Jackson-McCabe concluded that James is better characterized as "moral exhortation rather than as a 'wisdom writing.'"[3] Quoting from John J. Collins, Jackson-McCabe further argued that James's apocalyptic worldview was "distinguished primarily by an increased importance attached to the supernatural agents and a world beyond this one, and by the hope for judgment and vindication beyond death.[4] Hartin examined the Wisdom Traditions reflected in James and the function of eschatology in the epistle. He concluded that James is not pure wisdom, but uses wisdom and prophetic forms and contains apocalyptic patterns of thought, which, however, "do not displace his focus on providing exhortations and advice to readers about how they are to lead their lives in the present."[5]

---

1. Hartin, "Who is Wise?" 483–503.
2. Jackson-McCabe, "A Letter," 504–17.
3. Ibid., 507.
4. Ibid., 508, quoting from Collins, "Wisdom, Apocalypticism, and Generic Compatibility," 170.
5. Hartin, "Who is Wise?" 499.

My purpose is to deal with the same sort of questions as they,[6] but with a more narrow focus on the question of the rich and the poor and social status in general. It is clear that James[7] appropriates motifs, ideas and forms that are at home in older Hebrew wisdom, apocalyptic, and prophetic literature and more recent Hellenistic moral literature.[8] The mere application of these scholarly categories to James, however, does not advance our understanding of the epistle very far.

JAMES'S APPROPRIATION OF SAYINGS OF JESUS

The tradition that informs James's theology most significantly is early Jesus proclamation, especially as it is otherwise preserved in the Sermon on the Mount/Plain. The parallels between James and the Synoptic Gospels have often been catalogued and studied.[9] In this study I will examine one such parallel in order to discover how James appropriated the teaching of Jesus.

> οὐχ ὁ θεός ἐξελέξατο τοὺς πτωχοὺς τῷ κόσμῳ πλουσίους
> ἐν πίστει καὶ κληρονόμους τῆς βασιλείας ἧς ἐπηγγείλατο
> τοῖς ἀγαπῶσιν αὐτόν.
>
> Has not God chosen those who are poor from the world's point of view to be rich in faith and to be heirs of the kingdom that he has promised to those who love him? (Jas 2:5b)

James's rebuke of those who show favoritism toward the rich represents a conflation of at least two closely related traditions: that God has chosen the poor and that he has promised that the poor will inherit the kingdom. The first is reflected also in 1 Cor 1:27: "God has chosen the foolish things of the world to shame the wise, and God has chosen the weak things of the world to put the strong things to shame." Both Paul and James independently adopt the tradition that God chooses those who are despised in this world.

---

6. Other writers have treated James with similar interests and observations. See, for example, Penner, *Epistle of James and Eschatology*.

7. The question of authorship of the letter remains unsolved. None of the proposed solutions (James the Lord's brother, some lesser-known James, or a pseudonymous author) has won widespread agreement.

8. See, for example, the discussion of Johnson, *Letter of James*, 16–24, 27–29.

9. Hartin, *James and the Q Sayings*. For a convenient table of the parallels, see Davids, *Epistle of James*, 47–48; or Koester, *Ancient Christian Gospels*, 72–73.

The second tradition overlaps with the first beatitude in both canonical versions. All versions of the beatitude include both of the key words of the saying in James: πτωχοί (poor) and βασιλεῖα (kingdom).

> Μακάριοι οἱ <u>πτωχοὶ</u> τῷ πνεύματι, ὅτι αὐτῶν ἐστὶν ἡ <u>βασιλεία</u> τῶν οὐρανῶν.
>
> Blessed are the poor in spirit because the kingdom of heaven is theirs. (Matt 5:3)

> Μακάριοι οἱ <u>πτωχοί</u>, ὅτι ὑμετέρα ἐστὶν ἡ <u>βασιλεία</u> τοῦ θεοῦ.
>
> Blessed are you poor because the kingdom of God is yours. (Luke 6:20)

> ⲡⲉϫⲉ ⲓ̅ⲥ̅ ϫⲉ 2ⲛ̅ⲙⲁⲕⲁⲣⲓⲟⲥ ⲛⲉ <u>ⲛ2ⲏⲕⲉ</u> ϫⲉ ⲧⲱⲧⲛ̅ ⲧⲉ <u>ⲧⲙⲛ̅ⲧⲉⲣⲟ</u> ⲛⲙ̅ⲡⲏⲩⲉ
>
> Jesus said, "Blessed are you poor because the kingdom of heaven is yours." (*Gos. Thom.* 54)

> Μακάριοι οἱ <u>πτωχοὶ</u> καί οἱ διωκόμενοι ἕνεκεν δικαιοσύνης, ὅτι αὐτῶν ἐστίν ἡ <u>βασιλεία</u> τοῦ θεοῦ.
>
> Blessed are the poor and those who are persecuted on account of righteousness because the kingdom of God is theirs. (Polycarp, *To the Philippians* 2:3d)

James expands on the beatitude in several ways. The addition of the phrase τῷ κόσμῳ has a function similar to that of Matthews' τῷ πνεύματι. Both restrict the characterization of "poor" by specifying a particular point of view. James is talking about those who are poor in the world's point of view. The addition of "to be rich in faith," has a similar function. Though someone may be poor in the world's point of view, from the (correct) standpoint of faith, they can be rich. The addition of κληρονόμοι (heirs) may have been imported from one of the other beatitudes in the Matthean version of the collection: Μακάριοι οἱ πραεῖς ὅτι αὐτοὶ κληρονομήσουσιν τὴν γῆν ("Blessed are the meek for they shall inherit the earth," Matt 5:5).[10] James's final expansion is the addition of "which he promised to those who love him." Here James makes explicit his identification of the poor with those who love God.

---

10. See also *Did.* 3:7, ἴσθι δέ πραΰς ἐπεὶ οἱ πραεῖς κληρονομήσουσι τὴν γῆν ("Be meek because the meek will inherit the earth").

The reference to the "royal law" (or more properly, the "king's law" [νόμον βασιλικόν]) of 2:8 and the kingdom promised to the poor in 2:5 imply the existence of a kingdom and a king. The adjective "royal" does not mean "fit for a king" but "of the king" and must mean that the law is understood by James as the law that governs the kingdom promised by Jesus to the poor. As far as James is concerned, it is the King's law that commands him to "love your neighbor as yourself."[11]

Thus, James has taken a beatitude of Jesus, conflated it (slightly) with another from the same collection (that the meek would *inherit the earth*), and applied it to his teaching on the treatment of the poor. The most obvious difference between James's allusion and the older collection of beatitudes is that the traditional pronouncement of blessing has become the basis for a rebuke. If Jesus has pronounced the poor blessed, then one ought not to dishonor the poor (v. 6), but honor them. This is in marked distinction to the treatment of the poor and rich that might normally be expected in "polite society" and that James has (to his dismay) observed. It is here that we may observe how James's theology controls his ethics.

THE IMPLIED SOCIAL SETTING

Several previous studies have dealt with the social situation that serves as a context for Jas 2:1-7.[12] All agree that this passage is an exhortation to impartiality in reference to socioeconomic status using judicial language. The exhortation itself is traditional and parallels may be found throughout Jewish and Christian literature. But James thinks of much more than a particularly low level of material wealth and social status when he speaks of the poor and the rich. These are not simply terms that describe a socioeconomic status, but also ethical categories. Indeed, in spite of the fact that James must indirectly admit that there are "rich" people among his "twelve tribes of the dispersion" (1:1), he systematically avoids calling them "brothers."[13] This reluctance may have originated

---

11. I find the argument of Luke Timothy Johnson that the quotation of Lev 19:18 in Jas 2:8 is but one piece of an elaborate complex of references to Leviticus 19 less than totally convincing ("The Use of Leviticus 19," 391–401). In any case, James understands the law in terms of the promised kingdom, not in terms of Moses.

12. See, for examples, Dibelius, *James*, 128–32; Ward, "Partiality," 87–97; Vouga, *L'Épitre de Saint Jacques*, 72; and Johnson, *Letter of James*, 220.

13. This has often been noted and is probably due to the fact that for James πλούσιος ("rich") is a boundary marker that excludes the rich from the Christian com-

in the social condition of most early Christians, but it has also become a theological conviction. Thus the implied social setting has less to do with social entities than with theological constructions of reality.

THE THEOLOGICAL BASIS

Part of the reason for James's antipathy toward rich people is undoubtedly based on experience. In 2:6–7 James catalogues three offenses committed by rich people. (1) They oppress the addressees; (2) they "drag" the addressees into court; (3) they blaspheme the name of Jesus.[14] The first two have sometimes been understood in terms of persecution of Christians. Dibelius argues that these should be understood not as an actual "Christian persecution," but as economic and legal action taken by the rich against Christians for economic reasons similar to those in Acts 16:19 or Acts 19:24 or because of irritation with Christian propaganda.[15] As Johnson correctly observes, however, there need not be any anti-Christian activity alluded to at all, since "[i]t is universal enough a characteristic of the world's rich to oppress and humiliate the poor by 'legal' means."[16] While the charge of blasphemy is directed against religious opponents, the complaints against the other two offenses are not criticisms of religious competitors; they address social exploitation. This observation is important because James's theological position is based not on religious competition, but on competition between two very different understandings of social ethics. The exploitative actions of the rich are not offensive because they are directed against Christians in particular, but because they represent the norms of a demonic society.

James has similar criticisms of rich people in the two parallel passages, 4:13–17 and 5:1–6. The passages are held together by their content (criticisms of actions characteristic of rich people) and introductory particles ("Come now" plus vocative). The first is directed against "those

---

munity. Vouga notes the further movement from the third person to the second person (*Jacques*, 25). Though James's real audience surely included people of relative wealth, his implied audience seems to exclude them.

14. In each case the subject ("the rich," "they," "they") is emphatic, either by position or by the use of the emphatic pronoun. For parallels to "the fair name which is called over you" from the DSS, see 4Q418 81 i 12 (ו)כול הנקרא לשמו קודש ("And everyone who is called by [his] name"), and 4Q285 1:9–10 ושם קודשו נקרא ע[ליכם ("And his Holy name is called ov[er you").

15. Dibelius, *James*, 139–40.

16. Johnson, *James*, 226.

who say" that they will travel and make a profit by buying and selling, and it criticizes them for failing to recognize their temporality and for their pretentious, evil boasting. They are advised to change their attitude to one of submission to what "the Lord wills." This advice is in marked contrast with the far more severe advice in the next passage addressed to "the rich" who are advised to weep and wail because of their impending doom. They are condemned because of economic exploitation (they have withheld the rightful wages of their agricultural workers) and because they have condemned and murdered the righteous.[17] If, as was suggested above (n. 13), πλούσιος ("rich") is a boundary marker, then we may conclude that pretentiousness, while sinful, does not exclude one from the community upon which the name of Jesus is named (2:7). The blatant injustice named in 5:1–6, however, does merit the label "rich" and marks those who practice it as bound for judgment.

James's condemnation of economic exploitation is apparently based on the Deuteronomic obligation to act toward the needy with justice and kindness, based on God's justice and love for the poor. According to Deut 10:18–19, God is one "who executes justice for the orphan and the widow, and who loves the strangers, providing them food and clothing. You shall also love the stranger, for you were strangers in the land of Egypt." A similar ethic is found in the Psalms, which occasionally discuss God's care for the poor. According to Ps 72:12–13, for example, "For he delivers the needy when they call, the poor and those who have no helper. He has pity on the weak and the needy, and saves the lives of the needy." Job echoes this sentiment in his final defense where he affirms the impropriety of failing to feed and clothe the poor, the orphan, and the widow or of acting unjustly toward them (Job 31:16–23). This is apparently also in imitation of God's treatment of the poor: "But he saves the needy from the sword of their [the wicked's] mouth, from the hand of the mighty. So the poor have hope, and injustice shuts its mouth" (Job 5:15–16). Ben Sira's advice to his readers explicitly mentions kindness to the poor as a form of imitation of God.

> My child, do not cheat the poor of their living, and do not keep needy eyes waiting. Do not grieve the hungry, or anger one in need ... Give a hearing to the poor, and return his greeting with deference. Deliver the oppressed from his oppressors; let not

---

17. Presumably the charge of murder is due to the fact that one who lacks an income runs the risk of starvation (cf. Sir 34:21–22).

> right judgment be repugnant to you. To the fatherless be as a father, help the widows in their husbands' stead; then God will call you a son of his, and he will be more tender to you more than a mother. (Sir 4:1–10)

The prophets contain similar criticism for those who oppress the poor. Amos proclaims judgment for those who "trample on the needy, and bring to ruin the poor of the land" (Amos 8:4) along with those who are impatient at not being able to do business on the Sabbath and those who use false weights (v. 5). Many other examples could be cited. The Epistle of Enoch contains extremely harsh criticisms of the rich:

> Woe to you, you rich, for you have trusted in your riches, and from your riches you will be parted, because you have not remembered the Most High in the days of your riches. You have committed blasphemy and unrighteousness and have become ready for the day of slaughter and for the day of darkness and for the day of the great judgment (*1 Enoch* 94:8–9).[18]

The precise nature of their unrighteousness, however, is not always clear. In only one case is it clear that oppression of the poor is one of the crimes of the rich:

> Woe unto you, you sinners, for your riches make you appear righteous, but your hearts convict you of being sinners, and this word shall be a testimony against you for a memorial of your evil deeds. Woe to you who eat the finest of the wheat and drink new wine, the choicest of the wine and tread underfoot the poor in your might. (*1 Enoch* 96:4–5)

In this passage one of the actions that belies the appearance of righteousness is the oppression of the poor. More often, however, it is the persecution of the righteous for which the rich are condemned (*1 Enoch* 95:7). Thus *1 Enoch* may differ from the other examples cited in that its real concern is not so much with economic exploitation of the poor as with social dominance by those who are deemed unrighteous by the Enochic writer.

James's acceptance of the attitude displayed in these traditions is clear in 5:1–6 where the rich are advised to weep and lament in view of their impending judgment. Their injustice has been noted by God and will be judged. In this passage God is the arbiter of injustice done by the

---

18. All translations of *1 Enoch* are taken from Black, *Book of Enoch*.

rich; the implication is that God's care for the poor is grounds for the judgment of those who oppress the poor. In the light of this assurance, James advises his readers to be patient "because the Lord's coming is near" (Jas 5:8).

James has also another theological vantage point for developing his ethics of wealth and poverty. The occasional use of the term עֲנָוִים (humble/poor/pious) in some of the Psalms has apparently led to a similar use of the term "poor" in some of the Psalms of Solomon.[19] The term is apparently used as a self-designation in certain of the sectarian Qumran texts, possibly because the writers may have identified their piety with a lack of desired social status. This is especially clear in Pesher Habakkuk and the pesher on Psalm 37: "The interpretation of the word concerns the Wicked Priest, to pay him the reward for what he did to the poor. . . . God will sentence him to destruction, exactly as he intended to destroy the poor" (4QpHab 12:2–6). And "And the poor shall inherit the land and enjoy peace in plenty. Its interpretation concerns the congregation of the poor who will tolerate the period of distress and will be rescued from all the snares of Belial" (4QpPs37 2:9–11).[20]

What is distinctive about James's exhortation to impartiality is not simply that he adopts the identification of poverty and piety (which he seems to do in part), but that he applies his apocalyptic interpretation of the contours of reality to the problem. The eschatology of James is relatively conventional. He appeals to eschatology in order to encourage the pious and to threaten the wicked. Eschatology, however, does not provide the theological foundation for the statements of chapter 2. That foundation is provided by the apocalyptic division of the cosmos into above and below (3:15), God and this world (4:4), God and the devil (4:7; 3:15), and the contrast between desire, which leads to sin, and the word of truth, which gives "us" birth (1:14–18; cf. 4:1–4). James objects to far more than simple acts of exploitation. He objects to a whole cosmic structure that is in open conflict with God and which determines the false and evil social structure in which humans live.

---

19. For example, "And the devout shall give thanks in the assembly of the people, and God will be merciful to the poor to the joy of Israel" (*Pss. Sol.*10:6; see also 15:1; 18:2). Translations of the Psalms of Solomon are from Wright, "Psalms of Solomon," 639–70.

20. Translations of the DSS are from Martínez, *Dead Sea Scrolls*.

Dibelius is typical in his explanation of apocalypticism as the reason for Jesus' convictions regarding the poor (which have influenced James).

> If the proclaimer of this message and those who followed him lived in poverty, it was not because of thoroughgoing asceticism or strict proletarian consciousness, for Jesus consents to support from others and to being invited as a guest. The decisive element, again, is the apocalyptic expectation. He lives apart from active involvement in the economic functions of the world because he foresees the end of this world. Thanks to the situation in Galilee and the hospitality of his followers, this life of poverty never becomes penurious and proletarian.[21]

He is correct that apocalypticism has influenced this thinking, but he is not correct in emphasizing the "apocalyptic expectation." It was not the apocalyptic expectation of certain future events that influenced these attitudes; it was rather the apocalyptic understanding of the present.

James's appropriation of Jesus' beatitude contains a critical window onto his understanding of the meaning of poverty—James's addition of the little phrase τῷ κόσμῳ ("in the world's point of view"). Unlike Matthew, whose addition of τῷ πνεύματι ("in spirit") limits the scope of the word "poor" to poverty that cannot be measured in material terms, James adds a modifier that accepts the material sense of the word, but at the same time criticizes it as false. The conventional use of the word "poor" is inauthentic because it assumes the social order of the world in which the rich (those who have social as well as material status) are honored and the poor are dishonored and exploited. The fact that God has chosen the poor and dishonored of this world to be rich in faith and to inherit the kingdom is proof that the conventional criteria for assigning honor are false and in need of reversal. The importance of this view for James is evident also in his exhortation to the "lowly" brother (ὁ ἀδελφὸς ὁ ταπεινός) to boast in his exalted position, while the rich man (not "brother") should "boast" in his humiliation in view of the fact that he is about to perish (1:9–10). These verses are a clear declaration of the reversal of values that James believes is in force within the Christian community. Thus the addition of τῷ κόσμῳ clearly connects James's ethics concerning the poor with his wider conviction of the dualism of heaven and earth with its concomitant ethic of social reversal.

21. Debelius, *James*, 43.

One other passage confirms James's negative evaluation of the world. In 3:13—4:10, James contrasts two kinds of wisdom and the consequences of living by one or the other. According to 3:15, one kind of wisdom is "earthly, unspiritual, and demonic" (ἐπίγειος ψυχική δαιμονιώδης); the other "comes down from above" (ἄνωθεν κατερχομένη). The latter characterization should be understood in the context of 1:17 which proclaims that "every good and perfect gift is from above (ἄνωθεν), coming down (καταβαῖνον) from the Father of lights." Commentators have rightly understood this characterization of wisdom in the light of the traditional Jewish understanding of wisdom as a gift of God, the one who created wisdom and who is truly wise.[22] It is possible, however, that "coming down from above" is an allusion to a more concrete tradition of the descent of wisdom from heaven to earth to dwell among those who were to receive her (Sir 24:1–12; denied in *1 Enoch* 42:1–2).

James presses this contrast even more forcefully in the discussion of the opposition of the world to God that follows his characterization of wisdom. In his criticism of those who want to have things that they can squander on their own pleasures (4:3), James says that friendship with the world (κόσμος) is hatred toward God (4:4) and that God resists the proud but exalts the lowly (4:6, 10). The readers are accused of being "double-minded" (δίψυχοι) precisely because of their failed attempt to bring this diabolic cosmos (4:7) into harmony with God.

CONCLUSION

Moral exhortation (how one ought to live in this world) has probably always been one of the functions of apocalyptic literature. Our fascination with the temporal, eschatological aspects of apocalyptic texts and their outlandish descriptions of future judgment and heavenly journeys may sometimes blind us to the function of these mythical descriptions as symbols for an ethical system that involves the rejection of experienced social realities. The scholarly emphasis on the bizarre elements of apocalyptic may have also helped to obscure the fundamental concern with the "here and now" of all apocalyptic texts in so far as they seek to explain and redefine experienced reality and the moral obligations

---

22. E.g., Dibelius, *James*, 212; Johnson, *James*, 272; Vouga, *Jacques*, 105; and Davids, *James*, 152.

of those who live in that reality. The literary function of the mythical elements is to create an imaginative interpretation of the true structure of the cosmos. Texts, such as James, that deemphasize the geographic contours of heaven and hell and the details of future judgment, but that adopt the dualistic definition of reality that is characteristic of apocalyptic literature, should not be excluded from the category of apocalyptic. Some texts (those that belong to the genre of apocalypse) are characterized by descriptions of the apocalyptic construction of reality. Others, such as James, adopt that construction but focus on understanding one's rightful place within the apocalyptically defined cosmos. By interpreting Jesus' teachings within the context of an apocalyptic construction of reality, James has created a powerful social critique and a positive foundation for granting honor to those who otherwise lack it.

Epilogue

Through the process of ever broadening critical research and reflection that supports these essays, we were led repeatedly to rethink the assumptions, approaches, analyses, and fundamental concepts of biblical studies as they bear on wisdom and apocalyptic texts. As we join these essays together we offer further comments on a few key issues that we may not have sharpened or developed sufficiently and on certain implications that now appear more clearly.

JUDEAN SCRIBES AND THE CULTURAL REPERTOIRE THEY CULTIVATED

It seems clear from Sir 38:34—39:4 that learned scribes such as Ben Sira learned and cultivated torah and prophecies as well as various kinds of wisdom. From the Dead Sea Scrolls it is clear that the scribes (and priests?) of the Qumran community also cultivated torah, prophetic collections, and historical traditions, as well as wisdom. At least for mid- to late second-temple times, therefore, it seems that the standard typology in biblical studies according to which the priests cultivated torah, the disciples of prophets collected and expanded prophetic oracles, and learned scribes ("the wise") cultivated wisdom is inappropriate. If Ben Sira is typical, the scribes understood themselves to be responsible for exhorting their students to obey covenantal torah and as the heirs of prophecy as well as the purveyors of wisdom (Sir 39:5–11).

Whereas modern scholars standardly view wisdom and apocalyptic as different and separate traditions, genres, and even worldviews, ancient Judean scribes evidently understood themselves to be cultivating several different kinds of wisdom. By "wisdom" modern scholars generally mean proverbial wisdom. And indeed what appear to be the oldest sections of the book of Proverbs are collections of individual proverbs. The later sections of Proverbs (e.g., chapters 1–9) and the extensive proverbial material in Sirach, however, appear in short speeches of *instructional wisdom*, on a wide range of topics, from friendship to one's behavior in the presence of superiors to aiding the poor. Sirach, however, also includes poetic *reflection about wisdom* (Sirach 24) and *cosmological wisdom*, knowledge of the paths of the heavenly bodies and the patterns of weather. The Book of Luminaries (*1 Enoch* 72–82) is a brief encyclopedia of such cosmological wisdom. Both Sirach and the Book of Watchers include brief sections that use knowledge of the consistent, obedient behavior of the heavenly bodies as paradigms for human obedience to God. The Book of Watchers also draws extensively on such cosmological wisdom in its revelation of divine judgment of the rebel watchers as already orchestrated in the heaven and far reaches of the cosmos. Finally, something similar to what has been called *mantic wisdom* (with reference to Babylonian scribes' interpretation of dreams) was developed by Judean scribes into visions-and-interpretations of history to explain the origin of imperial violence and oppression and/or the current historical crisis of imperial persecution, as in "Enoch's" Animal Vision and Daniel 7, 8, 10–12. These visions-and-interpretations, which may have been a development on the basis of "mantic" wisdom, are the early texts of what has been labeled "apocalyptic" literature by modern scholars. Sirach does not include anything that resembles vision-interpretation, and seems to be suspicious of it. In the introduction to the book of Daniel, on the other hand, "Daniel" and the other young Judeans serving at the imperial court are trained "in every branch of wisdom" (Dan 1:4). And in the rest of the anthology that comprises the book of Daniel, the learned scribe "Daniel" is especially adept at the interpretation of visions. While not wishing to set up a new set of controlling concepts, it is clear that the texts themselves include and distinguish between different kinds of wisdom, one of which is close to what has been called "apocalyptic."

Given the continuity of scribal learning across the courts of the ancient Near East, we may wonder if "every branch of wisdom" includes all four of the kinds of wisdom mentioned above, and perhaps others as well. It would appear that scribes trained to serve in the Judean temple-state would have cultivated several kinds of wisdom, which they could then draw upon as appropriate to the occasion and function: instructional wisdom when teaching students/ protégés, cosmological wisdom when addressing religious-economic matters such as the annual calendar, reflection on wisdom as authoritative for the legitimation of the temple-state (Sirach 24), and interpretation of visions when seeking higher revelation about historical crises or future events. But they could also draw upon the other kinds of knowledge in the Judean cultural repertoire, such as torah rulings and prophetic oracles and various kinds of wisdom in combination with one or more kinds of wisdom.

QUESTIONS OF GENRE

The question of genres has been of central importance in recent discussion of second-temple Judean texts and of Gospel materials. Wisdom teaching, by which biblical scholars usually understand proverbial wisdom, is usually classified into micro-genres of particular sayings (such as "maxims"). The instructional wisdom in Proverbs 1–9 and Sirach, however, appears in short speeches, of which little or no formal analysis has been carried out.[1] Cosmological wisdom could take the form of a catalogue of knowledge or could be used in hymns to the Most High as creator. Reflective wisdom usually appeared in hymnic form. Thirty years ago, specialists on apocalyptic texts attempted to define a macro-genre that would cover apocalyptic literature generally. Most of the texts that address the crisis under Antiochus Epiphanes in the early second century, however, have the form of historical visions, or to be more precise, historical visions-and-interpretations. But some of those are included with or begin as "testaments." And some of the "apocalypses" include prophetic visions or commissionings familiar from several prophetic books. These observations suggest that we back away from any simplistic definition and dichotomy of "wisdom" and "apocalyptic" as genres, and remain open to discerning various combinations of forms from the various cultural traditions that second-temple scribes were apparently responsible for cultivating.

Similarly at the more popular level of the production of ("Gospel") texts from and for Jesus movements, it is difficult to discern and define distinctive genres. If collections or sequences of orally performed *logoi* ("words/ speeches") can be discerned through references in and/or the arrangement of materials in various texts, they cannot be characterized

---

1. Some first steps in Kirk, *Composition*, 93–104, 130–51; and Horsley, *Scribes, Visionaries*, 133–42.

as distinctively "sapiential" or the products of "sages." Many such collections were of (fragments of) prophetic oracles or speeches. The sequence of speeches in Q—which has standardly been given the misleading label of "the *sayings* source," as if it were merely a collection of individual "sayings"—bears most resemblance to prophetic speeches, including distinctive prophetic forms such as an oracle of lament or woes. It is not clear on what basis in second-temple Judean texts the speech in Mark 13 could be labeled an "apocalypse." If generic definitions are thought helpful, then all three of the Synoptic Gospels appear to be a combination of narrative and (interrupted by) speeches of Jesus that have more of a prophetic than an apocalyptic or sapiential character.

QUESTION(S) OF WORLDVIEW(S)

It has often been claimed that apocalyptic texts express a particular apocalyptic worldview or theology, even that a particular worldview is inherent in the genre of apocalypse.[2] It is also often assumed or claimed that wisdom sayings express a particular worldview or theology. We have come to think that such claims are questionable. Cosmological wisdom appears to lay out a view of the regular operations of the cosmos. Enoch texts classified as "apocalyptic," the Book of Watchers and Animal Vision, appear to have shared this worldview, according to which earthly affairs are under the divine governance of the Most High and any number of heavenly bodies/forces/messengers/watchers. This view of the cosmos as both under and included in the heavenly governance of the earthy was thus not "dualistic" and it was hardly distinctively "apocalyptic." It seems to stand in continuity with the worldview articulated in prophetic oracles and prophetic books, in which earthly/ historical affairs are under the oversight and governance of YHWH and the heavenly council of the "children-of-the-gods" (*bene-elohim*). Instructional wisdom does not appear to have articulated a worldview or theology, but it inculcated a conservative demeanor in the scribe-in-training whose role in life was to conserve the cultural tradition and serve the temple-state. The learned scribe thus had to "watch his words" vis-à-vis the aristocrats whom he served and on whom he was dependent.[3] The historical visions-and-interpretations that we classify as "apocalyptic" articulated

---

2. Recently, for example, Collins, "From Prophecy to Apocalypticism," 247, 257.
3. Carr, *Tablets of the Heart*; Horsley, *Scribes, Visionaries*, 67–69, 71–87, esp., 84.

a confidence that God will act in the near future to enforce his heavenly governance, enabling their addressees to persist in the traditional way of life in the face of imperial violence and persecution.

SCRIBAL ATTITUDES TOWARD THE HIGH PRIESTHOOD AND THE TEMPLE

So long as second-temple Judean texts are read as expressions of and evidence for the vague synthetic construct of "Judaism," the question of their stance toward the high priesthood and the Temple tends not to arise. It is simply assumed and restated repeatedly that all or most Jews were united around the Temple as well as the Torah. Consideration of the social location and role of learned scribes in the Judean temple-state, however, indicates that insofar as they were "in the middle" of things, they would understandably have held ambivalent attitudes toward the wealthy and powerful priestly aristocracy, including the incumbent high priest. But different texts exhibit different attitudes toward the high priesthood and the Temple.

The learned scribe Jesus ben Sira was hardly a neutral observer of Judean political-religious life. Significant sections of the book of Sirach are what today might be called propaganda for the incumbent Oniad high priesthood. The lengthy poetic "epic" of the heroic ancestral office-holders that climaxes with the paean of praise of the priestly aristocracy celebrating at the altar in the Temple (Sirach 44–50) is the "parade" example. But even the hymnic praise of Wisdom as a (semi-) divine heavenly figure (Sirach 24) is a remarkable legitimation of the Jerusalem Temple as *the* sacred site of divine presence. First Maccabees, which must have been produced by scribes under the high priest Simon in mid-second century BCE is now recognized as historical propaganda for the upstart Hasmonean dynasty.

In addition to his pro-Oniad propaganda, however, Ben Sira makes some remarkably forthright and even caustic comments, not just about scribal anxieties about their patrons' power, but about how the wealthy priestly aristocracy exploit and oppress the Judean peasantry. It should be no surprise then to find other scribes articulating several series of prophetic woes against the wealthy and powerful (priestly aristocracy) in the Epistle of Enoch. It is clear, once we read apocalyptic texts in historical political context, that the scribes who produced the historical visions-and-interpretations in Daniel 7–12 and the Enochic Animal Vision were engaged in a sustained struggle against their own high priestly aristocracy as well as against Antiochus Epiphanes. And less than a generation later numbers of scribes and priests adamantly condemned the incumbent high priesthood as they withdrew from Jerusalem to launch their new exodus and renewed covenant community at Qumran.

Those who recognize the opposition to the high priests in apocalyptic and other texts often insist, however, that the scribes did not oppose the Temple itself. When E. P. Sanders sought an explanation of how Jesus could pronounce God's judgment against the Temple, he claimed that Jesus was expecting a new (eschatological) temple and claimed that this expectation is attested in several prophetic and apocalyptic texts.[4] The book of Ezekiel, produced after the Babylonian destruction of Jerusalem, and the Temple Scroll from Qumran, from a time after the Daniel and Enoch texts, both speak of an ideal temple. But these are not expectations of a concrete new or "eschatological" temple-building. In claiming that there was a standard expectation of an eschatological temple, Sanders was building on a common scholarly assumption about certain apocalyptic texts. Closer examination of the passages Sanders cited, however, showed that late prophetic texts and the apocalyptic and other second-temple texts he cited do not include a rebuilt temple in their hopes for a restored Israel.[5] After the more extensive analysis of Daniel and Enoch texts in connection with the essays in Parts One and Two above, however, it seems clearer to us that they do not attest a new, eschatological temple. The *maskilim* who produced Daniel 7–12 were horrified at the attacks on the sacred building and rituals by Antiochus Epiphanes. Strikingly absent from these visions-and-interpretations, however, is any mention of a restored temple and/or high priesthood as part of the restoration of the (Judean) people. "Enoch's" Ten-Week Vision expects the restoration of the "house" of the Most High, evidently the people, but it lacks a temple. The Animal Vision even appears to condemn the whole Second Temple and its priesthood an illegitimate. The original "house," a symbol of the people, had a "tower," symbolizing the original Solomonic Temple. But the new "tower" had polluted bread on its table. And the (new) "house" that is restored and vastly expanded

---

4. Sanders, *Jesus and Judaism*, chap. 2.
5. Horsley, *Jesus and the Spiral of Violence*, 289–91.

following the judgment pointedly does not have a "tower."[6] In Qumran texts the community itself is understood as the true temple and (equivalent of) temple rituals.

These Judean scribal statements seem to be precursors of the final vision in the book of Revelation of the new Jerusalem coming down from heaven, symbolizing the restoration of the people (Rev 21). Given the presence of God and the Lamb, however, it has no need for a temple. Similarly in the contemporary *4 Ezra*, in the fourth and sixth visions (despite all the mourning over the destruction of the altar, Temple, etc. in the former), the new, gloriously restored Zion that symbolizes the restored people, does not appear to have a restored temple ("for no work of human building could endure in a place where the city of the Most High was to be revealed," 10:54).

SCRIBAL OPPOSITION TO IMPERIAL RULE

Previous interpretation of wisdom and apocalyptic literature as expressions of "Judaism"—particularly as "post-exilic" and focused on a rebuilt Temple—has tended to obscure the continuing subjection of Judea to the rule of one empire after another. One of our principal sources for second-temple "Judaism," moreover, the wisdom of Ben Sira, conveniently ignores imperial rule, which was contested among scribal circles, as we know from the books of Maccabees and the historical accounts of Josephus, as well as Daniel and "Enoch" texts. What Ben Sira does reveal, however, is the potential for and the basis of Judean scribal opposition to imperial rule. Contrary to a standard assumption and generalization in biblical studies, that learned scribes cultivated mainly or only wisdom, while prophetic materials were the province of prophets and Mosaic torah the turf of priests, Ben Sira insists that learned scribes also cultivated covenantal torah and prophecies. Insofar as wise scribes were professionally responsible for cultivating the whole repertoire of Judean culture, and personally committed to it, there was potential and basis for conflict with imperial rule if the latter became a threat to the traditional Judean way of life.

As is well rehearsed in the fields of biblical studies and Jewish history, this is just what happened under Seleucid rule in the early sec-

---

6. See further Tiller, *Animal Apocalypse*, 45–47; Horsley, *Scribes, Visionaries*, 166; *Revolt of the Scribes*, 69–72, 74–75.

ond century BCE and again under Roman rule. In graduate training we were taught that "apocalypticism," in its "otherworldly" orientation was "alienated from history," looking for the "end of the world" in a "cosmic catastrophe." Our analysis behind the essays in Parts One and Two above, however, indicated that virtually the opposite was true. The learned scribes who produced the visions-and-interpretations in the Animal Vision and Daniel 7, 8, and 10–12 were very much engaged in history. Committed to the traditional Judean way of life as articulated in the Judean cultural repertoire, which was the basis of their own sense of authority from God, they struggled against the invasion by the Seleucid emperor to enforce a "reform" in that way of life. What we call "apocalyptic" texts were their attempts to understand how history could have come to such a crisis on the basis of their familiarity with prophetic forms and their knowledge of mantic and cosmological wisdom. And on the basis of their commitment to Mosaic covenantal torah, they resisted the imperial repression of their way of life even when it meant martyrdom. Second-temple Judean apocalyptic texts are statements of opposition to Hellenistic and Roman imperial rule in which circles of dissident learned scribes also expressed conviction that God, still in control of history, would sit in judgment on empire and would restore the people to a life of independence and justice on a renewed earth.[7]

CHANGES IN "APOCALYPTIC" TEXTS AFTER THE ROMAN DESTRUCTION OF JERUSALEM

The essay on *4 Ezra* suggests that further exploration is needed of how "apocalyptic" texts composed after the tragic Roman devastation of Judea and Jerusalem differ from earlier texts, and how they develop and change traditions from earlier texts. The historical situation, of course, had changed dramatically for Judeans, with the Roman destruction of Jerusalem and the Temple. With the historical termination of the temple-state in Jerusalem, moreover, the social position of learned scribes as "retainers" serving the temple-state, albeit often dissident retainers, had disappeared and the professional role of the scribes was now unclear.

The best known apocalyptic texts that respond to the destruction of Jerusalem, *4 Ezra* and *2 Baruch*, are much longer and far more

---

7. More extensive development of this interpretation extending to other second-temple apocalyptic texts in Horsley, *Revolt of the Scribes*.

complex in their multiple forms and their mix of materials than any of the second-temple apocalyptic texts. Laments and mourning over the Roman destruction of Jerusalem replace much of the visionary review of the history of imperial oppression in the earlier Daniel and Enoch texts. The traditional strategies for applying visions-and-interpretations to the understanding of current events has been rejected or at least questioned. The scribal composers struggle to understand the significance of the destruction of Jerusalem in heated dialogues and arguments with divine messengers on issues such as sin, the severity of God's punishment, the covenantal Law, the future of the people, now focused on Jerusalem/ Zion. These are new issues that did not appear in earlier "apocalyptic" texts and new issues and forms that complicate, interrupt, and relativize the more coherent flow of historical vision-and-interpretation in Daniel 7, 8, 10–12 and the Animal Vision. Whereas God carried out the judgment of empires and the restoration of the earth and the people in second-temple apocalypses, "the Messiah" suddenly appears in *4 Ezra* and *2 Baruch*. Whereas a time of suffering is mentioned only briefly in previous texts (Dan 12:1b), such suffering receives more attention in the post-destruction texts (*4 Ezra* 5:1–13; *2 Baruch* 25–27). Similarly, while resurrection of the dead is mentioned only rarely and briefly in earlier apocalyptic texts (again only in Dan 12:2), it receives a bit more attention in *2 Baruch* (30:1–5; 50:2–3; 51; yet only brief references in *4 Ezra* 7:32, 37). Ironically, while *4 Ezra* appears in key ways as an "anti-apocalypse," many of the key features that comprise the modern scholarly construct of "apocalypticism," difficult to find in second-temple texts, appear in *4 Ezra* and *2 Baruch*. About the only sustained description of what might be called an "apocalyptic scenario" of "the end of days" comes in *2 Baruch* 25–32. This passage includes a key "sign," "determinism" of a foreordained sequence of events, and the appearance of "the Messiah." Of the key events that Schweitzer and Bultmann thought standard in the ubiquitous "apocalyptic scenario" of "Judaism" this is virtually the only sustained description of what became labeled as "the Great Tribulation" or "the woes/ birth pangs of the Messiah," and it includes the resurrection of the souls of the righteous at the Messiah's appearance. Of the other key events that Schweitzer and Bultmann found standard in the Jewish "apocalyptic scenario," however, the scenario in *2 Baruch* 25–32 does not include images of God's judgment, with the Son of Man as agent, and has an elaborate renewal of the earth, of God's creation, rather than the end of the world in cosmic catastrophe. So even these late "apocalyptic" texts do not fit easily into the modern synthetic construct of apocalypticism.

ARE SCRIBAL TEXTS SOURCES FOR POPULAR ATTITUDES AND EXPECTATIONS?

It has been assumed among Christian scholars for at least the last century that wisdom and particularly apocalyptic texts provide evidence for the views of Judeans and Galileans generally. Albert Schweitzer a century ago, followed by the neo-Schweitzerians of the last decade, for example, insisted, evidently on the basis of Judean apocalyptic texts, that John the Baptist, Jesus, and early Christians all shared the widespread apocalyptic expectations that supposedly permeated "Judaism."[8]

In the last few decades, however, at least some biblical scholars are recognizing that literacy in antiquity was very limited. In second-temple Judea it was confined mainly to circles of professional scribes. Direct knowledge of written texts was thus confined to scribal (and perhaps Jerusalem priestly) circles. Both early Enoch texts and Daniel were well known in the Qumran community. Probably even the oral-memorial cultivation of texts such as the books of the Pentateuch and Daniel and early Enoch books was confined to scribes and priests.[9] Ben Sira gives the sense that while he exhorted his students to aid the poor, scribes did not have much interaction with artisans and farmers. The various kinds of wisdom, moreover, were esoteric knowledge that was the special province of professional intellectuals, the learned scribes. As in other such societies, villagers who comprised the vast majority of the society cultivated their own popular Israelite tradition orally in their local communities. They probably knew that written texts existed and that what was "written" had a certain kind of authority. And the popular tradition included many parallels to the official texts (exodus narratives, covenantal commandments, Elijah-Elisha stories, etc.) But it seems unlikely that they had direct knowledge of these texts. It seems particularly unlikely that villagers would have known the instructional wisdom directed specifically to scribes-in-training and the purity codes designed for priests serving in the Temple.

---

8. Schweitzer, *The Quest of the Historical Jesus*, 367; Allison, "The Eschatology of Jesus."

9. See Horsley, *Scribes, Visionaries*, chaps 5, 6.

But what about the visions-and-interpretations that were addressed to the crisis under Antiochus Epiphanes? The vision-and-interpretation in Daniel 10–12 anticipates that, at the height of the crisis in Jerusalem, when Antiochus Epiphanes was cracking down on the *maskilim* who were resisting his repressive measures, "the wise among the people shall give understanding to many" (Dan 11:33–35). Insofar as learned scribes served in the temple-state located in Jerusalem, it seems unlikely that they would suddenly become missionaries to the outlying village communities. On the other hand, in the small city of Jerusalem itself during the crisis it would have been surprising if the ordinary people of the city did not know what the *maskilim* were doing and know of the confidence in God that motivated their leading role in resistance to Antiochus' persecution.

The Gospels, including the parallel speeches in Matthew and Luke standardly attributed to Q, do not display the features and lore of texts produced by professional scribes/sages. Insofar as the Gospels and their component materials reflect a prophet and movement(s) that originated in the villages of Galilee, they are clearly popular texts. This poses questions about whether scribal texts, sapiential or apocalyptic, can be taken as sources for the attitudes and views of ordinary people such as the popular prophetic and messianic movements and Jesus and his followers and whether the Gospels or Gospel materials can be interpreted directly from scribal texts. Josephus' brief accounts of the popular prophetic (and messianic) movements and their leaders give no indication that they shared the scribal lore and perspective found in Daniel and early Enoch texts, hence there is no basis in the sources for labeling them "apocalyptic."[10] From Josephus' accounts it seems clear that these prophetic (and messianic) figures and their movements were informed by social memories of Moses, Joshua, Elijah, or the young David in Israelite popular tradition. It thus seems questionable whether Judean apocalyptic texts can be used as sources for projecting the meaning of Jesus' teaching in Gospel sources.[11] Even the principal Jesus-interpreter

---

10. "Two Types of Popular Prophets;" etc.

11. Horsley, *Jesus and the Spiral*, 140–43. Urged by a senior mentor not to omit discussion of "apocalypticism" as an influence on Jesus and his mission, I hypothesized that insofar as scribes/sages had come to experience some of the same indignities under imperial rule that peasants had long endured perhaps the texts they composed in protest would have been parallel to popular views. After closer reading of Ben Sira's instructional speeches and other scribes' visions-and-interpretations, however, I now believe I was overestimating the potential similarity of scribal and popular views.

who agreed that Jesus and other popular leaders belonged to the "little tradition" (in contrast with the elite "great tradition"), however, used the label of "apocalyptic" prophets. He projected popular "apocalyptic" views, however, on the basis of the scribal *Psalms of Solomon* (which is not even usually classified as "apocalyptic"). And he projected Jesus' supposedly popular "sapiential" understanding of "the kingdom of God" on the basis of phrases in the Wisdom of Solomon and the treatises of Philo of Alexandria (elite Hellenistic Jewish intellectual reflection on heavenly Wisdom influenced by Platonic philosophy).[12] It seems even clearer now, however, after the investigation of second-temple scribal texts and then popular Gospel texts, that scribal texts cannot be used as direct sources for popular views and attitudes.

LACK OF TEXTUAL EVIDENCE FOR EITHER THE APOCALYPTIC JESUS OR THE SAPIENTIAL JESUS

There are thus no direct sources that might indicate that ordinary Judeans and Galileans held views and cultivated teachings that resembled or corresponded to scribal wisdom and/or apocalyptic texts – unless it might be the Gospels. That is just what Schweitzer claimed in his influential presentation of Jesus as completely caught up in the supposed Jewish apocalyptic scenario of the end of the world. Aware that most Jewish apocalyptic texts were either two hundred years earlier or several decades later, he claimed that Paul's letters and the Gospels of Mark and Matthew were the best sources for Jewish apocalypticism right at the time of Jesus.[13] Taking particular Gospel passages, such as the mission speech in Matthew, somewhat literally, he took the imminent "Parousia of the Son of Man" as the eschatological judge as the key apocalyptic event, to be preceded by the time of tribulation and followed by the resurrection of the dead as the complete transformation to otherworldly life. A hundred years later neo-Schweitzerians are again arguing that Jesus preached this apocalyptic scenario that he shared with other Jews at the time, including John the Baptist and the early Christians.[14] Recent neoliberal interpreters find the same preaching of an apocalyptic judgment by a vengeful God in the Baptist's preaching, but turn to wisdom texts to argue for a sapiential Jesus. Our investigations in the essays

---

12. Crossan, *Historical Jesus*, 284–92.
13. Schweitzer, *Quest of the Historical Jesus*, 366–71.
14. Allison, "The Eschatology of Jesus."

above, however, have found little or no indication in either apocalyptic texts or in Gospel texts of the supposedly standard "apocalyptic scenario" of the end of the world. Both the scribal apocalyptic texts and the Gospels anticipate God's judgment of oppressive imperial and/or local client rulers and both expect or anticipate the restoration or renewal of Israel. But neither scribal apocalyptic texts nor the earliest Gospel texts (Mark and Q) offer much attestation of the principal themes or events of the supposed apocalyptic scenario. The Gospel of Matthew comes the closest. As for the hypothesis of a sapiential Jesus, as even Kloppenborg pointed out, the material in the "clusters" of Q that he categorized as "sapiential" is not comparable to instructional wisdom in scribal texts.[15] There appears to be no basis in either the apocalyptic texts or in the earliest Gospel sources for the apocalyptic Jesus understood according to the modern scholarly construct of apocalypticism as articulated by Schweitzer (or Bultmann). And there is no basis in the Gospels for the hypothesis of Jesus as a sage understood in terms of the instructional wisdom propounded by learned scribes such as Ben Sira.

As Jesus traditions in the Gospels appear less and less susceptible of interpretation in terms of the modern scholarly construct of "apocalyptic" and Judean instructional wisdom (what is usually meant by "wisdom" or "sapiential), it would appear more promising to explore the Israelite prophetic tradition for illumination of Jesus' mission and the development of Gospel traditions. Many of the forms, images, and motifs that have been classified as "apocalyptic" in studies of Jesus and the Gospels were integral to the Israelite prophetic tradition. It is clear that the learned scribes who produced early Enoch texts and the visions-and-interpretation in Daniel drew upon and adapted prophetic forms and images. It is equally clear that the Gospels, especially Mark and the Q speeches, represent Jesus, like John the Baptist, primarily as a prophet in the tradition of the Israelite prophets. The learned scribes and the popular prophets operated in different "social locations" with significantly different "social roles." But they both adapted traditional prophetic forms of speech and they both continued the prophets' condemnation of oppression by domestic and foreign imperial rulers. As evident both in apocalyptic texts and the Gospels, both scribal circles and the popular prophet Jesus were convinced and declared that God would sit in judgment on the empire(s) and restore the people.

15. Kloppenborg, *Formation of Q*.

Bibliography

Allison, Dale C. "The Eschatology of Jesus." In *The Encyclopedia of Apocalypticism 1*, edited by John J. Collins, 267-302. New York: Continuum, 1998.
Argall, Randall A. *1 Enoch and Sirach: A Comparative Literary and Conceptual Analysis of the Themes of Revelation, Creation, and Judgment.* EJL 8. Atlanta: Scholars, 1995.
Bagnall, Roger. *The Administration of the Ptolemaic Possessions Outside Egypt.* Columbia Studies in the Classical Tradition 4. Leiden: Brill, 1976.
Bartelmus, R. *Heroentum in Israel und seiner Umwelt.* ATANT 65. Zurich: Theologischer Verlag, 1979.
Baumgarten, Albert I. *The Flourishing of Jewish Sects in the Maccabean Era: An Interpretation.* JSJSup 55. Leiden: Brill, 1997.
Beasley-Murray, G. R. *Jesus and the Last Days: The Interpretation of the Olivet Discourse.* Peabody, MA: Hendrickson, 1993.
Berquist, Jon L. *Judaism in Persia's Shadow: A Social and Historical Approach.* 1995. Reprinted, Eugene, OR: Wipf & Stock, 2003.
Bickerman, Elias. "La charte sélucide de Jérusalem." *Revue des etudes juives* 197 (1935) 4-35.
———. *The Jews in the Greek Age.* Cambridge: Harvard University Press, 1988.
Black, Matthew. *The Book of Enoch or 1 Enoch: A New English Edition.* Studia in Veteris Testamenti Pseudepigrapha 7. Leiden: Brill, 1985.
Blenkinsopp, Joseph. "Temple and Society in Achaemenid Judah." In *Second Temple Studies I: Persian Period*, edited by Philip Davies, 22-53. JSOTSup 117. Sheffield: Sheffield Academic, 1991.
———. "The Mission of Udjahorresnet and Those of Ezra and Nehemiah." *JBL* 106 (1987) 409-21.
Boring, M. Eugene. *Sayings of the Risen Jesus: Christian Prophecy in the Synoptic Tradition.* Cambridge: Cambridge University Press, 1982.
Bousset, Wilhelm. *Die Religion des Judentums im neutestamentliche Zeitalter.* Berlin: Reuther & Reichard, 1903.
Boyarin, Daniel. "Placing Reading: Ancient Israel and Medieval Europe." In *The Ethnography of Reading*, edited by Jonathan Boyarin, 10-37. Berkeley: University of California Press, 1993.
Brandenburger, Egon. *Markus 13 und die Apokalyptik.* FRLANT 134. Göttingen: Vandenhoeck & Ruprecht, 1984.
———. *Die verbogenheit Gottes im weltgeschehen: Das literarische und theologische Problem des 4. Esrabuches.* ATANT 68. Zurich: Theologischer Verlag, 1981.
Bryan, David. *Cosmos, Chaos and the Kosher Mentality.* JSPSup 12. Sheffield: Sheffield Academic, 1995.

Bultmann, Rudolf. *The History of the Synoptic Tradition*. Translated by John Marsh. New York: Harper & Row, 1963.

———. *New Testament Theology*. Translated by Kendrick Grobel. New York: Scribner, 1950–55.

———. *Primitive Christianity in Its Contemporary Setting*. Translated by R. H. Fuller. New York: Meridian, 1956.

Burridge, Kenelm. *New Heaven and New Earth: A Study of Millenarian Activities*. Pavilion Series: Social Anthropology. New York: Schocken, 1969.

Cameron, Ron. "The Gospel of Thomas and Christian Origins." In *The Future of Early Christianity: Essays in Honor of Helmut Koester*, edited by Birger A. Pearson, 381–92. Minneapolis: Fortress, 1991.

Carney, Thomas F. *The Shape of the Past: Models and Antiquity*. Lawrence, KS: Coronado, 1975.

Carr, David M. *Writing on the Tablet of the Heart: Origins of Scripture and Literature*. Oxford: Oxford University Press, 2005.

Chaney, Martin L. "Systemic Study of the Israelite Monarchy." *Semeia* 37 (1986) 53–76.

Charles, R. H. *The Book of Enoch or 1 Enoch*. 2nd ed. 1912. Reprinted, Mokelumne Hill, CA: Health Research, 1964.

Charlesworth, James H., editor. *The Messiah: Developments in Earliest Judaism and Christianity*. Minneapolis: Fortress, 1992.

Chesnutt, Randall D. "George Nickelsburg's *Jewish Literature Between the Bible and the Mishnah*: Retrospect and Prospect." In *George W. E. Nickelsburg in Perspective: An Ongoing Dialogue of Perspective*, edited by Jacob Neusner and Alan Jeffery Avery-Peck, 2:343–56. JSJSup 80. Leiden: Brill, 2003.

Collins, Adela Yarbro. "The Son of Man in the Sayings Source." In *To Touch the Text: Biblical and Related Studies in Honor of Joseph A. Fitzmyer S.J.*, edited by Maurya P. Horgan and Paul J. Kobelski, 369–89. New York: Crossroad, 1989.

———. *The Beginning of the Gospel: Probing Mark in Context*. Minneapolis: Fortress, 1992.

Collins, John C. "Wisdom, Apocalypticism, and Generic Compatibility." In *In Search of Wisdom: Essays in Memory of John G. Gammie*, edited by Leo G. Perdue, et al., 165–85. Louisville: Westminster John Knox, 1993.

Collins, John J., editor. *Apocalypse: The Morphology of a Genre*. Semeia 14. Missoula: Scholars, 1979.

———. *The Apocalyptic Imagination: An Introduction to the Jewish Matrix of Christianity*. New York: Crossroad, 1984.

———. "Daniel and His Social World." *Int* 39 (1985) 131–43.

———. *Daniel: With an Introduction to Apocalyptic Literature*. FOTL 20. Grand Rapids: Eerdmans, 1984.

———, editor. *The Encyclopedia of Apocalypticism*. Vol. 1, *The Origins of Apocalypticism in Judaism and Christianity*. New York: Continuum, 1998.

———. "An Enochic Testament? Comments on George Nickelsburg's Hermeneia Commentary." In *George W. E. Nickelsburg in Perspective: An Ongoing Dialogue of Perspective*, edited by Jacob Neusner and Alan Jeffery Avery-Peck, 2:373–78. JSJSup 80. Leiden: Brill, 2003.

———. "From Prophecy to Apocalypticism: The Expectation of the End." In *The Encyclopedia of Apocalypticism*, Vol. 1, edited by John J. Collins, 129–61. New York: Continuum, 1998.

———. "Genre, Ideology, and Social Movements in Jewish Apocalypticism." In *Mysteries and Revelations*, edited by John J. Collins and James H. Charlesworth, 11–32. JSPSup 9. Sheffield: Sheffield Academic, 1991.

———. *The Scepter and the Star: The Messiahs of the Dead Sea Scrolls and Other Ancient Literature*. New York: Doubleday, 1995.

———. "Wisdom, Apocalypticism, and Generic Compatibility." In *In Search of Wisdom: Essays in Memory of John G. Gammie*, edited by Leo G. Perdue et al., 165–85. Louisville: Westminster John Knox, 1993.

Crawford, Sidonie White. "Rewritten Pentateuch." In *Encyclopedia of the Dead Sea Scrolls*, edited by Lawrence H. Schiffman and James C. VanderKam, 2:775–76. Oxford: Oxford University Press, 2000.

Crenshaw, James L. "The Primacy of Listening in Ben Sira's Pedagogy." In *Wisdom, You Are My Sister: Studies in Honor of Roland E. Murphy*, edited by Michael L. Barre, 277–87. Catholic Biblical Quarterly Monograph Series 27. Washington, DC: Catholic Biblical Association of America, 1997.

Cross, Frank M. "New Directions in the Study of Apocalyptic." *Journal of Theology and Church* 6 (1969) 157–65.

Crossan, John Dominic. *The Historical Jesus: The Life of the Mediterranean Jewish Peasant*. San Francisco: HarperCollins, 1991.

———. *In Fragments: The Aphorisms of Jesus*. 1983. Reprint, Eugene, OR: Wipf & Stock, 2008.

Davids, Peter H. *The Epistle of James: A Commentary on the Greek text*. New International Greek Testament Commentary. Grand Rapids: Eerdmans, 1982.

Davies, Philip R. "Reading Daniel Sociologically." In *The Book of Daniel in the Light of New Findings*, edited by A. S. van der Woude, 345–61. Bibliotheca ephemeridum theologicarum Lovaniensium 106. Leuven: Peeters, 1993.

———. "The Social World of Apocalyptic Writings." In *The World of Ancient Israel: Social, Anthropological, and Political Perspectives*, edited by R. E. Clements, 251–71. Cambridge: Cambridge University Press, 1989.

DeJonge, Marianus. "The Use of the Word 'Anointed' in the Time of Jesus." *NovT* 8 (1966) 132–48.

Dibelius, Martin. *A Commentary on the Epistle of James*. Revised by Heinrich Greeven. Translated by Michael A. Williams. Hermeneia. Philadelphia: Fortress, 1976.

Doran, Robert. "Serious George, or the Wise Apocalypticist—Response to 'Tobit and Enoch: Distant Cousins with a Recognizable Resemblance.'" In *George W. E. Nickelsburg in Perspective: An Ongoing Dialogue of Learning*, edited by Jacob Neusner and Alan Jeffery Avery-Peck, 1:254–62. JSJSup 80. Leiden: Brill, 2003.

Eisenberg, Sheldon R. "Millenarianism in Greco-Roman Palestine." *Religion* 4 (1974) 35.

Elliott, John. "Social-Scientific Criticism of the New Testament: More on Methods and Models." *Semeia* 35 (1986) 1–33.

Eshel, Hanan. *The Dead Sea Scrolls and the Hasmonean State*. Studies in the Dead Sea Scrolls and Related Literature. Grand Rapids: Eerdmans, 2008.

Fox, Michael V. "Wisdom and the Self-Presentation of Wisdom Literature." In *Reading from Left to Right: Essays on the Hebrew Bible in Honour of David J. A. Clines*, edited by J. Cheryl Exum and H. G. M. Williamson, 153–72. JSOTSup 373. Sheffield: Sheffield Academic, 2003.

Gager, John G. *Kingdom and Community: The Social of Early Christianity*. Prentice-Hall Studies in Religion Series. Englewood Cliffs, NJ: Prentice-Hall, 1975.

Gebhardt, Oscar. "Die 70 Hirten des Buches Henoch und ihre Deutungen mit besonderer Rücksicht auf die Barkochba-Hypothese." *Archiv für wissenschaftliche Erforschung des Alten Testaments* 2 (1872) 163–246.

Gera, Dov. "The Tobiads: Fiction and History." In *Judaea and Mediterranean Politics, 219 to 161 B.C.E.*, 36–57. Brill's Series in Jewish Studies 8. Leiden: Brill, 1998.

Goodblatt, David. *The Monarchic Principle: Studies in Jewish Self-Government in Antiquity*. Texte und Studien zum antiken Judentum 38. Tübingen: Mohr/Siebeck, 1994.

Gottwald, Norman K. *The Politics of Ancient Israel*. Library of Ancient Israel. Louisville: Westminster John Knox, 2000.

Grabbe, Lester. "The Social Setting of Early Jewish Apocalypticism." *JSP* 4 (1989) 27–47.

Green, William Scott. "Writing with Scripture: The Rabbinic Uses of the Hebrew Bible." In *Writing with Scripture: The Authority and Uses of the Hebrew Bible in the Torah of Formative Judaism*, edited by Jacob Neusner, 7–23. Minneapolis: Fortress, 1989.

Gruen, Eric S. *Heritage and Hellenism: The Reinvention of Jewish Tradition*. Hellenistic Culture and Society 30. Berkeley: University of California Press, 1998.

Gruenwald, Ithamar. "The Commentary on 1 Enoch." In *George W. E. Nickelsburg in Perspective: An Ongoing Dialogue of Perspective*, Vol. 2, edited by Jacob Neusner and Alan Jeffery Avery-Peck, 395–408. JSJSup 80. Leiden: Brill, 2003.

Hanson, Paul D. *The Dawn of Apocalyptic*. Philadelphia: Fortress, 1975.

Harris, William V. *Ancient Literacy*. Cambridge: Harvard University Press, 1989.

Hartin, Patrick J. *James and the Q Sayings of Jesus*. JSNTSup 47. Sheffield: JSOT Press, 1991.

———. "'Who is wise and understanding among you?' (James 3:13): An Analysis of Wisdom, Eschatology, and Apocalypticism in the Epistle of James." In *Society of Biblical Literature 1996 Seminar Papers* 35, edited by David J. Lull, 483–503. Atlanta: Scholars, 1996.

Hartman, Lars. *Prophecy Interpreted: The Formation of Some Jewish Apocalyptic Texts and of the Eschatological Discourse Mark 13 Par*. Coniectanea biblica: New Testament Series 1. Lund: Gleerup, 1966.

Hellholm, David, editor. *Apocalypticism in the Mediterranean World and the Near East*. Tübingen: Mohr/Siebeck, 1983.

Hengel, Martin. *Judaism and Hellenism: Studies in their Encounter in Palestine during the Early Hellenistic Period*. 2 vols. Translated by John Bowden. Philadelphia: Fortress, 1974.

Hezser, Catherine. *Jewish Literacy in Roman Palestine*. Texts and Studies in Ancient Judaism 81. Tübingen: Mohr/Siebeck, 2001.

Hoffmann, Paul. *Studien zur Theologie der Logienquelle*. 2nd ed. Neutestamentlich Abhandlungen 8. Münster: Aschendorf, 1975.

Hofmann, J. Chr. K. von. *Der Schriftbefweis: Ein theologischer Versuch*. 2 vols. 2nd ed. Nördlingen: Beck, 1857–60.

Horsley, Richard A. "Empire, Temple, and Community—but no Bourgeoisie." In *Second Temple Studies I*, edited by Philip Davies, 163–74. JSOTSup 117. Sheffield: Sheffield Academic, 1991.

———. *Galilee: History, Politics, People*. Harrisburg, PA: Trinity, 1995.

———. *Hearing the Whole Story: The Politics of Plot in Mark's Gospel*. Louisville: Westminster John Knox, 2001.

———. *Jesus and the Spiral of Violence: Popular Jewish Resistance in Roman Palestine*. 1987. Reprinted, Minneapolis: Fortress, 1993.

---. *The Liberation of Christmas: The Infancy Narratives in Social Context.* 1989. Reprinted, Eugene, OR: Wipf & Stock, 2006.
---. "'Like One of the Prophets of Old': Two Types of Popular Prophets at the Time of Jesus." *CBQ* 47 (1985) 435–63.
---. "'Messianic' Figures and Movements in First-Century Palestine." In *The Messiah: Developments in Earliest Judaism and Christianity,* edited by James H. Charlesworth, 276–95. Minneapolis: Fortress, 1992.
---. "Popular Messianic Movements around the Time of Jesus." *CBQ* 46 (1984) 471–93.
---. "Q and Jesus: Assumptions, Approaches, and Analyses." In *Early Christianity, Q, and Jesus,* edited by John S. Kloppenborg and Leif E. Vaage. *Semeia* 55 (1991) 175–209.
---. "Questions about Redactional Strata and the Social Relations in Q." In *Society of Biblical Literature 1989 Seminar Papers,* edited by David J. Lull, 186–203. Atlanta: Scholars, 1989.
---. *Revolt of the Scribes: Resistance and Apocalyptic Origins.* Minneapolis: Fortress, 2010.
---. *Scribes, Visionaries, and the Politics of Second-Temple Judea.* Louisville: Westminster John Knox, 2007.
---. "Social Conflict in the Synoptic Sayings Source Q." In *Conflict and Invention: Literary, Rhetorical, and Social Studies on the Sayings Gospel Q,* edited by John S. Kloppenborg, 37–52. Valley Forge, PA: Trinity, 1995.
---. "Social Relations and Social Conflict in the Epistle of Enoch." In *For a Later Generation: The Transformation of Tradition in Israel, Early Judaism, and Early Christianity,* edited by Randal A. Argall, et al, 100–115. Harrisburg, PA: Trinity, 2000.
---. *Sociology and the Jesus Movement.* New York: Crossroad, 1989.
Horsley, Richard A., and Jonathan A. Draper. *Whoever Hears You Hears Me: Prophets, Performance, and Tradition in Q.* Harrisburg, PA: Trinity, 1999.
Horsley, Richard A., and John S. Hanson. *Bandits, Prophets, and Messiahs: Popular Movements in the Time of Jesus.* 1985. Reprinted, Harrisburg, PA: Trinity, 1999.
Horsley, Richard A., and Patrick Tiller. "Ben Sira and the Sociology of the Second Temple." In *Second Temple Studies III: Studies in Politics, Class, and Material Culture,* edited by Philip R. Davies and John M. Halligan, 74–107. JSOTSup 340. London: Sheffield Academic, 2002.
Isenberg, Sheldon R. "Millenarianism in Greco-Roman Palestine." *Religion* 4 (1974) 26–46.
Jackson-McCabe, Matt A. "A Letter to the Twelve Tribes of Israel in the Diaspora: Wisdom and 'Apocalyptic' Eschatology in the Letter of James." In *Society of Biblical Literature 1996 Seminar Papers* 35, edited by David J. Lull, 504–17. Atlanta: Scholars, 1996.
Jacobson, Arland D. "Apocalyptic and the Synoptic Sayings Source Q." In *The Four Gospels 1992: Festschrift Franz Neirinck,* edited by F. van Segbroeck et al., 403–19. Bibliotheca ephemeridum theologicarum Lovaniensium 100. Louvain: Louvain University Press, 1994.
Jaffee, Martin. *Torah in the Mouth: Writing and Oral Tradition in Palestinian Judaism, 200 BCE—400 CE.* Oxford: Oxford University Press, 2001.

Joachim Schaper. "The Jerusalem Temple as an Instrument of the Achaemenid Fiscal Administration." *Vetus Testamentum* 45 (1995) 528–39.

Johnson, Luke Timothy. *The Letter of James*. AB 37A. New York: Doubleday, 1995.

———. "The Use of Leviticus in the Letter of James." *JBL* 101 (1982) 391–401.

Jokiranta, Jutta M. "'Sectarianism' of the Qumran 'Sect': Sociological Notes." *Revue de Qumran* 20 (2001) 223–39.

Kautsky, John H. *The Politics of Aristocratic Empires*. Chapel Hill: University of North Carolina Press, 1982.

Kelber, Werner H. *The Kingdom in Mark*. Philadelphia: Fortress, 1974.

———. *Mark's Story of Jesus*. Philadelphia: Fortress, 1979.

———. *The Oral and Written Gospel: The Hermeneutics of Speaking and Writing in the Synoptic Tradition, Mark, Paul, and Q*. Philadelphia: Fortress, 1983.

Kirk, Alan. *The Composition of the Sayings Source: Genre, Synchrony, and Wisdom Redaction in Q*. NovTSup 91. Leiden: Brill, 1998.

Klijn, A. F. J. "2 (Syriac Apocalypse of) Baruch." In *OTP* 1 (1983) 621–52.

Kloppenborg, John S. "The Formation of Q Revisited: A Response to Richard Horsley." In *Society of Biblical Literature 1989 Seminar Papers*, edited by David J. Lull, 204–15. Atlanta: Scholars, 1989.

———. *The Formation of Q: Trajectories in Ancient Wisdom Collections*. Studies in Antiquity and Christianity 2. Philadelphia: Fortress, 1987.

———. "Literary Convention, Self-Evidence, and the Social History of the Q People." *Semeia* 55 (1991) 77–102.

———. "Symbolic Eschatology and the Apocalypticism of Q." *HTR* 80 (1987) 287–306.

Koch, Klaus. *Ratlos vor der Apokalyptik*. Gütersloh: Gütersloher, 1970.

———. *The Rediscovery of Apocalyptic: A Polemical Work on a Neglected Area of Biblical Studies and Its Damaging Effects on Theology and Philosophy*. SBT 2/22. Naperville, IL: Allenson, 1972.

———. "Response to 'The Apocalyptic Construction of Reality in 1 Enoch.'" In *George W. E. Nickelsburg in Perspective: An Ongoing Dialogue of Learning*, edited by Jacob Neusner and Alan Jeffery Avery-Peck, 1:44–55. JSJSup 80. Leiden, Brill, 2003.

Koester, Helmut. *Ancient Christian Gospels: Their History and Development*. Philadelphia: Trinity, 1990.

———. "Apocryphal and Canonical Gospels." *HTR* 73 (1980) 105–30.

———. "GNOMAI DIAPHOROI: The Origin and Nature of Diversification in the History of Early Christianity." *HTR* 58 (1965) 279–318. Reprinted in James M. Robinson and Helmut Koester, *Trajectories through Early Christianity*, 114–57. 1971. Reprinted, Eugene, OR: Wipf & Stock, 2006.

———. "One Jesus and Four Primitive Gospels." *HTR* 61 (1968) 203–47. Reprinted in James M. Robinson and Helmut Koester, *Trajectories through Early Christianity*, 158–204. 1971. Reprint, Eugene, OR: Wipf & Stock, 2006.

Kraft, Robert A. *The Apostolic Fathers*. Vol. 3, *The Didache and Barnabas*. New York: Nelson, 1965.

Kurtz, Mark R. "The Social Construction of Judea in the Greek Period." In *Society of Biblical Literature 1999 Seminar Papers*, edited by David J. Lull, 54–76. Atlanta: Society of Biblical Literature, 1999.

Landau, Y. H. "A Greek Inscription Found near Hefzibah." *Israel Exploration Journal* 16 (1966) 54–70.

Lenski, Gerhard. *Power and Privilege: A Theory of Social Stratification*. New York: McGraw-Hill, 1966.
Lührmann, Dieter. *Die Redaktion der Logienquelle*. Wissenschaftliche Monographien zum Alten und Neuen Testament 33. Neukirchen-Vluyn: Neukirchner, 1969.
Mack, Burton L. "The Kingdom that Didn't Come: A Social History of the Q Tradents." In *Society of Biblical Literature 1988 Seminar Papers*, edited by David J. Lull, 608–35. Atlanta: Scholars, 1988.
———. *A Myth of Innocence: Mark and Christian Origins*. Philadelphia: Fortress, 1988.
———. *Wisdom and Hebrew Epic: Ben Sira's Hymn in Praise of the Fathers*. Chicago: University of Chicago Press, 1985.
Manson, T. W. *The Sayings of Jesus*. London: SCM, 1937. Reprinted, 1949.
Marcus, Ralph. *Josephus*. 9 vols. Cambridge: Harvard University Press, 1961.
Martin, François. *Le Livre d'Hénoch*. Documents pour l'étude de la Bible: Les Apocryphes de l'Ancien Testament. Paris: Letouzey & Ané, 1906.
Martinez, Florentino Garcia. *The Dead Sea Scrolls Translated: The Qumran Texts in English*. Translated by W. G. E. Watson. Leiden: Brill, 1994.
Mendels, Doron. *The Land of Israel as a Political Concept in Hasmonean Literature: Recourse to History in Second Century B.C. Claims to the Holy Land*. Texte und Studien zum Antiken Judentum 15. Tübingen: Mohr/Siebeck, 1987.
Metzger, Bruce M. "The Fourth Book of Ezra." In *OTP* 1 (1983) 516–59.
Middendorp, Th. *Die Stellung Jesu Ben Siras zwischen Judentum und Hellenismus*. Leiden: Brill, 1973.
Moore, Stephen D. *The Gospels and Literary Criticism*. New Haven: Yale University Press, 1990.
Myers, Ched. *Binding the Strong Man: A Political Reading of Mark's Story of Jesus*. Maryknoll, NY: Orbis, 1989.
Neirynck, F. "Recent Developments in the Study of Q." In *LOGIA: Les Paroles Jesu: Mémorial M. Coppens*, Joël Delobel, 19–75. Bibliotheca Ephemeridum theologicarum Lovaniensium 59. Louvain: Louvain University Press, 1982.
Neusner, Jacob, and Alan Jeffery Avery-Peck, editors. *George W. E. Nickelsburg in Perspective: An Ongoing Dialogue of Learning*. 2 vols. JSJSup 80. Leiden: Brill, 2003.
Neusner, Jacob, William S. Green, and Ernest Frerichs, editors. *Judaisms and Their Messiahs at the Turn of the Christian Era*. Cambridge: Cambridge University Press, 1987.
Newsom, Carol A. "Enoch 83–90: The Historical Résumé as Biblical Exegesis." Unpublished seminar paper, Harvard University, 1975.
———. "'Sectually Explicit' Literature from Qumran." In *The Hebrew Bible and Its Interpreters*, edited by William Henry Propp, Baruch Halpern, and David Noel Freedman, 167–87. Bibilical and Judaic Studies 1. Winona, IN: Eisenbrauns, 1990.
Neyrey, Jerome H. *The Social World of Luke-Acts: Models for Interpretation*. Peabody, MA. Hendrickson, 1991.
Nickelsburg, George W. E. "Apocalyptic and Myth in 1 Enoch 6–11." *JBL* 96 (1977) 383–405.
———. *1 Enoch*. Vol. 1, *A Commentary on the Book of 1 Enoch chapters 1–36; 81–108*. Hermeneia. Minneapolis: Fortress, 2001.
———. "Enoch, Levi and Peter: Recipients of Revelation in Upper Galilee." *JBL* 100 (1981) 575–600.

———. "The Epistle of Enoch and the Qumran Literature." *Journal of Jewish Studies* 33 (1982) 333–48.
———. "The Genre and Function of the Passion Narrative." *HTR* 73 (1980) 153–184.
———. *Jewish Literature between the Bible and the Mishnah*. 2nd ed. Philadelphia: Fortress, 2005.
———. "Riches, the Rich, and God's Judgment in 1 Enoch 92–105 and the Gospel of Luke." *NTS* 25 (1979) 324–44.
———. "Salvation Without and With a Messiah: Developing Beliefs in Writings Ascribed to Enoch." In *Judaisms and Their Messiahs at the Turn of the Christian Era*, edited by Jacob Neusner, et al., 49–68. Cambridge: Cambridge University Press, 1987.
———. "Social Aspects of Palestinian Jewish Apocalypticism." In *Apocalypticism in the Mediterranean World and the Near East*, edited by David D. Hellholm, 639–52. Tübingen: Mohr/Siebeck, 1983.
Nickelsburg, George W. E., and James C. VanderKam. *1 Enoch*. Vol. 2, *A Commentary on the Book of 1 Enoch chapters 37–82*. Hermeneia. Minneapolis: Fortress, 2011.
Olyan, Saul M. "Ben Sira's Relationship to the Priesthood." *HTR* 80 (1987) 261–86.
Penner, Todd C. *The Epistle of James and Eschatology: Rereading an Ancient Christian Letter*. JSNTSup 121. Sheffield: Sheffield Academic, 1996.
Perrin, Norman. *The New Testament: An Introduction*. New York: Harcourt Brace, 1974.
Plöger, Otto. *Theocracy and Eschatology*. Translated by S. Rudman. Richmond: John Knox, 1968.
Porter, Paul A. *Metaphors and Monsters: A Literary-critical Study of Daniel 7 and 8*. Coniectanea biblica: Old Testament Series, 20. Uppsala: Gleerup, 1983.
Rad, Gerhard von. *Old Testament Theology*. Vol. 2, *The Theology of Israel's Prophetic Traditions*. Translated by D. M. G. Stalker. New York: Harper & Row, 1965.
Robinson, James M. "LOGOI SOPHON: On the Gattung of Q." In *Trajectories through Early Christianity*, 71–113. 1971. Reprinted, Eugene, OR: Wipf & Stock, 2006.
———. *Matthew's Jewish-Christian Community*. Chicago: University of Chicago Press, 1994.
———. *The Problem of History in Mark*. SBT 1/21. London: SCM, 1957.
Robinson, James M., and Helmut Koester. *Trajectories through Early Christianity*. 1971. Reprinted, Eugene, OR: Wipf & Stock, 2006.
Rostovtzeff, Michael. *The Social and Economic History of the Hellenistic World*. 3 vols. Oxford: Clarendon, 1941.
Saldarini, Anthony J. *Pharisees, Scribes, and Sadducees in Palestinian Society: A Sociological Approach*. 1988. Reprinted, Grand Rapids: Eerdmans, 2001.
Sanders, Jack T. *Ben Sira and Demotic Wisdom*. SBL Monograph Series 28. Chico, CA: Scholars, 1983.
Schenk, Wolfgang. *Synopse zur Redenquelle der Evangelien: Synopse und Rekonstruktion in deutscher Übersetzung mit kurzen Erläuterungen*. Düsseldorf: Patmos, 1981.
Schultz, Siegfried. *Q: Die Spruchquelle der Evangelisten*. Zurich: Theologischer Verlag, 1972.
Schwartz, Seth. "On the Autonomy of Judaea in the Fourth and Third Centuries B.C.E." *JJS* 45 (1994) 157–68.
Schweitzer, Albert. *The Quest of the Historical Jesus: A Critical Study of Its Progress from Reimarus to Wrede*. Translated by W. Montgomery. New York: Macmillan, 1910.

———. *The Quest of the Historical Jesus*. 1st complete edition. Edited by John Bowden. Translated by W. Montgomery, J. R. Coates, Susan Cupitt, and John Bowden. Minneapolis: Fortress, 2001.
Scott, Bernard B. *Hear Then the Parable: A Commentary on the Parables of Jesus*. Minneapolis: Fortress, 1989.
Sellew, Philip H. "Early Collections of Jesus' Words: The Development of Dominical Discourses." Ph.D. diss., Harvard University, 1985.
Schürer, Emil. *The History of the Jewish People in the Age of Jesus Christ (175 BC–AD 135)*. Edinburgh: T. & T. Clark, 1973–87.
Skehan, Patrick W., and A. A. DiLella. *The Wisdom of Ben Sira*. AB 39. Garden City, NY: Doubleday, 1987.
Smith, Jonathan Z. *Map Is Not Territory: Studies in the History of Religions*. Studies in Judaism in Late Antiquity 23. Leiden: Brill, 1978.
Stone, Michael E. *Features of the Eschatology of IV Ezra*. Harvard Semitic Studies 35. Atlanta: Scholars, 1989.
———. *Fourth Ezra: A Commentary on the Book of Fourth Ezra*. Hermeneia. Minneapolis: Fortress, 1990.
———. "Ideal Figures and Social Context: Priest and Sage in the Early Second Temple Age." In *Ancient Israelite Religion: Essays in Honor of Frank Moore Cross*, edited by Patrick D. Miller et al., 575–86. Philadelphia: Fortress, 1987.
———. "Lists of Revealed Things in the Apocalyptic Literature." In *Magnalia Dei, The Mighty Acts of God: Essays on the Bible and Archaeology in Memory of G. Ernest Wright*, edited by Frank Moore Cross et al., 414–52. Garden City, NY: Doubleday, 1976.
Suter, D. "Fallen Angel, Fallen Priest: The Problem with Family Purity in *1 Enoch* 6–16." *Hebrew Union College Annual* 50 (1979) 115–35.
Tannehill, Robert C. *The Narrative Unity of Luke-Acts: A Literary Interpretation*. Vol. 1, *The Gospel according to Luke*. Philadelphia: Fortress, 1986.
Tanzer, Sarah J. "Response to 'Wisdom and Apocalypticism in Early Judaism: Some Points for Discussion.'" In *George W. E. Nickelsburg in Perspective: An Ongoing Dialogue of Learning*, edited by Jacob Neusner and Alan Jeffery Avery-Peck, 1:288–99. JSJSup 80. Leiden: Brill, 2003.
Taylor, James Ellis. "Seleucid Rule in Palestine." PhD diss., Duke University, 1979.
Tcherikover, Victor. *Hellenistic Civilization and the Jews*. Translated by S. Appelbaum. New York, NY: Atheneum, 1979.
———. "Palestine under the Ptolemies." *Mizraim* 4/5 (1937) 9–90.
Theissen, Gerd. *The Sociology of the Jesus Movement*. Translated by John Bowden. Philadelphia: Fortress, 1978.
Thrupp, Sylvia L., editor. *Millennial Dreams in Action: Studies in Revolutionary Religious Movements*. New York: Schocken, 1970.
Tiller, Patrick. *A Commentary on the Animal Apocalypse of 1 Enoch*. EJL 4. Atlanta: Scholars, 1993.
———. "George Nickelsburg's '1 Enoch: A Commentary on the Book of 1 Enoch: Chapters 1–36; 81–108.'" In *George W. E. Nickelsburg in Perspective: An Ongoing Dialogue of Perspective*, edited by Jacob Neusner and Alan Jeffery Avery-Peck, 2:365–72. JSJSup 80. Leiden, Brill, 2003.
———. "Sirach and the Politics of Seleucid Judea." Paper presented at the annual meeting of the New England Region of the SBL, Boston, MA, 2002.

Tödt, Heinz Eduard. *The Son of Man in the Synoptic Tradition*. Translated by Dorothea M. Barton. Philadelphia: Westminster, 1965.

Tov, Emanuel. "Biblical Texts as Reworked in Some Qumran Manuscripts with Special Attention to 4QRP and 4QParaGen-Exod." In *The Community of the Renewed Covenant: The Notre Dame Symposium on the Dead Sea Scrolls*, edited by Eugene Ulrich and James VanderKam, 112–28. Christianity and Judaism in Antiquity Series 10. Notre Dame: Notre Dame University Press, 1994.

Ulrich, Eugene. *The Dead Sea Scrolls and the Origins of the Bible*. Studies in the Dead Sea Scrolls and Related Literature. Grand Rapids: Eerdmans, 1999.

VanderKam, James C. *Enoch and the Growth of the Apocalyptic Tradition*. Catholic Biblical Quarterly Monograph Series 16. Washington, DC: Catholic Biblical Association of America, 1984.

———. "Response to George Nickelsburg, '1 Enoch: A Commentary on the Book of 1 Enoch: Chapters 1–36; 81–108.'" In *George W. E. Nickelsburg in Perspective: An Ongoing Dialogue of Perspective*, edited by Jacob Neusner and Alan Jeffery Avery-Peck, 2:379–86. JSJSup 80. Leiden: Brill, 2003.

Vermes, Geza. *Scripture and Tradition: Haggadic Studies*. Studia post-Biblica 4. Leiden: Brill, 1961.

Volz, Paul. *Jüdische Eschatologie von Daniel bis Akiba*. Tübingen: Mohr/Siebeck, 1903.

Vouga, François. *L'Epitre de Saint Jacques*. Commentaire du Nouveau Testament 13a. Geneva: Labor et Fides, 1984.

Walker, William O. "The Son of Man: Some Recent Developments." *CBQ* 45 (1983) 601–18.

Ward, Roy Bowen. "Particularity in the Assembly: James 2:2–4." *HTR* 62 (1969) 87–97.

Weissenrieder, Annette, and Robert B. Coote. *The Interface of Orality and Writing: Speaking, Seeing, Writing in the Shaping of New Genres*. Wissenschaftliche Untersuchungen zum Neuen Testament 260. Tübingen: Mohr/Siebeck, 2010.

Wilder, Amos N. "Apocalyptic Imagery and Earthly Circumstance." *NTS* 5 (1958–59) 229–45.

Wills, Lawrence M. *The Jew in the Court of the Foreign King: Ancient Jewish Court Legends*. Harvard Dissertations in Religion 26. Minneapolis: Fortress, 1990.

Wilson, Bryan R. *Magic and the Millennium: A Sociological Study of Religious Movements of Protest among Tribal and Third-World Peoples*. New York: Harper & Row, 1973.

Wire, Antoinette Clark. *The Case for Mark Composed in Performance*. Biblical Performance Criticism Series 3. Eugene, OR: Cascade Books, 2011.

Worsley, Peter. *The Trumpet Shall Sound: A Study of "Cargo" Cults in Melanesia*. 2nd ed. New York: Schocken, 1968.

Wright, Benjamin G. III. "'Fear the Lord and Honor the Priest': Ben Sira as Defender of the Jerusalem Priesthood." In *The Book of Ben Sira in Modern Research: Proceedings of the First International Ben Sira Conference, 28–31 July 1996, Soesterberg, Netherlands*, edited by Pancratius C. Beentjes, 189–222. Beihefte zur Zeitschrift für die alttestamentliche Wissenschaft 255. Berlin: de Gruyter, 1997.

Youtie, Herbert C. "*Aggramatos*: As Aspect of Greek Society in Egypt." *Harvard Studies in Classical Philology* 75 (1971) 161–76.

———. "*Hypografeus*: The Social Impact of Illiteracy in Graeco-Roman Egypt." *Zeitschrift für Papyrologie und Epigraphie* 17 (1975) 201–21.

Scripture Index

HEBREW BIBLE

Exodus
20	189, 245
22:25–27	187
22:25	122, 128
24:7	93

Leviticus
19	246, 283n11
25:36–38	128

Numbers
22–24	53

Deuteronomy
10:18–19	285
15:7–8	187
32:8	238
33:4	93

Joshua
24	189, 245

Judges
5:4–5	237

1 Samuel
2:8	28

1 Kings
12	128
22	237

2 Chronicles
36:20–21	79

Ezra
	52, 61, 125
7:25–26	62

Nehemiah
	52, 61, 125, 154
2:9	62
2:19	83
4:3	83
4:7	83
5:1–12	74, 128
5:1–5	124, 128
5:4	62
5:7–11	124
5:14	62
6	62
6:1	83
6:14	83
6:17–19	83
10:26–29	62
10:40	62
10:35	85n8
13:28–30	62
13:31	85n8

Job

	137
5:15–16	285
28:25–27	135
31:16–23	285
38	135

Psalms

	253, 269n34, 287
37	287
72:12–13	285

Proverbs

	8, 53, 146, 291–92
1–9	146, 152, 165, 178, 292, 293
8	146
10–29	67
10:1—22:16	165–66
22:17—24:34	165

Qoheleth

2:6	20

Isaiah

	11, 144, 258, 278
1:2–3	184
7:22	243
8:21	224, 260
13	237, 262
13:10	225
13:13	224, 260
14:30	224, 260
19:2	224, 260
24–27	237
26:16–19	234
34	262
34:4	225
35:5–6	185, 243, 247
40:1–13	237
40:3	256
52–53	166
55–66	62
61:1	185, 243, 247
65:17–22	248
65:17	237
65:19–25	237

Jeremiah

	258, 278
25	107–9
22:13–19	124

Ezekiel

	70, 252, 260, 296
1:1	132
5:12	224, 260
32	262
32:7–8	225
34	107
34:8	110
34:16	107
37	234

Daniel

	6, 9, 16, 51, 56–58, 67–68, 76–80, 94, 98–99, 113, 138, 143, 146–47, 152–53, 156–57, 159, 164, 166–67, 178, 212–15, 221, 224, 232, 259–60, 292, 296–301, 303
1–6	76–77, 79
1	77, 146, 166
1:3–7	117
1:4	76, 292
1:5	76
1:8–16	76
1:20	76
2	76, 77, 212
2:2	76
2:10	76
2:12	76
2:19	76
2:27	76

Daniel (cont.)

2:28	76
4:6	76
4:9	76
5	77
5:7	76
5:8	76
5:11–12	76
5:12	76
7–12	76, 147, 166, 234–35, 296
7–8	107
7	10, 72, 76, 77, 143, 173, 202, 212, 218, 225, 228, 232, 236, 238, 244, 254, 256, 258, 270, 272, 292, 298–99
7:9–12	237
7:11–12	233
7:13	173, 218, 225, 263–64
7:27	77
8	76, 143, 237–38, 258, 292, 298–99
8:13	78
9	77
9:2	76
9:24–27	108
9:27	78, 260, 261
10–12	12, 76, 131, 143, 154, 236, 238, 261, 270, 272, 292, 298–99
10–11	258
11–12	254
11:31	78, 260, 261
11:33–35	166, 301
11:35	77
12	77, 228
12:1–3	234, 278
12:1	77–78, 224, 266, 235, 260, 275, 299
12:2	234, 239
12:3	78, 234–35, 237, 254, 259
12:11	260, 261

Joel

	232, 237, 278
2	262
2:10	225

Amos

	144
2:6	74, 129
2:6–8	44, 50, 93, 123
4:4–5	123
5:21–24	123
6:1	127
6:4–6	74, 127
8:4, 5	286

Micah

	128
2:1–2	74, 128
7:6	171, 193, 251, 266

Habakkuk

	144

Haggai

	62

Zechariah

1:12–17	79
2:6	225
11	107, 110
13:5–6	225
13:5	225
13:9–13	225
13:9	225
13:23	225
13:25	225
13:28–37	225
13:33	225
13:37	225

Malachi

	62, 185, 256
3:1	185, 256

APOCRYPHA

4 Ezra
4n6, 6, 7n13, 16, 132–40, 151, 212, 234–35, 274, 297–99

1–2	133
3–14	132
4:21	137
4:22	137
4:26–32	267
5:1–13	299
5:35	133
5:36–37	137
6:34	138
6:42	137
7:26–31	138
7:32	235n15, 299
7:37	235n15, 299
7:63	137
7:75–101	138
7:102–15	138
7:132–140	138
9:3	224, 260
9:26—10:59	132
10:54	297
11:1—12:39	132
11–12	134
12:37–39	139
13	275
13:31	224, 260
14:5–7	135
14:17–18	139
14:34–36	139
14:46	139
14:47	134
15–16	133

Judith
	86
4:8	86
11:14	86
15:8	86

Wisdom of Solomon
8, 164, 166, 178, 302

1–5	166
6–9	166
11–19	166

Sirach
19–34, 39–55, 57, 58, 67–75, 77, 79, 88–95, 97–99, 117, 130n16, 142, 146, 148, 152, 160, 165–66, 178–79, 188, 205, 213, 215, 292–93, 295

1–22	93
1:1–20	67
1:1–5	55
3:21–24	55, 67
3:30—4:10	59
4:1–10	34, 50, 70, 93, 285–86
4:11–19	67
4:1–9	44
4:1–4	123
4:7	28-30, 33, 60, 68, 92, 120
4:8–10	61
4:9	26, 32, 44, 119, 123
4:15	28, 68
4:17	29, 123
4:27	28–29, 32
6:11	33, 47
6:18–31	67
6:33–34	68
6:34	29, 32, 59–60, 118, 119
7:14	27, 29–31, 91, 118, 59–60, 119
7:15	33, 44
7:20–21	47
7:21	33
7:29	69, 89

Scripture Index

Sirach (cont.)

7:29–31	31–32, 39, 42, 59–60, 69, 119
7:32–36	32
7:32	34, 50, 70
7:4–7	123
7:4–6	29–30
7:4	27
7:6	28
8:1–2	26, 30, 60, 68, 92, 118, 120
8:2	30
8:8–9	68
8:8	26, 31, 48, 60, 92, 118–20
8:9	91
8:14	28–29, 60, 92, 120
9	92
9:17—10:5	48, 120
9:17	28
10:1	28
10:10	27
10:1–2	28–29, 59, 92, 118
10:2	29
10:3	27, 29, 59, 92, 118
10:4	89
10:5	29
10:19–25	92
10:24	27
11:1	28, 68
11:7–9	32, 119
11:10–19	46, 122
13:3–4	61, 121
13:8–11	33
13:9–11	60, 92, 120
13:9	28, 33, 68, 120
13:17–24	34
13:18–23	44
13:18–19	61, 121
13:19	44, 59
13:24–25	46, 122
13:26b	92
14:20–27	67
15:1–10	67
15:10	28
15:5–6	68
15:5	30, 32, 60, 91, 93, 119
16:26–30	67
17:1–24	67
18:1–14	67
19:20–24	67
20:29	30
21:5	93
21:8	46, 122
21:17	32, 60, 68, 119–20
23–31	93
23:14	68
23:24	91
24	10, 93, 146, 292, 293, 295
24:1–12	289
24:1–33	93
24:8–12	93
24:19d	93
24:23	93
24:30–31	20
24:32–33	68
24:33	92-93
25:4–5	91
25–27	67
26:29—27:3	21
26:29—27:2	33, 39, 46, 122
29:1–20	44, 59, 121
29:1–13	50n48, 70, 186
29:1–8	34
29:1–2	44
29:8–12	44
29:8–9	61, 123
29:14–15	44
29:22	34
30–34	93
30:27	28–29, 59, 118
31:3–8	122
31:3–5	46
31:12–24	33, 60, 92, 120
31:27	33
32:3	92
32:9	27
33:16–19	68

Sirach (cont.)

33:16	94
33:19	27, 68
33:25–33	33, 47
33:31	33
34:11	30, 91
34:12	60, 119–20
34:1–8	55
34:9–13	68
34:21–27	32, 61, 123
34:21–22	285n17
34:24–27	34, 44, 50, 93
34:25–27	130
35:1–26	123
35:1–15	32
35:1–13	69
35:1–12	31, 119
35:12–20	93
35:16–26	32, 34
35:18–19	89
36:3	94
36:9	89
36:11	89
36:13–14	89
37:11	33, 46, 122
37:18	28
37:22–24	68
37:23	48, 68, 120
38:1–8	47
38:2	27
38:24—39:11	26, 31, 58, 60, 68, 92, 118, 119, 214
38:24–34	43, 121
38:24–25	33
38:24	48
38:27–34	59
38:27–32	45
38:27–30	33
38:32—39:4	120
38:32–33	31, 48, 68, 92
38:32	30, 91
38:33	28, 31, 41, 68
38:34	89
38:34—39:4	48, 291
38:34–39:1	61
39:1–11	76
39:1–4	32, 152, 214
39:1–3	89, 120, 227
39:1–2	94
39:2–3	76
39:4	29, 41, 59, 68, 89–90, 118
39:6	120
39:7b	89
39:8b	89
39:10	68
39:5–11	291
39:5	89
39:6	68, 89
39:16–35	67, 90
39:23	90
40:12–13	30
42:2	32, 70, 119–20
42:5	33, 46–47, 122
42:15–25	67
42:16	67
42:17	55
42:19	67
42:25	24
40:28	34
43	135
43:1–33	67
43:32–33	68
44–50	23, 27, 69, 124, 130, 295
44–49	61, 155
44:4	28
45:15–16	60
45:15	30, 91
45:17	24, 48, 91, 120
45:20–22	42, 59, 119
45:20–21	31, 40, 60, 119
45:25	91
45:3	27
45:5	24, 48, 91, 120
45:6–7	60
47:8–10	24, 91
47:11	24

Sirach (cont.)

47:13	24, 91
48:17	24, 91
50	42, 119
50:1–21	59
50:1–4	66
50:1	39
50:2–4	24, 91
50:2	27
50:5–13	40, 59, 119
50:12	39
50:13	30, 91
50:18	92
50:20	30, 91
50:27	88
51:23	88

2 Baruch

	6, 7n13, 136–37, 212, 234–35, 298–99
25–32	299
25–27	299
27	224, 260
30:1–5	299
48:3–4	136
50–51	235n15
50:2–3	299
51	268, 299
57:2	235n15
59:5–11	135
70:8	224, 260
73	235n15

1 Maccabees

	86, 119, 160
12	87
12:6	41, 60, 86, 119
14:20b	86n9

2 Maccabees

	86–88, 95
3:4	66
4:11	85, 88
4:28	87n11
4:40	88, 95
4:44	86

~

PSEUDEPIGRAPHA

Assumption of Moses

10:3–5	225

1 Enoch

	11, 51, 56–57, 67–68, 71–73, 76–77, 81–82, 94, 96–97, 117, 126, 134, 139, 142–46, 156, 167, 214–15, 247

The Book of Watchers (1–36)

	52–55, 71–72, 75, 96–98, 106, 109–11, 143, 233n11, 292, 294
1–5	53
1:2	72
5–11	238
5:8	73
6–11	52, 157
9–10	106
9	106
10:4–5	106
10:4–8	233
10:9	106
10:16—11:2	233
12–16	53, 157
12:3–4	96, 117
12:4	71
13:3–7	71, 96
13:8	72
14:2	72
14:8	72
14:18–23	72
15:1	71, 96, 117
17–36	53, 135

Book of Watchers (cont.)

19:3	72
20	105
24–25	233

Similitudes of Enoch (37–69)

212, 219, 232, 234, 273

41:1–7	135
42:1–2	289
45:4–6	233
48:10	233
51:4–5	233
60:11–22	135

Astronomical Book (72–82)

53n52, 71, 135, 146, 238n19, 292

81:1–2	71, 96
81:5	105
82:1–3	96
82:1–2	147
82:1	71, 96
82:2–3	73

The Dream-Visions (83–90)

71, 143

Animal Vision (85–90)

54, 71–73, 75, 80, 97–98, 103–12, 126, 131, 138, 143, 160, 179, 212, 233–34, 236–37, 244, 258, 261, 292, 294, 296, 298–99

85:2	147
86:1—87:1	238
87:2	105
89:39	73
89:50	73
89:51	104
89:59—90:27	72
89:59—60	104
89:59	238
89:61	96, 105
89:66	73
89:68	96
89:72–80	126
89:73–74	73
89:73	110
89:74	108
89:76–77	96
90:6–14	75
90:7	108
90:14	105
90:17	105, 106
90:19	238
90:20–25	233
90:22	105, 106
90:24–25	105
90:26–27	233
90:29	73
90:33	234

Epistle of Enoch (91–108)

71, 73–75, 78, 97–98, 113–17, 121, 126–27, 129–31, 143–44, 152, 154, 160, 234, 244, 286, 295

91–104	131
91:1–4	96
91:2	147
91:11–17	55, 97, 131, 236
91:11–13	114
91:11	131
91:12	233
91:15	233
91:18–19	147
92–105	71, 98, 114
92:1	71, 96, 117

Ten-Week Vision

55, 71, 73, 75, 80, 97, 114, 126, 131, 138, 160, 233, 236–37, 296

93	55, 97
93:1–10	236

Ten-Week Vision (cont.)

93:2	96
93:7	73
93:8	73
93:9	73, 126, 131
93:9–10	114
93:10	131
93:11–14	135, 137
93:13	73
94–104	131
94:6–7	74, 114, 127, 130
94:7	74, 129
94:8–9	286
94:9	114
95:6	74, 129
95:7	114, 286
96:4–5	286
96:5–6	74, 114, 127
96:5	97
96:8	74, 127
97:2	74, 127
97:6	74, 129
97:8—98:2	114
97:8–9	130
97:8	74, 129
97:10	74, 129
98:1–3	126
98:4	74, 127, 129
98:7–8	74, 129
98:9	73, 114, 126
98:11	114
98:12	74, 129
98:13	128
98:15	114
99:2	114, 126
99:6–9	129
99:7	114, 129
99:10	74, 114, 127, 130
99:13	130
99:14	114
99:15	74, 129
100:5	73, 126
100:8	74, 128
102:9	74, 129
103:3	74, 127
103:9–15	114, 127
103:9	74, 127
103:11–12	74, 127
103:13	130
103:14–15	129
104:2	234

2 Enoch

	137, 143
23:1	135
40:1–13	135
40:1	137

Psalms of Solomon

	142, 159, 212, 234, 287, 302
3:12	234
10:6	287n19
15:1	287n19
17	150, 157
18:2	287n19

Testament of Moses

	156, 212, 237, 258, 261
1–5	236
8–10	236
9–10	237, 272
10	255, 256, 263
10:1	233
10:3–7	232, 233, 237
10:8–9	234

Testaments of the Twelve Patriarchs

	212, 252

NEW TESTAMENT

Matthew

    1, 6, 11, 144, 149, 154–55, 163, 173, 176–77, 190, 208n2, 210, 224, 230, 241–42, 247–48, 261, 264–75, 279, 301–3

3:7–12	244
5–7	154, 189
5	204
5:3	282
5:5	282
5:11	249
5:38–48	203
6:12	248
8:12	251
10:20	266
10:23	6, 266, 268
10:29–31	266
10:34–36	266
10:37–39	266
10:40–42	266
11:33–35	266
12:2	266
13:18–23	267
13:24–30	267
13:36–43	267
13:39	270
13:40	270
13:49	270
19:28	185, 253
16:17–19	265
16:27–28	268–69
18	268
18:15–20	265
19:28–29	268–69
21:43	269n34, 270
22:1–14	265
22:1–7	270
23	144
23:4	184
23:13	184
23:25–26	184
23:37–38	270
23:37	251
24–25	268–73, 279
24	204
24:3	270
24:5–28	272
24:12	267
24:14	271
24:15	261, 270
24:16–28	271
24:30–31	271, 272
24:32–35	272
24:36–44	272
24:36	271, 272
24:37—25:30	272
24:48	272
25	6
25:5	272
25:6	272
25:19	272
26:47–56	274
27:50–53	274
28:2	274
28:18	271
28:19–20a	271
28:20	270
28:20b	271

Mark

    1, 6, 144, 149, 154–55, 177, 180, 189, 196, 207–31, 235, 241, 249, 255–75, 279, 302–3

1–10	258
1–9	209
1:2–3	256
1:13	219
1:15	209, 255
1:16	182
1:20	182
1:21–28	219, 257
1:22–27	256
1:24	257

Mark (cont.)

1:32–34	257
1:39	257
2:1—3:5	256
2:1–12	219
2:10	218
2:15–17	228
2:18–20	228
2:20	210
2:21–22	228
2:23–28	227
2:28	218
3:1–6	219
3:6	216, 256
3:11–12	257
3:13–19	256
3:15	257
3:22–27	219, 228, 257
3:22	220
3:31–35	216
4–8	216
4	226, 267
4:10–20	227
4:11	228
4:35—8:26	256
4:15	219
4:21	228
4:30–32	219
5:1–20	220
5:7	257
5:10–13	257
6	247
6:4	228
6:7–13	256
6:17–29	256
7:1–23	227
7:1–13	239
7:1–5	256
8–10	216
8:12	192 n. 6
8:28—9:10	209
8:38	264
8:31	218, 258
8:34–9:1	226, 263
8:34–38	222, 225
8:38	192n6, 208–10, 218, 264
9:1	210, 218, 256, 258, 275
9:2–8	256
9:9	218
9:12	218
9:19	192n6
10	216
10:2–45	154
10:2–9	209, 227, 256
10:17–31	256
10:30	258
10:33–34	218
10:33	258
10:45	218
11–12	226
11:1–10	258
11:12–23	208
11:15–19	258
11:27—13:2	258
12:1–9	208
12:18–27	208
12:38–40	208
13	11, 13, 204, 207–9, 220–22, 226, 259–61, 273, 275, 276, 294
13:1–2	208
13:2	226, 260
13:3–4	226
13:4	210
13:5–27	261, 270
13:5–13	226
13:5–9	262
13:5–8	260
13:5–6	263
13:6	262
13:7–8	221, 223–25, 260
13:7	209, 222, 224, 260, 261
13:9–13	262, 263
13:10	221
13:13	220, 275
13:14–27	226, 263

Mark (cont.)

13:14–23	260, 262
13:14–20	221, 223, 260, 262
13:14	221–23, 260, 261, 276
13:14b–18	223–24, 262
13:17	224
13:18–37	263
13:19–20	224
13:19	275
13:21–22	223, 262
13:23	270
13:24–27	221, 225, 260, 263
13:24–25	209, 224, 262
13:26–27	218, 262, 264
13:26	209-210, 225
13:27	275
13:28–37	226, 263
13:28–31	225, 263
13:30	192n6, 260, 275
13:32	209
14–15	258
14:21	218
14:25	210
14:41	218
14:62	208-210, 264
16:8	263

Luke

	1, 144, 149, 163, 169, 176–77, 190, 208n2, 241, 275–77, 279, 301
3:7–9	183, 244
3:9	193
3:16–17	183, 244
3:17	193
4	155
4:15	275
6:20–21	195
6:20	182, 282
6:22	172
6:27–36	195
7:18–28	193
7:24–28	183
7:31–35	193
7:34	172
9:23–27	275
9:58	172
9:59–60	183
9:61–62	183
10:2–16	183, 204
10:4	182-83
10:5–8	195
10:13–15	193
11:2–4	204, 248
11:3	182
11:4	248
11:9–13	182
11:14–26	192
11:29–32	173, 192, 201
11:30	172
11:39–52	183, 192
11:39–40	184
11:42	184
11:47–51	201
11:49–51	164, 192n6, 201
12	200–201
12:2–12	200
12:8–9	173
12:40	173
12:13–14	182
12:22–32	181
12:22–31	182, 195, 200
12:33	182
12:35–48	276
12:35–38	186
12:35	204
12:39–40	200
12:40	170, 193, 204
12:42–46	186, 193, 200
12:49–56	198
12:49–53	276
12:49	193, 198
12:51–53	193
12:54–56	193
12:56	198
13:28–30	193, 199
13:28–29	183, 276

Luke *(cont.)*

13:34–35	193, 199, 201, 276
14:15	276
14:16–24	193, 199
14:26–27	199
14:26	183
14:34–35	199
15:4–7	199
16:1–9	128
16:13	182, 199
16:17	182, 199
16:18	182, 199
17:1–6	199
17:1–4	204
17:20–37	276
17:20–21	276
17:22	276
17:23–37	193, 199, 201
17:24	170, 173
17:25	276
17:26	170, 173
17:27	193
17:28–30	253
17:29	193
17:30	170, 173
19:11	276
19:41–44	276
21:8–19	276
21:19	275
21:20–21	261
21:20	224, 276
21:23b	275
21:27–28	275
21:32	275
21:34–36	276
22:28–30	185
22:30	253
24:19	276
24:21	276

John

	1, 8

Acts

	271
16:19	284
19:24	284

1 Corinthians

	1, 226
1:27	281
2:6–7	208
2:8–9	196
10:30	208
13	226
15	235n15
15:52	272

Philippians

2:9–11	259
3:20–21	259

1 Thessalonians

4:16–17	272

James

	280–90
1:1	283
1:9–10	288
1:14–18	287
1:17	289
2	287
2:1–8	283–84
2:5	281, 283
2:7	285
3:13—4:10	289
3:15	287, 289
4:1–4	287
4:3	289
4:4	287, 289
4:6	289
4:7	287, 289
4:10	289
4:13–17	284–87
5:1–6	284–87

Revelation
21 297

DEAD SEA SCROLLS

Damascus Rule (Document)
  154, 245

Jubilees
  98, 139, 155–56, 160, 252

Temple Scroll
  155–56, 160, 296

Genesis Apocryphon   155
1QM 17 (*War Scroll*) 219, 220, 249
4QMMT   155–56
4Q418 81 i 12   284n14
4Q285 1:9–10   284n14
4QpPs37 2:9–11   287
4QEna   52n49
4QpHab 12:2–6   287
1QS (*Community Rule*) 12, 154, 245, 249, 255, 265
3–4   219
4:18–25   219
6:6–8   148
8:1–4   253

GRECO-ROMAN WRITINGS

Clement of Alexandria
Stromata
3:16   133

Diodorus Siculus
40.3   63, 83

Hecataeus of Abdera
  63, 82

Josephus
  12, 14, 48, 83–84, 86, 154, 188, 190, 222, 234, 240, 247, 253, 262, 269n34, 274, 297, 301

Antiquities
  30, 41, 60, 64-65, 84-85, 88, 95, 119, 188, 253
10.66, 107   253
12.138–144   65, 84, 95
12.140–41   85
12.142   30n26, 41, 60, 85, 119
12.145–46   85
12.157–236   64
12.158–161   64, 84
12.163   65, 84
12.184   64, 84
12.239–40   88, 95
16.203   188

Contra Apion
1.187–89   63, 83

War
1.479   188
6:296–99   274

Pseudo–Aristeas
96–98   63

Pseudo-Hecataeus	63, 83	31	228
		35	203, 228
Pseudo-Philo		39	202, 203
Biblical Antiquities		47	198, 228
	156	51	196
19.10	135	54	282
		73	203
		85	196
Zeno Papyri	19, 64, 82, 83	89	203
		91	198
		102	202
		104	228
		111	196

EARLY CHRISTIAN WRITINGS

Polycarp

To the Philippians

2:3	282

Q (Synoptic Sayings Source)

1, 13–14, 144, 149, 155, 163–90, 191–206, 213, 217, 241–58, 254, 265, 268, 270, 272, 273, 275, 276, 279, 294, 301, 303

Barnabas

18–20	203

Didache

	203–5, 243
1:3a	204
1:3b–6	204
1–5	203
3:7	282 n. 10
8:2–3	204
11–13	204
15:3–4	204

Q/Luke

3:7–9	168, 176, 185, 192, 199, 242, 245, 252
3:9	171
3:9–11	200
3:9, 17	254
3:16–17	168, 176, 192, 199, 200, 205, 242, 245
3:17	171
4:11	255
4:26–32	255
6:20–49	176, 178, 186, 189, 195, 199–201, 203, 245, 250
6:20–26	177, 187
6:20–21	178

Gospel of Thomas

175, 191, 195–98, 201–3, 205–6, 228, 241, 243

1	175
3	175
5–6	202, 203
10	198
11	196
14	198
15–20	196
16	198
17	196
18	196
19	196
21	198, 202

Q/Luke (cont.)

6:20	176, 243
6:21	243
6:22	249, 250
6:23	255
6:27–45	199
6:27–38	176, 199, 246
6:27–36	186, 248
6:27–35	185, 203
6:27–31	186
6:37–38	186
6:41–42	186
6:43–49	246
6:46–49	176, 185, 199
7:1–10	168, 169, 192, 242
7:18–35	168, 178, 186, 192, 199–200, 205, 242, 246
7:18–28	169, 205, 245, 250
7:22	243, 247
7:27	185
7:28	176, 243
7:31–35	169, 170, 247
7:35	255
8:34—9:1	256
9:57–62	176, 250
7:18–35	178, 199–200, 205
7:18–28	250
7:22	185
7:31–35	202
9:57—10:16	178, 247
9:57	250
9:58	249
10	203
10:1–16	176, 178, 195
10:2–16	174, 200
10:8–11	244
10:9	176, 200, 243
10:11	176, 200
10:13–15	169
10:14–15	256
10:17–25	256
10:21–24	176, 247
10:23–24	171, 250
10:24	185, 243
10:12–16	244
11:2–4	174, 187, 195, 199–201, 243, 248
11:2	176
11:9–13	174, 186, 195, 199–201, 248
11:14–52	192, 199
11:14–26	168, 169, 242, 245, 248
11:14–23	203
11:14–22	178
11:14–20	202, 243
11:17–22	249
11:19–36	170
11:20	176, 178, 200
11:29–32	168, 169–70, 193, 201, 242, 249
11:29–30	178
11:30	249, 250
11:31–32	169, 243, 244, 249, 250
11:37–52	144, 242, 244, 250
11:39–52	168, 176, 178, 185, 199, 201, 205, 242
11:42	184
11:43	184
11:46	184
11:47–51	186
11:47–48	184
11:49–51	166, 170, 185, 193, 201, 250, 255
11:49–50	205
11:52	184
12:2–12	195, 200, 205, 225, 250, 251, 255
12:2–9	203
12:2	202
12:3–9	202
12:3, 11	250
12:4–5	250
12:8–9	173, 201, 202, 218, 250, 264
12:13–14	194

Q/Luke (cont.)

12:22–31	195, 201, 205, 243, 251
12:31	176, 200
12:33	194
12:39–59	168, 173, 192, 242
12:39–46	169
12:(39–)40	251
12:39	170
12:40	173, 201
12:41–46	251
12:49–59	200, 205
12:49–56	251
12:49	171, 178, 254
12:51–56	170
12:51–53	169, 171, 178, 198, 225, 251
12:52	202
12:54–56	171
12:54–55	170
12:57–59	169, 170
13:18–21	176, 200, 251
13:28–29	169, 176, 178, 200, 201–2, 205, 244, 245, 251–52, 253
13:29	252
13:34–35	178, 183, 186, 201–2, 205, 244, 251–53
13:34	205, 251
14:16–24	178
14:25	256
14:26	186
16:18	186
17	252
17:1–4	186
17:23–37	171, 173, 176, 192, 199, 204, 206
17:23–35	168, 169, 242
17:23–30	202
17:23–24	252
17:23	253
17:24	173, 201, 202
17:26–30	252
17:26	173, 201, 202
17:27	171, 254
17:29	171
17:30	173, 201, 202
17:33–34	252
17:37	252
17:37b	170
22:28–30	176, 178, 199, 200, 205, 269n34
22:30	253
24:27	252
24:37	252
24:39	252
29:2	186
29:4–7	186
29:8–11	187

Q/Matthew

6:11–12	195

www.ingramcontent.com/pod-product-compliance
Lightning Source LLC
Chambersburg PA
CBHW030433300426
44112CB00009B/974